To Barbara —

the complete baking cookbook

Happy Baking!

350 recipes from cookies and cakes to muffins and pies

Enjoy —

George Geary

George Geary

Robert ROSE

To my Father — Born on Lincoln's birthday and just as honest!

For complete cataloguing information, see page 443.

Disclaimers

The recipes in this book have been carefully tested by our kitchen and our tasters. To the best of our knowledge, they are safe and nutritious for ordinary use and users. For those people with food or other allergies, or who have special food requirements or health issues, please read the suggested contents of each recipe carefully and determine whether or not they may create a problem for you. All recipes are used at the risk of the consumer.

We cannot be responsible for any hazards, loss or damage that may occur as a result of any recipe use.

For those with special needs, allergies, requirements or health problems, in the event of any doubt, please contact your medical adviser prior to the use of any recipe.

Editors: Jennifer MacKenzie and Carol Sherman
Proofreader: Sheila Wawanash
Indexer: Gillian Watts
Design and Production: Kevin Cockburn/PageWave Graphics Inc.
Photography: Colin Erricson
Food Styling: Kathryn Robertson and Kate Bush
Prop Styling: Charlene Erricson
Illustrations: Kveta/Three in a Box

Cover image: Marble Layer Cake (page 178)
Page 3: Sour Cherry Lattice Pie (page 122)

We acknowledge the financial support of the Government of Canada through the Book Publishing Industry Development Program (BPIDP) for our publishing activities.

Published by Robert Rose Inc.
120 Eglinton Avenue East, Suite 800, Toronto, Ontario, Canada M4P 1E2
Tel: (416) 322-6552 Fax: (416) 322-6936

Printed in Canada

1 2 3 4 5 6 7 8 9 TCP 15 14 13 12 11 10 09 08 07

Contents

Acknowledgments

I could not have produced this book without the help of many. I thank all of you wholeheartedly.

I thank my parents for every word of encouragement and support. They have been with me every step of the way. My Mom, with her support — if my books were not so heavy, she would carry them and show strangers on the streets. Dad with all of his great wisdom. Both of my sisters, Monica and Pattie, for surrounding me with love. My grandmother for not teaching me how to make any pastry, having to learn it for myself so I could teach the masses. I miss your Chocolate Cream Pie, Gammie. Neil for putting up with me, my travel and work schedule for 25 years. You always have such great things to say about my work. Jonathan for dropping anything and everything to lend a helping hand. Teri Pittam for being my right and left hand — photographer, prep, kitchen assistant and primary recipe tester. Adam for keeping my website perfect. Sean and Chris from Sephno Systems for keeping my computers up and running even at 1 a.m. Also, for always being close by to try what was coming out of the oven. Everyone at the Corona Starbucks for knowing when I want to drink and asking how the book is coming. All of the United Airline gate agents at Ontario International, who always make sure I get on my flights on time, even phoning me at home about delays.

My recipe testers, friends and colleagues, Carnie, Katrina, Carol Ann and Randy. Thank you, Alice and Elaine, for being my friends and colleagues, you both have made the world a better "chocolate" place. Val, Annette and Martha at the LA Fairplex for all of your help and dedication, plus keeping me grounded in Pomona every September!

Lisa Ekus-Staffer, my great friend for many years who eventually became my literary agent. Bob Dees, my publisher and friend who has put up with me for four books now! Thank you for your trust in my work and visions. My senior editors, Jennifer MacKenzie and Carol Sherman, for their guidance and the extra hours spent on this project. Sheila Wawanash for her careful copy edit. The entire staff at PageWave Graphics for making this book truly a piece of art. Photographer Colin Erricson for photos that you want to eat! Food stylists Kathryn Robertson and Kate Bush for making the pastries look like I made them myself. Jill Snider for baking my recipes and Charlene Erricson for the prop styling. Illustrator Kveta for drawing my illustrations perfectly and better than pictures!

And finally, thanks to all of my students, the cooking schools and directors throughout the country who bring me into their kitchens.

Introduction

I am asked weekly, "Why did you get into the culinary field?" Simple answer, "I never go hungry." Plus, "I make people happy."

When I get on a plane for a long trip I try not to tell the person next to me what I do or I will be hearing about how their grandmother made the best cakes. For 6 hours! Everyone has a food story. Food makes people happy. Pastry even more so. I cannot think of anything negative to say about being a pastry chef. You make birthday cakes, not death cakes. You create wedding cakes, not divorce cakes. See? It's all happy!

From my first pastry job to my last, at Disney, I am the happiest when I'm in the kitchen baking. I assure you that many of the recipes you make from this book will become family favorites. Many already have with my students!

Baking is therapeutic. It feels great to make a crust, cake or dessert from scratch. I'm the first to tell you it takes time. You won't be able to create a dessert in 5 minutes. If you're in a hurry, then by all means, purchase a dessert. If time permits, however, make some pastry. You will not only taste the difference, but you'll also know exactly what's in your finished pastry.

— *George Geary*

Electric Equipment

My Dad always said, "You get what you pay for!" Buy the best you can afford. Before you purchase equipment, comparison shop and research your needs.

Mixers

HAND-HELD MIXER

A hand-held mixer is great for small jobs. It allows easy access around the bowl when beating egg whites and whipping cream. It also makes it easier to mix ingredients in hot pots that are still on the stove. Many of the recipes in this book will work, with a little additional effort, with a hand mixer.

STAND MIXER

Select a stand mixer that's sturdy and comes with a rounded bowl and whip and paddle attachments. Professional quality is not essential, but a 6-quart KitchenAid® is a delight to use and takes care of most mixing needs. I have two brands of stand mixers in my kitchen, KitchenAid® and Viking®. My 15-year-old KitchenAid® is still running strong. I suggest that you get a 5- or 6-quart mixer. My Viking® is 1000 horsepower and can handle a double batch of bread dough. The noise is a factor when I run this machine, but I like it for big jobs.

Mixer Parts: Most stand mixers come with three attachments: whip, paddle and dough hook. The whip is used mainly to create air in cream or egg whites and is not strong enough to handle mixing anything that is not primarily liquid. It also is the most common item that needs replacing, as some people use it for creaming butter, which causes the whip to break. The paddle is used for almost everything else, such as cutting butter into flour for scones. You can cream butter and sugar as well with the paddle. The dough hook is for yeast breads.

USING A MIXER

The variables between different mixer brands and speeds mean that one manufacturer's medium might be another's high. Therefore, I do not indicate the speed in the recipes, but instead give you a visual indicator of what to look for. In my mixer, I tend to mix ingredients on medium speed, but if you see your ingredients flying out of the bowl, turn your speed down.

When mixing air into ingredients, such as butter and sugar, the mixer speed should be high enough so the butter and sugar get light in color and become fluffy.

Food processor

Select a sturdy processor that is large enough to handle the volume of the recipes you use most often. All of the recipes in this book use an 11-cup processor. I also own a 14-cup Cuisinart® — both have worked well for me over many years.

Hand Tools

The first step in creating a perfect recipe every time is having the proper tools. The wrong size of pan or poor-quality tools will cause problems that are not easy to solve. Many of the tools that you'll need will have other uses in your kitchen and last a long time, so it's worth purchasing quality equipment the first time. You'll never have to replace it.

Rubber spatulas

A rubber spatula is the perfect tool for scraping a bowl clean. It also allows for the most thorough mixing of ingredients, the least waste of ingredients when turning them into the baking pan and an easy cleanup. The new silicone spatulas are heatproof up to 800°F (427°C) and ultra-efficient because they can go from the mixing bowl to the stovetop. Commercial-quality spatulas are usually more flexible and durable than grocery-store brands.

Whisks

To achieve perfectly beaten egg whites or whipped cream, use a sturdy whisk. They come in many sizes for different jobs. If you buy only one whisk, select a medium-size one. I also use a whisk to blend dry ingredients together to help remove any lumps.

Liquid measuring cups

The most accurate way to measure liquid ingredients is with a glass or Pyrex® measuring cup with a pouring spout. They are widely available in sizes ranging from 1 cup (250 mL) to 8 cups (2 L). Place the measure on a flat surface and add the liquid until it reaches the desired level. When checking for accuracy, bend down so that your eye is level with the measure. Angled liquid measures are now available that allow you to measure the ingredients without bending because the markings are inside the cup for easy viewing. They are made of sturdy plastic or stainless steel. Pyrex® cups can also be used in the microwave to melt butter and heat water.

Dry measuring cups

The most accurate way to measure dry ingredients is with metal nesting measuring cups. They usually come in sets of four to six cups in sizes ranging from ¼ cup (50 mL) to 1 cup (250 mL). Spoon the dry ingredient into the appropriate cup and then level off by sliding the flat side of a knife or spatula across the top of the cup. The exceptions are brown sugar and shortening, which need to be packed firmly in the cup for correct measurement.

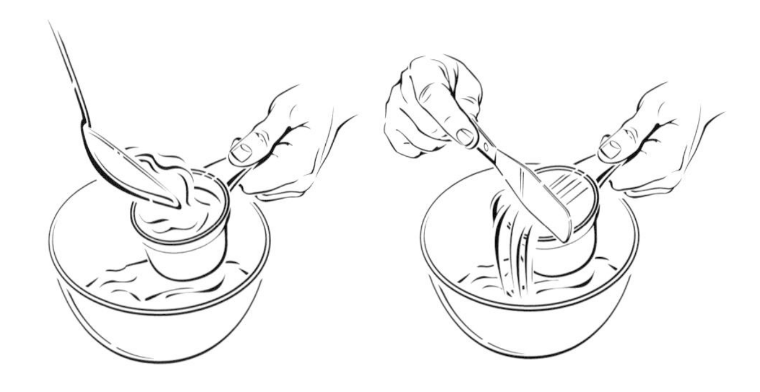

Adjustable, push-up style cup

This is a push-up-style measuring cup that measures messy items such as peanut butter, shortening and sour cream. You scoop the ingredients into the top and level off. Push the bottom up and the ingredient comes out.

Measuring spoons

The most accurate measuring spoons are metal. A set of sturdy spoons ranging from $\frac{1}{8}$ tsp (0.5 mL) to 1 tbsp (15 mL) is necessary for measuring small amounts of both liquid and dry ingredients.

Mixing bowls

A nested set of small, medium and large mixing bowls will be used countless times. Having the right size bowl for the job, whether it's beating egg whites or whipping a quart (1 L) of cream, helps the cooking process. Ceramic, glass and stainless steel all have their merits, but I think stainless steel is the most versatile, although when making a citrus-based recipe, such as lemon curd, it may add a metallic taste.

Microplane® zester/grater

A Microplane® zester/grater with a handle is the best tool for quickly making zest from lemons or other citrus fruits. It is also good for grating hard cheeses and chocolate.

THE PROPER WAY TO ZEST CITRUS

1. Hold fruit underneath the Microplane's cutting edge.
2. Drag Microplane across the fruit once, rotating fruit so you can see where you have zested. I have seen so many "chefs" on television do this incorrectly by dragging the fruit across the Microplane. If you zest across the fruit more than once you will get the bitter pith part of the citrus.
3. The Microplane captures the zest and is now ready to use in recipes.

Blending fork

Also called a granny fork or pastry fork, the blending fork is a very handy tool. It has so many uses but is often overlooked. It looks like an overgrown fork with triangular tines. I use this tool instead of a pastry blender when making pie or quiche crusts because it doesn't allow the dough to get trapped.

Rolling pins

There are two main types of rolling pins: with and without handles. I have seen many new rolling pins made with special surfaces, which I feel are a waste of good money. I rely on a traditional wooden pin. My favorite is the French box or French tapered rolling pin (see illustration, below). You use the palm of your hands instead of gripping the handles. The rolling surface on most handled pins is not large enough for a piecrust thus creating lines in your dough. You also do not have to be concerned with the handles separating from the pin.

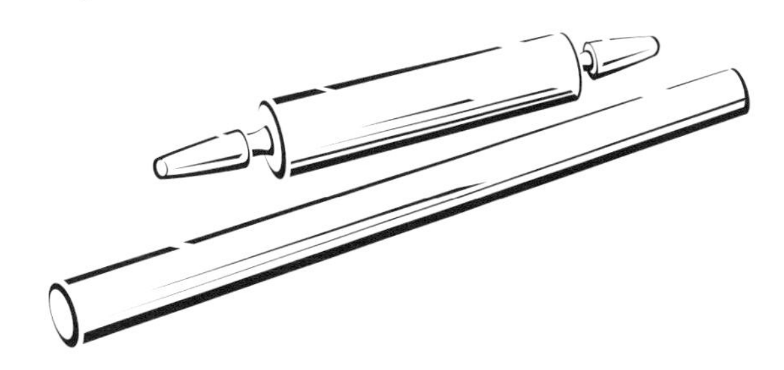

Pastry bags, tips and couplers

A pastry bag allows you to pipe beautiful garnishes and decorations to make perfect-looking baking. Pastry bags come in a variety of materials.

PASTRY BAGS

I like pastry bags made from poly plastic in a 12- to 16-inch (30 to 40 cm) size. They clean up easily and last for many uses. To wash, take out tip and coupler. Wash with warm soapy water inside and out and rinse. Place over a bottle to air-dry. Other types of pastry bags:

- *Canvas:* This bag is harder to use and after a few washings gets very stiff. If you use colored icings they may discolor the bag. Also, if you use the bag for something with a strong smell, such as deviled eggs, the aroma of eggs will permeate the bag and you will be unable to use it for pastry again.
- *Disposable:* I like to use this type for writing only because you don't need a tip. If you use a tip with these bags and your frosting is stiff you will have a difficult time piping out the design and sometimes the bag will split. Also, you can't use anything warm, such as chocolate or cream puff dough, in the bag or it will melt.

COUPLER

This is a handy item if you have a bag that you want to use for more than one use, such as writing and swirls. You can change the tip on the bag between uses without emptying the frosting.

To use a coupler: Cut your bag to fit the larger piece of the coupler with about one-third of the top showing. Insert the larger coupler piece into bag. Place tip on the end of the coupler in the bag and then screw top part of coupler over tip. You can fill pastry bag with frosting and change tip to fit your needs without replacing frosting.

TIPS

Every tip has a number on it. Some tips are named according to what they pipe out, such as a star or a writing tip.

- *American tips:* These are small and easy to use with a coupler.
- *French tips:* These are larger and are mainly used without a coupler.

Metal spatulas

Every year, *Pastry Art & Design* magazine writes about what pastry chefs around the world can't live without. For many years running an offset spatula has been one of the top items mentioned. My first pick is someone that does my cleanup and dishes; my second is the offset spatula.

An offset spatula has a long handle and a flexible metal blade that is set on an angle. Offset spatulas come in a variety of lengths and thicknesses. Choose one that feels comfortable in your hand. Here are some different types of spatulas and their uses:

- *10-inch (25 cm) narrow flat spatula:* Used to ice cake sides and smear fillings inside cookies.
- *8-inch (20 cm) wide flat spatula:* Used to ice cake sides and smear fillings inside cookies.
- *10-inch (25 cm) offset spatula:* Used to ice tops of cakes without your knuckles dragging into the icing. Great to smooth brownies or thick batters in pans prior to baking.

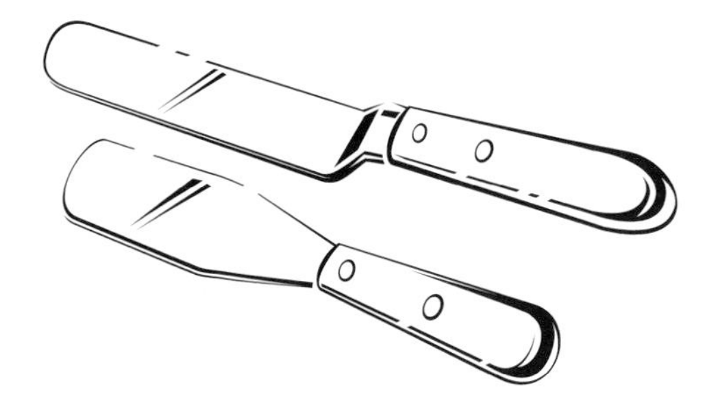

- *4-inch (10 cm) offset spatula:* Used to ice smaller cakes and cupcakes.
- *4-inch (10 cm) flat spatula:* Used to ice sides of smaller cakes.

Candy and general thermometers

There are many types and price ranges for thermometers. Here's a brief listing of some available:

- *Digital instant-read thermometer:* This is my favorite type. This thermometer has many functions. To use, you set the exact temperature you want. It will alarm when the desired temperature is achieved. You can also place the probe into a roast with the wire extending from the oven into a digital temperature/timer unit and it will alarm when your meat is done. It is also used as a kitchen timer.

  There are more simple stem thermometers with a digital read-out that are useful for candy making and for meats, though they cannot be put directly into the oven, as they will melt under heat.
- *Large candy thermometer:* For years this was the only type of thermometer you could find. Some do not list the register for some of the degrees, instead it has "hard ball," "soft ball," etc. on the register instead of the exact degrees.
- *Analog instant-read thermometer:* This thermometer gives you an exact read in a few seconds, but if you are cooking sugar it may not give you the correct reading in a timely fashion and you may burn the sugar.

Silpats

This fairly new invention was originally only available in France for pastry chefs. Silpat is a silicone-covered fiberglass mesh, sold as a baking-pan liner. They are now widely available at specialty kitchenware and well-stocked housewares stores. They are available in various sizes and require no greasing. One side has a texture that helps prevent the mat from moving when on a baking sheet. I also like to use the textured side when I am dipping bonbons into chocolate to prevent them from sliding around the sheet.

Dishers/scoopers

Traditionally, dishers are used in commercial bakeries and in food service, but they are very handy for home baking, too. The size number is determined by the number of portions of food you would get from 1 quart (1 L) using that specific disher. Here are the volume equivalents for the different scoops:

Scoop Size	Amount
#6	⅔ cup (150 mL)
#8	½ cup (125 mL)
#10	6 tbsp + 2 tsp (100 mL)
#12	⅓ cup (75 mL)
#16	¼ cup (60 mL)
#20	3 tbsp + 1 tsp (50 mL)
#24	2 tbsp + 2 tsp (40 mL)
#30	2 tbsp (30 mL)
#40	1 tbsp + 2 tsp (25 mL)
#50	1 tbsp + ¾ tsp (19 mL)
#60	1 tbsp + ¼ tsp (16 mL)
#70	2¾ tsp (14 mL)
#100	2 tsp (10 mL)

Torches

You can find fancy torches for crème brûlée or browning meringues. I use a propane blowtorch to brown my meringue tops on pies and tarts. I like the industrial-size ones that are available in hardware stores. They allow me to brown the meringue evenly, which is not always possible with an oven broiler. The cost is about a third of the small ones from specialty kitchenware stores. Not only do the small ones cost more, they are much lower in power and not as effective. Purchase one that has an automatic trigger. Then just purchase new gas tanks for the trigger system.

Apple peeler

I love these hand-crank machines. You can peel, core and slice a bushel of apples in less time than it takes to do a half a dozen with a hand peeler or paring knife.

Baking Pans

The note to purchase once and use forever bears repeating for baking pans. Invest in quality pans; they conduct heat more efficiently, so cooking is more even and the desired results are achieved on top and bottom. Stay with a light metal as the darker pans conduct too much heat into the baked goods causing a dark crust.

Have an assortment of baking pans on hand for the most flexibility in making a variety of recipes. A good selection of pans would include:

- Two 8-by 1½-inch (20 by 4 cm) metal tart pans with removable bottoms
- Two 9-by 2-inch (23 cm) round baking pans with straight sides
- 9-inch (23 cm) metal pie plate
- 10-inch (25 cm) deep-dish ceramic pie plate
- 10-inch (3 L) metal Bundt pan

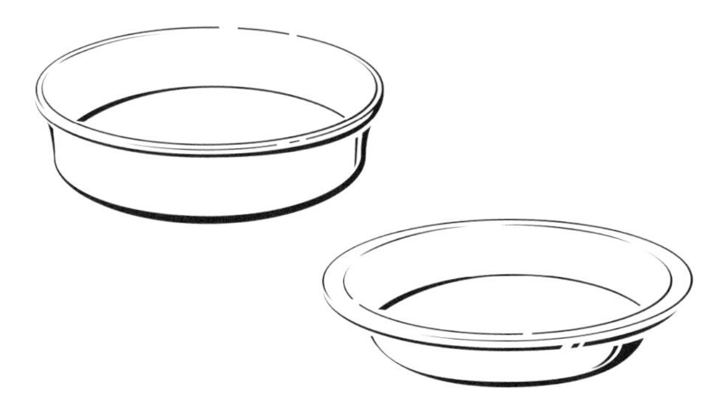

- 10-inch (3 L) metal angel food cake pan
- 13-by 9-by 2-inch (3 L) metal baking pan
- 9-by 2-inch (2 L) square metal baking pan
- Two 17-by 11-inch (43 by 28 cm) jelly roll pan or half-sheet pan (also called baking sheets or rimmed baking sheets)
- Regular and mini metal muffin tins
- 9-inch (23 cm) cheesecake pan with 3-inch (7.5 cm) sides
- 10-inch (25 cm) cheesecake pan with 3-inch (7.5 cm) sides

Common Ingredients

Dairy Products

LIQUID MILK PRODUCTS

- *Milk:* I prefer to use whole milk in the recipes. Lower-fat milk may alter the texture and taste of the final product.
- *Cream:* There are many different creams on the market under names that include heavy, whipping, table, etc. Make sure you use the liquid cream that you would whip to make whipped cream. It is normally 35% fat.
- *Half-and-half (10%) cream:* This is a lighter cream than whipping (35%) but more rich than whole milk and contributes tenderness and texture to baked items. You can use half-and-half (10%) cream in place of whole milk in recipes. You can substitute whipping (35%) cream in recipes that call for half-and-half; however, you cannot use half-and-half if whipping (35%) cream is called for.

CANNED MILKS

- *Evaporated milk:* Canned unsweetened milk, from which 60% of the water has been removed. Unopened cans can be stored at cool room temperature for up to 1 year. Once opened, it must be consumed within 5 to 7 days.
- *Sweetened condensed milk:* Whole milk and sugar is heated until 60% of the water evaporates. This milk has a sugar content of 40 to 45%.

Canada and the U.S. label sweetened condensed milk cans differently by size and weight. Make sure you use the exact amount called for. In the U.S. the cans are 14 oz (396 g) by weight or 1⅓ cups (300 mL). In Canada, the cans are listed by volume as 300 mL.

CREAM CHEESE

Cream cheese is a fresh cheese made from cow's milk and by law must contain 33% milk fat and no more than 55% moisture to be classified as such.

Light or lower-fat cream cheese has about half the calories of regular cream cheese. Whipped cream cheese, which is soft because it has air whipped into it, has slightly fewer calories. Nonfat cream cheese, of course, has no calories from fat and is best used on a bagel or sandwich, not for baking.

Use a name-brand cream cheese. Some of the store brands have added ascorbic gum acids and moisture, which diminish the texture and quality of the baked goods.

Eggs

The recipes in this book were tested using large eggs. Eggs are easier to separate when cold. After separating, allow eggs to come to room temperature before using. Leftover egg whites and yolks will keep for up to 2 days in a covered container in the refrigerator. Both can be frozen as well. Refrigerate eggs in the carton in which they came for up to a month.

If you don't have large eggs, beat the eggs and measure carefully to substitute as follows: One large egg equals about ¼ cup (50 mL).

Butter and Oils

BUTTER

I use unsalted butter throughout the book. Many students ask me, "Why do you use unsalted butter in your recipes?" I then ask them, "Do you know how much salt is in salted butter?" No one has the answer for me. Percentages differ with each manufacturer. I like to know exactly how much salt is in the food I'm making. Unsalted butter allows me to control the salt by adding however much I think the recipe needs. Also, salt is a preservative, so the salted butter can sit on the grocer's shelf much longer. Within the last few years we have seen a large influx of European butters, which are sometimes double in price. Unless you are making a recipe, such as butter cookies or a butter crust, I do not feel the extra cost is worth it. I suggest you use a regular name-brand butter and not a store brand one, as it may have added moisture.

VEGETABLE SHORTENING

Many are worried about trans-fats in vegetable shortening. Moderation is the key in using shortening. Now, trans-fat-free shortening is available, but it may change the taste and texture of baked goods. The recipes in this book that call for vegetable shortening were tested using the traditional type.

OILS

I use canola oil when I'm frying items such as donuts, and any mild vegetable oil in cookies, cakes, etc. Check the taste of the oil prior to use. Oils go rancid very quickly in a warm kitchen.

Flour

The sack of flour that you see on the store shelf is a recipe all by itself. Most bakeries have flourmills that create flour to their specifications. I try to always use the flours that are most readily available in local stores.

Hard wheat flour is grown in spring and has a higher protein content than soft wheat, which is grown in winter. The protein in flour is the factor that determines the gluten content, contributing to the strength of a dough or batter.

You may run across many different brands and types. Here are the main flours you will find:

- *Whole Wheat Flour:* Light brown in color, it should never be the only flour in your recipe. It is mainly used for breads. If you use only whole wheat flour the results will be a hard brick instead of a loaf of bread or muffin. Use only about 50% whole wheat and the remainder a softer flour, such as cake or pastry.
- *High-Gluten Bread Flour:* Generally made from hard wheat, this flour contains the most amount of gluten-forming protein. Gluten is what gives the elasticity to your yeast baked goods. You want a higher gluten level for breads.
- *All-Purpose Flour:* This flour is made from a combination of hard and soft wheats. It has less gluten-forming protein than bread flour and can be used interchangeably with unbleached all-purpose flour. It may bleach naturally as it ages, or be chemically treated.
- *Unbleached All-Purpose Flour:* It can be used interchangeably with all-purpose flour. It has the natural color of the milled wheat.
- *Pastry Flour:* This is a more difficult flour to find in stores. I seem to locate it in health food stores in the bulk sections. It has some gluten, but not as much as all-purpose. If you cannot locate it, mix 50% cake and 50% all-purpose to get the blend of gluten needed for the recipe.
- *Cake Flour:* Milled from soft wheat with more moisture, it is perfect for cakes when you want less gluten for a more tender product. Cake flour is sometimes hard to find, as it is often sold in a box that looks like a cake mix. Look for it close to the biscuit mix.
- *Cake & Pastry Flour:* This flour is available in some areas and is made from soft wheat. It can be used interchangeably for both cake flour and pastry flour.
- *Nut Flours (almond, pecan, hazelnut):* Again, these flours are found in health food stores. You can make your own with a food processor by adding 10% by volume of all-purpose flour to your toasted nuts. Process until flour-like.

STORING FLOURS

I place mine in my pantry in a sealed container and store away from light. I do not use the freezer to store my flours, as the added moisture from the freezer can create a different product. If you tend to get bugs in your flour, you're not baking enough!

Sugars

Sugar has many uses besides sweetening. As an ingredient in pastry dough, it adds tenderness. It adds body to help egg whites become meringues. It is a natural preservative that allows jelly and jam to have a long shelf life. Heat makes it turn brown, so it adds an attractive color to many baked goods and candy.

GRANULATED SUGAR

Granulated, or white sugar, is the most common form of sugar. When it is pulverized, which is easily done in a blender or food processor, it is called superfine sugar. Because superfine sugar melts so quickly, it is used for sweetening cold liquids and in delicate sweets such as meringues. When it is crushed to an even finer powder with a bit of cornstarch added, it is called powdered sugar or confectioner's (icing) sugar, which is excellent for icings and candy or as a decoration.

BROWN SUGAR

Light and brown sugars are created when white sugar is mixed with molasses. The light variety is lighter in taste, but both have nutritional value from the molasses, while white sugar has none. There's also some calcium, phosphorus, iron, potassium and sodium, making brown sugar a popular addition in cookies and cereal.

Unless a recipe specifies, you can use either light or dark. Because it is very moist and tends to clump, brown sugar should be packed tightly in a measuring cup to get the exact amount required.

Store brown sugar in an airtight container or in the refrigerator. If the sugar becomes too hard, restore its moisture by placing an apple slice in the container, by warming the sugar in a low oven with a few drops of water for 20 minutes, or by microwaving it at Medium (50%) power 20 seconds at a time until softened. Granulated and liquid brown sugars are good for cereal or fruit but should not be substituted in baking recipes because of their different moisture contents.

LIQUID SUGARS

Liquid sugars come in a variety of different flavors and can be used to add sweetness to baked goods. Store in a cool, dry place for the best shelf life.

- Honey is made by bees from flower nectar and therefore is a natural sugar, but that doesn't mean it has fewer calories. It actually has a few more. Because it is sweeter, use less honey if substituting it for other liquid sweeteners.
- Molasses made from sugarcane or sugar beet syrup is available in three varieties: light (fancy), dark (cooking) and blackstrap. Light molasses is typically used as table syrup, while dark molasses provides the distinctive sweet flavor of gingerbread and Boston baked beans. Blackstrap molasses is only slightly more nutritious than the lighter versions and not commonly used in baking.
- Corn syrup is made from cornstarch and is available in light and dark varieties. Popular in baking, it does not crystallize and it makes baked products brown more quickly than granulated sugar. The dark version is best used when color doesn't matter and the caramel flavor is an asset to the recipe. Both types are used as table syrups and in frostings, candy and jam.

Nuts

Nuts provide good nutritional value, including a generous amount of the good monounsaturated fat. But because of the high fat content, they have the corresponding high calories, too. They add flavor and texture to baked goods. Refrigerate or freeze shelled nuts that won't be used right away. For the best results, defrost and toast before proceeding with the recipe. To toast nuts, preheat oven to 350°F (180°C). Spread nuts on a baking sheet and bake for 6 to 8 minutes, depending on the size of nuts, checking a few times to make sure they don't burn. Allow to cool before chopping.

NUT BUTTERS

All nuts can be made into a spreadable butter. When a recipe calls for peanut butter, try using almond butter instead. To make a nut butter, place toasted cooled nuts in a work bowl of a food processor fitted with metal blade. Process until desired consistency, 2 to 4 minutes. Keep leftovers refrigerated for up to 3 weeks. Different varieties of nut butters are available in health food, specialty food and well-stocked grocery stores.

Flavorings and Spices

VANILLA EXTRACTS

Pure vanilla extract is created by soaking vanilla beans in bourbon or vodka and then aging the liquid. The flavor and aroma are unmistakable. Do not scrimp on the quality, nor delete vanilla from your recipes. Vanilla enhances all the other ingredients. Vanilla is the only edible part of a certain species of orchid. (For a list of companies for vanilla extract, see Sources, page 442.) There are three types of vanilla extracts as listed by region.

- *Madagascar*: For baking, this is by far the best. Whenever vanilla is going to be heated in your baking, such as when making a cake or custard, use this vanilla.
- *Mexico*: Mexican vanilla beans are good quality; however, some vanilla extract sold in Mexico is not real and contains harmful ingredients, even though it is labeled "real." Be cautious when buying vanilla from Mexico and make sure it is genuine. It should state on the label that it contains "no coumarin." If the price seems too good to be true, it probably isn't real vanilla. Many companies purchase beans from Mexico and produce the extract outside of Mexico. These are generally good-quality extracts.
- *Tahiti*: For unbaked sweets and dessert, such as ice creams and frostings. Tahitian vanilla beans tend to have a "flowery" aroma and taste.

Imitation vanilla is created with man-made products and barely resembles what it attempts to imitate. Despite being one-tenth the cost of the real thing, it is not worth substituting for pure vanilla extract.

FLAVORED OILS, EXTRACTS AND FLAVORINGS

Citrus oils are all-natural essences cold-pressed from the rind of the fruit. Extracts and flavorings don't come close to the remarkable intensity of these oils. It takes approximately 220 oranges, 330 lemons or 400 limes to fill a 5-oz (150 mL) bottle.

Extracts and flavorings are made by infusing alcohol with the rind of the fruit. It can dissipate if left open and change flavor in heat.

SPICES

Keep spices tightly sealed and store in a cool, dry, dark place. For the best flavor, purchase whole spices and grind them as you need them. Use ground spices within 2 years and whole spices within 3. For a list of companies for spices, see Sources, page 442.

Chocolates

I feel chocolate is like wine. Many enjoy store brands and some only use European brands. In the past few years chocolate companies have started listing the cocoa percentages on the outside of the packaging so you don't have to search for it. The higher the percentage, the more cocoa liquor or mass in the chocolate and the less sugar. I use a variety of chocolates in my baking. Try a recipe with a high-quality chocolate and no tropical oils every time and you can't lose. Only use chocolate chips when it is stated, as they react differently in baking. Use block or bars and chop the chocolate up when called for in everything else. (For Melting Chocolate, see page 250.)

- *Unsweetened chocolate:* Made without sugar, it is pure chocolate liquor that has been cooled and formed into bars.
- *Cocoa Powder:* I use Dutch-process cocoa powder. It is processed with alkali, which neutralizes the cocoa powder's natural acidity. The resulting cocoa powder is darker and richer — some are a "brick red" color.
- *White chocolate:* Not really a chocolate, white chocolate is a mixture of cocoa butter, milk solids, vanilla and lecithin. It does not contain chocolate liquor. Make sure the oil or fat in the product is cocoa butter. Any "tropical" oils, such as palm kernel, coconut, cottonseed, etc., will create an off-taste.
- *Milk chocolate:* It must contain at least 10% chocolate liquor and 12% milk solids.
- *Semisweet and bittersweet chocolate:* These chocolates can be used interchangeably in most recipes without any change to the outcome other than the taste. Bittersweet must contain at least 35% chocolate liquor. Semisweet must contain at least 15 to 35% chocolate liquor. To make the truffles in the recipes come out with a favorable taste, I suggest 55 to 70%, any higher may result in a bitter-tasting confection. There are some extremely bitter varieties (80 to 95%) available and these are best used only when unsweetened chocolate is needed.

Apples

I am often asked what kind of apples to use for baking. My favorite is Gravenstein apples from the Sonoma, California, area. They are rarely found outside of this area and do not ship well and bruise easily. Like most great apples and produce, you cannot beat locally farmed produce in season. When going to your market for produce talk with the farmer or grower as to which is the best for what your use is.

When making apple pies I tend to mix my apples, with sweet and tart varieties.

- *Sweet baking apples:* Golden Delicious, Braeburn, Jonagold, Ida Red, Gravenstein
- *Tart apples:* Granny Smith, Cortland, Empire, Northern Spy, Crispin (Mutsu), McIntosh (McIntosh tend to soften when baked and do not hold their shape as well as the other tart apples)

Quadruple Chocolate Chip Cookies & Ultimate Chocolate Chunk Cookies for a Crowd

Cookies, Bars & Squares

Cookies

Bar Cookies & Brownies

Cookies

Cookies are one of the simplest baked goods to create and are probably one of our first baking experiences. Just the word "cookies" brings so many fond memories of childhood. Whether you were taught how to measure by your mother or grandmother, I'd bet the first recipe you ever made was the one for Toll House Cookies that was printed on the bag of Nestlé chocolate chips. I recall dumping that big bag of chips into the buttery batter. I couldn't wait until the chips were blended so I could sneak a chunk of that thick raw batter. Years later, as a professional baker, I decided to make those cookies again. The yield says 60 cookies, but I only got about 24 to 36 cookies. The one time I did make it to 60, the cookies were the size of dimes. I started taking polls of students in my baking classes to see if anyone could reach 60. Never. With every recipe in this book you will obtain the yield stated.

When I was the pastry chef for the Walt Disney Company one of the new cast members (as Disney calls its employees) saw me sneak a bite of raw dough. Jeff looked at me in horror and said, "You're going to get worms!" I looked at this latest addition to the baking team and replied, "I bet your mom used to tell you that when you were young, making cookies. Trust me. She waited until you left the kitchen and would sneak the dough herself. Ask her." The next day, Jeff looked a little sheepish. "You were right," was the first thing he said to me that morning. I told him that the first rule in chef school is that the chef is always right. And the second rule is, if the chef is wrong, refer to rule number one.

Remember, the chocolate chip cookie dough ice cream was created in the 1970s and it is still one of the most popular favors. Even less-than-perfect homemade cookies are better than any boxed cookies (although I can't resist an Oreo once in awhile).

12 Simple Rules to Perfect Cookies

1. Measure all your ingredients perfectly (see page 6).
2. Do not substitute. Use only the specific ingredients called for unless the recipe has a substitution listed in the recipe.
3. Use only fresh nuts. Go to a health food store with a bulk section or bulk food store with a high turnover and purchase only what you need. Freeze any remainders. When buying in bulk, use your nose — check for any strong or rancid aroma when you open the container and avoid those nuts. If you are using nuts often, warehouse stores sell good-quality nuts in large packages at reasonable prices.
4. Bring fats, such as butter, shortening, etc., to room temperature before mixing the other ingredients, unless otherwise specified.
5. Preheat the oven to the correct temperature. (Purchase an oven thermometer if you think your oven is off, and then have it calibrated or adjust the setting accordingly.)
6. If you have a convection oven, reduce the temperature by 25°F (14°C) and reduce the cooking time by 20% and all cookies can be baked perfectly. Other baked goods, such as scones, muffins and biscuits, work well with convection baking. Items that need to be baked longer than 20 minutes, such as pies, cakes and cheesecakes, do not work well.
7. Never grease, oil or spray baking pans prior to baking, or the cookies will become "ice skaters" and the cookie dough will run together once the pans become heated.
8. Use parchment paper or a silicone baking mat, such as Silpat.
9. I like to use a heavy-gauge baking sheet that is light in color, also known as a half

bun pan, half sheet pan or jelly-roll pan, that measures about 17-by 11-inches (43 by 28 cm) and has ½-inch (1 cm) sides. The sizes between brands may vary slightly, but something close to this size is the most useful. It's the perfect size for a silicone sheet. I don't like to use cookie sheets because they don't have rims. When you remove the cookies from the oven, they tend to slide off the pan and onto the floor. Some bakers and authors claim that the type of pan I like to use prevents the proper "airflow" for baking the cookies. If your oven has a problem flowing heat over the sides of a pan that is only about ½ inch (1 cm) deep, then I say you need to have your oven calibrated now! Nonstick pans are not necessary since I recommend parchment or Silpat.

10. Use a disher, also known as an ice cream scoop, portion scoop or a spring loaded cookie scoop, to portion the dough perfectly. (For volume equivalents, see page 9.)
11. If you want to bake two sheets of cookies at the same time, rotate the pans partway through the baking just in case your oven has "hot spots."
12. Let the cookies cool on the pan slightly, then use an offset spatula or large metal spatula to transfer them onto a cooling rack.

Dealing with Cookie Dough

All cookie recipes can be doubled if your mixer or food processor allows for the capacity. I like to freeze the extra dough. Roll it into a log and wrap it in wax paper or parchment paper and then foil. Label the contents and freeze. Frozen dough keeps for approximately 2 months before losing flavor and quality. Most dough can be sliced frozen and placed directly on the prepared baking pan and baked according to the recipe directions.

Storing and Freezing Cookies

Nearly everyone collects something. My passion is antique cookie jars. My favorite is a replica of one from my childhood — a Gilner Gingerbread Boy — just like the one my grandmother had. I only recall chocolate chip cookies being stored in his body, so mine also has only chocolate chip cookies in it. I do think cookie jars are the best way to store cookies. To keep soft cookies soft, place a slice of bread in the cookie jar with the cookies.

If you don't have enough time to bake all of the cookie dough, roll it into a log and wrap in plastic wrap, then foil. Freeze for up to 3 months.

Shipping Cookies

During the holiday months I am often asked how to ship cookies. If the cookies are large, place two back-to-back and wrap the pair in plastic wrap. Continue until all the cookies are wrapped and then pack them snugly in a tin. Use edible unbuttered popcorn to fill in any spaces. Place the tin in a shipping box. If cookies are small and crisp, I suggest packing them in a single layer with paper between each cookie. You can also wrap the cookies in groups. Again, place in a tin and pack as described above.

Top 5 Favorite Cookies sold at Disneyland

1. Chocolate Chip
2. Oatmeal Raisin
3. Peanut Butter
4. White Chocolate Chip Macadamia
5. Snickerdoodle

Using a Disher

1. Firmly press the disher into the dough and use the side of the mixing bowl to pack the dough into the scoop.

2. Remove any excess dough from the disher for a perfect portion.

3. Place the portion on the prepared baking sheet. Most cookie recipes will allow 9 to 12 cookies to be baked on each pan.
4. Press the dough firmly into the pan with the palm of your hand or the bottom of a drinking glass, to about ¼-inch (0.5 cm) thickness. If the dough starts to stick to your hand, wet your palm and press lightly again. Do not press the dough with your fingers because the impressions they leave will create a "ripple" effect on top of the dough and will pass the look on to the finished product. (For volume equivalents for dishers, see page 9.)

Bar Cookies and Brownies

Bar cookies are fast and easy. An entire recipe can be baked in one batch in one pan. Then just let cool and cut. Now they're ready for the kids and you. A rich, fudgey brownie with a glass of ice-cold milk is what childhood memories are made of.

Top Reasons for Brownie Problems and How to Resolve Them

1. *Hard brownies:* Two things cause hard-textured brownies. The first one is overbaking. Most people have been taught that when a toothpick inserted into the center of the brownies comes out clean they are done. Technically, at this point they are overdone by at least 5 minutes. When a recipe gives the baking time as 22 to 26 minutes, check at 18 minutes. The toothpick will be wet-looking. Bake for 4 more minutes, and the toothpick should include some moist crumbs. And then the brownies are finished — they continue to bake as they cool. The second problem is overmixing. Once the flour hits the moisture in the recipe, it starts to react. You don't want the gluten in the flour to be overdeveloped — the more you mix, the more the gluten starts to develop and toughen.
2. *Underbaked:* If the brownies are underbaked when you cut into them, just return them to a preheated 350°F (180°C) oven until done.
3. *Old brownies or ones you know you won't use:* Dry the brownies out in a 250°F (120° C) oven; let cool and then grind them into crumbs in a food processor. Use the crumbs to decorate the sides of cakes or as a topping for ice cream sundaes.

Brownie Facts and Information

1. *Nuts and/or chocolate chips:* Add up to 1 cup (250 mL) of chips or nuts to an average brownie recipe for a 13-by 9-inch (3 L) pan. (If a recipe calls for an 8-inch/2 L square pan, add up to ½ cup/125 mL chips or nuts.)
2. *Preparing the pan:* I like to use a light-colored metal 13-by 9-inch (3 L) baking pan with 2-inch (5 cm) sides. Cut a piece of foil at least 4-inches (10 cm) longer than the pan. Place the pan on the work surface bottom-side up. Place the foil on the pan, letting the foil hang over each end by at least 2 inches (5 cm). Shape the foil around the bottom of the pan, molding the corners neatly. Lift the foil off, flip the pan right-side up and fit the molded foil into the pan. Spray the foil and add a piece of fitted parchment paper to the bottom. When the bars are completely cool, pull on the sides and ends of the foil, which act as handles and remove the whole thing from the pan and place it on a cutting board. Peel the foil down from the sides to cut the brownies. This method works well, as it always seems that when you make bars and try to get that first bar out they tend to break and crumble, and it protects the pan from being scored by the knife, giving it a much longer useful life.

   If you want to freeze the brownies, fold the excess foil over the top of the uncut bars/brownies and fit another piece of foil over top to enclose, if necessary, and freeze whole.
3. *Quantities:* All the brownie and bar recipes can be cut in half and baked in a 9-inch (2.5 L) square baking pan. Decrease the baking time by 25%. If there is an odd number of eggs in the recipe and you would like to cut the recipe in half, refer to Eggs on page 11.
4. *Cutting bars and brownies:* Most of the recipes make 24 bars. To cut the bars or brownies, use a chef's knife, dip it in hot water and then dry it. Cut the cooled panful in half lengthwise and then crosswise to make 4 equal sections. Cut each section into 6 equal pieces for 24 bars.

Almond Raspberry Kiss Cookies

MAKES ABOUT 24 COOKIES

The flavors of raspberry, chocolate and almond make this an all-time favorite.

Tip

Make sure the candies are unwrapped so you don't waste time while the cookie is hot. You want to place the candies on a hot cookie. The candies will not stick to a cooled cookie.

Variation

Replace almond-filled Hershey Kisses with the new peanut butter and dark chocolate varieties.

- Preheat oven to 350°F (180°C)
- Baking sheets, lined with parchment paper or Silpats
- #40 disher or scoop

2¼ cups	all-purpose flour	550 mL
1 tsp	baking soda	5 mL
¼ tsp	salt	1 mL
½ cup	unsalted butter, softened	125 mL
½ cup	vegetable shortening	125 mL
½ cup	granulated sugar	125 mL
½ cup	packed brown sugar	125 mL
1	egg	1
1 tsp	almond extract	5 mL
1 tsp	vanilla extract	5 mL
24	almond-filled Hershey Kisses, unwrapped (see Tip, left)	24
¼ cup	raspberry preserves	50 mL
1 tbsp	corn syrup	15 mL

Mixer Method

1. In a bowl, whisk together flour, baking soda and salt. Set aside.
2. In a mixer bowl fitted with paddle attachment, cream butter, shortening, granulated sugar and brown sugar until fluffy, for 2 minutes. Add egg, almond and vanilla extracts and mix until blended. Using a wooden spoon, gradually stir in flour mixture until incorporated. Refrigerate for 10 minutes or until firm.
3. Using disher, scoop dough and place on prepared baking sheets, about 2 inches (5 cm) apart. Press down with palm of your hand. Bake in preheated oven until light brown, 7 to 12 minutes. Immediately top each cookie with an almond-filled kiss, pressing down gently. Let cool on baking sheets for 10 minutes before transferring to a wire rack to cool completely.
4. In a small bowl, combine raspberry preserves and corn syrup. Drizzle over cooled cookies.

Food Processor Method

1. In a bowl, whisk together flour, baking soda and salt. Set aside.
2. In work bowl fitted with metal blade, process butter, shortening, granulated sugar and brown sugar until fluffy, for 20 seconds. With motor running, add egg, almond and vanilla extracts through the feed tube and process for 10 seconds. Add flour mixture and process until blended, for 10 seconds. Proceed with Step 3 left.

Biscotti with Walnuts

MAKES ABOUT 24

A wonderful helper, friend and great actress, Carol Ann Suzi, makes this Blue Ribbon award-winning biscotti every year for the Baked Foods Competition at the Los Angeles County Fair. She was kind enough to share her recipe for my book.

Tip

Make sure you bake loaves one day and then slice biscotti the next day. They are easier to cut when they are set.

Variation

California Biscotti: Replace walnuts with pistachios.

- Preheat oven to 350°F (180°C)
- Baking sheets, lined with parchment paper or Silpat

1¼ cups	unsalted butter, softened	300 mL
1¼ cups	granulated sugar	300 mL
4	eggs, beaten	4
3¾ cups	all-purpose flour	925 mL
¼ cup	baking powder	50 mL
½ cup	orange juice	125 mL
1 tsp	vanilla extract	5 mL
1 lb	walnuts, chopped (about 3½ cups/875 mL)	500 g
1	egg	1
2 tbsp	water	25 mL

1. In a mixer bowl fitted with paddle attachment, cream butter and sugar until fluffy, for 3 minutes. Add 4 eggs, one at a time, beating for about 30 seconds between each addition. Using a wooden spoon, gradually add flour, baking powder, orange juice and vanilla until incorporated. Fold in walnuts.
2. On a lightly floured work surface, divide dough into 4 pieces. Knead each piece and free-form into an 8-by 3-inch (20 by 7.5 cm) loaf. Place loaves on prepared baking sheets, at least 2 inches (5 cm) apart.
3. In a small bowl, whisk egg and water. Brush each loaf with egg wash.
4. Bake in preheated oven until firm to the touch, 25 to 30 minutes. Let cool on the pan and refrigerate overnight.
5. Preheat oven to 350°F (180°C). Cut each loaf on an angle into ½-inch (1 cm) slices. Place on baking sheets, at least 2 inches (5 cm) apart. Bake until firm and dry, 10 to 12 minutes. Let cool on baking sheets for 10 minutes before transferring to a wire rack to cool completely.

Almond Cookies

MAKES ABOUT 24 COOKIES

These little cookies are perfect with a strong espresso or caffé Americano.

Tip

If the almond paste is hard and dried out, place in the food processor with the granulated sugar called for in the recipe. Process until smooth.

- Preheat oven to 350°F (180°C)
- Baking sheets, lined with parchment paper or Silpats
- #60 disher or scoop

1 cup	all-purpose flour	250 mL
½ cup	almond flour	125 mL
½ tsp	baking powder	2 mL
½ tsp	baking soda	2 mL
2	drops almond extract	2
Pinch	salt	Pinch
½ cup	unsalted butter, softened	125 mL
1 cup	granulated sugar	250 mL
1	egg	1
7 oz	almond paste, cut into small pieces (see Tip, left)	210 g
24	whole blanched almonds (approx.)	24

Mixer Method

1. In a bowl, whisk together all-purpose flour, almond flour, baking powder, baking soda, almond extract and salt.
2. In a mixer bowl fitted with paddle attachment, cream butter and sugar until fluffy, for 2 minutes. Add egg and mix until incorporated, about 1 minute. Add almond paste and mix on low speed until well blended, for 2 minutes. Using a wooden spoon, stir in flour mixture until incorporated. Refrigerate for 20 minutes or until firm.
3. Using disher, scoop dough and place on prepared baking sheets, about 2 inches (5 cm) apart. Press down with palm of your hand. Place an almond on each cookie. Bake in a preheated oven until light brown, 9 to 12 minutes. Let cool on baking sheets for 10 minutes before transferring to a wire rack to cool completely.

Food Processor Method

1. In work bowl fitted with metal blade, process butter, sugar and almond paste until smooth, about 2 minutes. With motor running, add egg through the feed tube and process for 10 seconds. Add all-purpose flour, almond flour, baking powder, baking soda, almond extract and salt. Process for 30 seconds or until blended. Proceed with Step 3 above.

Amaretti Cookies

MAKES ABOUT 36 COOKIES

These little Italian cookies can be made easily and without too many ingredients. They are simple and tasty.

Tip

Make sure you have the brush and water handy when the cookies come out of the oven.

Variation

You can drizzle 2 oz (60 g) melted semisweet chocolate on top of the cooled cookies.

- Preheat oven to 375°F (190°C)
- Baking sheets, lined with parchment paper
- Pastry bag, fitted with large round tip

7 oz	almond paste, cut into small pieces	210 g
1 cup	granulated sugar	250 mL
2	egg whites	2
2 tbsp	granulated sugar	25 mL
2 tbsp	water	25 mL

1. In a mixer bowl fitted with paddle attachment, beat almond paste and 1 cup (250 mL) of the granulated sugar until it looks like wet sand, for 4 minutes.
2. Add egg whites in two additions, beating between each addition. After all the egg whites have been added, beat until smooth, about 3 minutes.
3. Working in batches as necessary, place batter in prepared pastry bag. Pipe mixture onto prepared baking sheets, 1 inch (2.5 cm) apart. The mounds should each be 1 to 1½ inches (2.5 to 4 cm) in diameter.
4. Place a moistened tea towel briefly on top of cookies to dampen them. Sprinkle 2 tbsp (25 mL) sugar on top. Bake in preheated oven until light brown, 15 to 18 minutes.
5. When the cookies are removed from the oven they will be stuck to the parchment paper. Turn paper over and brush the underside with water. The cookies will now easily come off the parchment paper.

Amish Cookies

MAKES ABOUT 48 COOKIES

Bakeries in the Amish area of Ohio and Pennsylvania all have their versions of tender little butter cookies. They're so good you can't eat just one. Here is a perfect recipe for them.

Tip

You can freeze the logs for up to 3 months. That way you will always have cookies ready for baking.

Variation

Sandwich cookies with a filling of Cream Cheese Icing (page 226).

- Preheat oven to 375°F (190°C)
- Baking sheets, lined with parchment paper or Silpats

4½ cups	all-purpose flour	1.125 L
1 tsp	baking soda	5 mL
1 tsp	cream of tartar	5 mL
1 cup	unsalted butter, softened	250 mL
1 cup	vegetable oil	250 mL
1 cup	granulated sugar	250 mL
1 cup	confectioner's (icing) sugar	250 mL
2	eggs	2
1 tsp	vanilla extract	5 mL

Mixer Method

1. In a large bowl, whisk together flour, baking soda and cream of tartar. Set aside.
2. In a mixer bowl fitted with paddle attachment, cream butter, oil, granulated sugar and confectioner's sugar until fluffy, for 3 minutes. Add eggs and vanilla and mix just to incorporate. Using a wooden spoon, gradually stir in flour mixture until blended.
3. Divide dough into quarters. Roll each quarter into logs about 1 inch (2.5 cm) in diameter and wrap in plastic wrap, then foil. Chill for 2 hours or freeze for 45 minutes.
4. With a sharp knife, cut each log into about 12 equal portions and place on prepared baking sheets, about 2 inches (5 cm) apart. Bake in preheated oven until light brown, 8 to 10 minutes. Let cool on baking sheets for 10 minutes before transferring to a wire rack to cool completely.

Food Processor Method

1. In a large bowl, whisk together flour, baking soda and cream of tartar. Set aside.
2. In work bowl fitted with metal blade, process butter, oil, granulated sugar and confectioner's sugar until blended, for 10 seconds. With motor running, add eggs and vanilla though the feed tube and process until blended, for 10 seconds. Add flour mixture and process just until combined, for 1 minute. Proceed with Step 3 above.

Blue Ribbon Double Chocolate Cookies

MAKES ABOUT 24 LARGE COOKIES

You will win a blue ribbon with your family when you make these award-winning cookies.

Variation

You can use an array of chips that are available these days. Try butterscotch or milk chocolate chips in place of the white and semisweet.

- Preheat oven to 350°F (180°C)
- Baking sheets, lined with parchment paper or Silpats
- #24 disher or scoop

3¾ cups	all-purpose flour	925 mL
1 tsp	baking soda	5 mL
½ tsp	salt	2 mL
1¼ cups	unsalted butter, softened	300 mL
2 cups	granulated sugar	500 mL
2	eggs	2
2 tsp	vanilla extract	10 mL
2 cups	white chocolate chips	500 mL
1 cup	semisweet chocolate chips	250 mL

Mixer Method

1. In a bowl, whisk together flour, baking soda and salt. Set aside.
2. In a mixer bowl fitted with paddle attachment, cream butter and sugar until fluffy, for 3 minutes. Add eggs, one at a time, and mix until incorporated. Beat in vanilla. Using a wooden spoon, gradually add flour mixture until blended. Stir in white and chocolate chips.
3. Using a disher, scoop dough and place on prepared baking sheets, about 2 inches (5 cm) apart. Press down with palm of your hand. Bake in preheated oven until light brown, 12 to 16 minutes. Let cool on baking sheets for 10 minutes before transferring to a wire rack to cool completely.

Food Processor Method

1. In a bowl, whisk together flour, baking soda and salt. Set aside.
2. In work bowl fitted with metal blade, process butter and sugar until combined, for 1 minute. With motor running, add eggs through feed tube and process until blended, for 10 seconds. Add vanilla. Add flour mixture and process for about 20 seconds or until combined. Transfer to a bowl and stir in white and chocolate chips by hand. Proceed with Step 3 above.

Belgian Dandoy Spice Cookies

MAKES 24 TO 48 COOKIES

Brussels has a long-standing relationship with this cookie. The best place to witness this is the Dandoy shop in the old city, run by the Dandoy family since 1829.

Tip

You can freeze the logs for up to 3 months. That way you will always have cookies ready for baking.

- Preheat oven to 350°F (180°C)
- Baking sheets, lined with parchment paper or Silpats
- Blending fork

1 cup	packed dark brown sugar	250 mL
3 tbsp	milk, preferably whole	45 mL
3 cups	all-purpose flour	750 mL
1½ tsp	ground cloves	7 mL
1½ tsp	ground cinnamon	7 mL
¾ tsp	ground ginger	4 mL
¾ tsp	ground nutmeg	4 mL
Pinch	baking powder	Pinch
Pinch	salt	Pinch
1¼ cups	unsalted butter, softened and cut into small pieces	300 mL
¼ cup	slivered blanched almonds	50 mL

Hand Method

1. In a small bowl, combine brown sugar and milk and stir until smooth. Set aside.
2. In a large bowl, sift together flour, cloves, cinnamon, ginger, nutmeg, baking powder and salt. With a blending fork or 2 knives, cut butter into flour mixture until it looks like coarse meal. Add brown sugar mixture and almonds and stir well. Wrap in foil or plastic wrap and refrigerate overnight. (Shape into 2 logs if you do not have wooden molds.)

Food Processor Method

1. In a small bowl, combine brown sugar and milk and stir until smooth. Set aside.
2. In work bowl fitted with metal blade, process flour, cloves, cinnamon, ginger, nutmeg, baking powder and salt until combined, for 10 seconds. Add butter around work bowl and pulse 20 times until crumbly. Add brown sugar mixture and process for 15 seconds until dough holds together. Transfer dough to a large bowl and blend almonds into dough by hand. Wrap in foil or plastic wrap and refrigerate overnight. (Shape into two logs if you do not have wooden molds.)

If using a wooden mold

Brush carvings in mold well with a stiff brush, but do not wash. (You should never grease or wash carved moulds. The wood will warp.) Dust well with flour. Press enough chilled dough into the mold to fill it completely. With a small knife, cut around the edge of the pattern, removing the trimmings. Carefully invert filled mold onto baking sheets. Tap lightly to release the dough onto baking sheets. Repeat until baking sheet is full, leaving 1 inch (2.5 cm) between cookies. Bake in preheated oven until light brown, 15 to 25 minutes, depending on the mold size.

Without a mold

On a lightly floured surface, cut each log into ¼-inch (0.5 cm) slices and place on prepared baking sheets, about 2 inches (5 cm) apart. Bake in preheated oven until edges are light brown, 9 to 12 minutes.

Boysenberry Chews

MAKES 36 COOKIES

Living close to where the boysenberry was created in Buena Park, California, I decided to create this cookie chew using their famous preserves.

Tip

Make sure the melted chocolate mixture has cooled to the touch prior to adding to the butter mixture or it will curdle.

Variation

If boysenberry preserves are difficult to locate you can use raspberry or strawberry.

- Preheat oven to 375°F (190°C)
- Baking sheets, lined with parchment paper or Silpats
- #60 disher or scoop

4 oz	unsweetened chocolate, chopped	125 g
½ cup	milk, preferably whole	125 mL
½ cup	unsalted butter, softened	125 mL
2 cups	granulated sugar	500 mL
1	egg, beaten	1
2 cups	all-purpose flour	500 mL
½ tsp	baking soda	2 mL
1½ cups	sweetened flaked coconut	375 mL
1 cup	boysenberry preserves	250 mL
½ cup	chopped pecans	125 mL

Mixer Method

1. In a saucepan over low heat, melt chocolate and milk, stirring until chocolate has melted. Set aside.
2. In a mixer bowl fitted with paddle attachment, cream butter and sugar until fluffy, for 2 minutes. Beat in egg for 30 seconds. Blend in melted chocolate mixture on low speed for 2 minutes. Using a wooden spoon, stir in flour, baking soda, coconut, boysenberry preserves and chopped nuts. If batter is too soft, refrigerate for 15 minutes.
3. Using disher, scoop dough and place on prepared sheets, about 2 inches (5 cm) apart. Press down with palm of your hand. Bake in preheated oven until light brown, 10 to 12 minutes. Let cool on baking sheets for 10 minutes before transferring to a wire rack to cool completely.

Food Processor Method

1. In a saucepan on low heat, melt chocolate and milk together, stirring until chocolate has melted. Set aside.
2. In work bowl fitted with metal blade, process butter and sugar until light and creamy, about 10 seconds. With motor running, add egg and melted chocolate mixture through the feed tube and process for 10 seconds, until combined. Add flour and baking soda and process for 10 seconds or until blended. Transfer to a large bowl. Fold in coconut, boysenberry preserves and chopped nuts by hand. If batter is too soft, refrigerate for 15 minutes. Proceed with Step 3 above.

Butter Crispy Cookies

MAKES 30 COOKIES

These are the best butter cookies you could make. I love the crunch of these cookies.

Tip

Make sure you slowly add the sugar into the butter or the cookies will not be as crunchy as they should be.

Variation

Roll the dough in colored sugars for holiday-themed cookies.

- Preheat oven to 325°F (160°C)
- Baking sheets, lined with parchment paper or Silpats
- #50 disher or scoop

1 cup	unsalted butter, softened	250 mL
10 tbsp	granulated sugar, divided	150 mL
	Grated zest of 1 lemon	
2 cups	all-purpose flour	500 mL
½ tsp	salt	2 mL
¼ cup	granulated sugar	50 mL

Mixer Method

1. In a mixer bowl fitted with paddle attachment, cream butter until fluffy, for 3 minutes. With mixer running, spoon 10 tbsp (150 mL) sugar, 1 tbsp (15 mL) at a time, into butter. Using a wooden spoon, stir in lemon zest, all-purpose flour and salt until well blended. Refrigerate for 20 minutes.
2. Place ¼ cup (50 mL) granulated sugar in a shallow dish. Using disher, scoop dough and roll in sugar. Place on prepared baking sheets, about 2 inches (5 cm) apart. Press down with palm of your hand. Bake in preheated oven until light brown, 12 to 16 minutes. Let cool on baking sheets for 10 minutes before transferring to a wire rack to cool completely.

Food Processor Method

1. In work bowl fitted with metal blade, process butter for 15 seconds. With motor running, add 10 tbsp (150 mL) sugar, 1 tbsp (15 mL) at a time, through the feed tube and process until incorporated. Add lemon zest, all-purpose flour and salt and process until well blended, for 3 minutes. Refrigerate for 35 minutes. Proceed with Step 2 above.

Cashew Butter Cookies

MAKES ABOUT 48 COOKIES

If you love peanut butter cookies, you will really love the richness of these cashew butter cookies.

Variation

Cashew Chocolate Chip Cookies: Stir in 1 cup (250 mL) semisweet chocolate chips to dough by hand.

- Preheat oven to 350°F (180°C)
- Baking sheets, lined with parchment paper or Silpats (see Tip, page 73)
- #60 disher or scoop

1¾ cups	all-purpose flour	425 mL
1 tsp	baking soda	5 mL
½ tsp	salt	2 mL
½ cup	vegetable shortening	125 mL
½ cup	cashew butter	125 mL
¾ cup	granulated sugar, divided	175 mL
½ cup	packed brown sugar	125 mL
1	egg	1
2 tbsp	milk, preferably whole	25 mL
1 tsp	vanilla extract	5 mL
1 cup	whole roasted cashews (approx.)	250 mL

Mixer Method

1. In a bowl, whisk together flour, baking soda and salt. Set aside.
2. In a mixer bowl fitted with paddle attachment, cream shortening, cashew butter, ½ cup (125 mL) of the granulated sugar, brown sugar, egg, milk and vanilla until light and fluffy, for 3 minutes. Using a wooden spoon, gradually stir in flour mixture until incorporated. Refrigerate for 10 minutes.
3. Place remaining ¼ cup (50 mL) of granulated sugar in a shallow dish. Using disher, scoop dough and roll in sugar. Place on prepared baking sheets, about 2 inches (5 cm) apart. Press down with palm of your hand. Place 2 cashews on top of each cookie. Bake in preheated oven until golden brown, 10 to 12 minutes. Let cool on baking sheets for 10 minutes before transferring to a wire rack to cool completely.

Food Processor Method

1. In work bowl fitted with metal blade, process flour, baking soda, salt, shortening, cashew butter, ½ cup (125 mL) of the granulated sugar, brown sugar, egg, milk and vanilla until light and creamy, about 2 minutes. Refrigerate dough for 20 minutes. Proceed with Step 3 above.

Butter Pecan Shortbread Cookies

MAKES ABOUT 24 COOKIES

These fast cookies have only four ingredients. They're perfect for when you're out of eggs.

Tip

Toast and cool pecans prior to adding to dough or the taste will not be nutty. Place pecans in a single layer on a baking sheet. Bake at 350°F (180°C) for about 8 minutes or until fragrant.

Variation

Replace pecans with ⅔ cup (150 mL) of chocolate chips.

- Preheat oven to 350°F (180°C)
- Baking sheets, lined with parchment paper or Silpats
- #70 disher or scoop

¾ cup	unsalted butter, softened	175 mL
½ cup	granulated sugar	125 mL
1½ cups	all-purpose flour	375 mL
½ cup	chopped pecans, toasted (see Tip, left)	125 mL

Mixer Method

1. In a mixer bowl fitted with paddle attachment, cream butter and sugar until fluffy, for 3 minutes. Using a wooden spoon, stir in flour and pecans until blended.
2. Using disher, scoop dough and place on prepared baking sheets, about 2 inches (5 cm) apart. Press down with palm of your hand. Bake in preheated oven until edges are light brown, 12 to 16 minutes. Let cool on baking sheets for 10 minutes before transferring to a wire rack to cool completely.

Food Processor Method

1. In work bowl fitted with metal blade, process butter and sugar until smooth, for 10 seconds. Add flour and process for 10 seconds, until blended. Transfer dough to a bowl and fold in pecans by hand. Refrigerate for 20 minutes or until firm. Proceed with Step 2 above.

Candied Ginger Cookies

MAKES ABOUT 24 COOKIES

When I discovered a new product, ginger nibs, I knew I wanted to create a new ginger cookie just for them.

Tip

Ginger nibs are small pieces or nibs of candied ginger. If you don't have ginger nibs, use candied ginger and cut into small pieces.

- Preheat oven to 325°F (160°C)
- Baking sheets, lined with parchment paper or Silpats
- #50 disher or scoop

1 cup	unsalted butter, softened	250 mL
2⁄3 cup	granulated sugar	150 mL
2 cups	all-purpose flour	500 mL
1 tsp	ground cinnamon	5 mL
1 tsp	ground ginger	5 mL
1⁄2 tsp	salt	2 mL
2 tsp	vanilla extract	10 mL
1 tbsp	candied ginger nibs (see Tip, left)	15 mL

Mixer Method

1. In a mixer bowl fitted with paddle attachment, cream butter and sugar until fluffy, for 2 minutes. Using a wooden spoon, gradually stir in flour, cinnamon, ground ginger, salt and vanilla until incorporated. Refrigerate for 15 minutes.
2. Using disher, scoop dough and place on prepared baking sheets, about 2 inches (5 cm) apart. Press down with palm of your hand. Place a ginger nib on each. Bake in preheated oven until golden brown, 14 to 16 minutes. Let cool on baking sheets for 10 minutes before transferring to a wire rack to cool completely.

Food Processor Method

1. In work bowl fitted with metal blade, process butter and sugar until fluffy, for 15 seconds. Add flour, cinnamon, ground ginger, salt and vanilla and process until incorporated, for 10 seconds. Refrigerate for 20 minutes. Proceed with Step 2 above.

Cherry Almond Butter Cookies

MAKES 36 COOKIES

Every country I travel to claims to have invented this cookie. It is a simple tea cookie that I love to make during the holiday season.

Tip

Use green and red cherries during the holiday season.

Variation

You can make chocolate star cookies by replacing 1/3 cup (75 mL) of the biscuit mix with unsweetened Dutch-process cocoa powder and adding 1 tbsp (15 mL) extra butter.

- Preheat oven to 350°F (180°C)
- Baking sheets, lined with parchment paper or Silpats
- 12-inch (30 cm) pastry bag, fitted with a large star tip

3/4 cup	granulated sugar	175 mL
1/4 cup	unsalted butter, softened	50 mL
2	eggs	2
1/8 tsp	almond extract	0.5 mL
2 3/4 cups	dry biscuit mix, such as Bisquick or other dry biscuit mix	675 mL
1	jar (8 oz/250 mL) maraschino cherries	1

1. In a mixer bowl fitted with paddle attachment, cream sugar and butter until light and fluffy, for 3 minutes. Add eggs and almond extract until blended. Using a wooden spoon, stir in biscuit mix just until blended.
2. Working in batches as necessary, place dough in prepared pastry bag. Pipe stars on prepared baking sheets, about 2 inches (5 cm) apart.
3. Thoroughly drain maraschino cherries on paper towels. Cut each in half. Place one half on each cookie star, cut-side down. Bake in preheated oven until edges color a little, 10 to 12 minutes. Let cool on baking sheets for 10 minutes before transferring to a wire rack to cool completely.

Chinese Almond Cookies

MAKES ABOUT 30 COOKIES

No need to buy Chinese almond cookies when making them is so easy and they taste even better than store-bought!

Variation

Replace ½ cup (125 mL) all-purpose flour with same amount of finely ground almonds for a crunchy cookie.

- Preheat oven to 325°F (160°C)
- Baking sheets, lined with parchment paper or Silpats
- #60 disher or scoop

1 cup	unsalted butter, softened	250 mL
1 cup	granulated sugar	250 mL
2	eggs, beaten	2
1 tbsp	almond extract	15 mL
2½ cups	all-purpose flour	625 mL
⅛ tsp	salt	0.5 mL
½ tsp	baking soda	2 mL
1	egg yolk	1
2 tsp	warm water	10 mL
30	whole blanched almonds (approx.)	30

Mixer Method

1. In a mixer bowl fitted with paddle attachment, cream butter and sugar until light and fluffy, for 2 minutes. Add eggs and almond extract and mix until well blended, for 2 minutes. Using a wooden spoon, stir in flour, salt and baking soda until soft dough forms. Refrigerate for 10 minutes.
2. Using disher, scoop dough and place on prepared baking sheets, about 2 inches (5 cm) apart. Press down with palm of your hand. In a small bowl, whisk egg yolk and warm water. Brush egg wash over each cookie. Place an almond on each cookie. Bake in preheated oven until light brown and egg wash is shiny, 20 to 22 minutes. Let cool on baking sheets for 10 minutes before transferring to a wire rack to cool completely.

Food Processor Method

1. In work bowl fitted with metal blade, process butter and sugar until creamy, for 1 minute. With motor running, add eggs and almond extract through feed tube and process until well blended, for 10 seconds. Add flour, salt and baking soda and process until a soft dough forms, for 20 seconds. Refrigerate for 20 minutes. Proceed with Step 2 above.

Chocolate Chip Cookies

MAKES ABOUT 18 LARGE COOKIES

I have probably made hundreds and hundreds of chocolate chip cookies in my day. These are thick and chewy. I dislike nuts in my chocolate chip cookies, but you can include them if you like.

Tip

Make sure you remove dough from food processor before adding chocolate chips and nuts or they will become pulverized.

Variation

White Chocolate Chip Macadamia Cookies: Use 1½ cups (375 mL) white chocolate chips in place of the chocolate chips and 1½ cups (375 mL) toasted macadamia nuts, coarsely chopped, for the nuts.

- Preheat oven to 325°F (160°C)
- Baking sheets, lined with parchment paper or Silpats
- #24 disher or scoop

2⅛ cups	all-purpose flour	525 mL
½ tsp	salt	2 mL
½ tsp	baking soda	2 mL
¾ cup	unsalted butter, melted and cooled	175 mL
1 cup	packed brown sugar	250 mL
1	egg	1
2 tsp	vanilla extract	10 mL
2 cups	semisweet or milk chocolate chips	500 mL
1 cup	chopped nuts, toasted, optional	250 mL

Mixer Method

1. In a bowl, whisk together flour, salt and baking soda. Set aside.
2. In a mixer bowl fitted with paddle attachment, beat butter and sugar until very smooth. With mixer running, add egg and vanilla. Using a wooden spoon, stir in flour mixture until incorporated. Fold in chocolate chips and nuts, if using. Refrigerate for 10 minutes.
3. Using disher, scoop dough and place on prepared baking sheets, about 2 inches (5 cm) apart. Press down with palm of your hand. Bake in preheated oven until light brown, 14 to 18 minutes. Let cool on baking sheet for 10 minutes before transferring to a wire rack to cool completely.

Food Processor Method

1. In a bowl, whisk together flour, salt and baking soda. Set aside.
2. In work bowl fitted with metal blade, process butter and sugar until blended, for 15 seconds. With motor running, add egg and vanilla through the feed tube and process until incorporated, for 10 seconds. Add flour mixture and process until a soft dough forms, for 20 seconds. Transfer dough to a large bowl and fold in chips and nuts, if using. Refrigerate for 20 minutes. Proceed with Step 3 above.

Chocolate-Drizzled Meringue Cookies

MAKES 48 COOKIES

I noticed huge meringue cookies in a pastry window in London and was dazzled. This recipe makes a smaller version of those giant cookies, but you can make the large version if you prefer.

Variations

For huge "London" meringues: Dollop one-half of the meringue in 2 mounds on each of 2 prepared baking sheets, making 4 large mounds. Proceed with drying instructions in Step 3. Decrease melted chocolate to 2 oz (60 g). Drizzle over meringues.

Add 1 tsp (5 mL) peppermint extract into whipped meringues to make mint meringues.

- Preheat oven to 200°F (100°C)
- Baking sheets, lined with parchment paper or Silpats
- 14-inch (35 cm) pastry bag, fitted with a large star tip

6	egg whites, at room temperature	6
1 tsp	cream of tartar	5 mL
½ tsp	salt	2 mL
1½ cups	granulated sugar, divided	375 mL
4 oz	semisweet chocolate, melted and slightly cooled	125 g

1. Prior to starting, make sure your cooking utensils and mixer are free of any oil and are dry and clean. This is important because egg whites won't get stiff if there is any oil on the bowl or whip.
2. In a mixer bowl fitted with whip attachment, whip egg whites, cream of tartar and salt until frothy, about 4 minutes. Place on high speed and beat until whip starts to leave streak marks in egg whites. Gradually beat in half of sugar, 1 tbsp (15 mL) at a time, beating well between each addition. Remove bowl from mixer. Using a rubber spatula, gently fold in remaining sugar just until incorporated.
3. Place meringue in prepared pastry bag. Pipe cookies the size of 2-inch (5 cm) stars onto prepared baking sheets. Place in oven. Turn oven off and dry meringues overnight, until firm to the touch.
4. Using a fork, drizzle melted chocolate over top of dried meringues.

Chocolate Chunk Cookies

MAKES ABOUT 36 LARGE COOKIES

Sometimes I like making chocolate cookies with chunks of chocolate in them instead of the traditional chips.

- Preheat oven to 325°F (160°C)
- 2 baking sheets, lined with parchment paper or Silpats
- #24 disher or scoop

4¼ cups	all-purpose flour	1.05 L
1 tsp	salt	5 mL
1 tsp	baking soda	5 mL
1½ cups	unsalted butter, melted and cooled	375 mL
1 cup	packed brown sugar	250 mL
1 cup	granulated sugar	250 mL
2	eggs	2
1 tbsp	vanilla extract	15 mL
2 cups	semisweet or milk chocolate chunks (12 oz/375 g)	500 mL

Mixer Method

1. In a large bowl, whisk together flour, salt and baking soda. Set aside.
2. In a mixer bowl fitted with paddle attachment, beat butter, brown sugar and granulated sugar until incorporated. With mixer running, add eggs and vanilla on low speed until incorporated. Using a wooden spoon, gradually stir in flour mixture until incorporated. Fold in chocolate chunks. Refrigerate for 10 minutes.
3. Using disher, scoop dough and place on prepared baking sheets, about 2 inches (5 cm) apart. Press down with palm of your hand. Bake in preheated oven until light brown, 14 to 18 minutes. Let cool on baking sheets for 10 minutes before transferring to a wire rack to cool completely.

Food Processor Method

1. In a large bowl, whisk together flour, salt and baking soda. Set aside.
2. In work bowl fitted with metal blade, process butter, brown sugar and granulated sugar until blended, for 15 seconds. With motor running, add eggs and vanilla through the feed tube and process until incorporated, for 10 seconds. Add flour mixture and process until a soft dough forms, for 20 seconds. Transfer dough to a large bowl and fold in chocolate chunks by hand. Refrigerate for 20 minutes. Proceed with Step 3 above.

Chocolate Snowballs

MAKES ABOUT 38 COOKIES

Rich and a reminder of winter! These snowball cookies look great on a brunch table.

- Preheat oven to 350°F (180°C)
- Baking pans sheets, lined with parchments paper or Silpats
- #40 disher or scoop

1¼ cups	unsalted butter, softened	300 mL
⅔ cup	granulated sugar	150 mL
1 tsp	vanilla extract	5 mL
2 cups	all-purpose flour	500 mL
½ cup	unsweetened Dutch-process cocoa powder, sifted	125 mL
1 cup	hazelnuts, chopped and toasted	250 mL
1 cup	semisweet chocolate chips	250 mL
½ cup	confectioner's (icing) sugar	125 mL

Mixer Method

1. In a mixer bowl fitted with paddle attachment, cream butter, sugar and vanilla until light and fluffy, for 3 minutes. Using a wooden spoon, gradually stir in flour and cocoa powder until incorporated. Fold in hazelnuts and chocolate chips. Refrigerate for 1 hour.
2. Using disher, scoop dough and roll into perfect balls. Place on prepared baking sheets, about 2 inches (5 cm) apart. Bake in preheated oven until slightly firm, 16 to 18 minutes. Let cool on baking sheets for 10 minutes before transferring to a wire rack to cool completely. Place confectioner's sugar in a shallow dish and roll the cooled chocolate balls.

Food Processor Method

1. In work bowl fitted with metal blade, process butter, sugar and vanilla for 20 seconds, until blended. Add flour and cocoa powder and process until incorporated, 3 minutes. Transfer dough to a bowl and fold nuts and chips into batter. Refrigerate for 1 hour. Proceed with Step 2 above.

Citrus White Chocolate Macaroons

MAKES ABOUT 18 MACAROONS

Fresh orange and lemon zest make this macaroon perfect for springtime.

Variation

Melt 3 oz (90 g) white chocolate and drizzle evenly on top of each cooled macaroon.

- Preheat oven to 300°F (150°C)
- Baking sheets, lined with parchment paper or Silpats
- #40 disher or scoop

4 cups	sweetened shredded coconut	1 L
3/4 cup	sweetened condensed milk	175 mL
1	egg white, lighten beaten	1
1/2 cup	white chocolate chunks	125 mL
1 tsp	grated lemon zest	5 mL
1 tsp	grated orange zest	5 mL
1 tsp	vanilla extract	5 mL

1. In a large bowl, combine coconut, condensed milk, egg white, chocolate chunks, lemon zest, orange zest and vanilla and mix until all coconut is moistened.
2. Using disher, scoop macaroons and place on prepared baking sheets, about 2 inches (5 cm) apart. Bake in preheated oven until light brown and firm to the touch, about 20 minutes. Let cool on baking sheets for 10 minutes before transferring to a wire rack to cool completely.

Coconut Macaroons

MAKES ABOUT 36 MACAROONS

Fast and easy to make and perfect for the kids to help — all you use is a bowl and spoon.

Variation

You can add ¾ cup (175 mL) mini chocolate chips or dried cranberries to the batter.

- Preheat oven to 300°F (150°C)
- Baking sheets, lined with parchment paper or Silpats
- #40 disher or scoop

8 cups	sweetened shredded coconut (about 1¾ lbs/875 g)	2 L
1	can (14 oz/396 g or 300 mL) sweetened condensed milk	1
2	egg whites, lighten beaten	2
1 tsp	vanilla extract	5 mL
1 tsp	almond extract	5 mL
Pinch	salt	Pinch

1. In a large bowl, combine coconut, condensed milk, egg whites, vanilla and almond extracts and salt and mix until all coconut is moistened.
2. Using disher, scoop macaroons and place on prepared baking sheets, about 2 inches (5 cm) apart. Bake in preheated oven until light brown and firm to the touch, about 20 minutes. Let cool on baking sheets for 10 minutes before transferring to a wire rack to cool completely.

French Chocolate Cookies

MAKES ABOUT 24 COOKIES

These small and elegant cookies are perfect to serve with cappuccino.

Tip

After cookies have cooled, refrigerate and then dip in chocolate so they firm up faster.

Variation

You can use any kind of chopped and toasted nuts for decoration.

- Preheat oven to 350°F (180°C)
- Baking sheets, lined with parchment paper or Silpats
- #70 disher or scoop

3⁄4 cup	unsalted butter, softened	175 mL
1⁄2 cup	granulated sugar	125 mL
1 1⁄4 cups	all-purpose flour	300 mL
1⁄2 cup	unsweetened Dutch-process cocoa powder, sifted	125 mL
4 oz	bittersweet chocolate, melted and cooled	125 g
1 cup	pecans, finely chopped and toasted (see Tip, page 36)	250 mL

Mixer Method

1. In a mixer bowl fitted with paddle attachment, cream butter until light and fluffy, for 3 minutes. Gradually add sugar and continue beating until fluffy, about 3 minutes. Using a wooden spoon, gradually stir in flour and cocoa powder until well blended.
2. Using disher, scoop dough and place on prepared baking sheets, about 2 inches (5 cm) apart. Press down with palm of your hand. Bake in preheated oven until edges start to firm, 18 to 20 minutes.
3. Let cool completely on baking sheets. Dip half of each cookie into melted chocolate and then pecans. Let cool on parchment paper until chocolate is set.

Food Processor Method

1. In work bowl fitted with metal blade, process butter and sugar until fluffy, about 2 minutes. Add flour and cocoa powder and process until incorporated, for 1 minute. Refrigerate for 20 minutes. Proceed with Step 2 above.

Gingersnaps

MAKES ABOUT 24 COOKIES

This is the best gingersnap cookie recipe invented. The four different spices work in unison to create the crunchiest, snappiest, most flavorful ginger cookie ever! Make a double batch of these cookies, then grind them to a powder in a food processor and use for the crust on the French Apple Cheesecake (see recipe, page 168).

- Preheat oven to 375°F (190°C)
- Baking sheets, lined with parchment paper or Silpats
- #40 disher or scoop

2¼ cups	all-purpose flour	550 mL
2 tsp	baking soda	10 mL
1 tsp	ground cinnamon	5 mL
1 tsp	ground ginger	5 mL
½ tsp	salt	2 mL
½ tsp	ground cloves	2 mL
¼ tsp	ground allspice	1 mL
¼ cup	unsalted butter, softened	50 mL
1 cup	packed light brown sugar	250 mL
1	egg	1
¼ cup	dark (cooking) molasses	50 mL
¼ cup	granulated sugar	50 mL

Mixer Method

1. In a large bowl, whisk together flour, baking soda, cinnamon, ginger, salt, cloves and allspice. Set aside.
2. In a mixer bowl fitted with paddle attachment, cream butter and brown sugar until light and fluffy, for 2 minutes. Add egg and molasses and mix until blended, for 2 minutes. Using a wooden spoon, gradually stir in flour mixture until blended, 2 minutes. Refrigerate for 10 minutes.
3. Place granulated sugar in a shallow dish. Using disher, scoop dough and roll in sugar. Place on prepared baking sheets, about 2 inches (5 cm) apart. Press down with palm of your hand. Bake in preheated oven until tops start to crack a bit, 8 to 10 minutes. Let cool on baking sheets for 10 minutes before transferring to a wire rack to cool completely.

Food Processor Method

1. In a large bowl, whisk together flour, baking soda, cinnamon, ginger, salt, cloves and allspice. Set aside.
2. In work bowl fitted with metal blade, process butter and brown sugar until blended, for 10 seconds. With motor running, add egg and molasses through the feed tube and process until incorporated, for 10 seconds. Add flour mixture and process until blended, for 10 seconds. Refrigerate for 20 minutes. Proceed with Step 3 above.

Greek Butter Cookies

MAKES ABOUT 24 COOKIES

Little bites of Greek cookies are perfect for a cookie tray.

Tip

If you don't have pastry flour, substitute ¾ cup (175 mL) each all-purpose and cake flours. For more information about different flours, see page 12.

- Preheat oven to 350°F (180°C)
- Baking sheets, lined with parchment paper or Silpats
- #70 disher or scoop

½ cup	unsalted butter, softened	125 mL
¾ cup	confectioner's (icing) sugar, divided	175 mL
1	egg yolk	1
1½ cups	pastry flour (see Tip, left)	375 mL
¼ tsp	ground nutmeg	1 mL

Mixer Method

1. In a mixer bowl with paddle attachment, cream butter and ¼ cup (50 mL) of the confectioner's sugar until fluffy, about 2 minutes. Add egg yolk and mix until incorporated, for 1 minute. Using a wooden spoon, stir in flour and nutmeg until blended. Refrigerate for 20 minutes.
2. Using disher, scoop dough into rounds and roll between your palms. Place dough balls on prepared baking sheets, about 2 inches (5 cm) apart. Bake in preheated oven until light brown, 18 to 20 minutes. Let cool on baking sheets for 10 minutes before transferring to a wire rack to cool completely. Place remaining ½ cup (125 mL) confectioner's sugar in a shallow dish and roll cooled cookies.

Food Processor Method

1. In work bowl fitted with metal blade, process butter, ¼ cup (50 mL) of the confectioner's sugar, egg yolk, pastry flour and nutmeg until blended, for 1 minute. Refrigerate for 20 minutes or until firm. Proceed with Step 2 above.

Lemon Shortbread Cookies

MAKES ABOUT 30 COOKIES

You can have a batch of these fast and easy shortbreads ready in less than 20 minutes.

Tip
If lemon oil is not available, increase the lemon zest to 2 medium lemons.

- Preheat oven to 300°F (150°C)
- Baking sheets, lined with parchment paper or Silpats
- #50 disher or scoop

1 cup	unsalted butter, softened	250 mL
½ cup	confectioner's (icing) sugar	125 mL
1 tsp	vanilla extract	5 mL
2 cups	all-purpose flour	500 mL
	Grated zest of 1 lemon	
1 tsp	lemon oil (see Tip, left)	5 mL
¼ tsp	salt	1 mL

Mixer Method

1. In a mixer bowl fitted with paddle attachment, cream butter and confectioner's sugar until fluffy, for 3 minutes. Beat in vanilla. Using a wooden spoon, gradually stir in flour, zest, oil and salt and mix just until incorporated. Refrigerate for 10 minutes.
2. Using disher, scoop dough and place on prepared baking sheets, about 2 inches (5 cm) apart. Press down with palm of your hand. Bake in preheated oven until firm, but not yet starting to brown, 20 to 22 minutes. Let cool on baking sheets for 10 minutes before transferring to a wire rack to cool completely.

Food Processor Method

1. In work bowl fitted with metal blade, process butter and confectioner's sugar until fluffy, for 30 seconds. Add vanilla, flour, zest, oil and salt and process just until incorporated, for 20 seconds. Refrigerate for 15 minutes.

Island Macaroons

MAKES ABOUT 18 MACAROONS

One bowl and no mixer. How can cookies be easier?

Variation

Add ¾ cup (175 mL) toasted and crushed macadamia nuts to macaroons.

- Preheat oven to 300°F (150°C)
- Baking sheets, lined with parchment paper or Silpats
- #40 disher or scoop

4 cups	sweetened shredded coconut (14 oz/420 g)	1 L
¾ cup	sweetened condensed milk	175 mL
1	egg white	1
½ cup	white chocolate chunks	125 mL
½ cup	dried apricots, chopped fine	125 mL
1 tsp	vanilla extract	5 mL
½ tsp	rum extract	2 mL

1. In a large bowl, combine coconut, condensed milk, egg white, chocolate chunks, apricots, vanilla and rum extracts and mix until all coconut is moistened.
2. Using disher, scoop mixture and place on prepared baking sheets, about 2 inches (5 cm) apart. Bake in preheated oven until light brown and firm to the touch, about 20 minutes. Let cool on baking sheets for 10 minutes before transferring to a wire rack to cool completely.

Lavender Snap Tea Cookies

MAKES 30 COOKIES

The slight hint of lavender in these cookies is perfect for tea.

Tip

If you can't find lavender sugar you can make your own. Purchase ¼ cup (50 mL) dried lavender at a health food or specialty food store (make sure it is not treated with preservatives) and process with 2 cups (500 mL) granulated sugar in work bowl of food processor with metal blade for 30 seconds.

- Preheat oven to 325°F (160°C)
- Baking sheets, lined with parchment paper or Silpats
- #50 disher or scoop

1 cup	unsalted butter, softened	250 mL
5 tbsp	granulated sugar, divided	75 mL
5 tbsp	lavender sugar, divided (see Tip, left)	75 mL
2 cups	all-purpose flour	500 mL
½ tsp	salt	2 mL
¼ cup	granulated sugar	50 mL
30	dried lavender flowers	30

Mixer Method

1. In a mixer bowl fitted with paddle attachment, beat butter until creamy, for 3 minutes. With mixer running, add 5 tbsp (75 mL) granulated sugar and lavender sugar into butter, 1 tbsp (15 mL) at a time. Using a wooden spoon, gradually stir in flour and salt until well blended. Refrigerate for 20 minutes.
2. Place ¼ cup (50 mL) granulated sugar in a shallow dish. Using disher, scoop dough and roll in sugar. Place on prepared baking sheets, about 2 inches (5 cm) apart. Press down with palm of your hand. Lightly press a lavender flower on top of each unbaked cookie. Bake in preheated oven until light brown, 12 to 16 minutes.

Food Processor Method

1. In work bowl fitted with metal blade, process butter until creamy, for 15 seconds. With motor running, add 5 tbsp (75 mL) granulated sugar and lavender sugar, 1 tbsp (15 mL) at a time, through the feed tube and process until incorporated. Add flour and salt and process or until well blended, for 30 seconds. Refrigerate for 35 minutes. Proceed with Step 2 above.

Macadamia Crunch Cookies

MAKES ABOUT 24 LARGE COOKIES

Macadamia nuts are so rich it's best to eat only one of these delicious cookies.

- Preheat oven to 325°F (160°C)
- Baking sheets, lined with parchment paper or Silpats
- #24 disher or scoop

2 cups	all-purpose flour	500 mL
½ cup	old-fashioned rolled oats	125 mL
1 tsp	baking soda	5 mL
½ tsp	ground nutmeg	2 mL
1 cup	unsalted butter, softened	250 mL
¾ cup	granulated sugar	175 mL
½ cup	packed brown sugar	125 mL
2	eggs	2
2 tbsp	milk, preferably whole	25 mL
2 tsp	vanilla extract	10 mL
2 cups	macadamia nuts, finely chopped	500 mL

Mixer Method

1. In a bowl, whisk together flour, oats, baking soda and nutmeg. Set aside.
2. In a mixer bowl fitted with paddle attachment, cream butter, granulated sugar and brown sugar until fluffy, for 2 minutes. Add eggs, one at a time, and mix until blended, for 2 minutes. Beat in milk and vanilla. Using a wooden spoon, gradually stir in flour mixture until incorporated. Fold in macadamia nuts.
3. Using disher, scoop dough and place on prepared baking sheets, about 2 inches (5 cm) apart. Press down with palm of your hand. Bake in preheated oven until light brown, 10 to 14 minutes. Let cool on baking sheets for 10 minutes before transferring to a wire rack to cool completely.

Food Processor Method

1. In a bowl, whisk together flour, oats, baking soda and nutmeg. Set aside.
2. In work bowl fitted with metal blade, process butter, granulated sugar and brown sugar until fluffy, for 10 seconds. With motor running, add eggs, vanilla and milk through the feed tube and process until blended, for 10 seconds. Add flour mixture and process just until incorporated, for 10 seconds. Transfer to a bowl and fold in macadamia nuts by hand. Proceed with Step 3 above.

Maple Sugar Cookies

MAKES 60 COOKIES

I like to serve these cookies with Lavender Snap Tea Cookies and Vanilla Rose Cookies with Rose Crème Filling (see recipes, pages 53 and 75) for a great trio of flavors.

Tip

Maple sugar is available at specialty gourmet stores and health food and well-stocked grocer stores. See also Sources, page 442.

- Preheat oven to 325°F (160°C)
- Baking sheets, lined with parchment paper or Silpats (see Tip, page 73)
- #50 disher or scoop

2 cups	unsalted butter, softened	500 mL
10 tbsp	granulated sugar	150 mL
10 tbsp	granulated maple sugar (see Tip, left)	150 mL
4 cups	all-purpose flour	1 L
1 tsp	salt	5 mL
½ cup	granulated sugar	125 mL

Mixer Method

1. In a mixer bowl fitted with paddle attachment, beat butter until creamy, for 3 minutes. With mixer running, add 10 tbsp (150 mL) granulated sugar and maple sugar, 1 tbsp (15 mL) at a time, into butter until fluffy. Using a wooden spoon, gradually stir in flour and salt until blended. Refrigerate for 20 minutes.
2. Place ½ cup (125 mL) granulated sugar in a shallow dish. Using disher, scoop dough and roll in sugar. Place on prepared baking sheets, about 2 inches (5 cm) apart. Press down with palm of your hand. Bake in preheated oven until light brown, 12 to 16 minutes. Let cool on baking sheets for 10 minutes before transferring to a wire rack to cool completely.

Food Processor Method

1. In work bowl fitted with metal blade, process butter until creamy, for 15 seconds. With motor running, add 10 tbsp (150 mL) granulated sugar and maple sugar, 1 tbsp (15 mL) at a time, through the feed tube and process until incorporated. Add flour and salt and mix until blended, for 30 seconds. Refrigerate for 35 minutes. Proceed with Step 2 above.

Mexican Wedding Cakes

MAKES ABOUT 48 COOKIES

Similar to Russian tea cakes, these buttery cookies (also known as Mexican Wedding Cookies) were first made in the mid-1950s.

Tip

Make sure cookies are cooled before rolling in confectioner's sugar. If the cookies are hot the sugar will just dissolve into cookies.

- Preheat oven to 325°F (160°C)
- Baking sheets, lined with parchment paper or Silpats
- #70 disher or scoop

½ cup	unsalted butter, softened	125 mL
½ cup	granulated sugar	125 mL
1⅓ cups	all-purpose flour	325 mL
1 cup	pecans, finely chopped	250 mL
¼ tsp	vanilla extract	1 mL
Pinch	salt	Pinch
¼ cup	confectioner's (icing) sugar, sifted	50 mL

Mixer Method

1. In a mixer bowl fitted with paddle attachment, cream butter and granulated sugar until fluffy, for 2 minutes. Using a wooden spoon, gradually stir in flour, pecans, vanilla and salt and mix until well blended. If dough is too soft, refrigerate for 20 minutes.
2. Using disher, scoop dough and roll into balls between your palms. Place on prepared baking sheets, about 2 inches (5 cm) apart. Bake in preheated oven until light brown, 12 to 15 minutes.
3. Let cool on baking sheets for 10 minutes before transferring to a wire rack to cool completely. Place confectioner's sugar in a shallow dish and roll cooled cookies in sugar.

Food Processor Method

1. In work bowl fitted with metal blade, process butter, granulated sugar, flour, pecans, vanilla and salt until smooth, for 2 minutes. Refrigerate for 20 minutes. Proceed with Step 2 above.

Oatmeal Raisin Cookies

MAKES ABOUT 46 LARGE COOKIES

These cookies remind me of the big cookies of my elementary school days.

- Preheat oven to 375°F (190°C)
- Baking sheets, lined with parchment paper or Silpats
- #24 disher or scoop

2⅓ cups	all-purpose flour	575 mL
2¼ tsp	baking powder	11 mL
1½ tsp	ground cinnamon	7 mL
1¼ tsp	salt	6 mL
½ tsp	baking soda	2 mL
1½ cups	vegetable shortening	375 mL
1⅓ cups	packed light brown sugar	325 mL
1 cup	granulated sugar	250 mL
2	eggs	2
2 tbsp	water	25 mL
2 tsp	vanilla extract	10 mL
4½ cups	quick-cooking rolled oats	1.125 L
2 cups	golden raisins	500 mL

Mixer Method

1. In a bowl, whisk together flour, baking powder, cinnamon, salt and baking soda. Set aside.
2. In a mixer bowl fitted with paddle attachment, cream shortening, brown and granulated sugars, eggs, water and vanilla until light and fluffy, for 3 minutes. Using a wooden spoon, gradually stir in flour mixture just until incorporated. Gradually stir in oats and raisins.
3. Using disher, scoop dough and place on prepared baking sheets, about 2 inches (5 cm) apart. Press down with palm of your hand. Bake in preheated oven until light brown, 10 to 12 minutes. Let cool on baking sheets for 10 minutes before transferring to a wire rack to cool completely.

Food Processor Method

1. In a bowl, whisk together flour, baking powder, cinnamon, salt and baking soda. Set aside.
2. In work bowl fitted with metal blade, process shortening, brown and granulated sugars, eggs, water and vanilla until creamy, for 2 minutes. Add flour mixture and process until incorporated, for 10 seconds. Fold in oats and raisins. Refrigerate for 20 minutes. Proceed with Step 3 above.

Orange Cranberry Cookies

MAKES ABOUT 24 COOKIES

The sweet citrus taste of orange and tart cranberry complement each other in this cookie.

Tip

If your cranberries are hard, pour hot water over them to soften. Drain off water and pat dry.

Variation

Try golden raisins in place of cranberries.

- Preheat oven to 325°F (160°C)
- Baking sheets, lined with parchment paper or Silpats
- #40 disher or scoop

1½ cups	all-purpose flour	375 mL
1 tsp	cream of tartar	5 mL
½ tsp	baking soda	2 mL
½ cup	unsalted butter, softened	125 mL
1 cup	packed brown sugar	250 mL
2	eggs	2
2 tsp	grated orange zest	10 mL
1 tsp	orange-flavored liqueur	5 mL
½ cup	dried cranberries (see Tip, left)	125 mL

Mixer Method

1. In a bowl, whisk together flour, cream of tartar and baking soda. Set aside.
2. In a mixer bowl fitted with paddle attachment, cream butter, brown sugar, eggs, orange zest and liqueur until fluffy, for 3 minutes. Using a wooden spoon, gradually stir in flour mixture until incorporated. Fold in dried cranberries. If dough is sticky, refrigerate for 15 minutes.
3. Using disher, scoop dough and place on prepared baking sheets, about 2 inches (5 cm) apart. Press down with palm of your hand. Bake in preheated oven until light brown, 10 to 12 minutes. Let cool on baking sheets for 10 minutes before transferring to a wire rack to cool completely.

Food Processor Method

1. In a bowl, whisk together flour, cream of tartar and baking soda. Set aside.
2. In work bowl fitted with metal blade, process butter, sugar, eggs, orange zest and liqueur until blended, for 20 seconds. Add flour mixture and process until blended, for 10 seconds. Transfer to a bowl and fold in cranberries by hand. Refrigerate for 30 minutes. Proceed with Step 3 above.

Orange Butter Cookies

MAKES ABOUT 48 COOKIES

I always bake these cookies when I can first start to smell the aroma of the orange blossoms close to my home.

- Preheat oven to 350°F (180°C)
- Baking sheets, lined with parchment paper or Silpats (see Tip, page 73)
- #60 disher or scoop

4½ cups	all-purpose flour	1.125 L
1½ tsp	baking soda	7 mL
1½ tsp	cream of tartar	7 mL
1 tsp	salt	5 mL
¾ cup	unsalted butter, softened	175 mL
¾ cup	vegetable oil	175 mL
1¾ cups	granulated sugar, divided	425 mL
2	eggs	2
1 tsp	vanilla extract	5 mL
1 tsp	orange extract	5 mL
	Grated zest of 1 orange	

Mixer Method

1. In a large bowl, whisk together flour, baking soda, cream of tartar and salt. Set aside.
2. In a mixer bowl fitted with paddle attachment, cream butter, oil, 1½ cups (375 mL) of the sugar and eggs until well blended, for 2 minutes. Beat in vanilla, orange extract and orange zest. Using a wooden spoon, gradually stir in flour mixture until blended. Refrigerate for 20 minutes.
3. Place remaining sugar in a shallow dish. Using disher, scoop dough and roll in sugar. Place on prepared baking sheets, about 2 inches (5 cm) apart. Press dough down with palm of your hand. Bake in preheated oven until light brown, 10 to 12 minutes.

Food Processor Method

1. In a large bowl, whisk together flour, baking soda, cream of tartar and salt. Set aside.
2. In work bowl fitted with metal blade, process butter, oil, 1½ cups (375 mL) of the sugar, eggs, vanilla, orange extract and orange zest until blended, for 20 seconds. Add flour mixture and process until blended, for 10 seconds. Refrigerate for 30 minutes. Proceed with Step 3 above.

Palmiers

MAKES ABOUT 48 COOKIES

Sometimes called palm trees or elephant ears, these cookies are simple to make with ingredients you most likely have on hand.

Tips

After you make cookie logs you can freeze them unbaked for future use. Wrap in plastic wrap and then foil and freeze for up to 2 months. Cut while still frozen.

Resist the temptation to eat these cookies before they are completely cool because the caramelized sugar can burn your mouth if you try to eat the cookies while hot.

Variation

Add 2 tsp (10 mL) ground cinnamon to sugar.

- Preheat oven to 425°F (220°C)
- Baking sheets, lined with parchment paper or Silpats
- French rolling pin

1	package (18 oz/540 g) puff pastry	1
1 cup	granulated sugar or coarse sugar, divided	250 mL
½ cup	water	125 mL

1. Unwrap 2 sheets of puff pastry and thaw in the refrigerator for 90 minutes. (To check if puff pastry is thawed, hold unfolded sheets, and if limp, it's ready. If you unfold dough while it is still frozen it will break.) If necessary, roll out thawed pastry into two 14-by 10-inch (35 by 25 cm) sheets.
2. Sprinkle about ¼ cup (50 mL) of the sugar over a flat work surface. Unfold one sheet and place on top of sugar. Roll it out just a bit to make the sheet smooth. Brush with a light coating of water and then press about ¼ cup (50 mL) of sugar over the surface. Using a rolling pin, roll over sugar to press lightly into dough.
3. *To fold pastry:* Starting at each long edge, fold about 1½ inches (4 cm) in towards middle. Continue folding each side toward the center in this manner to create a "folded cinnamon roll" style log. Repeat with second sheet of dough. Cut each log crosswise into 24 slices. Place cookies on prepared baking sheets and spread two rolls of each cookie apart slightly. Bake in preheated oven until golden brown, 10 to 12 minutes. Let cool completely on baking sheets.

Peanut Butter Cookies

MAKES ABOUT 60 COOKIES

Packed with nutty taste, peanut butter cookies are a favorite.

Tip

If you don't have a large stand mixer, follow the directions in Step 1 and 2 for Cashew Butter Cookies (page 34) to make dough. Proceed with Step 2, right.

Variation

Peanut Chocolate Chip Cookies: Stir 1 cup (250 mL) semisweet chocolate chips into dough by hand.

- Preheat oven to 350°F (180°C)
- Baking sheets, lined with parchment paper or Silpats (see Tip, page 73)
- #40 disher or scoop

3 cups	all-purpose flour	750 mL
1½ cups	granulated sugar, divided	375 mL
1 cup	packed brown sugar	250 mL
2 tsp	baking soda	10 mL
1 tsp	salt	5 mL
1 cup	vegetable shortening	250 mL
1 cup	creamy peanut butter	250 mL
¼ cup	milk, preferably whole	50 mL
1½ tsp	vanilla extract	7 mL
2	eggs	2
1 cup	finely chopped peanuts	250 mL

Mixer Method

1. In a mixer bowl fitted with paddle attachment, combine flour, 1 cup (250 mL) of the granulated sugar, brown sugar, baking soda, salt, vegetable shortening, peanut butter, milk, vanilla and eggs on low speed until stiff dough forms, for 4 minutes. Refrigerate for 10 minutes.
2. Place remaining ½ cup (125 mL) of granulated sugar in a shallow dish. Using disher, scoop dough and roll in sugar. Then roll in chopped peanuts. Place on prepared baking sheets, about 2 inches (5 cm) apart. Press down with palm of your hand. Bake in preheated oven until golden brown, 10 to 12 minutes. Let cool on baking sheets for 10 minutes before transferring to a wire rack to cool completely.

Food Processor Method

1. In work bowl fitted with metal blade, process flour, 1 cup (250 mL) of the granulated sugar, brown sugar, baking soda, salt, vegetable shortening, peanut butter, milk, vanilla and eggs until light and creamy, about 20 seconds. Refrigerate for 20 minutes. Proceed with Step 2 above.

Pineapple Island Cookies

MAKES ABOUT 24 COOKIES

Crushed pineapple makes these cookies so moist and packed with flavor.

- Preheat oven to 350°F (180°C)
- Baking sheets, lined with parchment paper or Silpats
- #40 disher or scoop

2 cups	all-purpose flour	500 mL
1 tsp	baking soda	5 mL
1 tsp	baking powder	5 mL
1 tsp	salt	5 mL
½ cup	unsalted butter, softened	125 mL
1 cup	granulated sugar	250 mL
1	egg	1
½ cup	crushed pineapple, drained	125 mL
1 tbsp	rum	15 mL

Mixer Method

1. In a bowl, whisk together flour, baking soda, baking powder and salt. Set aside.
2. In a mixer bowl fitted with paddle attachment, cream butter and sugar until light and fluffy, for 2 minutes. Add egg, pineapple and rum and mix until blended. Using a wooden spoon, gradually stir in flour mixture until incorporated. Refrigerate for 10 minutes.
3. Using disher, scoop dough and place on prepared baking sheets, about 2 inches (5 cm) apart. Press down with palm of your hand. Bake in preheated oven until light brown, 12 to 14 minutes. Let cool on baking sheets for 10 minutes before transferring to a wire rack to cool completely.

Food Processor Method

1. In a bowl, whisk together flour, baking soda, baking powder and salt. Set aside.
2. In work bowl fitted with metal blade, process butter and sugar until creamy, for 10 seconds. Add egg, pineapple and rum and process until blended, for 10 seconds. Add flour mixture and process until incorporated, for 10 seconds. Refrigerate for 20 minutes. Proceed with Step 3 above.

Quadruple Chocolate Chip Cookies

MAKES ABOUT 50 COOKIES

My best cookie ever! I make this cookie in every cooking school where I teach. Just the title alone excites the class.

Tips

Store cookies in an airtight container for up to 4 days. You can also freeze them in resealable plastic bags for up to 1 month.

Purchase new baking soda when you haven't baked for a few months. Do not use soda kept in the refrigerator or freezer as a deodorizer because it may take on the taste of fish or other items.

Variations

Try mint or peanut butter chips in place of the other varieties in this recipe.

For larger cookies, scoop by level ¼ cup (50 mL) to yield 32 cookies.

- Preheat oven to 350°F (180°C)
- Baking sheets, lined with parchment paper or Silpats (see Tip, right)
- #24 disher or scoop

3 cups	all-purpose flour	750 mL
¾ cup	unsweetened Dutch-process cocoa powder, sifted	175 mL
1 tsp	baking soda	5 mL
½ tsp	salt	2 mL
1¼ cups	unsalted butter, softened	300 mL
2 cups	granulated sugar	500 mL
2	eggs	2
2 tsp	vanilla extract	10 mL
2 cups	white chocolate chips	500 mL
1 cup	semisweet chocolate chips	250 mL
1 cup	milk chocolate chips	250 mL

Mixer Method

1. In a bowl, whisk together flour, cocoa, baking soda and salt. Set aside.
2. In a mixer bowl fitted with paddle attachment, cream butter and sugar until light and fluffy, for 2 minutes. Add eggs and vanilla and mix until incorporated. Using a wooden spoon, gradually stir in flour mixture until well blended, 3 minutes. Fold in white, semisweet and milk chocolate chips. Refrigerate for 10 minutes.
3. Using disher, scoop dough and place on prepared baking sheets, about 2 inches (5 cm) apart. Press down with palm of your hand or the bottom of a drinking glass. Bake in preheated oven until edges are firm, 12 to 18 minutes. Let cool on baking sheets for 10 minutes before transferring to a wire rack to cool completely.

Food Processor Method

1. In a bowl, whisk together flour, cocoa, baking soda and salt. Set aside.
2. In work bowl fitted with metal blade, process butter and sugar until creamy, about 10 seconds. With motor running, add eggs and vanilla through the feed tube and process for 10 seconds. Scrape work bowl to incorporate the whole mixture. Add flour mixture and process just until combined, about 1 minute. Transfer to a large bowl. Fold in white, semisweet and milk chocolate chips by hand. If dough is very soft, refrigerate until firm, about 20 minutes. Proceed with Step 3 left.

Tip

This large recipe will need to be baked in batches. After cooling cookies as instructed, let baking sheets cool down completely before re-using to bake more cookies. Also, between batches keep your dough cool in refrigerator if your kitchen is warm.

Thumbprint Jam Cookies

MAKES ABOUT 24 COOKIES

You can make an array of flavors with this basic thumbprint cookie.

Tip

Make sure you use a thick preserve or jam because a jelly does not have enough fruit and will spread as the cookie bakes.

- Preheat oven to 300°F (150°C)
- Baking sheets, lined with parchment paper or Silpats
- #40 disher or scoop

1 cup	unsalted butter, softened	250 mL
3⁄4 cup	granulated sugar	175 mL
2 tsp	vanilla extract	10 mL
1 tsp	almond extract	5 mL
2 1⁄4 cups	all-purpose flour	550 mL
1⁄2 cup	finely chopped nuts, such as almonds or other nuts	125 mL
1⁄3 cup	preserves, such as raspberry or your favorite (see Tip, left)	75 mL

Mixer Method

1. In a mixer bowl fitted with paddle attachment, cream butter and sugar until light and fluffy, for 2 minutes. Beat in vanilla and almond extracts. Using a wooden spoon, gradually stir in flour until incorporated.
2. Using disher, scoop dough and roll in chopped nuts. Place dough on prepared baking sheets, about 2 inches (5 cm) apart. Press down and make a little well in center with your finger or thumb. Fill each well with about 1⁄2 tsp (2 mL) of preserves. Bake in preheated oven until light brown, 18 to 24 minutes. Let cool on baking sheets for 10 minutes before transferring to a wire rack to cool completely

Food Processor Method

1. In work bowl fitted with metal blade, process butter, sugar, vanilla and almond extracts until creamy, for 10 seconds. Add flour and process just until incorporated, for 20 seconds. If dough is soft, refrigerate until firm, about 20 minutes. Proceed with Step 2 above.

Pumpkin Harvest Cookies

MAKES ABOUT 36 COOKIES

You can use fresh or canned pumpkin to make this autumn cookie.

- Preheat oven to 350°F (180°C)
- Baking sheets, lined with parchment paper or Silpats
- #60 disher or scoop

2½ cups	all-purpose flour	625 mL
2 tsp	ground cinnamon	10 mL
1 tsp	each baking powder and baking soda	5 mL
1 tsp	ground nutmeg	5 mL
½ tsp	salt	2 mL
½ cup	unsalted butter, softened	125 mL
1½ cups	granulated sugar	375 mL
1	egg	1
1 cup	canned or fresh pumpkin purée (not pie filling)	250 mL
1 tsp	vanilla extract	5 mL
1 cup	semisweet chocolate chips	250 mL
1 cup	pecans, toasted and chopped	250 mL

Mixer Method

1. In a large bowl, whisk together flour, cinnamon, baking powder, baking soda, nutmeg and salt. Set aside.
2. In a mixer bowl fitted with paddle attachment, cream butter and sugar until light and fluffy, for 2 minutes. Add egg and mix until incorporated. Beat in pumpkin and vanilla. Using a wooden spoon, gradually stir in flour mixture until well blended. Fold in chocolate chips and pecans. Refrigerate for 10 minutes.
3. Using disher, scoop dough and place on prepared baking sheets, leaving dough in mounds. Bake in preheated oven until light brown, 12 to 15 minutes. Let cool on sheets for 10 minutes before transferring to a rack to cool completely.

Food Processor Method

1. In a large bowl, whisk together flour, cinnamon, baking powder, baking soda, nutmeg and salt. Set aside.
2. In work bowl fitted with metal blade, process butter and sugar until creamy, for 10 seconds. Add egg, pumpkin and vanilla and process until blended, for 20 seconds. Add flour mixture and process until well blended, for 20 seconds. Transfer to a bowl and fold in chocolate chips and pecans by hand. Refrigerate for 20 minutes. Proceed with Step 3 above.

Snickerdoodles

MAKES ABOUT 24 LARGE COOKIES

I recall my elementary school making big snickerdoodles for the lunchroom. When I eat these it takes me back to third grade.

- Preheat oven to 375°F (190°C)
- Baking sheets, lined with parchment paper or Silpats
- #20 disher or scoop

2¾ cups	all-purpose flour	675 mL
2 tsp	cream of tartar	10 mL
1 tsp	baking soda	5 mL
½ tsp	salt	2 mL
1 cup	unsalted butter, softened	250 mL
1¾ cups	granulated sugar, divided	425 mL
2	eggs	2
2 tsp	ground cinnamon	10 mL

Mixer Method

1. In a large bowl, whisk together flour, cream of tartar, baking soda and salt. Set aside.
2. In a mixer bowl fitted with paddle attachment, cream butter and 1½ cups (375 mL) of the sugar until fluffy, for 3 minutes. Add eggs, one at a time, and mix for 30 seconds between each until incorporated. Using a wooden spoon, gradually stir in flour mixture until blended. Refrigerate for 20 minutes.
3. In a shallow dish, combine remaining ¼ cup (50 mL) of sugar and cinnamon. Using disher, scoop dough and roll in sugar mixture. Place on prepared baking sheets, about 2 inches (5 cm) apart. Press down with palm of your hand. Bake in preheated oven until light brown, 8 to 10 minutes. Let cool on baking sheets for 10 minutes before transferring to a wire rack to cool completely

Food Processor Method

1. In a large bowl, whisk together flour, cream of tartar, baking soda and salt. Set aside.
2. In work bowl fitted with metal blade, process butter and 1½ cups (375 mL) of the sugar until creamy, for 10 seconds. With motor running, add eggs, one at a time, through the feed tube and process until incorporated, for 10 seconds. Add flour mixture and process until blended, for 20 seconds. Refrigerate for 20 minutes. Proceed with Step 3 above.

Sugar and Spice Cookies

MAKES ABOUT 40 COOKIES

I like to make these as one-bite cookies so I can get the entire flavor of the cookie in one bite.

- Preheat oven to 350°F (180°C)
- Baking sheets, lined with parchment paper or Silpats
- #60 disher or scoop

1¾ cups	all-purpose flour	425 mL
3 tsp	ground cinnamon, divided	15 mL
2 tsp	baking powder	10 mL
1½ tsp	ground nutmeg, divided	7 mL
¼ tsp	salt	1 mL
½ cup	unsalted butter, softened	125 mL
1¼ cups	granulated sugar, divided	300 mL
1 tbsp	freshly squeezed lemon juice	15 mL
1	egg	1
2 tbsp	milk, preferably whole	25 mL

Mixer Method

1. In a bowl, combine flour, 2 tsp (10 mL) of the cinnamon, baking powder, 1 tsp (5 mL) of the nutmeg and salt. Set aside.
2. In a mixer bowl fitted with paddle attachment, cream butter and 1 cup (250 mL) of the sugar until fluffy, for 3 minutes. Add lemon juice, egg and milk and mix until incorporated, for 1 minute. Using a wooden spoon, gradually stir in flour mixture until blended. Refrigerate for 20 minutes.
3. In a shallow dish, combine remaining ¼ cup (50 mL) of sugar, 1 tsp (5 mL) of cinnamon and ½ tsp (2 mL) of nutmeg. Using disher, scoop dough and roll in sugar mixture. Place on prepared baking sheets, about 2 inches (5 cm) apart. Press down with palm of your hand. Bake in preheated oven until light brown, 10 to 12 minutes. Let cool on baking sheets for 10 minutes before transferring to a wire rack to cool completely.

Food Processor Method

1. In a bowl, combine flour, 2 tsp (10 mL) of the cinnamon, baking powder, 1 tsp (5 mL) of the nutmeg and salt. Set aside.
2. In work bowl fitted with metal blade, process butter and 1 cup (250 mL) of sugar and butter until creamy, for 10 seconds. With motor running, add lemon juice, egg and milk through the feed tube and process until incorporated for 10 seconds. Add flour mixture and process until blended, for 30 seconds. Refrigerate for 20 minutes. Proceed with Step 3 above.

Sugar Cookies

MAKES ABOUT 24 LARGE COOKIES

I like to take two cookies and sandwich ice cream between them.

- Preheat oven to 350°F (180°C)
- Baking sheets, lined with parchment paper or Silpats
- #24 disher or scoop

1¼ cups	all-purpose flour	300 mL
2 tsp	baking powder	10 mL
¼ tsp	salt	1 mL
½ cup	unsalted butter, softened	125 mL
1¼ cups	granulated sugar, divided	300 mL
1	egg	1
1 tsp	vanilla extract	5 mL

Mixer Method

1. In a bowl, combine flour, baking powder and salt. Set aside.
2. In a mixer bowl fitted with paddle attachment, cream butter and 1 cup (250 mL) of the sugar until light and fluffy, for 3 minutes. Add egg and vanilla and mix until incorporated. Using a wooden spoon, stir in flour mixture until blended. Refrigerate for 20 minutes.
3. Place remaining sugar in a shallow dish. Using disher, scoop dough and roll in sugar. Place on prepared baking sheets, about 2 inches (5 cm) apart. Press down with palm of your hand. Bake in preheated oven until light brown, 10 to 12 minutes. Let cool on baking sheets for 10 minutes before transferring to a wire rack to cool completely.

Food Processor Method

1. In a bowl, combine flour, baking powder and salt. Set aside.
2. In work bowl fitted with metal blade, process butter and 1 cup (250 mL) of the sugar until creamy, for 10 seconds. With motor running, add egg and vanilla through the feed tube and process until incorporated, for 10 seconds. Add flour mixture and process for 30 seconds until blended. Refrigerate for 20 minutes. Proceed with Step 3 above.

Tangy Lemon Butter Cookies

MAKES ABOUT 24 COOKIES

You can sandwich these cookies with Fresh Lemon Curd (see recipe, page 284) or just swirl some on top.

- Preheat oven to 325°F (160°C)
- Baking sheets, lined with parchment paper or Silpats
- #40 disher or scoop

3 cups	all-purpose flour	750 mL
1 tsp	baking soda	5 mL
1 tsp	cream of tartar	5 mL
Pinch	salt	Pinch
½ cup	unsalted butter, softened	125 mL
½ cup	vegetable oil	125 mL
1 cup	granulated sugar	250 mL
1	egg	1
½ tsp	vanilla extract	2 mL
½ tsp	lemon extract	2 mL
1 tsp	grated lemon zest	5 mL

Mixer Method

1. In a bowl, combine flour, baking soda, cream of tartar and salt. Set aside.
2. In a mixer bowl fitted with paddle attachment, cream butter, oil, sugar and egg until light and fluffy, for 2 minutes. Add vanilla and lemon extracts and zest and mix until incorporated. Using a wooden spoon, gradually stir in flour mixture until blended. Refrigerate for 20 minutes.
3. Using disher, scoop dough and place on prepared baking sheet, about 2 inches (5 cm) apart. Press down with palm of your hand. Bake in preheated oven until light brown, 10 to 12 minutes. Let cool on baking sheets for 10 minutes before transferring to a wire rack to cool completely.

Food Processor Method

1. In a bowl, combine flour, baking soda, cream of tartar and salt. Set aside.
2. In work bowl fitted with metal blade, process butter, oil, sugar, egg, vanilla and lemon extracts and zest until creamy, for 20 seconds. Add flour mixture and process until blended for 30 seconds. Refrigerate for 30 minutes. Proceed with Step 3 above.

Ultimate Chocolate Chunk Cookies for a Crowd

MAKES ABOUT 72 COOKIES

If you need a big batch of cookies, make these. If you only need a few, freeze the remaining dough for future use (see Storing and Freezing Cookies, page 19*).*

Tip

This large recipe will need to be baked in batches. After cooling cookies as instructed, let baking sheets cool down completely before re-using to bake more cookies. Also, between batches keep your dough cool in refrigerator if your kitchen is warm.

- Preheat oven to 325°F (160°C)
- Baking sheets, lined with parchment paper or Silpats
- #24 disher or scoop

6 cups	high-gluten bread flour	1.5 L
1½ tsp	baking soda	7 mL
½ tsp	salt	2 mL
2½ cups	unsalted butter, softened	625 mL
2½ cups	packed light brown sugar	625 mL
2	eggs	2
1½ tbsp	vanilla extract	22 mL
3⅓ cups	semisweet chocolate chunks (1¼ lbs/625 g)	825 mL

1. In a large bowl, whisk together flour, baking soda and salt. Set aside.
2. In a mixer bowl fitted with paddle attachment, cream butter and brown sugar until light and fluffy, for 3 minutes. Add eggs and vanilla until incorporated. Using a wooden spoon, gradually stir in flour mixture just until incorporated. Fold in chocolate chunks.
3. Using disher, scoop dough and place on prepared baking sheets, about 2 inches (5 cm) apart. Press down with palm of your hand. Bake in preheated oven until light brown, 12 to 14 minutes. Let cool on baking sheets for 10 minutes before transferring to a wire rack to cool completely.

Vanilla Rose Cookies with Rose Crème Filling

MAKES 30 SANDWICHED COOKIES

The slight hints of rose petals and vanilla enhance this sandwiched cookie.

Tip

If filling is too thick, you can add drops of milk until it is spreadable.

- Preheat oven to 325°F (160°C)
- Baking sheets, lined with parchment paper or Silpats
- #50 disher or scoop

2 cups	unsalted butter, softened	500 mL
10 tbsp	granulated sugar	150 mL
10 tbsp	vanilla rose sugar	150 mL
4 cups	all-purpose flour	1 L
1 tsp	salt	5 mL
1/2 cup	granulated sugar	125 mL
8 oz	cream cheese, softened	250 g
1 1/2 cups	confectioner's (icing) sugar	375 mL
1 tsp	rose water (see Sources, page 442)	5 mL
	Milk, if necessary (see Tip, left)	

Mixer Method

1. In a mixer bowl fitted with paddle attachment, cream butter until creamy, for 3 minutes. With mixer running, spoon 10 tbsp (150 mL) granulated sugar and vanilla rose sugar, 1 tbsp (15 mL) at a time, into butter until fluffy. Using a wooden spoon, gradually stir in flour and salt until well blended. Refrigerate for 20 minutes.
2. Place 1/2 cup (125 mL) granulated sugar in a shallow dish. Using disher, scoop dough and roll in sugar. (You should have 60 cookies.) Place on prepared baking sheets, about 2 inches (5 cm) apart. Bake in preheated oven until light brown, 12 to 16 minutes. Let cool on baking sheets for 10 minutes before transferring to a wire rack to cool completely.
3. In a clean mixer bowl fitted with paddle attachment, blend cream cheese, confectioner's sugar and rose water until fluffy (see Tip, left). Place 2 tsp (10 mL) crème on bottom of half of cooled cookies and sandwich two together.

Food Processor Method

1. In work bowl fitted with metal blade, process butter until creamy, for 15 seconds. With motor running, add sugar and vanilla rose sugar, 1 tbsp (15 mL) at a time, through the feed tube and process until incorporated. Add flour and salt and mix for 30 seconds. Refrigerate for 35 minutes. Proceed with Step 2 above.

7-Layer Bars

MAKES ABOUT 24 BARS

Here's an adapted recipe first printed on Eagle Brand sweetened condensed milk cans. In the '60s, these cookies were referred to as Magic Bars because it was magic how the sweetened condensed milk pulled all the ingredients together into a bar cookie.

Tip

Make sure you spray the sides of the pan with nonstick spray, as the mixture gets sticky after it bakes and is hard to release.

Variation

You can change the chips in the recipe to your favorite type.

- Preheat oven to 350°F (180°C)
- 13-by 9-inch (3 L) metal baking pan, lined with foil, sprayed with nonstick spray, then lined with parchment paper

½ cup	unsalted butter, melted	125 mL
2 cups	graham cracker crumbs	500 mL
1 cup	semisweet chocolate chips	250 mL
1 cup	butterscotch chips	250 mL
1½ cups	sweetened flaked coconut	375 mL
1 cup	chopped pecans	250 mL
1	can (14 oz/396 g or 300 mL) sweetened condensed milk	1

1. In a bowl, combine butter and graham crackers until moistened. Press into bottom of prepared baking pan. Sprinkle chocolate chips, butterscotch chips, coconut and pecans over top. Pour condensed milk evenly over top.
2. Bake in preheated oven until coconut is light brown, 25 to 30 minutes. Let cool in baking pan for 1 hour before cutting into bars.

Apple Bars

MAKES ABOUT 24 BARS

Crisp apples make the best bars for this fall treat.

Variations

Use pears instead of apples when they're in season.

If you are out of lemon juice, try orange juice instead.

- Preheat oven to 350°F (180°C)
- 13-by 9-inch (3 L) metal baking pan, lined with foil, sprayed with nonstick spray, then lined with parchment paper

3 cups	chopped peeled baking apples (about 2 large)	750 mL
2 tbsp	freshly squeezed lemon juice	25 mL
2 cups	quick-cooking rolled oats	500 mL
1½ cups	graham cracker crumbs	375 mL
½ cup	unsalted butter, softened	125 mL
2 tbsp	granulated sugar	25 mL
2 cups	chopped pecans	500 mL
1 cup	flaked sweetened coconut	250 mL
1	can (14 oz/396 g or 300 mL) sweetened condensed milk	1

1. In a bowl, combine apples and lemon juice and cover with water. Set aside.
2. In a large bowl, stir together oats, graham cracker crumbs, butter and sugar until well blended. Press firmly into prepared baking pan. Drain apples and place on top of crumbs. Then sprinkle pecans and coconut over top. Pour condensed milk evenly over top. Bake in preheated oven until light brown, 30 to 35 minutes. Let cool completely in baking pan before cutting into bars.

Almond Pumpkin Bars

MAKES ABOUT 24 BARS

These bars are just like small pumpkin cheesecakes. I love them in the fall.

Tip

You can use 2 tsp (10 mL) pumpkin pie spice in place of cinnamon, nutmeg, cloves and allspice.

Variations

Try chopped pecans in place of almonds.

- Preheat oven to 350°F (180°C)
- 13-by 9-inch (3 L) metal baking pan, lined with foil, sprayed with nonstick spray, then lined with parchment paper

Crust

2½ cups	gingersnap cookie crumbs (see recipe, page 48, or store-bought)	625 mL
½ cup	unsalted butter, melted	125 mL

Filling

3	packages (each 8 oz/250 g) cream cheese, softened	3
1	package (8 oz/250 g) small curd cottage cheese	1
¾ cup	granulated sugar	175 mL
4	eggs	4
½ cup	pumpkin purée (not pie filling)	125 mL
1 tsp	ground cinnamon	5 mL
½ tsp	ground nutmeg	2 mL
¼ tsp	ground cloves	1 mL
¼ tsp	ground allspice	1 mL
1 tsp	almond-flavored liqueur	5 mL
½ cup	slivered almonds	125 mL

Mixer Method

1. *Crust:* In a bowl, combine gingersnap crumbs and butter. Press into bottom of prepared pan and freeze until filling is ready.
2. *Filling:* In a mixer bowl fitted with paddle attachment, beat cream cheese and cottage cheese until soft, about 3 minutes. Add sugar and mix until blended. Add eggs, one at a time, beating for 30 seconds between each addition. Add pumpkin, cinnamon, nutmeg, cloves, allspice and almond liqueur and mix until incorporated.
3. Pour filling over crust. Sprinkle almonds over top. Bake in preheated oven until firm, 25 to 30 minutes. Let cool completely in baking pan before cutting into bars.

Food Processor Method

1. *Crust:* In a bowl, combine gingersnap crumbs and butter. Press into bottom of prepared pan and freeze until batter is ready.
2. *Filling:* In work bowl fitted with metal blade, process cream cheese and cottage cheese until creamy, for 30 seconds. Add sugar and process until blended, for 10 seconds. With motor running, add eggs, one at a time, through the feed tube and process for 10 seconds. Add pumpkin, cinnamon, nutmeg, cloves, allspice and almond liqueur and process until incorporated, for 10 seconds. Proceed with Step 3 left.

Beware of the Brownies

MAKES ABOUT 48 BROWNIES

My good friend, singer and author Carnie Wilson, gave me this brownie recipe for the book. She's a great cook and baker and the flavors here are perfect for the richest brownie treat ever.

- Preheat oven to 350°F (180°C)
- 13-by 9-inch (3 L) metal baking pan, lined with foil, sprayed with nonstick spray, then lined with parchment paper

1½ cups	unsalted butter, softened, divided	375 mL
⅔ cup	unsweetened Dutch-process cocoa powder, divided	150 mL
2 cups	granulated sugar	500 mL
4	eggs	4
2 tsp	vanilla extract, divided	10 mL
1½ cups	all-purpose flour	375 mL
1 tsp	salt, divided	5 mL
1¼ cups	chunky peanut butter	300 mL
⅓ cup	milk, preferably whole	75 mL
8	large marshmallows, cut into small pieces	8
1 lb	confectioner's (icing) sugar	500 g
½ cup	caramel sauce	125 mL
½ cup	peanuts, chopped	125 mL

1. In a small saucepan over low heat, melt 1 cup (250 mL) of the butter and ⅓ cup (75 mL) of the cocoa powder. Stir until smooth. Set aside to cool.
2. Meanwhile, in a mixer bowl fitted with paddle attachment, blend granulated sugar, eggs and 1 tsp (5 mL) of the vanilla until creamy, for 2 minutes. Add cocoa mixture. Using a wooden spoon, stir in flour and ½ tsp (2 mL) of the salt until incorporated. Pour into prepared baking pan. Bake in preheated oven until a toothpick inserted into center comes out with a few moist crumbs, 25 to 30 minutes.
3. As soon as the brownies come out of the oven, carefully spread peanut butter over top. Let cool completely in baking pan, about 1 hour.
4. In a large saucepan over low heat, melt remaining butter. Add remaining cocoa, milk and marshmallows and stir until melted and smooth. Stir in remaining salt and vanilla. Gradually stir in confectioner's sugar until smooth. Frost top of cooled brownies.
5. Pour caramel sauce over top and spread evenly. Sprinkle nuts over top. Cut into 48 small bars.

Black and White Brownies

MAKES ABOUT 24 BROWNIES

Dark and white chocolates create a flavorful and colorful brownie.

Variation

Try coarsely chopping chocolate bars in place of the chips to create a chunky effect.

- Preheat oven to 350°F (180°C)
- 13-by 9-inch (3 L) metal baking pan, lined with foil, sprayed with nonstick spray, then lined with parchment paper

1/2 cup	unsalted butter, softened	125 mL
4 oz	unsweetened chocolate, coarsely chopped	125 g
4	eggs	4
2 cups	granulated sugar	500 mL
1/2 tsp	salt	2 mL
2 tsp	vanilla extract	10 mL
1 cup	all-purpose flour	250 mL
1 cup	semisweet chocolate chips	250 mL
1 cup	white chocolate chips	250 mL

1. In a small saucepan over low heat, melt butter and unsweetened chocolate. Stir until smooth. Set aside.
2. In a mixer bowl fitted with paddle attachment, beat eggs, sugar, salt and vanilla until light, about 5 minutes. Add chocolate mixture and mix on low speed until incorporated. Using a wooden spoon, stir in flour until well blended. Fold in semisweet and white chocolate chips.
3. Spread batter into prepared baking pan. Bake in preheated oven until a toothpick inserted into the center comes out with a few moist crumbs, 35 to 40 minutes. Let cool completely in baking pan before cutting into bars.

5-Chocolate Brownies

MAKES ABOUT 24 BROWNIES

As a chocolaholic, I could not pack any more chocolate into this brownie. Should I just put chocolate sauce on top?

Tip

Use very high-quality chocolate (see Common Ingredients, page 14).

Variation

You can add up to 1 cup (250 mL) chopped nuts if you desire.

- Preheat oven to 325°F (160°C)
- 13-by 9-inch (3 L) metal baking pan, lined with foil, sprayed with nonstick spray, then lined with parchment paper

14 oz	unsweetened chocolate, chopped	425 g
1/4 cup	unsweetened Dutch-process cocoa powder	50 mL
1 1/2 cups	unsalted butter, softened	375 mL
3 cups	granulated sugar	750 mL
1 tsp	salt	5 mL
6	eggs	6
2 cups	all-purpose flour	500 mL
1 cup	white chocolate chips	250 mL
1 cup	milk chocolate chips	250 mL
1 cup	semisweet chocolate chips	250 mL

1. In a heatproof bowl set over a saucepan of simmering water, melt unsweetened chocolate with cocoa powder. Stir until smooth. Set aside to cool.
2. In a mixer bowl fitted with paddle attachment, cream butter, sugar and salt until incorporated, for 2 minutes. Add eggs and mix until fluffy, for 4 minutes. Beat in melted chocolate mixture. Using a wooden spoon, stir in flour until incorporated. Fold in chips.
3. Transfer to prepared baking pan. Bake in preheated oven until a toothpick inserted into the center comes out with a few moist crumbs and top is firm, 35 to 40 minutes. Let cool completely in baking pan before cutting into bars.

Buttermilk Brownie Muffins

MAKES 12 BROWNIE MUFFINS

These brownies make perfect single-size servings for lunches or children's parties.

Tip

Make a double batch and freeze brownies in single-serving sizes (see Storing and Freezing Cookies, page 19).

Variation

Add 1 cup (250 mL) chocolate chips into batter.

- Preheat oven to 375°F (190°C)
- 12-cup muffin tin, lined with paper cups

⅔ cup	unsalted butter, softened	150 mL
⅔ cup	water	150 mL
¼ cup	unsweetened Dutch-process cocoa powder	50 mL
1⅓ cups	all-purpose flour	325 mL
1⅓ cups	granulated sugar	325 mL
¾ tsp	baking soda	4 mL
½ tsp	salt	2 mL
1	egg, beaten	1
⅓ cup	buttermilk	75 mL
1 tsp	vanilla extract	5 mL

Mixer Method

1. In a small saucepan over medium heat, melt butter, water and cocoa powder. Whisk until fully melted, about 2 minutes. Remove from heat and let cool.
2. In a mixer bowl fitted with paddle attachment, combine flour, sugar, baking soda and salt on low speed until blended, for 1 minute. Add egg, buttermilk and vanilla and mix until blended, for 3 minutes. Add cocoa mixture and continue to mix until incorporated, for 2 minutes.
3. Divide batter evenly into prepared muffin tin. Bake in preheated oven until a toothpick inserted in center comes out with a few moist crumbs, 18 to 20 minutes. Let cool in muffin tin on wire rack for 20 minutes before transferring to a wire rack to cool completely.

Food Processor Method

1. In a small saucepan over medium heat, melt butter, water and cocoa powder. Whisk until fully melted, about 2 minutes. Remove from heat and let cool.
2. In work bowl fitted with metal blade, process flour, sugar, baking soda and salt until combined, for 10 seconds . With motor running, add eggs, buttermilk and vanilla through the feed tube and process until blended, for 10 seconds. Add cocoa mixture and process until incorporated, for 10 seconds. Proceed with Step 3 above.

Butterscotch Blondies

MAKES ABOUT 24 THICK BARS

Blondies are brownies without the chocolate. Sometimes I think why bother, but believe it or not there are some people who don't enjoy chocolate!

Tip

If using cashews or any other nut, make sure they are unsalted or the bars will be too salty.

Variation

You can use any chopped nut in place of the cashews.

- Preheat oven to 350°F (180°C)
- 13-by 9-inch (3 L) metal baking pan, lined with foil, sprayed with nonstick spray, then lined with parchment paper

4 cups	butterscotch chips (1½ lbs/750 g)	1 L
1 cup	unsalted butter, softened	250 mL
3 cups	all-purpose flour	750 mL
2 tsp	baking powder	10 mL
2 tsp	salt	10 mL
3 cups	packed brown sugar	750 mL
6	eggs	6
2 tsp	vanilla extract	10 mL
1 cup	unsalted cashews, chopped	250 mL

1. In a heatproof bowl set over a saucepan of simmering water, melt butterscotch chips and butter. Stir until smooth. Set aside and let cool.
2. In a bowl, combine flour, baking powder and salt. Set aside.
3. In a mixer bowl fitted with paddle attachment, beat cooled butterscotch mixture with brown sugar until smooth, about 4 minutes. Add eggs, one at a time, beating for 20 seconds between each egg addition. Beat in vanilla. Using a wooden spoon, stir in flour mixture until incorporated. Stir in cashews.
4. Spread evenly in prepared pan. Bake in preheated oven until a toothpick inserted comes out with a few moist crumbs, about 30 minutes. Let cool completely in baking pan before cutting into squares.

Butterscotch Caramel Brownies

MAKES ABOUT 24 THICK BARS

Rich butterscotch and deep rich chocolate combine to make this a winner.

Tip

Make sure to chop the unsweetened chocolate well so it will melt faster.

Variation

You can add up to 1 cup (250 mL) of chopped nuts into the batter.

- Preheat oven to 350°F (180°C)
- 13-by 9-inch (3 L) metal baking pan, lined with foil, sprayed with nonstick spray, then lined with parchment paper

4 cups	butterscotch chips (1½ lbs/750 g)	1 L
¾ cup	unsalted butter, softened	175 mL
4 oz	unsweetened chocolate, chopped	125 g
3 cups	packed brown sugar	750 mL
6	eggs	6
2 tsp	vanilla extract	10 mL
3 cups	all-purpose flour	750 mL
2 tsp	baking powder	10 mL
2 tsp	salt	10 mL
1 cup	caramel sauce	250 mL

1. In a heatproof bowl set over a saucepan of simmering water, melt butterscotch chips, butter and unsweetened chocolate. Stir until smooth. Set aside and let cool.
2. In a mixer bowl fitted with paddle attachment, beat cooled butterscotch mixture and brown sugar until smooth, about 4 minutes. Add eggs, one at a time, beating for 20 seconds between each egg addition. Beat in vanilla. Using a wooden spoon, stir in flour, baking powder and salt until incorporated.
3. Spread evenly in prepared pan. Bake in preheated oven until a toothpick inserted comes out with a few moist crumbs, about 30 minutes. Let cool completely in baking pan. Spread caramel sauce over top of cooled brownies. Cut into bars.

Cake Brownies

MAKES ABOUT 24 BROWNIES

This is a one-saucepan recipe. You won't have much to clean up and you should have everything handy in your pantry.

Tip

Make sure you don't heat the butter and chocolate over high or the mixture will taste burnt.

Variation

Add 1 cup (250 mL) dried cherries to the batter in place of the pecans.

- Preheat oven to 350°F (180°C)
- 13-by 9-inch (3 L) metal baking pan, lined with foil, sprayed with nonstick spray, then lined with parchment paper

4 oz	unsweetened chocolate, chopped into small pieces	125 g
2⁄3 cup	unsalted butter	150 mL
2 cups	granulated sugar	500 mL
4	eggs	4
1 1⁄2 cups	all-purpose flour	375 mL
1 tsp	baking powder	5 mL
1 tsp	salt	5 mL
1 cup	pecans, chopped	250 mL
	Old-Fashioned Chocolate Fudge Frosting (see recipe, page 233) or confectioner's (icing) sugar, optional	

1. In a large saucepan over medium heat, melt chocolate and butter. Stir until smooth. Remove from heat.
2. Whisk in sugar and eggs, one at a time, until incorporated. Stir in flour, baking powder and salt until well blended, about 3 minutes. Gently stir in pecans. Pour into prepared pan, spreading batter to edges. Bake in preheated oven until a dull crust forms, 28 to 30 minutes. Let cool completely in baking pan before cutting into bars.
3. Frost with Old-Fashioned Chocolate Fudge Frosting or dust with confectioner's sugar, if desired.

Chocolate Raspberry Brownies

MAKES ABOUT 24 BROWNIES

Raspberries are the perfect fruit to accompany this rich chocolate brownie.

Tips

Store brownies wrapped in plastic wrap for up to 5 days. You can also freeze them wrapped in foil for up to 1 month.

If the raspberries are large, cut them into smaller pieces.

Variation

You can use 1 cup (250 mL) seedless raspberry preserves in place of the raspberries.

- Preheat oven to 350°F (180°C)
- 13-by 9-inch (3 L) metal baking pan, lined with foil, sprayed with nonstick spray, then lined with parchment paper

1¼ cups	granulated sugar	300 mL
¾ cup	unsalted butter, melted	175 mL
2	eggs	2
1 tsp	vanilla extract	5 mL
1½ cups	all-purpose flour	375 mL
½ cup	unsweetened Dutch-process cocoa powder, sifted	125 mL
1 tsp	baking powder	5 mL
¼ tsp	baking soda	1 mL
1 cup	milk, at room temperature	250 mL
1 cup	fresh or frozen raspberries, thawed and drained if frozen (see Tips, left)	250 mL
	Bittersweet Fudge Frosting, optional (see recipe, page 233)	

1. In work bowl of food processor fitted with metal blade, process sugar, butter, eggs and vanilla until combined, about 20 seconds. Add flour, cocoa powder, baking powder and baking soda and process until it begins to gather, 20 to 30 seconds. With motor running, add milk in a thin steady stream through the feed tube until incorporated.
2. Transfer mixture to a bowl and carefully fold in raspberries. Spread into prepared baking pan. Bake in preheated oven until a toothpick inserted into the center comes out with a few moist crumbs and top is firm, 25 to 35 minutes. Let cool completely in baking pan before cutting into bars.
3. Frost with Bittersweet Fudge Frosting, if desired.

Cranberry Pecan Bars

MAKES ABOUT 24 BARS

Fresh cranberries are not just for sauce! Try these bars on your fall pastry table.

- Preheat oven to 350°F (180°C)
- 13-by 9-inch (3 L) metal baking pan, lined with foil, sprayed with nonstick spray, then lined with parchment paper

4	egg whites	4
2 cups	granulated sugar	500 mL
2 cups	all-purpose flour	500 mL
2⁄3 cup	unsalted butter, melted	150 mL
12 oz	fresh cranberries (3 cups/750 mL)	375 g
1 cup	pecans, chopped	250 mL

1. In a mixer bowl fitted with whip attachment, whip egg whites on high speed until tripled in volume, about 5 minutes. Reduce speed to medium. Gradually sprinkle sugar into eggs. Gradually add flour, spoonfuls at a time, mixing on low speed until incorporated. Add butter and mix until blended. Remove bowl from mixer. With rubber spatula, clean sides and bottom of bowl, folding in any unmixed ingredients. Fold cranberries and pecans into batter.
2. Spread into prepared baking pan. Bake in preheated oven until golden brown and a toothpick inserted into center comes out clean, 40 to 45 minutes. Let cool completely in baking pan before cutting into bars.

Raspberry Bars

MAKES ABOUT 24 BARS

This was one of the first desserts I made on morning television. They were a hit with the hosts and producers of the show.

Tip

Make sure you use thick preserves or jam because jelly preserves will bleed too much and cookie bar won't be firm.

Variation

You can use an array of preserves, such as strawberry or boysenberry, in place of raspberry.

- Preheat oven to 350°F (180°C)
- 13-by 9-inch (3 L) metal baking pan, lined with foil, sprayed with nonstick spray, then lined with parchment paper

2¼ cups	quick-cooking rolled oats	550 mL
2¼ cups	all-purpose flour	550 mL
1½ cups	packed brown sugar	375 mL
1½ tsp	baking powder	7 mL
1⅓ cups	cold unsalted butter, cut into small pieces	325 mL
1½ cups	raspberry preserves (see Tip, left)	375 mL

1. In a mixer bowl fitted with paddle attachment, combine oats, flour, brown sugar and baking powder. Stir on low speed for 30 seconds until blended. With mixer running, add butter, a few pieces at a time, and mix until crumbly, about 3 minutes. Press two-thirds of the crumb mixture into prepared baking pan.
2. Smooth preserves over crumb base. Sprinkle with remaining crumb mixture. Bake in preheated oven until light brown and preserves are bubbling, 18 to 24 minutes. Let cool completely in baking pan before cutting into bars.

Deep Rich Chocolate Brownies

MAKES ABOUT 24 BROWNIES

Cakes, cookies and brownies made with mayonnaise were popular in the 1970s. Here is a great fudgy brownie recipe you serve without a frosting.

Tips

Be sure to use good-quality semisweet chocolate and not chocolate chips for this recipe.

If chocolate is not cooled completely prior to adding it to other ingredients it will harden batter and make it difficult to spread.

Variation

You can use the same amount of nut flour in place of ground nuts.

- Preheat oven to 350°F (180°C)
- 13-by 9-inch (3 L) metal baking pan, lined with foil, sprayed with nonstick spray, then lined with parchment paper

2 cups	mayonnaise	500 mL
8	eggs	8
1½ cups	granulated sugar	375 mL
1½ cups	almonds or pecans, finely ground	375 mL
½ cup	all-purpose flour	125 mL
1½ lbs	semisweet chocolate, melted and cooled (see Tip, left)	750 g
½ cup	confectioner's (icing) sugar	125 mL

1. In a large bowl, whisk together mayonnaise, eggs, sugar, almonds and flour. Fold in chocolate.
2. Pour into prepared baking pan. Bake in preheated oven until firm and a toothpick inserted into center comes out with a few moist crumbs, 35 to 45 minutes.
3. Let cool completely in baking pan before cutting into bars. Sprinkle with confectioner's sugar.

Granola Bars

MAKES ABOUT 18 BARS

I got tired of the cost of the dried-out granola bars you find in stores. I created my own for a healthy treat.

Tip

After cutting into bars, wrap each bar in its own plastic wrap and store in a cool, dry place or a cookie jar for easy serving.

Variation

You can replace dates with any dried fruit.

- Preheat oven to 350°F (180°C)
- 13-by 9-inch (3 L) metal baking pan, lined with foil, sprayed with nonstick spray, then lined with parchment paper

⅓ cup	unsalted butter, softened	75 mL
¾ cup	honey	175 mL
½ cup	packed brown sugar	125 mL
2 cups	old-fashioned rolled oats	500 mL
1 cup	natural bran	250 mL
1 cup	sunflower seeds	250 mL
1 cup	dates, pitted and chopped	250 mL
½ cup	pecans, toasted and chopped	125 mL
¼ cup	sesame seeds	50 mL
2 tsp	ground cinnamon	10 mL

1. In a small saucepan over medium heat, melt butter. Stir in honey and brown sugar. Bring to boil, about 3 minutes. Simmer over low heat for 5 minutes. Let cool slightly.
2. In a large bowl, combine rolled oats, bran, sunflower seeds, dates, pecans, sesame seeds and cinnamon. Gradually stir in sugar mixture. Firmly press into prepared baking pan. Bake in preheated oven until golden brown, 15 to 18 minutes. Let cool completely in baking pan before cutting into bars.

Key Lime Bars

MAKES ABOUT 24 BARS

Key limes from Florida make this a pucker-up bar.

Tip

If Key limes are not available, you can use bottled Key lime juice (see Sources, page 442) and regular lime zest.

Variation

After pouring filling over crust, swirl 2 oz (60 g) cooled melted semisweet chocolate into the Key lime batter.

- Preheat oven to 350°F (180°C)
- 13-by 9-inch (3 L) metal baking pan, lined with foil, sprayed with nonstick spray, then lined with parchment paper

Crust

2¼ cups	all-purpose flour	550 mL
½ cup	granulated sugar	125 mL
1 cup	unsalted butter, softened	250 mL
1 tbsp	grated Key lime zest	15 mL
1 tbsp	Key lime juice (see Tip, left)	15 mL

Filling

4	eggs	4
2 cups	granulated sugar	500 mL
¼ cup	all-purpose flour	50 mL
½ tsp	baking powder	2 mL
1 tbsp	grated Key lime zest	15 mL
¼ cup	Key lime juice	50 mL

Mixer Method

1. *Crust:* In a large bowl, combine flour and sugar. Stir in butter, lime zest and lime juice until blended. Pat into bottom of prepared baking pan. Bake in preheated oven until golden brown, 20 to 24 minutes.
2. *Filling:* In a mixer bowl fitted with whisk attachment, beat eggs, sugar, flour, baking powder, lime zest and lime juice until well combined. Pour over top of hot crust.
3. Return to preheated oven and bake until set and sides are light brown, 25 to 30 minutes. Let cool completely in baking pan before cutting into bars.

Food Processor Method

1. *Crust:* In a large bowl, combine flour and sugar. Stir in butter, lime zest and lime juice until blended. Pat into bottom of prepared baking pan. Bake in preheated oven until golden brown, 20 to 24 minutes.
2. *Filling:* In work bowl fitted with metal blade, process eggs, sugar, flour, baking powder, lime zest and lime juice until well combined, for 10 seconds. Pour over top of hot crust. Proceed with Step 3 above.

Lemon Macadamia Bars

MAKES ABOUT 24 BARS

Try these tart and refreshing bars for a summer picnic.

Tips

When using macadamia nuts, try to find the unsalted ones. If you can only locate salted, rub the nuts with a dish towel to remove the excess salt.

Bars can be wrapped in plastic wrap and then foil and refrigerated for up to 3 days or frozen for up to 2 months.

Variation

Replace macadamia nuts with cashews or skinned toasted hazelnuts.

- Preheat oven to 350°F (180°C)
- 13-by 9-inch (3 L) metal baking pan, lined with foil, sprayed with nonstick spray, then lined with parchment paper

Crust

2 cups	biscuit mix, such as Bisquick or other dry biscuit mix	500 mL
1/4 cup	macadamia nuts, finely chopped (see Tips, left)	50 mL
1/2 cup	granulated sugar	125 mL
2/3 cup	unsalted butter, softened	150 mL
1 tbsp	grated lemon zest	15 mL

Filling

4	eggs	4
2 cups	granulated sugar	500 mL
3 tbsp	all-purpose flour	45 mL
1/2 tsp	baking powder	2 mL
1 tbsp	grated lemon zest	15 mL
1/4 cup	freshly squeezed lemon juice	50 mL
1/4 cup	chopped macadamia nuts	50 mL

1. *Crust:* In a large bowl, combine biscuit mix, macadamia nuts and sugar. Stir in butter and lemon zest until blended. Pat into bottom of prepared baking pan. Bake in preheated oven until golden brown, about 22 minutes.
2. *Filling:* In a large bowl, whisk together eggs, sugar, flour, baking powder, lemon zest and lemon juice until well combined. Pour over top of hot crust. Sprinkle with macadamia nuts. Return to preheated oven and bake until sides are light brown, 25 to 30 minutes. Let cool completely in baking pan before cutting into bars.

Lemon Oatmeal Bars

MAKES ABOUT 24 BARS

Make these with fresh lemons so you get a really tart-tasting bar!

Tip

Make sure the butter is cut into small pieces so it will incorporate well.

Variation

You can add ½ cup (125 mL) fresh berries chopped into mixture to create berry bars. Fold berries by hand into batter after adding vanilla.

- Preheat oven to 375°F (190°C)
- 13-by 9-inch (3 L) metal baking pan, lined with foil, sprayed with nonstick spray, then lined with parchment paper

1¼ cups	all purpose flour	300 mL
1 cup	unsalted butter, softened, cut into small pieces	250 mL
¾ cup	quick-cooking rolled oats	175 mL
⅔ cup	granulated sugar	150 mL
½ cup	milk, preferably whole	125 mL
1	egg	1
2 tbsp	grated lemon zest, divided	25 mL
1 tsp	baking soda	5 mL
1 tsp	vanilla extract	5 mL
1 cup	confectioner's (icing) sugar	250 mL
2 tbsp	freshly squeezed lemon juice	25 mL

Mixer Method

1. In a mixer bowl fitted with paddle attachment, beat flour, butter, oats, sugar, milk, egg, 1 tbsp (15 mL) of the lemon zest, baking soda and vanilla until fluffy, for 3 minutes. Press into prepared baking pan. Bake in preheated oven until firm and light brown, 18 to 22 minutes. Let cool completely in baking pan.
2. In a small bowl, whisk together confectioner's sugar, lemon juice and remaining zest until smooth, about 3 minutes. Drizzle over cooled bars. Cut into bars.

Food Processor Method

1. In work bowl fitted with metal blade, combine flour, butter, oats, sugar, milk, egg, 1 tbsp (15 mL) of the lemon zest, baking soda and vanilla. Pulse until smooth, 30 times. Press into prepared baking pan. Bake in preheated oven until firm and light brown, 18 to 22 minutes. Let cool completely in baking pan. Proceed with Step 2 above.

Lemon Raspberry Nut Bars

MAKES ABOUT 24 BARS

Tart, sweet and nutty — all these flavors in one cookie bar.

Tip

If you're make the filling prior to the crust being baked completely, make sure you whisk the filling before pouring over the crust.

Variation

Try blackberries in place of the raspberries.

- Preheat oven to 350°F (180°C)
- 13-by 9-inch (3 L) metal baking pan, lined with foil, sprayed with nonstick spray, then lined with parchment paper

Crust

2 cups	all-purpose flour	500 mL
1/4 cup	pecans, finely chopped	50 mL
1/2 cup	granulated sugar	125 mL
1 cup	unsalted butter, softened	250 mL
1 tbsp	grated lemon zest	15 mL

Filling

4	eggs	4
2 cups	granulated sugar	500 mL
2 tbsp	all-purpose flour	25 mL
1/2 tsp	baking powder	2 mL
1 tbsp	grated lemon zest	15 mL
1/4 cup	freshly squeezed lemon juice	50 mL
1/2 cup	raspberries, cut into small pieces	125 mL

Mixer Method

1. *Crust:* In a mixer bowl fitted with paddle attachment, combine flour, pecans and sugar. Add butter and lemon zest and mix until blended. Pat into bottom of baking pan. Bake in preheated oven until golden brown, 20 to 24 minutes.
2. *Filling:* In a large bowl, whisk together eggs, sugar, flour, baking powder, lemon zest and lemon juice until well combined. Pour over hot crust. Sprinkle raspberries over top. Return to preheated oven and bake until set, 25 to 30 minutes. Let cool completely in baking pan before cutting into bars.

Food Processor Method

1. *Crust:* In work bowl fitted with metal blade, pulse flour, pecans and sugar 10 times, until combined. Add butter and lemon zest and process until blended, for 10 seconds. Pat into bottom of prepared baking pan. Bake in preheated oven until golden brown, 20 to 24 minutes.
2. *Filling:* In work bowl fitted with metal blade, process eggs, sugar, flour, baking powder, zest and juice for 10 seconds until well combined. Pour over hot crust. Sprinkle raspberries over top. Return to preheated oven and bake until set, 25 to 30 minutes. Let cool completely in baking pan before cutting.

Mocha Squares with Fudge Glaze

MAKES ABOUT 48 SQUARES

These are perfect for a small treat after a hearty meal.

- Preheat oven to 350°F (180°C)
- 13-by 9-inch (3 L) metal baking pan, lined with foil, sprayed with nonstick spray, then lined with parchment paper

Squares

½ cup	unsalted butter	125 mL
2 oz	unsweetened chocolate, cut into small pieces	60 g
¾ cup	all-purpose flour	175 mL
¾ cup	granulated sugar	175 mL
1 tbsp	instant coffee granules	15 mL
2 tbsp	milk, preferably whole	25 mL
½ tsp	baking powder	2 mL
¼ tsp	salt	1 mL
2	eggs	2

Glaze

½ cup	whipping (35%) cream	125 mL
4 oz	semisweet chocolate, cut into small pieces	125 g

1. *Squares:* In a large saucepan over low heat, melt butter and unsweetened chocolate, stirring frequently, until smooth, about 4 minutes. Whisk in flour, sugar, coffee granules, milk, baking powder, salt and eggs until well blended, about 3 minutes. Pour into prepared pan, spreading out to the sides. Bake in preheated oven until a toothpick inserted in the center comes out clean, 18 to 22 minutes. Let cool completely in baking pan.
2. *Glaze:* In a small saucepan over medium heat, bring cream to a boil. Remove from heat. Add chocolate and stir until smooth. Refrigerate for 20 minutes, until firm. Spread over cooled squares. Cut into 48 squares.

Peanut Butter Chocolate Bars

MAKES ABOUT 24 BARS

My mom is hooked on anything peanut butter and chocolate and these are no exception.

Tip

Make sure the butter is soft before blending with peanut butter. If cold, it won't blend with the peanut butter.

Variation

Try using chunky peanut butter for a more crunchy texture.

- Preheat oven to 350°F (180°C)
- 13-by 9-inch (3 L) metal baking pan, lined with foil, sprayed with nonstick spray, then lined with parchment paper

2⅔ cups	all-purpose flour	650 mL
1 cup	unsweetened Dutch-process cocoa powder, sifted	250 mL
1 tsp	baking powder	5 mL
⅔ cup	creamy peanut butter	150 mL
½ cup	unsalted butter, softened	125 mL
1½ cups	packed brown sugar	375 mL
1½ cups	granulated sugar	375 mL
2	eggs	2
2 tsp	vanilla extract	10 mL
1¼ cups	chopped peanuts	300 mL

Mixer Method

1. In a bowl, combine flour, cocoa powder and baking powder. Set aside.
2. In a mixer bowl fitted with paddle attachment, blend peanut butter and butter until fluffy, for 2 minutes. Add brown and granulated sugars and beat until light in color, about 2 minutes. Add eggs, one at a time, and mix until incorporated. Beat in vanilla. Using a wooden spoon, stir in flour mixture. Fold in peanuts.
3. Spread into prepared pan. Bake in preheated oven until the top is firm, 28 to 32 minutes. Let cool completely in baking pan before cutting into bars.

Food Processor Method

1. In a bowl, combine flour, cocoa powder and baking powder. Set aside.
2. In work bowl fitted with metal blade, process peanut butter and butter until creamy, for 15 seconds. Add brown and granulated sugars, eggs and vanilla and process until smooth, about 30 seconds. Add flour mixture and process until incorporated for 20 seconds. Transfer to a bowl and fold in peanuts by hand. Proceed with Step 3 above.

Peanut Butter and Jelly Bars

MAKES ABOUT 24 BARS

You will think back to your childhood days with this moist and flavorful cookie bar.

Tip

Sometimes the batter may need more time in the freezer to firm up.

Variation

Add 2 tsp (10 mL) almond extract to the batter for a rich almond bar.

- Preheat oven to 375°F (190°C)
- 13-by 9-inch (3 L) metal baking pan, lined with foil, sprayed with nonstick spray, then lined with parchment paper

2½ cups	all-purpose flour	625 mL
1½ tsp	baking powder	7 mL
1 cup	packed brown sugar	250 mL
1 cup	unsalted butter, softened, cut into small pieces	250 mL
2	eggs	2
1 tsp	vanilla extract	5 mL
½ cup	chunky peanut butter	125 mL
½ cup	jelly, such as raspberry or strawberry	125 mL

Mixer Method

1. In a mixer bowl fitted with paddle attachment, mix flour, baking powder and brown sugar on low speed until combined, about 1 minute. Add butter, a few pieces at a time, on low speed, until it resembles coarse meal, about 3 minutes. Add eggs and vanilla and mix until well blended, about 2 minutes.
2. Smooth half of batter into prepared baking pan. Place in freezer for 5 minutes to firm up.
3. Dollop peanut butter and jelly over top of firm batter. Drop remaining batter by spoonfuls over top, leaving areas of the jelly–peanut butter mixture exposed. Bake in preheated oven until light brown, 28 to 32 minutes. Let cool completely in baking pan before cutting into bars.

Food Processor Method

1. In work bowl fitted with metal blade, pulse flour, baking powder and brown sugar until blended, about 5 times. With motor running, add butter, a few pieces at a time, until it resembles coarse meal. Add eggs and vanilla thorough the feed tube and process until well blended, about 15 seconds.
2. Smooth half of batter into prepared baking pan. Place in freezer for 15 minutes to firm up. Proceed with Step 3 above.

Pecan Bars

MAKES ABOUT 24 BARS

These bars are just like pecan pie without the fuss of making a pie.

- Preheat oven to 350°F (180°C)
- 13-by 9-inch (3 L) metal baking pan, lined with foil, sprayed with nonstick spray, then lined with parchment paper

Crust		
1½ cups	all-purpose flour	375 mL
¾ cup	packed brown sugar	175 mL
½ cup	unsalted butter, softened	125 mL
Pinch	salt	Pinch
Filling		
¼ cup	unsalted butter, melted	50 mL
1 cup	packed brown sugar	250 mL
3	eggs	3
1¼ cups	pure maple syrup	300 mL
1 cup	pecan halves	250 mL

1. *Crust:* In work bowl of a food processor, pulse flour, brown sugar, butter and salt until crumbly, 20 times. Pat into prepared baking pan, pressing into corners. Bake in preheated oven until sides are firm, for 10 minutes. Set aside until filling mixture is ready.
2. *Filling:* In a large bowl, whisk butter, brown sugar, eggs and maple syrup until blended. Pour over top of baked crust. Sprinkle with pecans.
3. Bake in preheated oven until a knife inserted into center comes out clean, 22 to 24 minutes. Let cool completely in baking pan before cutting into bars.

Sinful Coffee Rum Brownies

MAKES ABOUT 24 BROWNIES

These are adult brownies packed with flavor and rum.

Tip

If you wait until the brownies cool to brush with liqueur you may have to poke holes in the brownies to soak up the liquid.

Variation

Use raspberry liqueur in place of the coffee-flavored for a raspberry brownie.

- Preheat oven to 325°F (160°C)
- 13-by 9-inch (3 L) metal baking pan, lined with foil, sprayed with nonstick spray, then lined with parchment paper

1½ cups	all-purpose flour	375 mL
½ tsp	baking soda	2 mL
½ tsp	salt	2 mL
⅔ cup	unsalted butter, softened	150 mL
1 cup	granulated sugar	250 mL
¼ cup	rum	50 mL
12 oz	semisweet chocolate, chopped	375 g
2 tsp	vanilla extract	10 mL
4	eggs, beaten	4
1½ cups	pecans, chopped	375 mL
½ cup	coffee-flavored liqueur	125 mL

1. In a small bowl, combine flour, baking soda and salt. Set aside.
2. In a large saucepan over medium heat, melt butter, sugar and rum, stirring until sugar has dissolved, about 3 minutes. Add chocolate and vanilla, stirring until chocolate has completely melted. Remove from heat and beat in eggs. Stir in flour mixture until blended. Stir in nuts.
3. Spread into prepared baking pan. Bake in preheated oven until a toothpick inserted into center comes out with a few moist crumbs, 25 to 30 minutes.
4. As soon as brownies come out of oven, lightly brush the coffee-flavored liqueur over top. Let cool completely in baking pan before cutting into bars.

Triple-Chocolate Bar Cookies

MAKES ABOUT 24 BARS

Three chocolates make up this rich bar. I always say you cannot have too much chocolate in your diet.

Tip

Wrap bars in plastic wrap and store in a cool, dry place for up to 1 week.

Variations

Try butterscotch chips in place of the milk chocolate chunks.

You can also try walnuts or macadamia nuts in place of the pecans.

- Preheat oven to 325°F (160°C)
- 13-by 9-inch (3 L) metal baking pan, lined with foil, sprayed with nonstick spray, then lined with parchment paper

2/3 cup	unsalted butter, softened	150 mL
3/4 cup	granulated sugar	175 mL
1/2 cup	packed brown sugar	125 mL
2	eggs	2
2 tsp	vanilla extract	10 mL
2 1/4 cups	biscuit mix, such as Bisquick or other dry biscuit mix	550 mL
1/4 cup	unsweetened Dutch-process cocoa powder	50 mL
1 cup	semisweet chocolate chunks (6 oz/175 g)	250 mL
3/4 cup	milk chocolate chunks (4 oz/125 g)	175 mL
1 cup	chopped pecans	250 mL

1. In a mixer bowl fitted with paddle attachment, cream butter and granulated and brown sugars until smooth. Beat in eggs, one at a time, until incorporated. Beat in vanilla. Scrape down side of bowl with a rubber spatula.
2. Using a wooden spoon, stir in biscuit mix and cocoa powder just until combined. Fold in semisweet and milk chocolate chunks and pecans. With a moistened spatula, spread batter into prepared baking pan. Bake in preheated oven until center is firm, 24 to 32 minutes. Let cool completely in baking pan before cutting into bars.

Turtle Brownies

MAKES ABOUT 24 BROWNIES

I created Turtle Brownies for many of the bakeries I worked in years back. They are still a favorite of adults.

- Preheat oven to 350°F (180°C)
- 13-by 9-inch (3 L) metal baking pan, lined with foil, sprayed with nonstick spray, then lined with parchment paper

28 oz	soft caramels (about 100)	850 g
1¾ cups	evaporated milk	375 mL
¾ cup	unsalted butter, melted	175 mL
3 oz	unsweetened chocolate, chopped	90 g
2 cups	packed brown sugar	500 mL
4	eggs	4
1 tsp	vanilla extract	5 mL
1¼ cups	all-purpose flour	300 mL
1 tsp	baking powder	5 mL
¼ tsp	salt	1 mL
1 cup	semisweet chocolate chips	250 mL
½ cup	pecan halves, toasted	125 mL

1. In a saucepan over low heat, melt caramels and evaporated milk, stirring until smooth, about 6 minutes. Set aside.
2. In a large saucepan over medium heat, melt butter. Remove from heat. Add unsweetened chocolate, stirring until fully melted. Whisk in brown sugar, eggs and vanilla until blended. Stir in flour, baking powder and salt until incorporated. Spread half into prepared baking pan. Dollop caramel mixture over batter. Sprinkle with about half of chocolate chips and pecans. Dollop remaining batter over top. Sprinkle remaining chips and nuts over top.
3. Bake in preheated oven until firm to the touch, 24 to 30 minutes. Let cool completely in baking pan before cutting into bars.

Key Lime Pie

Pies, Tarts & Cobblers

Pie Pastry Doughs & Crusts

Double-Crust Pies

Single-Crust Pies

Tarts

Cobbler, Crisps & Buckles

Pies

The thought of making a pie from scratch astounds most first-time bakers. In the fall every year I offer a Pie Making Workshop. I have taught it throughout the country to great success. I want the world to know how to make pies that their grandmothers never taught them. I think there was something lost in the last generation. At the holidays, grandma would bring the pies. It was a secret to the entire family how she masterminded the filling, the flaky crust and the decorations on the top.

Everyone I meet talks about how their grandmother made the best pies. And they'll say that they don't have the recipe because she never measured. Really, nobody measures a crust's ingredients precisely, as the moisture in the air is a determining factor — but who I am to tell someone reliving the flavors of their childhood?

My grandmother's specialty was pumpkin. I think I was about 10 one October when I helped her take pumpkin pies to a fall bazaar where she was selling them for charity. My aunt would tell me how people would line up to buy grandmother's pies and this I had to see for myself. Sure enough, the first four people in line purchased grandmother's pies. I thought to myself, what's so special about these pies? And I asked her what she did that was special. "Do you use fresh pumpkin? Have a special crust recipe?" No. She used the crust recipe on the shortening label and the pumpkin — and recipe — out of a can.

So here I want to show you the simple ways to make a perfect pie and crust.

Simple Steps to Perfect Pie Crust and Pies

1. Never use a mixer to make a pie pastry dough, and use a food processor only when you have first mastered making a crust by hand. Everyone's first pie should be by hand, so you can handle the dough and know what to look for and get a feel for the correct texture.
2. Measure dry ingredients into a large bowl, cut cold fat (butter, shortening, etc.) into small chunks, about ¼-inch (0.5 cm) in size. The liquid used should be ice cold. If I am using water, I will fill up a glass measuring cup with water and ice cubes. I pour in the water (holding back the ice cubes) until the desired moisture content has been achieved.
3. Use a blending fork by pressing down on the chunks of fat, until they are the size of small peas. You should add water or liquid by large spoonfuls. Then use the fork to toss mixture gently but thoroughly until it starts to bind together. Once you see it starting to bind, use your hands to press the dough together, being sure not to work the dough too much or let it get too warm from the heat of your hands.
4. Press the dough into a disk and wrap in plastic. Refrigerate while you are making the filling or for about 15 minutes. The dough should be chilled and slightly firm but not hard. If the dough is too hard to roll out, place on rolling surface at room temperature for a few minutes to warm up.
5. *Your work area:* I would love to replace one section of my kitchen with wooden counters for pastry making. Instead I have an island that is made of butcher block. It is perfect for pastry making. Pastry tends to stick to marble and tile, so if you don't have a large wooden work surface, I suggest that you buy a large wooden rolling board that you can find in most kitchenware stores.
6. *Rolling the dough:* Follow the steps (page 110) for my perfect rolling techniques.

7. *Dusting your work area with flour:* Grandmothers would say, "Don't use too much flour or your crust will be tough." But most beginner pastry makers will under-flour their work area, thus causing a sticky dough that is difficult to roll because it sticks to the pin and table. I recommend sprinkling plenty of flour over the work area, since you can always dust off the excess with a pastry brush later if you need to.
8. If you are making a custard pie such as pumpkin with a fluid filling, I suggest that you pull the oven rack out slightly and place your prepared pie crust (unfilled) on the rack. Use a container with a pouring spout to pour the filling into the crust while the pan is on the rack; now you only have a few inches to push the rack into the oven, instead of walking from the counter to the oven and spilling or sloshing the filling up the sides of the pie crust.

Perfect Tools for Pie Making

- *Blending fork* (*see page 7*): I like how the fork "digs" into the ingredients prior to the water being added and then how you blend the ingredients once the water has been added. Using a pastry blender, you will find that the mixture will get caught up in the blender and you will have to stop often and pull it out of your "blades."
- *Rolling pin:* I favor a "French box" or "French tapered" rolling pin. They look like a wooden dowel without handles. With the handled rolling pins, many new bakers tend to tighten their grip around the handles while they are rolling their dough, which creates pressure and squishes the dough rather than letting the rolling pin do the work. With the French rolling pins you use the palms of your hands to roll the dough out, thus not adding too much pressure on the dough. Also, most rolling pins with handles have only 9 inches (23 cm) of rolling surface, so if you are making a pie that is more than 7 inches (17.5 cm) you will not have ample rolling surface. Your dough will have line marks from the ends of the pin, which I call lawn mower marks because they look like the perfect lines up and down grass that's been recently mowed. That's fine for a lawn, but not for a pie crust.
- *Pie pans/dishes:* My personal favorite is ceramic. These are not allowed for use in commercial bakeries as they can break and the pieces end up in the pie. My least favorite are glass pie dishes. As with ceramic, the health department frowns on these for commercial use. Personally, I find them too shallow and I don't like the shape.

For average homes, light-colored metal pie pans are best. However, you do need to pay close attention to metal pans and make sure they are the correct size for your recipe. Double-check the actual size, rather than the printed label or stamp in the pan, by measuring the top of the pan from the inside rim to rim. Be wary of reusing some of the foil pans that you get when you buy a commercial pie. I was surprised that they are often 7 inches (17.5 cm) in diameter. If you use these pans for my recipes you will have a great deal of crust and filling left over.

There are two-piece pie pans with holes in the bottom of one piece that are good for a blind-baked crust (unfilled crusts). These are available at specialty kitchenware stores and are handy if you bake unfilled crusts often.

- *Pie weights:* Many recipes will specify to use pie weights to blind-bake pie crusts. I don't like to use pie weights as it seems like a waste of time and money for them. If you roll your dough out correctly (see below) you will be fine without them.
- *Wooden rolling board:* A wooden rolling board especially made for pastry has a backsplash to prevent flour from spilling off the board and a lip at the front that hooks on the counter to hold the board in place. This is handy to have if you plan to make pastry often. Rolling boards are available at specialty kitchenware and baking supply stores. As an alternative, a large butcher block cutting board makes a good rolling surface and is readily available at most kitchenware stores. Be sure to get one that is large enough to fit a rolled-out pie crust with extra room all around for maneuvering your rolling pin. And keep at least one side exclusively for rolling pastry so strong flavors from other foods don't transfer to the pastry.
- *Torch:* I use a propane blowtorch to brown my meringue tops on pies and tarts. This allows me to brown the meringue evenly, which is not always possible with an oven broiler. I prefer the torch that I purchase from a hardware store. The cost is about a third of the small ones from specialty kitchenware stores. Not only do the small ones cost more, they are much lower in power and not as effective.

Perfect Pie Crust Rolling

1. Dust your work surface with flour. Take the disk of dough out of the refrigerator and press it down with palm of your hand.
2. Looking at the dough, I refer to it as a "clock." Starting in the center of the dough, take the rolling pin and roll the dough from center point to the 12 o'clock position.

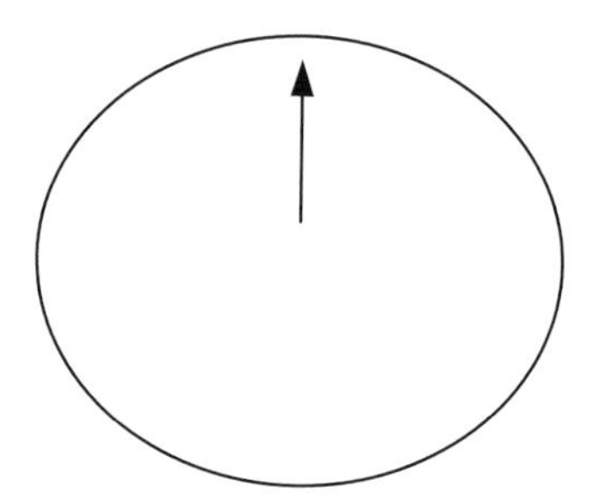

3. Take the pin, place it back in center position, and now roll down to the 6 o'clock position.

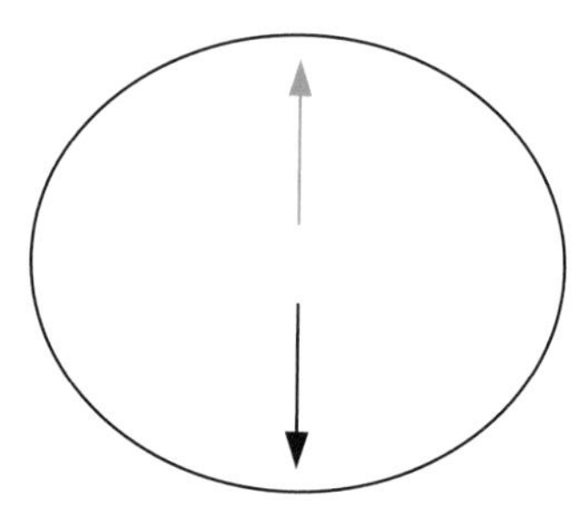

4. Turn the dough 45 degrees (so now your rolling pin is at the 3 and 9 o'clock positions). You may have to add flour to the underside of the dough. This is so you can see if the dough is sticking.
5. Take the pin, place it in the center of the dough, roll dough from center point to 12 o'clock position.

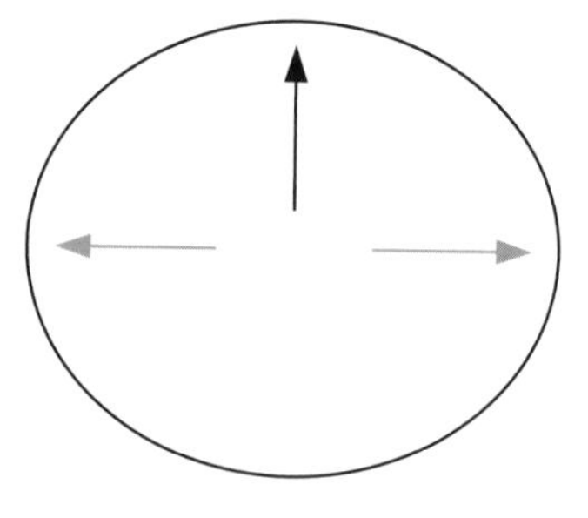

6. Take the pin, place it back in center position, and now roll down to the 6 o'clock position. You should have made a "plus" pattern.
7. Take the pin, place it back in center position and roll to 10 o'clock.

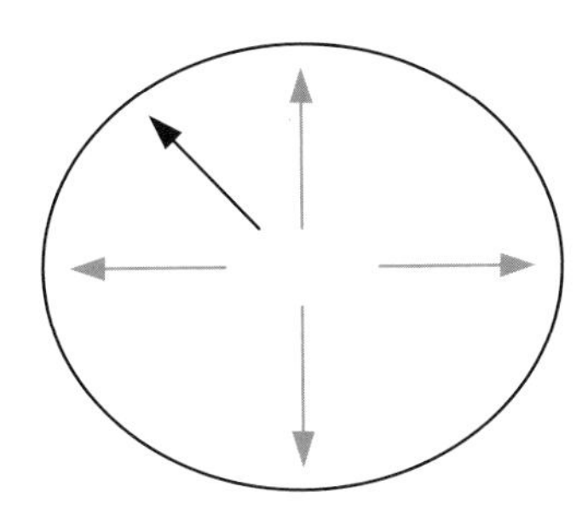

8. Take the pin, place it back in center position and roll to 4 o'clock.

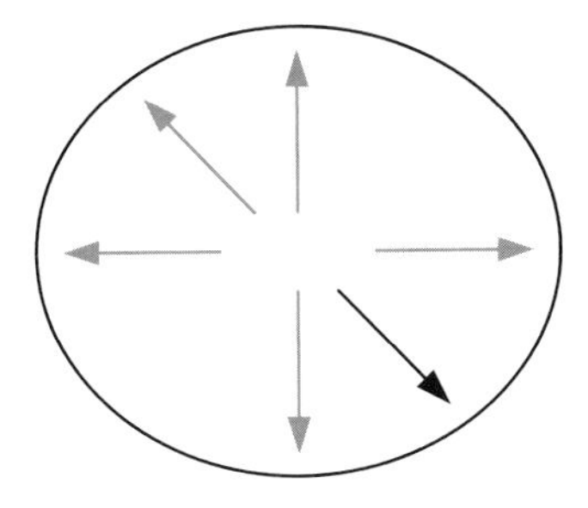

9. Take the pin, place it back in center position and roll to 2 o'clock.

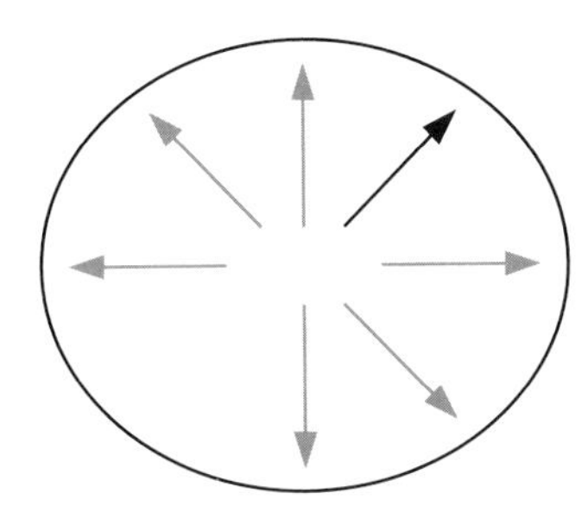

10. Take the pin, place it back in center position and roll to 8 o'clock. You should now have made an "x" pattern. Feel for any areas of the dough that seem thicker and, starting with the pin always in the center, roll outwards over the thick areas.

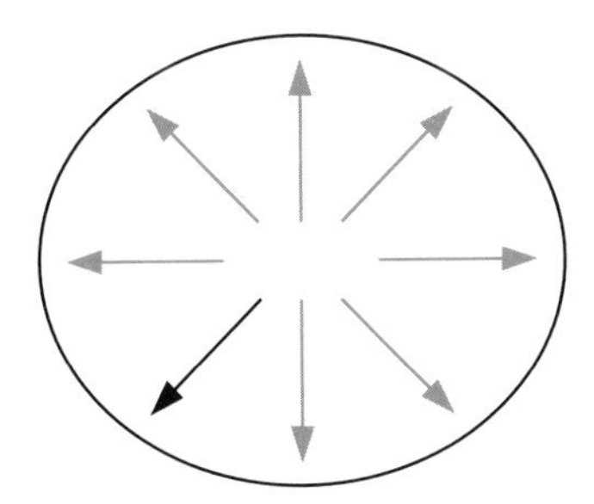

Top 5 flavors of pie according to the American Pie Council

1. Pumpkin
2. Apple
3. Cherry
4. Lemon Meringue
5. Pecan, Chocolate Cream, Mincemeat (three-way tie)

11. To transfer the dough to the pie pan, roll the dough loosely up around your pin.
12. Hold the pin over the front edge of the pie pan and unroll the dough out over the pan. Be sure not to touch the pan while unrolling the dough, as the rim of the pie pan can cut the dough. I like to pick up the dough a bit at the edges and gently lay it into the pan. Do not push it in firmly as this will cause it to shrink during baking.
13. Fill the bottom crust.
14. Repeat Steps 1 to 10 to roll the top crust. After you have finished rolling the top crust, use a small decorative cookie cutter and make a cut-out in the center of the dough. Fill the hole with flour so that there is a marker left on the work surface. Roll the dough up around the pin as in Step 11, rolling toward you and without moving the pin from the place where you finish rolling. Move the pie pan to the work surface where the pastry circle was, placing the center of the pan directly over the flour marker on the surface. Unroll the dough and the cut-out on the top pastry will be dead center.
15. Press the sides of the pan where the dough overhangs. If you are using a metal pan the dough will cut without a knife. Fold the edge of the top crust over the edge of the bottom and crimp the side of the dough to seal in the filling.

Tips for a Perfect Lattice Crust

1. Prepare your double-crust dough and let it chill for 10 minutes.
2. Roll out one disk of dough as for a single-crust pie and line a 9-inch (23 cm) pie pan, leaving the excess hanging over the sides.
3. Roll out the other disk on parchment paper into a rectangle that's slightly larger than 14-by 9-inches (35 by 23 cm). Trim the dough to an exact 14-by 9-inch (35 by 23 cm) rectangle. Cut 8 strips that are 14 inches (35 cm) long and ¾ inch (2 cm) wide. If the dough gets soft, slide the parchment and dough onto a baking sheet and chill briefly before continuing. Reserve extra rolled dough to cut more strips if any break while assembling the lattice. Loosely place 5 strips horizontally across filled pie.

4. Pull back the second and fourth strips, to the left. Add a center strip.

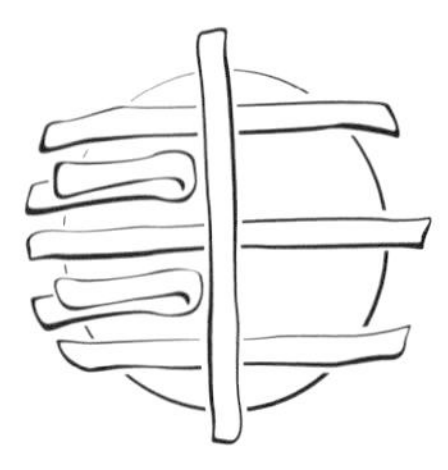

5. Pull back the first, third and fifth strips, to the left, add the right strip.

6. Pull back the first, third and fifth strips, to the right, add the left strip.

7. With all strips in place, pinch ends of the lattice strips together with the bottom around edge of the pie. Cut off excess dough.

Baking Perfect Pies Troubleshooting

CRUSTS

Bottom too soggy or looks raw. Bake pies on a pizza stone. Twenty minutes prior to baking your pie, place pizza stone in middle of oven, at 500°F (260°C). Before placing pie in the oven, reduce the temperature according to the recipe requirements.

Crust looks raw. The oven was not at the correct temperature. Be sure to preheat the oven, checking the temperature with an oven thermometer, before placing pie in the oven.

Top of crust is light in color. If you have a convection oven, place fan on for 5 minutes or until crust is light brown. If you don't have a convection option, you can use a torch or the broiler and carefully brown the top crust.

FILLING

The filling is too runny. You need to add more thickener. Fruit naturally varies in pectin levels and amounts of juice, so you may need more thickener.

How can I tell when my custard type pie is fully baked? Start by checking your pie at the first of the two times indicated. If a knife inserted in the center comes out runny with a little bit of firm pieces attached, the pie needs an additional 10 minutes. If you only see firm pieces but the knife is still not clean, it needs additional 5 minutes. You never want the knife to come out clean the first time because it may be overbaked at this point.

Tips for Making Tart Crust

1. After the mixture has been processed in the food processor, it will be very loose. Place the mixture on a work surface. With palm of your hand, smear the mixture and you will see it start to hold together.

2. In a French removable-bottom tart pan, press a little piece of dough at a time into the sides, working around the entire tart pan.

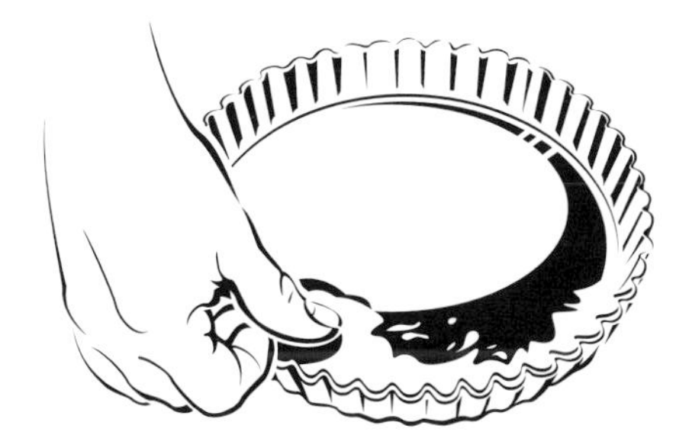

3. Using your knuckles, press the dough into the corner to make the excess dough rise up. Using a bench scraper, scrape the excess dough even with the rim of the tart pan.

4. Now fill in the bottom of the pan, trying to make it as even as possible.

5. Use the tines of a fork to poke the bottom and sides if you need to prebake tart shell.

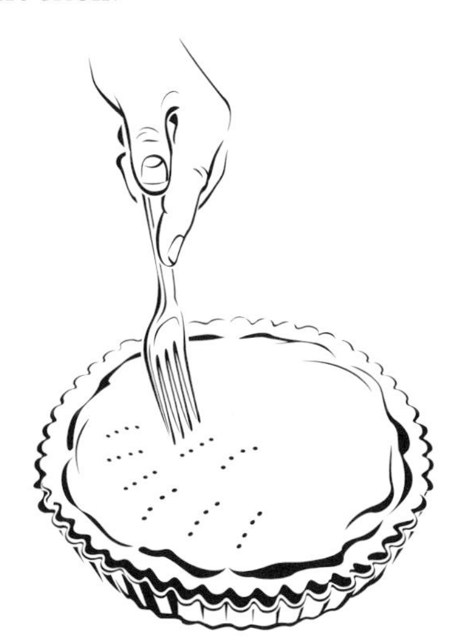

All-Butter Pie Pastry Dough

MAKES ENOUGH DOUGH FOR ONE 9-INCH (23 CM) SINGLE-CRUST PIE

Here is a classic recipe that will suit all of your pie-making needs. Once you master making the dough by hand, try the food processor version and in less than 5 minutes you can have a flaky pie crust.

Tip

If your dough forms a ball in the food processor work bowl, it may be too tough. To save the dough, turn the machine off and sprinkle dough with 1/4 cup (50 mL) all-purpose flour. Pulse 5 times, then proceed with Step 2.

Variations

Flaky Pie Pastry Dough: Replace butter with cold vegetable shortening.

You can double this recipe for a double-crust pie. Just be careful when you add the water as you will not need twice, as much as single-crust recipe.

- Blending fork

3/4 cup	cake flour	175 mL
1/2 cup	all-purpose flour	125 mL
1 tbsp	granulated sugar	15 mL
1/2 tsp	salt	2 mL
7 tbsp	cold unsalted butter, cut into small chunks	105 mL
3 to 4 tbsp	ice water (approx.)	45 to 60 mL

Hand Method

1. In a large bowl, using a blending fork, blend together cake flour, all-purpose flour, sugar and salt. Add butter and blend until mixture resembles coarse crumbs.
2. Add ice water, by spoonfuls, while tossing mixture with fork. Add only enough water to make dough stick together. Press dough into a ball.
3. Flatten into a disk and wrap with plastic wrap. Refrigerate until firm enough to roll out for your pie, for about 20 minutes. (To roll out dough, see page 110.) For pre-baking instructions, see Tip, page 116, or fill and bake according to recipe directions.

Food Processor Method

1. In a food processor fitted with metal blade, process cake and all-purpose flours, sugar and salt until combined, about 10 seconds. Remove lid and distribute butter evenly over top. Cover and pulse until mixture resembles coarse crumbs, about 20 times. Place water in a container with a pouring spout and, with motor running, slowly pour through the feed tube in a steady stream just until dough begins to gather. You may not use all the water, which is fine.
2. Turn out dough onto a clean surface and gather into a ball. Proceed with Step 3 above.

Chocolate Pie Pastry Dough

MAKES ENOUGH DOUGH FOR ONE 9-INCH (23 CM) SINGLE-CRUST PIE

Try a rich chocolate crust instead of a regular flaky crust. It will enhance any berry or pumpkin-type pie.

Tip

Pre-baking is needed when making a pie that does not require the filling to be baked in the pie (such as Lemon Meringue) but the crust needs to be baked prior to adding the filling. To pre-bake: Preheat the oven to 350°F (180°C). Prick bottom and sides of pie shell with tines of fork. Bake until light brown, 15 to 20 minutes. Check crust about halfway to see if crust is puffing up. If it is, prick bottom crust with a fork or pat down with scrunched-up paper towel. Return to oven to finish baking.

- Blending fork

1½ cups	all purpose flour	375 mL
2 tbsp	unsweetened Dutch-process cocoa powder, sifted	25 mL
1 tbsp	granulated sugar	15 mL
¼ tsp	salt	1 mL
½ cup	vegetable shortening, cut into small pieces	125 mL
3 to 4 tbsp	ice water	45 to 60 mL

1. In a large bowl, using a blending fork, blend together flour, cocoa, sugar and salt. Add shortening and blend until dough resembles coarse crumbs.
2. Add ice water, by spoonfuls, while tossing mixture with fork. Add only enough water to make dough stick together. Press dough into a ball. Flatten into a disk and wrap with plastic wrap. Refrigerate until firm enough to roll out for your pie, about 20 minutes. (To roll out dough, see page 110.)
3. For pre-baking instructions, see Tip, left, or fill and bake according to recipe directions.

Uses

- Chocolate Pecan Bourbon Pie (page 130)
- Pumpkin Kahlua Pie (page 134)
- Triple Chocolate Cream Pie (page 138)

Chocolate Tart Pastry Dough

MAKES 2 TART SHELLS

I like using the contrasting color of the chocolate with the Pumpkin Chocolate Swirl Tarts (page 145).

Tips

Freeze unbaked dough in an airtight container for up to 1 month.

I don't use pie weights when blind-baking tart shells. I check the tart partway through the baking and then press any bloating down with a fork or scrunched-up paper towel.

To bake as 2-inch (5 cm) or 3-inch (7.5 cm) tarts, follow baking directions in Tips for Buttery Tart Pastry Dough (page 120).

Variation

Try adding 1 tsp (5 mL) ground cinnamon in the dough if you are making something that cinnamon will enhance.

- Two 8-inch (20 cm) metal tart pans with removable bottoms

2 cups	all-purpose flour	500 mL
½ cup	unsweetened Dutch-process cocoa powder	125 mL
½ cup	granulated sugar	125 mL
½ tsp	salt	2 mL
1 cup	cold unsalted butter, cut into small chunks	250 mL
2	egg yolks	2
¼ cup	cold water	50 mL

1. In a food processor fitted with metal blade, pulse flour, cocoa powder, sugar and salt until combined, about 5 times. Remove lid and distribute butter evenly over top. Cover and pulse until mixture resembles coarse crumbs, about 20 times.
2. In a container with a pouring spout, mix together egg yolks and cold water. With motor running, slowly pour mixture through the feed tube in a steady stream until dough begins to gather. Do not overprocess or let a ball form. The dough will be somewhat crumbly at this point. Place the dough on a board and press lightly with palm of your hand to warm up, if necessary.
3. Press half of the dough evenly into sides and bottoms of each pan. Trim excess dough from top.
4. *To bake with filling:* Fill crust with your favorite filling and follow recipe directions.
5. *To bake unfilled:* Prick bottom and sides of crust. Bake in preheated 425°F (220°C) oven until dry-looking, 18 to 22 minutes. Let cool completely. Fill with desired filling.

Uses

- Pumpkin Chocolate Swirl Tarts (page 145)

Graham Cracker Nut Crust

MAKES ONE 9-INCH (23 CM) SINGLE-CRUST PIE CRUST

This is not your typical cookie crust. The pecans make it richer and more delicious.

- 9-inch (23 cm) pie pan

1½ cups	graham cracker crumbs	375 mL
½ cup	ground toasted pecans	125 mL
4 tbsp	unsalted butter, melted	60 mL

1. In a bowl, combine graham crackers and pecans. Add butter and mix until mixture sticks together and resembles wet sand.
2. Press crust into bottom and up sides of pie pan. Place in freezer to firm up until your filling mixture is ready, about 20 minutes.

Uses

- Key Lime Pie (page 132)

Hazelnut Pie Pastry Dough

MAKES ENOUGH DOUGH FOR ONE 9-INCH (23 CM) SINGLE-CRUST PIE

Use this crust for pies with fall flavors. The rich hazelnut taste amplifies the filling of the pie tenfold.

- Blending fork

1½ cups	all-purpose flour	375 mL
¼ cup	ground toasted hazelnuts	50 mL
½ cup	cold unsalted butter, cut into small chunks	125 mL
3 to 4 tbsp	ice water	45 to 60 mL

1. In a large bowl, with a blending fork, blend together flour and hazelnuts Add butter and blend until mixture resembles coarse crumbs.
2. Add ice water, by spoonfuls, while tossing mixture with a fork. Add only enough water to make dough stick together. Press dough into a ball. Flatten into a disk and wrap with plastic wrap. Refrigerate until firm enough to roll out for your pie, about 20 minutes. (To roll out dough, page 110.)
3. For pre-baking instructions, see Tip, page 116, or fill and bake according to recipe directions.

Uses

- Chocolate Pecan Bourbon Pie (page 130)

Spiced Pie Pastry Dough

MAKES ENOUGH DOUGH FOR TWO 9-INCH (23 CM) SINGLE-CRUST PIES OR ONE DOUBLE-CRUST PIE

Years ago, I created this crust for a story I wrote for my hometown newspaper. It is still reprinted every holiday season.

Tips

Freeze dough in an airtight container for up to 1 month. Thaw in the refrigerator for at least 8 hours or overnight before rolling.

If your dough forms a ball in the food processor work bowl, it may be too tough. To save the dough, turn the machine off and sprinkle dough with 1⁄4 cup (50 mL) all-purpose flour. Pulse 5 times, then proceed with Step 2.

Variation

Try using 1⁄2 tsp (2 mL) ground cloves or mace in place of the nutmeg.

1 1⁄2 cups	cake flour	375 mL
1 1⁄2 cups	all-purpose flour	375 mL
2 tsp	ground cinnamon	10 mL
2 tsp	granulated sugar	10 mL
1 tsp	freshly grated nutmeg	5 mL
1⁄2 tsp	salt	2 mL
1 cup	cold unsalted butter, cut into small chunks	250 mL
1⁄2 cup	ice water	125 mL

1. In a food processor fitted with metal blade, process cake and all-purpose flours, cinnamon, sugar, nutmeg and salt until combined, about 10 seconds. Remove lid and distribute butter evenly over top. Cover and pulse until mixture resembles coarse crumbs, about 10 times. Place water in a container with a pouring spout and, with motor running, slowly pour through the feed tube in a steady stream until dough begins to gather. You may not use all the water, which is fine.
2. Turn out dough onto a clean surface and form into 2 balls. Flatten into disks and wrap in plastic wrap. Refrigerate until firm enough to roll out for your pie, 10 to 20 minutes. (To roll out dough, see page 110.)
3. For pre-baking instructions, see Tip, page 116, or fill and bake according to recipe directions.

Uses

- Apple Spice Pie (page 121)
- Deep Harvest Walnut Pie (page 129)
- Double-Crust Peach Pie (page 125)
- Rustic Apple Cherry Pie (page 136)

Buttery Tart Pastry Dough

MAKES 2 TART SHELLS

A tart crust, unlike a pie crust, needs to be able to stand on its own outside of a pan. This rich and buttery crust will enhance your tart pastries.

Tips

Freeze unbaked dough in an airtight container for up to 1 month.

You can also use this dough for small individual tart shells.

For small tarts (2-inch/5 cm or 3-inch/7.5 cm), press dough into tart shells and prick all over with a fork. Place on a baking sheet and bake in a preheated 375°F (190°C) oven for 14 to 18 minutes or until dry-looking.

Variation

Savory Buttery Tart Pastry: You can make a savory tart shell by omitting the sugar and adding 1/4 cup (50 mL) additional all-purpose flour.

- Two 8-inch (20 cm) metal tart pans with removable bottoms

2 1/2 cups	all-purpose flour	625 mL
1/4 cup	granulated sugar	50 mL
1/2 tsp	salt	2 mL
1 cup	cold unsalted butter, cut into small chunks	250 mL
2	egg yolks	2
3 tbsp	cold water	45 mL

1. In a food processor fitted with metal blade, pulse flour, sugar and salt until combined, about 5 times. Remove lid and distribute butter evenly over top. Cover and pulse until mixture resembles coarse crumbs, about 20 times.
2. In a container with a pouring spout, mix together egg yolks and cold water. With motor running, slowly pour mixture through the feed tube in a steady stream until dough begins to gather. Do not overprocess or let a ball form. The dough will be somewhat crumbly at this point. Transfer dough to a board and press lightly with palm of your hand to warm up. It is now ready to press out into tart pans, if desired.
3. Press half of the dough evenly into sides and bottoms of each pan. Trim excess dough from top.
4. For pre-baking instructions, see Tip, page 116, or fill and bake according to recipe directions.

Uses

- Blueberry Tarts (page 141)
- Fresh Berry Tarts (page 143)
- Lemon Curd Tarts (page 144)
- Pear Almond Crème Tarts (page 146)
- Pumpkin Chocolate Swirl Tarts (page 145)

Apple Spice Pie

SERVES 6 TO 8

You can create this pie faster than going to the store or bakery and purchasing one.

Tip

I like to use a mixture of three different types of baking apples in my pie. To make your own mixture, see Apples, page 15.

Variation

This pie would also work with a lattice crust top (for instructions, see page 112). Follow the instructions for Sour Cherry Lattice Pie, Step 3, page 122.

- Preheat oven to 400°F (200°C)
- 9-inch (23 cm) pie pan

1	recipe Spiced Pie Pastry Dough (see recipe, page 119)	1
6	large baking apples, peeled, cored and quartered (see Tip, left)	6
1/4 cup	freshly squeezed lemon juice	50 mL
1 cup	granulated sugar	250 mL
3 tbsp	all-purpose flour	45 mL
1 1/2 tsp	ground cinnamon	7 mL
1/2 tsp	freshly grated nutmeg	2 mL
2 tbsp	unsalted butter, melted	25 mL
2 tsp	water	10 mL
2 tsp	coarse sugar	10 mL

1. On a lightly floured surface, roll out half of the dough and fit into bottom of pie pan. Roll the remaining half into a 1/4-inch (0.5 cm) thick circle for the top. Set aside. (To roll out dough, see page 110.)
2. In a food processor fitted with slicing blade and with motor running, slice apples. Transfer to a bowl filled with enough water to cover apple slices and lemon juice. Set aside.
3. In a large bowl, blend together sugar, flour, cinnamon and nutmeg until fully incorporated. Drain apples and add to sugar mixture. Toss to fully coat apple slices. Fill bottom crust with apple mixture. Drizzle butter over top. Place top pastry crust over filling. Seal and crimp edges, trimming off any excess dough. Using a knife, make several slits in the top of the dough, or use a small cookie cutter to cut a design from the center of the pie for steam to escape.
4. Brush top with water and sprinkle with coarse sugar. Bake in preheated oven until light brown and filling is bubbly, 40 to 55 minutes. Let cool on a wire rack for at least 1 hour before cutting.

Sour Cherry Lattice Pie

SERVES 6 TO 8

Cherries seem to only be in season for a short time. When they are, have this recipe handy.

Variation

You can use 2 lbs (1 kg) frozen cherries in a pinch. Thaw out prior to use. Drain off juices before measuring.

- Preheat oven to 325°F (160°C)
- 9-inch (23 cm) pie pan

1	double recipe Flaky Pie Pastry Dough (see Variations, page 115)	1
6 cups	fresh sour cherries, stemmed and pitted	1.5 L
½ cup	granulated sugar	125 mL
½ cup	cornstarch	125 mL
1 tsp	freshly grated lemon zest	5 mL
½ tsp	almond extract	2 mL
¼ tsp	ground ginger	1 mL
⅛ tsp	ground cardamom	0.5 mL
2 tbsp	unsalted butter, softened	25 mL

1. On a lightly floured surface, roll out half of the dough and fit into bottom of pie pan, leaving edges untrimmed. Set aside. (To roll out dough, see page 110.)
2. In a large bowl, combine cherries, sugar, cornstarch, lemon zest, almond extract, ginger and cardamom. Stir together to coat evenly and let stand about 15 minutes, so the cherries start releasing juices. Spoon into bottom crust. Smooth top and dot with butter.
3. Roll out the second crust (see Tips for a Perfect Lattice Crust, page 112). Weave the strips over top of the cherry filling. Seal and crimp edges, trimming off any excess dough.
4. Place pie on a baking sheet to catch juices. Bake in preheated oven until top starts to brown and cherries are bubbly, 35 to 40 minutes. Let cool completely on a wire rack for at least 1 hour before cutting.

Double-Crust Berry Pie

SERVES 6 TO 8

The combination of the mixed berries make a perfectly sweet pie.

Variation

This pie would also work with a lattice crust top (for instructions, see page 112). Follow the instructions for Sour Cherry Lattice Pie, Step 3, page 122.

- Preheat oven to 400°F (200°C)
- 9-inch (23 cm) pie pan

1	double recipe Flaky Pie Pastry Dough (see Variations, page 115)	1
1 cup	granulated sugar	250 mL
1⁄3 cup	cornstarch	75 mL
1 tsp	salt	5 mL
1 lb	frozen mixed berries (about 3 1⁄2 cups/875 mL)	500 g

1. On a lightly floured surface, roll out half of the dough and fit into bottom of pie pan. Roll the remaining half into a 1⁄4-inch (0.5 cm) thick circle for the top. Set aside. (To roll out dough, see page 110.)
2. In a small bowl, combine sugar, cornstarch and salt.
3. In a large bowl, sprinkle berries with sugar mixture and stir to evenly coat. Spoon into bottom crust. Place top pastry crust over filling. Seal and crimp edges, trimming off any excess dough. Using a knife, make several slits in the top of the dough, or use a small cookie cutter to cut a design from the center of the pie for steam to escape.
4. Bake in preheated oven until top is light brown and center is bubbly, 55 to 65 minutes. Let cool on a wire rack for at least 1 hour before cutting.

Double-Crust Peach Pie

SERVES 6 TO 8

When fresh peaches are in season it's the best time to make a peach pie or peach ice cream. Better yet, make both for a perfect dessert.

Variation

This pie would also work with a lattice crust top (for instructions, see page 112). Follow the instructions for Sour Cherry Lattice Pie, Step 3, page 122.

- Preheat oven to 425°F (220°C)
- 9-inch (23 cm) pie pan

1	recipe Spiced Pie Pastry Dough (see recipe, page 119)	1
½ cup	granulated sugar	125 mL
2 tbsp	cornstarch	25 mL
½ tsp	ground cinnamon	2 mL
¼ tsp	ground nutmeg	1 mL
5 cups	sliced peeled fresh peaches	1.25 L
1 tbsp	freshly squeezed lemon juice	15 mL
2 tbsp	unsalted butter, melted	25 mL

1. On a lightly floured surface, roll out half of the dough and fit into bottom of pie pan. Roll the remaining half into a ¼-inch (0.5 cm) thick circle for the top. Set aside. (To roll out dough, see page 110.)
2. In a large bowl, combine sugar, cornstarch, cinnamon and nutmeg. Add peaches and lemon juice and stir to coat evenly with dry ingredients. Spoon into bottom crust. Place top pastry crust over filling. Seal and crimp edges, trimming off any excess dough. Using a knife, make several slits in the top of the dough, or use a small cookie cutter to cut a design from the center of the pie for steam to escape.
3. Brush top with melted butter. Bake in preheated oven until golden brown and center is bubbly, 40 to 50 minutes. Let cool on a wire rack for at least 1 hour before cutting.

Strawberry Rhubarb Pie

SERVES 6 TO 8

Strawberries are a sweet companion to rhubarb, which is generally too tart on its own for pie.

Variation

This pie would also work with a lattice crust top (for instructions, see page 112). Follow the instructions for Sour Cherry Lattice Pie, Step 3, page 122.

- Preheat oven to 425°F (220°C)
- 9-inch (23 cm) pie pan

1	double recipe All-Butter Pie Pastry Dough (see recipe, page 115)	1
1 cup	granulated sugar	250 mL
3 tbsp	all-purpose flour	45 mL
½ tsp	ground cinnamon	2 mL
2 cups	diced rhubarb	500 mL
2 cups	quartered strawberries	500 mL
1 tsp	freshly squeezed lemon juice	5 mL
2 tbsp	unsalted butter, melted	25 mL

1. On a lightly floured surface, roll out half of the dough and fit into bottom of pie pan. Roll the remaining dough into a ¼-inch (0.5 cm) thick circle for the top. Set aside. (To roll out dough, see page 110.)
2. In a large bowl, combine sugar, flour and cinnamon. Add rhubarb, strawberries and lemon juice. Stir to coat fruit evenly. Spoon into bottom crust. Place top pastry crust over filling. Seal and crimp edges, trimming off any excess dough. Using a knife, make several slits in the top of the dough, or use a small cookie cutter to cut a design from the center of the pie for steam to escape.
3. Brush with melted butter. Bake in preheated oven for 10 minutes. Reduce temperature to 350°F (180°C) and continue baking until golden brown, 25 to 30 minutes. Let cool on a wire rack for at least 1 hour before cutting.

Banana Blackberry Cream Pie

SERVES 6 TO 8

Sweet blackberries and bananas in rich vanilla custard make this a summer treat.

- 9-inch (23 cm) pie pan

1	recipe All-Butter Pie Pastry Dough (see recipe, page 115)	1
1 cup	granulated sugar	250 mL
1⁄3 cup	all-purpose flour	75 mL
1⁄8 tsp	salt	0.5 mL
2 cups	milk, preferably whole	500 mL
3	egg yolks, beaten	3
1 tsp	vanilla extract	5 mL
2 tbsp	unsalted butter	25 mL
2	large bananas, sliced	2
1⁄2 cup	blackberries, cut into small pieces	125 mL
1	recipe Classic Whipped Cream (see recipe, page 239)	1

1. On a lightly floured surface, roll out dough and fit into bottom of pie pan. (To roll out dough, see page 110.) For pre-baking instructions, see Tip, page 116. Let cool completely.
2. In a heavy saucepan, whisk together sugar, flour and salt. Add milk in a steady stream, stirring until combined. Cook over medium heat, stirring constantly, until bubbly, about 4 minutes.
3. In a small bowl, whisk together egg yolks and vanilla. Gradually whisk in about 1⁄4 cup (50 mL) of hot milk mixture and then return to saucepan. Cook over medium heat, whisking constantly, until thickened, for 2 minutes. Remove from heat and whisk in butter. Set aside.
4. Place sliced bananas and blackberries in bottom of cooled pie shell. Pour custard over top. Let cool on a wire rack for 20 minutes. Refrigerate until chilled and set, about 2 hours. Serve topped with Classic Whipped Cream.

Coconut Almond Pie

SERVES 6 TO 8

This pie makes a beautiful presentation with the toasted coconut and almond.

- Preheat oven to 350°F (180°C)
- 9-inch (23 cm) pie pan

1	recipe Flaky Pie Pastry Dough (see Variations, page 115)	1
1 cup	lightly packed brown sugar	250 mL
1 cup	pure maple syrup	250 mL
1⁄4 cup	unsalted butter, melted	50 mL
3	eggs, beaten	3
1⁄4 cup	whiskey	50 mL
1 cup	slivered almonds	250 mL
1⁄2 cup	flaked sweetened coconut	125 mL

1. On a lightly floured surface, roll out dough and fit into bottom of pie pan. Set aside. (To roll out dough, see page 110.)
2. In a bowl, whisk together brown sugar, maple syrup, butter, eggs and whiskey.
3. Sprinkle almonds and coconut over pastry shell. Pour sugar mixture over top, making sure that you submerge the nuts and coconut. Bake in preheated oven until a knife inserted into center comes out clean, 40 to 45 minutes. Let cool on a wire rack for at least 1 hour prior to cutting.

Deep Harvest Walnut Pie

SERVES 6 TO 8

Years ago when I was a regular food host on a national television show I created this pie for an upcoming fall season. The aroma of baking pie could be smelled throughout the audience.

- Preheat oven to 400°F (200°C)
- 9-inch (23 cm) pie pan

1	recipe Spiced Pie Pastry Dough (see recipe, page 119)	1
2	medium baking apples, such as Granny Smith or Pippin, peeled, cored and sliced into 12 thin slices	2
1 cup	granulated sugar	250 mL
½ cup	golden raisins	125 mL
½ cup	fresh cranberries	125 mL
½ cup	toasted chopped walnuts	125 mL
1 tbsp	ground cinnamon	15 mL
½ tsp	ground nutmeg	2 mL
¼ tsp	ground cloves	1 mL
2 tbsp	unsalted butter, melted	25 mL
2 tsp	water	10 mL
2 tsp	granulated sugar	10 mL

1. On a lightly floured surface, roll out half of the dough and fit into bottom of pie pan. Roll the remaining half into a ¼-inch (0.5 cm) thick circle for the top. Set aside. (To roll out dough, see page 110.)
2. In a large bowl, combine apples, 1 cup (250 mL) sugar, raisins, cranberries, walnuts, cinnamon, nutmeg and cloves. Stir to evenly coat apples and fruits. Spoon into bottom crust. Drizzle butter over top. Place top pastry crust over filling. Seal and crimp edges, trimming off any excess dough. Using a knife, make several slits in the top of the dough, or use a small cookie cutter to cut a design from the center of the pie for steam to escape.
3. Brush top with water and sprinkle with 2 tsp (10 mL) sugar. Bake in preheated oven until light brown and filling is bubbly, 45 to 50 minutes. Let cool on a wire rack for at least 1 hour before cutting.

Chocolate Pecan Bourbon Pie

SERVES 6 TO 8

Rich chocolate laced with bourbon and crunchy pecans highlight this pie. Serve with vanilla ice cream.

- Preheat oven to 350°F (180°C)
- 9-inch (23 cm) pie pan

1	recipe Hazelnut Pastry Dough or Chocolate Pie Pastry Dough (see recipes, pages 118 and 116)	1
1 cup	packed light brown sugar	250 mL
1 cup	pure maple syrup	250 mL
¼ cup	unsalted butter, melted	50 mL
3	eggs, beaten	3
¼ cup	bourbon	50 mL
1 cup	pecan halves	250 mL
6 oz	semisweet chocolate, cut into small pieces	175 g

1. On a lightly floured surface, roll out dough and fit into bottom of pie pan. Set aside. (To roll out dough, see page 110.)
2. In a bowl, whisk together brown sugar, maple syrup, butter, eggs and bourbon.
3. Sprinkle pecans and semisweet chocolate over pastry shell. Pour sugar mixture over top, making sure that you submerge pecans and chocolate pieces.
4. Bake in preheated oven until a knife inserted into center comes out clean, 40 to 45 minutes. Let cool on a wire rack for at least 1 hour before cutting.

Key Lime Pie

SERVES 6 TO 8

Fresh Florida Key limes are the best to use in this pie. If Key limes are unavailable, you can use Key lime juice in bottles (see Sources, page 442).

Tips

You can use regular limes in place of Key limes, the tartness will be lacking, but you will still have a terrific pie. Some bakeries will add a few drops of green food coloring to the mixture to make it green, real lime pies are yellow in color.

Caution: this recipe contains raw eggs. If the food safety is a concern for you, use pasteurized eggs or avoid this recipe.

4	egg yolks	4
1	can (14 oz/396 g or 300 mL) sweetened condensed milk	1
1 tsp	grated Key lime zest (see Tips, left)	5 mL
½ cup	Key lime juice	125 mL
½ tsp	cream of tartar	2 mL
1	Graham Cracker Nut Crust (see page 118)	1
1	recipe Classic Whipped Cream (see recipe, page 239) or Brown Sugar Meringue Icing (see recipe, page 223)	1

1. In a mixer bowl fitted with whip attachment, whip egg yolks on high until pale yellow, about 4 minutes. Add condensed milk, lime zest and juice and cream of tartar and mix just to blend.
2. Pour into prepared pie shell. Refrigerate for 2 hours or until chilled and set.
3. Top with Classic Whipped Cream or Brown Sugar Meringue Icing.

Lemon Meringue Pie

SERVES 6 TO 8

My sister Monica always asks for Lemon Meringue Pie instead of cake for her birthday. As a kid, I thought this request was strange. Now I have grown up and share her enthusiasm. She still loves this pie.

Tips

For further tips about meringue, see page 236.

While cooking the lemon filling it is important that you do not stop whisking or you will have burnt spots.

Browning: If using a torch, hold a few inches from meringue and wave it back and forth to desired brownness. If using your oven, place under broiler until desired brownness. The timing will depend on how far your pastry is from the heat. Watch it carefully.

- 9-inch (23 cm) pie pan

1	recipe Flaky Pie Pastry Dough (see Variations, page 115)	1
1½ cups	granulated sugar	375 mL
3½ tbsp	cornstarch	52 mL
3½ tbsp	all-purpose flour	52 mL
Pinch	salt	Pinch
1½ cups	hot water	375 mL
3	egg yolks, beaten	3
2 tbsp	unsalted butter	25 mL
½ tsp	freshly grated lemon zest	2 mL
⅓ cup	freshly squeezed lemon juice	75 mL
1	recipe Brown Sugar Meringue Icing (see recipe, page 223)	1

1. On a lightly floured surface, roll out dough and fit into bottom of pie pan. (To roll out dough, see page 110.) For pre-baking instructions, see Tip, page 116. Let cool completely.
2. In a heavy saucepan, whisk together sugar, cornstarch, flour and salt. Gradually add hot water in a steady stream, whisking until smooth. Cook over medium heat, whisking constantly, until mixture comes to a boil, about 6 minutes. Reduce heat and cook, whisking, for an additional 2 minutes. Remove from heat.
3. In a small bowl, gradually whisk about ½ cup (125 mL) of hot sugar mixture into egg yolks. Whisk back into saucepan. Return to medium heat and, cook, whisking, until thickened, for 2 minutes. Remove from heat. Add butter and lemon zest. Pour in lemon juice in a steady stream while whisking.
4. Pour mixture into prepared pie shell. While filling is still hot, top with Brown Sugar Meringue Icing. Place under a broiler or use a propane blowtorch to brown (see Tips, left).

Pumpkin Kahlúa Pie

SERVES 6 TO 8

A hint of coffee flavor accenting rich pumpkin is a perfect marriage of flavors.

- Preheat oven to 375°F (190°C)
- 9-inch (23 cm) pie pan

1	recipe All-Butter Pie Pastry Dough or Chocolate Pie Pastry Dough (see recipes pages 115 and 116)	1
1½ cups	pumpkin purée (not pie filling)	375 mL
¾ cup	granulated sugar	175 mL
2 tsp	ground cinnamon	10 mL
1 tsp	ground ginger	5 mL
½ tsp	ground cloves	2 mL
½ tsp	salt	2 mL
½ tsp	freshly grated nutmeg	2 mL
3	eggs, beaten	3
1 cup	milk, preferably whole	250 mL
¾ cup	evaporated milk	175 mL
¼ cup	coffee-flavored liqueur, such as Kahlúa	50 mL
	Classic Whipped Cream (see recipe, page 239)	

1. On a lightly floured surface, roll out dough and fit into bottom of pie pan. Set aside. (To roll out dough, see page 110.)
2. In a large bowl, whisk together pumpkin, sugar, cinnamon, ginger, cloves, salt and nutmeg. Whisk in eggs. Pour in milk and evaporated milk in a steady stream, whisking until fully incorporated. Whisk in liqueur, making sure everything is incorporated.
3. Pour mixture into prepared pie crust. Bake in preheated oven until a knife inserted into center comes out clean, 40 to 50 minutes (see Tip, page 135). Let cool completely on a wire rack for at least 1 hour before serving with Classic Whipped Cream.

Pumpkin Pecan Pie

SERVES 6 TO 8

I love making both pumpkin and pecan pies. Here they are together in one pie.

Tip

Check your pie at 40 minutes. If a knife comes out runny with a few firm pieces attached, the pie needs 10 minutes more; if you see only firm pieces but the knife is still not clean, it needs 5 additional minutes. You never want the knife to come out completely clean the first time because it might be overbaked at this point.

Variations

Reduce milk by ¼ cup (50 mL) and use coffee-flavored liqueur instead.

To make this filling by hand instead of a food processor, follow the method for filling in Step 2 of Pumpkin Kahlúa Pie, (page 134), chopping the pecans by hand first.

- Preheat oven to 375°F (190°C)
- 9-inch (23 cm) pie pan

½	recipe Spiced Pie Pastry Dough (see recipe, page 119)	½
½ cup	pecan halves	125 mL
1½ cups	pumpkin purée (not pie filling)	375 mL
¾ cup	packed light brown sugar	175 mL
2 tsp	ground cinnamon	10 mL
1 tsp	ground ginger	5 mL
½ tsp	ground cloves	2 mL
½ tsp	salt	2 mL
½ tsp	freshly grated nutmeg	2 mL
3	eggs, beaten	3
1¼ cups	milk, preferably whole	300 mL
¾ cup	evaporated milk	175 mL

1. On a lightly floured surface, roll out dough and fit into bottom of pie pan. Set aside. (To roll out dough, see page 110.)
2. In a food processor fitted with metal blade, pulse pecans until finely chopped, about 15 times. Do not overprocess or you will get pecan butter. Spread pecans over pastry.
3. In same work bowl fitted with metal blade, process pumpkin, brown sugar, cinnamon, ginger, cloves, salt and nutmeg until smooth, about 30 seconds. With motor running, add eggs through the feed tube. Then pour in milk and evaporated milk in a steady stream and process until incorporated.
4. Pour mixture over pecans in prepared pie shell. Bake in preheated oven until crust is firm and light brown and a knife inserted into the center of filling comes out clean, 40 to 50 minutes (see Tip, left). Let cool on a wire rack for at least 1 hour prior to cutting.

Rustic Apple Cherry Pie

SERVES 6 TO 8

I took advantage of this rustic way to make a pie when I accidentally dropped the pastry for the top crust and didn't have time to make more. Ever since that mishap, it's my favorite way to bake up this tasty apple-cherry combination in spiced pastry.

- Preheat oven to 400°F (200°C)
- Baking sheet, lined with parchment paper or Silpat

½	recipe Spiced Pie Pastry Dough (see recipe, page 119)	½
1 cup	granulated sugar	250 mL
3 tbsp	all-purpose flour	45 mL
1½ tsp	ground cinnamon	7 mL
½ tsp	ground nutmeg	2 mL
5	medium baking apples, such as Granny Smith or Pippin, peeled and sliced	5
½ cup	sweet cherries, pitted and drained	125 mL
2 tbsp	unsalted butter, melted	25 mL

1. On a lightly floured surface, roll out dough to a 12-inch (30 cm) circle. Place on prepared baking sheet, leaving flat. Set aside. (To roll out dough, see page 110.)
2. In a large bowl, combine sugar, flour, cinnamon and nutmeg. Add apples and cherries and stir evenly to coat. Mound fruit in center of pastry. Fold dough about 1½ inches (4 cm) toward center over fruit. (Some of the fruit will still be visible in the center.) Drizzle butter into center of fruit.
3. Bake in preheated oven until sides start to brown and center is bubbly, 45 to 50 minutes. Let cool on a wire rack for at least 1 hour prior to cutting.

Sweet Potato Pie

SERVES 6 TO 8

This pie originated in the South, where it's still a huge favorite. Make a little Southern tradition this fall season in your home!

- Preheat oven to 425°F (220°C)
- 9-inch (23 cm) pie pan

2	small sweet potatoes, peeled and cut into quarters	2
1	recipe Flaky Pie Pastry Dough (see Variations, page 115)	1
2 cups	milk, preferably whole	500 mL
2 tbsp	grated orange zest	25 mL
½ cup	packed dark brown sugar	125 mL
½ tsp	salt	2 mL
½ tsp	ground cinnamon	2 mL
½ tsp	ground nutmeg	2 mL
¼ cup	unsalted butter, softened	50 mL
3	eggs, separated	3

1. In a large saucepan of boiling water, cook sweet potatoes until tender, about 15 minutes. Drain and rinse under cold water. Using a potato masher, mash sweet potatoes and measure out 1½ cups (375 mL) (reserve any extra for another use). Set aside.
2. On a lightly floured surface, roll out dough and fit into bottom of pie pan. Set aside. (To roll out dough, see page 110.)
3. In a saucepan over medium heat, scald milk and orange zest until bubbles start to form around sides of pan and a "skin" forms on top, about 3 minutes. Whisk in sweet potato, brown sugar, salt, cinnamon, nutmeg and butter. Whisk egg yolks and add to saucepan in a steady stream, whisking constantly. Set aside.
4. In a mixer bowl fitted with whip attachment, whip egg whites until firm peaks form. Fold into sweet potato mixture. Pour into prepared pie crust.
5. Bake in preheated oven for 10 minutes. Reduce heat to 325°F (160°C) and continue baking until light brown and a knife inserted into center comes out clean (see Tip, page 135), 35 to 40 minutes. Let cool completely on a wire rack for at least 1 hour before cutting.

Triple-Chocolate Cream Pie

SERVES 6 TO 8

Three chocolates packed into this creamy pie make a chocoholic's dream.

- 9-inch (23 cm) pie pan

1	recipe Chocolate Pie Pastry Dough (see recipe, page 116)	1
1 cup	granulated sugar	250 mL
⅓ cup	all-purpose flour	75 mL
⅛ tsp	salt	0.5 mL
2 cups	milk, preferably whole, at room temperature	500 mL
3 oz	unsweetened chocolate, melted and cooled (see Melting Chocolate, page 250)	90 g
3	egg yolks, beaten	3
1 tsp	vanilla extract	5 mL
2 tbsp	unsalted butter, softened	25 mL
3 oz	milk chocolate, chopped (about ¾ cup/175 mL)	90 g
3 oz	semisweet chocolate, chopped (about ¾ cup/175 mL)	90 g
1	recipe Classic Whipped Cream (see recipe, page 239)	1

1. On a lightly floured surface, roll out dough and fit into bottom of pie pan. Set aside. (To roll out dough, see page 110.)
2. In a heavy saucepan, combine sugar, flour and salt. Gradually whisk in milk and unsweetened chocolate. Cook over medium heat, stirring constantly, until mixture starts to bubble, about 3 minutes. Remove from heat.
3. In a small bowl, gradually whisk ¼ cup (50 mL) of the hot chocolate mixture into egg yolks. Add egg yolk mixture to saucepan. Cook over medium heat, stirring constantly, until thickened, for 2 minutes. Remove from heat.
4. Whisk in vanilla and butter. Fold in milk chocolate and semisweet chocolate. Pour into prepared pie shell. Let cool on a wire rack for 20 minutes. Refrigerate until chilled and set, about 2 hours. Decorate with Classic Whipped Cream just before serving.

Whole Egg Custard Pie

SERVES 6 TO 8

Rich egg custard in a pie. Try this topped with fresh stone fruit or berries.

- Preheat oven to 350°F (180°C)
- 9-inch (23 cm) pie pan

1	recipe Flaky Pie Pastry Dough (see Variations, page 115)	1
1½ cups	milk, preferably whole	375 mL
1 cup	whipping (35%) cream	250 mL
4	eggs, beaten	4
½ cup	granulated sugar	125 mL
1 tbsp	vanilla extract	15 mL
⅛ tsp	salt	0.5 mL
¼ tsp	freshly grated nutmeg	1 mL

1. On a lightly floured surface, roll out dough and fit into bottom of pie pan. Set aside. (To roll out dough, see page 110.)
2. In a heavy saucepan over medium heat, scald milk and cream until bubbles form around sides of saucepan and a "skin" forms on top, about 3 minutes. Set aside.
3. In a large bowl, whisk together eggs, sugar, vanilla and salt. Gradually whisk in scalded milk mixture. Pour into prepared shell. Sprinkle top with nutmeg. Bake in preheated oven until knife inserted into center comes out clean, 35 to 40 minutes. Let cool on a wire rack for 20 minutes. Refrigerate until chilled and set, about 2 hours.

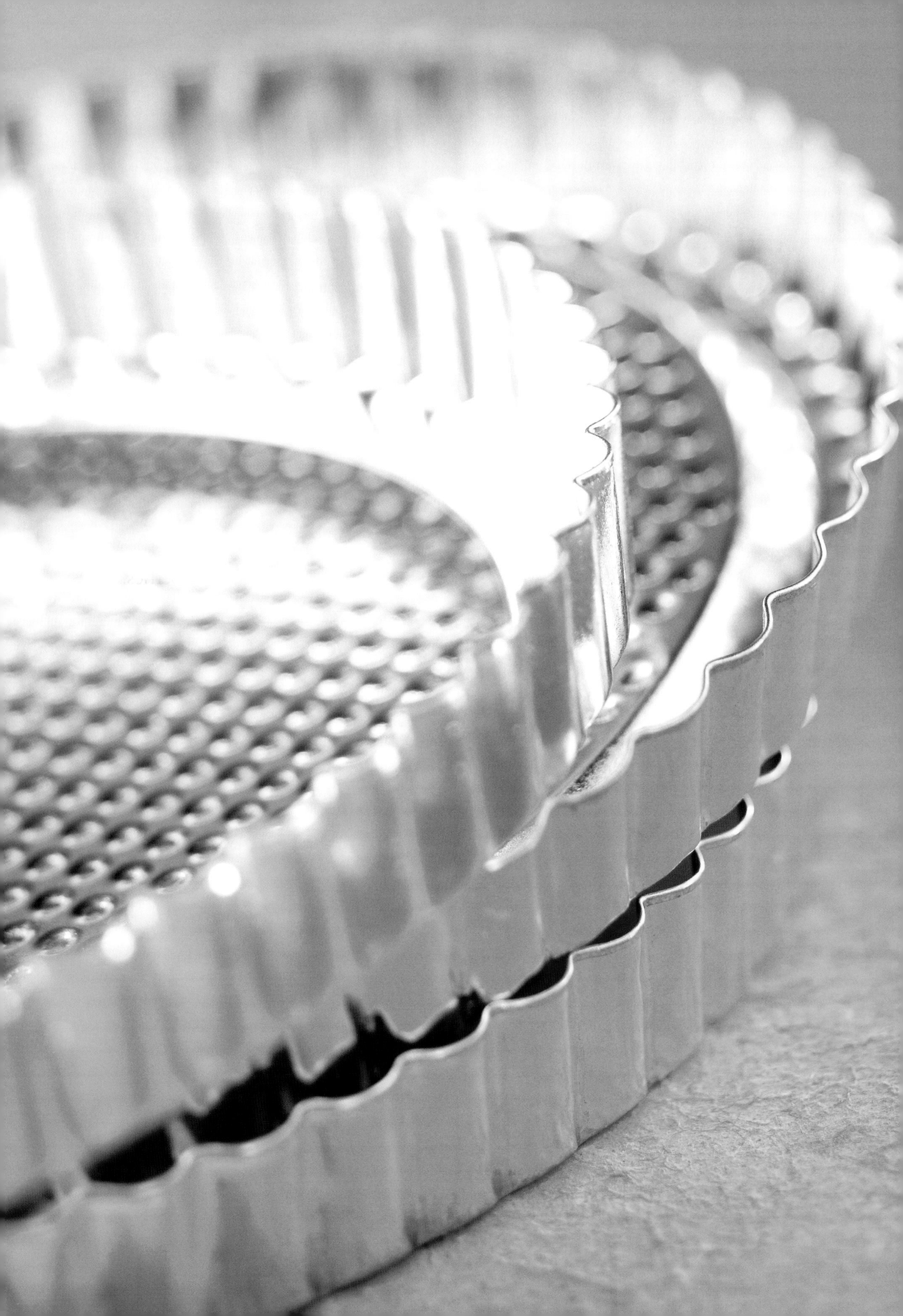

Blueberry Tarts

MAKES 8 TARTS

These tarts look great and you can make them any time of the year, since you can take advantage of frozen berries.

Tip

These tarts should not be prepared too far in advance, as the blueberry mixture starts to seep.

- Eight 3-inch (7.5 cm) tart pans

1	recipe Buttery Tart Pastry Dough (see recipe, page 120)	1
1/4 cup	granulated sugar	50 mL
1 1/2 tbsp	cornstarch	22 mL
12 oz	frozen blueberries (about 2 cups/500 mL)	375 g
2 tbsp	confectioner's (icing) sugar	25 mL

1. Press dough into tart pans. Bake according to Tips on page 120. Let cool completely.
2. In a saucepan over medium heat, bring 3/4 cup (175 mL) water and granulated sugar to a boil, stirring until sugar is dissolved, about 3 minutes.
3. In a small bowl, dissolve cornstarch and 1/4 cup (50 mL) water. Pour into boiling mixture and whisk until thickened, about 2 minutes. Remove from heat. Stir in blueberries.
4. Dust prepared tart shells with confectioner's sugar. Divide blueberry mixture evenly between tart shells. Dust again with confectioner's sugar. Serve immediately.

Chocolate Cream Tarts

MAKES 12 TARTS

These rich chocolate tarts will make any dessert table spectacular!

- Twelve 2-inch (5 cm) tart pans

1	recipe Buttery Tart Pastry Dough (see recipe, page 120)	1
1 cup	granulated sugar	250 mL
⅓ cup	all-purpose flour	75 mL
⅛ tsp	salt	0.5 mL
2 cups	milk, preferably whole	500 mL
4 oz	unsweetened chocolate, melted and cooled (see Melting Chocolate, page 250)	125 g
3	egg yolks, beaten	3
1 tsp	vanilla extract	5 mL
2 tbsp	unsalted butter	25 mL
1	recipe Classic Whipped Cream (see recipe, page 239)	1

1. Press dough into tart pans. Bake according to Tips on page 120. Let cool completely.
2. In a heavy saucepan, combine sugar, flour and salt. Gradually whisk in milk and chocolate. Cook over medium heat, stirring constantly, until mixture starts to bubble, about 2 minutes. Remove from heat.
3. In a small bowl, gradually whisk ¼ cup (50 mL) of the hot chocolate mixture into egg yolks. Add egg yolk mixture to saucepan. Cook over medium heat, stirring constantly, until thickened, for 2 minutes. Remove from heat and whisk in vanilla and butter.
4. Divide mixture evenly between tart shells. Let cool on a wire rack for 20 minutes. Refrigerate until chilled and set, about 2 hours. Decorate with Classic Whipped Cream.

Fresh Berry Tarts

MAKES 8 TARTS

Years back I used to work at a hotel where we would make hundreds of these berry tarts every Sunday for brunch.

Tips

Be sure to drain berries on paper towel after washing and pat them before assembling tarts.

If well chilled before serving, these tarts will last on a buffet table for about 1 hour.

- Eight 3-inch (7.5 cm) tart pans

1	recipe Buttery Tart Pastry Dough (see recipe, page 120)	1
1	recipe French Pastry Cream (see recipe, page 242)	1
4 cups	fresh berries, such as raspberries, strawberries or blackberries	1 L
¾ cup	currant jelly	175 mL
1 cup	Classic Whipped Cream (see recipe, page 239)	250 mL

1. Press dough into tart pans. Bake according to Tips on page 120. Let cool completely.
2. Fill prepared tart shells with pastry cream. Arrange berries over top. Set aside.
3. In a small saucepan over medium heat, bring jelly to a boil. Strain, if necessary, and brush over arranged berries. Pipe a swirl of Classic Whipped Cream over top of each tart. Refrigerate until serving.

Lemon Curd Tarts

MAKES 12 TARTS

This is by far one of my most popular desserts that is not predominantly chocolate.

Variation

Lemon Curd Meringue Tarts: Omit chocolate and top tarts with Brown Sugar Meringue (see recipe, page 223) and brown as directed.

- Twelve 3-inch (7.5 cm) tart pans
- Pastry bag, fitted with small piping tip

1	recipe Buttery Tart Pastry Dough (see recipe, page 120)	1
1	recipe Fresh Lemon Curd (see recipe, page 284)	1
2 oz	milk chocolate, chopped and melted (see Melting Chocolate, page 250)	60 g

1. Press dough into tart pans. Bake according to Tips on page 120. Let cool completely.
2. Divide lemon curd evenly between tart shells.
3. Fill pastry bag with melted chocolate and decorate each tart with "lines" and/or "teardrops" of piped chocolate.

Pumpkin Chocolate Swirl Tarts

MAKES 12 TARTS

These are beautiful on a pastry table in the fall.

- Preheat oven to 400°F (200°C)
- Twelve 3-inch (7.5 cm) tart pans
- Pastry bag, fitted with small piping tip

2	recipes Buttery Tart Pastry Dough or Chocolate Tart Pastry Dough (see recipes, pages 120 and 117)	2
3/4 cup	pumpkin purée (not pie filling)	175 mL
1/3 cup	packed brown sugar	75 mL
1 tsp	ground cinnamon	5 mL
1/2 tsp	ground ginger	2 mL
1/4 tsp	ground cloves	1 mL
1/4 tsp	salt	1 mL
1/4 tsp	freshly grated nutmeg	1 mL
2	eggs	2
1/2 cup	milk, preferably whole	125 mL
1/2 cup	evaporated milk	125 mL
3 oz	bittersweet chocolate, melted (see Melting Chocolate, page 250)	90 g

1. Press dough into tart pans. Set aside.
2. In a large bowl, whisk together pumpkin, sugar, cinnamon, ginger, cloves, salt and nutmeg. Whisk in eggs. Pour in milk and evaporated milk in a steady stream, whisking until fully incorporated.
3. Divide mixture evenly between tart shells. Bake in preheated oven until a knife inserted into the center of a tart comes out clean and crust is light brown, 20 to 28 minutes. Let cool completely.
4. Fill pastry bag with chocolate and top each tart with piped chocolate swirls.

Pear Almond Crème Tarts

MAKES 2 TARTS

These are the beautiful tarts that you see in French pastry shop windows. I'm always amazed at how expensive they are when they're so simple to make.

Tip

You can make the cream a few days prior to use. Cover and refrigerate and then stir before using.

Variations

Try using 6 fresh peaches, peeled, pitted and cut in half, or 1 cup (250 mL) canned peaches or cherries, drained, in place of the pears for each tart.

- Preheat oven to 375°F (190°C)
- Two 8-inch (20 cm) metal tart pans with removable bottoms

1	recipe Buttery Tart Pastry Dough (see recipe, page 120)	1
7 oz	almond paste	210 g
3⁄4 cup	granulated sugar	175 mL
1⁄3 cup	unsalted butter, softened	75 mL
3	eggs	3
1 tsp	vanilla extract	5 mL
3⁄4 cup	cake flour	175 mL
12	small canned pear halves, drained	12

1. Press dough into tart pans. Set aside.
2. In a food processor fitted with metal blade, process almond paste and sugar until softened, about 30 seconds. Add butter and process until incorporated. With motor running, add eggs and vanilla through the feed tube until well incorporated, about 20 seconds. Add flour and process until smooth, about 30 seconds.
3. Divide mixture evenly between tart shells. Slice each pear half vertically into 6 to 8 slices, trying to keep the pear looking like it's still intact. Place sliced pear over almond cream, pressing to fan pear. Do this five more times around the tart so you have 6 pear halves on each tart. Bake in preheated oven until crust is light brown and filling is set, 45 to 60 minutes.

Blueberry Crisp

SERVES 8 TO 10

Rich blueberries make this a perfect crisp when berries are plentiful.

- Preheat oven to 400°F (200°C)
- 13-by 9-inch (3 L) glass baking dish, buttered or sprayed with nonstick spray

Topping

1 cup	all-purpose flour	250 mL
1 cup	packed light brown sugar	250 mL
2/3 cup	old-fashioned rolled oats	150 mL
1/2 tsp	ground cinnamon	2 mL
1/4 tsp	salt	1 mL
2/3 cup	cold unsalted butter, cut into small chunks	150 mL

Filling

3 1/2 cups	fresh or frozen blueberries (1 1/2 lbs/750 g)	875 mL
1/2 cup	granulated sugar	125 mL
	Finely grated zest and juice of 1 lemon	
3 tbsp	all-purpose flour	45 mL

1. *Topping:* In a food processor fitted with metal blade, process flour, brown sugar, oats, cinnamon and salt for 5 seconds. Remove lid and distribute butter evenly over top. Cover and pulse until mixture resembles coarse crumbs, about 20 times. Set aside.
2. *Filling:* In a large bowl, combine blueberries, sugar, lemon zest and juice and flour. Stir to coat berries evenly. Transfer to prepared baking dish. Crumble topping over berries. Bake in preheated oven until bubbly around sides, 28 to 32 minutes. Serve warm.

Mixed Fruit Buckle

SERVES 12 TO 16

A buckle is a cake that is laced with large pieces of fruit. This is a good one for summer picnics.

- Preheat oven to 375°F (190°C)
- 13-by 9-inch (3 L) glass baking dish, buttered or sprayed with nonstick spray

Streusel Topping

1⅔ cups	all-purpose flour	400 mL
½ cup	granulated sugar	125 mL
¼ tsp	salt	1 mL
2 tsp	ground cinnamon	10 mL
½ cup	cold unsalted butter, cut in small chunks	125 mL

Cake

¾ cup	unsalted butter, softened	175 mL
2 cups	granulated sugar	500 mL
6	eggs	6
1 tbsp	vanilla extract	15 mL
1 tsp	almond extract	5 mL
2⅔ cups	all-purpose flour	650 mL
1 tbsp	baking powder	15 mL
1 tsp	salt	5 mL
8 cups	chopped peeled stone fruit, such as peaches, plums and nectarines	2 L

1. *Streusel Topping:* In a food processor fitted with metal blade, process flour, sugar, salt and cinnamon for 10 seconds. Remove lid and distribute butter evenly over top. Cover and pulse until mixture resembles coarse crumbs, about 20 times. Set aside.
2. *Cake:* In a mixer bowl fitted with paddle attachment, beat butter and sugar until smooth, about 3 minutes. Add eggs, one at a time, beating well between each addition. Beat in vanilla and almond extracts. Using a wooden spoon, gradually stir in flour, baking powder and salt just until incorporated. Add half the fruit to batter and fold in gently with a large rubber spatula. Spread batter into prepared dish and top evenly with rest of fruit. Sprinkle with Streusel Topping.
3. Bake in preheated oven until cake springs back in center when lightly pressed and toothpick comes out clean, 45 to 50 minutes. Let cool on a rack. Serve warm.

Tri-Berry Cobbler

SERVES 8 TO 10

This cobbler is ruby red in color and perfect for Valentine's Day.

- Preheat oven to 375°F (190°C)
- 8-cup (2 L) shallow baking dish, buttered or sprayed with nonstick spray

½ cup	unsalted butter	125 mL
1 cup	all-purpose flour	250 mL
1 cup	granulated sugar	250 mL
1½ tsp	baking powder	7 mL
1 cup	whipping (35%) cream	250 mL
3 cups	sliced strawberries (1 lb/500 g)	750 mL
1½ cups	raspberries (8 oz/250 g)	375 mL
1½ cups	blackberries (8 oz/250 g)	375 mL

1. In a large heavy saucepan over medium heat, melt butter. Stir in flour, sugar and baking powder until well blended. (It will be very dry at this point.) Gradually pour in cream in a steady stream, whisking until smooth. Set aside.
2. In prepared baking dish, combine strawberries, raspberries and blackberries. Drizzle batter back and forth over fruit. Bake in preheated oven until golden brown, 30 to 45 minutes. Serve warm.

Simple Peach Cobbler

SERVES 8 TO 10

A fast and easy dessert. Great paired with vanilla ice cream.

Variation

Use pears in place of the peaches.

- Preheat oven to 375°F (190°C)
- 8-cup (2 L) shallow baking dish, buttered or sprayed with nonstick spray

½ cup	unsalted butter	125 mL
1 cup	all-purpose flour	250 mL
1 cup	granulated sugar	250 mL
1½ tsp	baking powder	7 mL
1 cup	milk, preferably whole	250 mL
4 cups	fresh or frozen sliced peaches (1½ lbs/750 g)	1 L
1 tsp	ground cinnamon	5 mL

1. In a large heavy saucepan over medium heat, melt butter. Add flour, sugar and baking powder and stir well. (It will be very dry at this point.) Gradually pour in milk in a steady stream, whisking until smooth. Set aside.
2. Place peaches in prepared baking dish. Drizzle batter back and forth over fruit. Sprinkle with cinnamon. Bake in preheated oven until golden brown, 30 to 45 minutes. Serve warm.

Apple Crisp with Crumb Topping

SERVES 12 TO 16

In grade school I would swap anything for the cafeteria's signature apple crisp. This fruity dessert takes me back to those in the '70s.

Tips

Make sure the butter is cold from the refrigerator or topping will not be crumbly.

Use a food processor with a slicing blade to make quick work of slicing the apples. You don't even need to clean the bowl after making the topping.

Variation

You can add 1/4 cup (50 mL) nuts to the topping when processing flour mixture.

- Preheat oven to 350°F (180°C)
- 13-by 9-inch (3 L) glass baking dish, buttered

Topping

1 1/2 cups	all-purpose flour	375 mL
1/2 cup	lightly packed light brown sugar	125 mL
2 tbsp	granulated sugar	25 mL
1/2 tsp	ground cinnamon	2 mL
1/4 tsp	salt	1 mL
1/2 cup	cold unsalted butter, cut into small chunks	125 mL

Filling

1 cup	granulated sugar	250 mL
2 tbsp	all-purpose flour	25 mL
1 tsp	ground cinnamon	5 mL
1/2 tsp	freshly grated nutmeg	2 mL
1/4 tsp	ground cloves	1 mL
6	large baking apples, peeled and thinly sliced (see Apples, page 15)	6

1. *Topping:* In a food processor fitted with metal blade, pulse flour, brown and granulated sugars, cinnamon and salt until combined, about 5 times. Remove lid and distribute butter evenly over top. Cover and pulse until mixture resembles coarse crumbs, about 20 times. Transfer to a bowl. Set aside.
2. *Filling:* In a large bowl, combine sugar, flour, cinnamon, nutmeg and cloves. Add apples and toss to evenly coat. Transfer to prepared baking dish. Crumble topping over apples. Bake in preheated oven until brown and bubbly, 35 to 40 minutes. Serve warm.

Hummingbird Cake

Cakes

Cheesecakes

Two-Layer Cakes

One-Pan Cakes

Cupcakes & Jelly Rolls

Cakes

To me, cake has always meant birthdays. And my favorite birthday cake is a rich fudge cake with rich chocolate icing.

My grandmother used to make a cake called Heavenly Fudge Cake for my father's birthday. I never got to make the cake with my grandmother, but I have the recipe. However, it doesn't make anything close to what my dad said it was like. I suggest you learn to make those family recipes while you can and get them down on paper before it's too late and they're lost forever.

On my first day in pastry school, I was sent to the cake-making area. I was so proud of myself, pouring the huge mixing bowls full of chocolate cake batter into the prepared pans, then pounding the filled pans on the counter. The instructor came over and asked what I was doing. "Getting the air bubbles out of the cake, just like mom used to do." He asked if mom was a pastry chef. Well, no. He then went on to say she knew nothing about baking and I was to listen only to him. Pounding unbaked batter would result in fewer air pockets, and sometimes even make a cake fall. Why did we beat all that air into the batter to start with if we were going to just pound it all out? We need air to make the cake rise.

Tools

You must have the correct pans and tools — and techniques — if you want to make perfect cakes. Today, you will find pans in many sizes and shapes and a wide range of quality. Keep in mind the best pans and tools are not always the most expensive.

PANS

You want good-quality, heavy-gauge metal pans that are light in color. Dark pans conduct heat very badly, which results in darker crusts on your cakes. If you only have dark pans, reduce the oven temperature by 25°F (14°C) from that specified in the recipe.

After baking, I cool cakes in pans set on a wire rack, for exactly 10 minutes (20 minutes for specialty pans), and then invert onto the rack and remove the pan. Let cakes cool completely before proceeding with decorating.

- *Round pans:* The size and structure of round pans is a big factor to consider. First, measure the bottom of the pan: does it measure what your recipe calls for? Now measure the top rim. Both measurements should be same. Many pans will be different on the bottom, sometimes by as much as ½ inch (1 cm), so that pans can be nested. If you have pans like these, cakes will dome and the sides will be sloped. This makes for a strange shape when making a layer cake and makes it trickier to decorate.

  To prepare cake pans for baking, I spray with a nonstick spray that contains flour. It is available at large grocery stores and stores that sell specialty baking supplies (see Sources, page 442).
- *Tube, bundt and specialty-shaped pans:* My sister loves a castle cake for her birthday — and I have a pan for it. You can now find cake pans in many specialty shapes and sizes. Most specialty-shaped pans are tube-type pans. You can use any cake recipe and they will work fine; just check the volume of the specialty pan and make sure the batter will fit. Avoid filling a pan more than two-thirds full so there is room for the cake to rise. Even if your pan has a nonstick coating, I still suggest spraying it to make sure the cake turns out nicely. Most of these pans have fine details and patterns that make it difficult to get grease or butter and flour evenly into the crevices.

OFFSET SPATULA

One of the most important tools is an offset spatula. The handle sits above the icing surface so your knuckles are not drawn through your icing while you work.

Icing a Two-Layer Cake

I like to bake my cakes one day, freeze them overnight, then decorate the next day or up to 2 days later. It is so much easier to decorate a frozen cake. Don't worry, the cake will not be frozen solid, just firm and cold, making it much more sturdy and easy to handle. You can also cut a cake into layers more easily when its fresh out of the freezer.

The Art of Cutting the Perfect Cake Slice

Are you tired of your slice of cake crumbling on your spatula while you are serving it? Take a look at those perfect slices of cake in a cookbook or magazine and in comparison, yours looks like a two-year-old just cut the wedge out of a cake with a toy knife. Most photos of cakes and slices are not from the same cake. Food stylists have made that "first piece" of cake look terrific by having an extra cake to work with. We can't do that at home, but if you follow my easy tips, you can make perfect slices. Look at a cake as a clock:

1. Make a cut entirely through the cake from the 12 o'clock position to the 6 o'clock position.

2. From the first cut, start in the center and cut to the 3 o'clock position. You need to focus on one quarter of your cake at a time.

3. Slice each quarter into even-sized wedges, depending on how many pieces you want in total. For example, if you want 12 pieces, slice each quarter into three wedges. Do the remaining quarters the same way until the entire cake has been cut.

Common Myths and Facts about Cake Slicing

1. Cut perfect slices of cheesecake with dental floss or string.
   Myth: The dental floss or string can get caught on a nut or a piece of chocolate in the cake, thus shredding the fibers and leaving them in the cake.

2. Your knife should be wet.
   Myth and Fact: Not necessarily. A wet knife on a chocolate ganache-topped cake can leave water droplets on the cake slices, thus making the top of the cake look old.
3. Knife size and type matters.
   Fact: Put a knife in your hand and look at the top of the blade. You want a blade that is thin and the same thickness as the length of the blade. A blade that is at least 8 inches (20 cm) long is useful so it reaches at least halfway through the cake, and is even better if it is long enough to slice across the entire cake in one cut. Chef's knives are the best.
4. Your knife should be hot.
   Myth and Fact: Sometimes this is true. For a chocolate cake or cheesecake, it does make the cutting a little easier. But really in fact you need a clean blade after each cut, or the cake residue stays on the knife and is transferred to the other pieces of cake. So make sure you have a thin-bladed knife and wipe the blade clean after each cut.

Cutting a Cake to Make Two Layers

I get so tired of so many companies coming out with new-fangled ways to cut cakes into layers. I have seen some of these strange cutting devices that look like a musical instrument costing upwards of $40.00. And then where do you store these things? If you have a good serrated-edge knife you can cut any cake layer perfectly.

1. Place cake layer on flat surface. Place one hand on top of cake.
2. With only about 1 inch (2.5 cm) of tip of knife, gently saw knife tip around the middle of the side of the cake layer, keeping it parallel to the work surface and cutting only about 2 inches (5 cm) into the cake, without going through the center. Once you have cut around the circumference, use the outer cut as a guide and cut all the way through to the center of the cake. Now you have a perfectly cut cake. Depending on the depth of the cake, you can take these two pieces and cut them again in the same way, creating four layers out of one.

Freezing

FREEZING CHEESECAKES

If I am not in need of my cheesecake pan for a few days, I wrap the completely cooled cheesecake tightly with plastic wrap and then foil while it's still in the pan. Freeze for 3 days, then remove the cheesecake from the pan, place on a cake circle and rewrap with plastic and then foil. Cheesecakes can be frozen for up to 4 months. Thaw, unwrapped, for a day in refrigerator.

FREEZING CAKE LAYERS

Place completely cooled cake layer on a cake circle or a piece of cardboard cut to exactly the same size as the cake, wrap in plastic wrap and then foil. Freeze for up to 1 month. There's no need to thaw before decorating.

Blue Ribbon Cheesecake

SERVES 10 TO 12

I have won numerous awards with this recipe, also affectionately called "Patty's Favorite Cheesecake" after my mom, my biggest fan.

Tips

Zest lemons and limes before juicing and freeze the zest for another recipe.

This cheesecake freezes well for up to 4 months before decorating. Defrost in the refrigerator the day prior to use and then decorate.

Variation

If fresh berries are not available, spread 1 cup (250 mL) strawberry preserves on top.

- Preheat oven to 350°F (180°C)
- 9-inch (23 cm) cheesecake pan, ungreased, or springform pan with 3-inch (7.5 cm) sides, greased

Crust

1¼ cups	graham cracker crumbs	300 mL
¼ cup	unsalted butter, melted	50 mL

Filling

4	packages (each 8 oz/250 g) cream cheese, softened	4
1¼ cups	granulated sugar	300 mL
4	eggs	4
3 tbsp	freshly squeezed lemon juice	45 mL
1 tsp	vanilla extract	5 mL

Topping

½ cup	sour cream	125 mL
¼ cup	granulated sugar	50 mL
1 tbsp	freshly squeezed lemon juice	15 mL
½ tsp	vanilla extract	2 mL

Decoration

2 cups	fresh strawberries, sliced	500 mL

1. *Crust:* In a bowl, combine graham cracker crumbs and butter. Press into bottom of cheesecake pan and freeze.
2. *Filling:* In a large mixer bowl fitted with paddle attachment, beat cream cheese and sugar until very smooth, for 3 minutes. Add eggs, one at a time, beating after each addition. Stir in lemon juice and vanilla.
3. Pour over frozen crust, smoothing out to sides of pan. Bake in preheated oven until top is light brown and center has a slight jiggle to it, 45 to 55 minutes. Let cool on the counter for 10 minutes (do not turn the oven off). The cake will sink slightly.
4. *Topping:* In a small bowl, combine sour cream, sugar, lemon juice and vanilla. Pour into center of cooled cake and spread out to edges. Bake for 5 minutes more. Let cool on a wire rack for 2 hours. Cover with plastic wrap and refrigerate for at least 6 hours before decorating.
5. *Decoration:* Top with sliced strawberries when completely chilled.

Buckeye Cheesecake

SERVES 10 TO 12

I was introduced to buckeyes, great chocolate candies packed with peanut butter, on my first teaching trip to Ohio. They inspired this cheesecake.

Variation

Grate bittersweet chocolate on top of each individual serving.

- Preheat oven to 350°F (180°C)
- 9-inch (23 cm) cheesecake pan, ungreased, or springform pan with 3-inch (7.5 cm) sides, greased

Crust

1½ cups	peanut butter sandwich cookie crumbs	375 mL
¼ cup	all-purpose flour	50 mL
¼ cup	unsalted butter, melted	50 mL

Filling

4 oz	bittersweet chocolate, chopped	125 g
¼ cup	creamy peanut butter	50 mL
3	packages (each 8 oz/250 g) cream cheese, softened	3
1 cup	sour cream	250 mL
1½ cups	granulated sugar	375 mL
4	eggs	4
1 tsp	vanilla extract	5 mL

Topping

½ cup	sour cream	125 mL
¼ cup	granulated sugar	50 mL
¼ cup	creamy peanut butter	50 mL
1 tbsp	freshly squeezed lemon juice	15 mL
½ tsp	vanilla extract	2 mL

1. *Crust:* In a bowl, combine cookie crumbs, flour and butter. Press into bottom of cheesecake pan and freeze.
2. *Filling:* Melt chocolate in the top of a double boiler. When fully melted, add peanut butter and stir until blended. Set aside to cool slightly. In a mixer bowl fitted with paddle attachment, beat cream cheese, sour cream and sugar until very smooth, for 3 minutes. Add eggs, one at a time, beating after each addition. Stir in vanilla. Swirl melted chocolate mixture into batter. Pour over frozen crust, smoothing out to sides of pan. Bake until top is light brown and center has a slight jiggle to it, 45 to 55 minutes. Let cool on the counter for 10 minutes (do not turn the oven off). The cake will sink slightly.
3. *Topping:* In a small bowl, combine sour cream, sugar, peanut butter, lemon juice and vanilla. Pour into center of cooled cake, spreading out to edges. Bake for 5 minutes more. Let cool on a rack for 2 hours. Cover and refrigerate for 6 hours.

Caramel Pecan Cheesecake

SERVES 10 TO 12

A childhood fondness for turtle candies with crunchy pecans wrapped in rich caramel inspired this decadent cheesecake.

Tip

It's best not to spread the melted caramels right to the edge of the pan. Otherwise, it might stick and make it difficult to remove from the pan.

- Preheat oven to 350°F (180°C)
- 9-inch (23 cm) cheesecake pan, ungreased, or springform pan with 3-inch (7.5 cm) sides, greased

Crust

1¼ cups	chocolate sandwich cookie crumbs	300 mL
¼ cup	chopped pecans	50 mL
¼ cup	unsalted butter, melted	50 mL

Filling

1 cup	soft caramels	250 mL
2 tbsp	evaporated milk or whipping (35%) cream	25 mL
6 oz	bittersweet chocolate chunks	175 g
2	packages (each 8 oz/250 g) cream cheese, softened	2
1 cup	sour cream	250 mL
½ cup	granulated sugar	125 mL
3	eggs	3
1 tsp	vanilla extract	5 mL
1 cup	pecans, chopped and toasted	250 mL

1. *Crust:* In a bowl, combine cookie crumbs, pecans and butter. Press into bottom of cheesecake pan and freeze.
2. *Filling:* In a small saucepan over low heat, melt caramels and evaporated milk, stirring frequently, until smooth. Reserve about 3 tbsp (45 mL); cover and refrigerate. (When ready to use, reheat in the microwave or in a small pan over low heat until melted.) Pour remainder over frozen crust, spreading evenly and leaving a ½-inch (1 cm) border uncovered. Sprinkle chocolate chunks over melted caramel. Set aside. In a mixer bowl fitted with paddle attachment, beat cream cheese, sour cream and sugar until very smooth, for 3 minutes. Add eggs, one at a time, beating after each addition. Mix in vanilla. Fold in pecans by hand.
3. Pour over chocolate chunks, smoothing out to sides of pan. Bake in preheated oven until top is light brown and center has a slight jiggle to it, 45 to 55 minutes. Let cool on a wire rack for 2 hours. Cover with plastic wrap and refrigerate for at least 6 hours before decorating or serving.
4. *Decoration:* Drizzle the reserved caramel mixture over top of cake.

Deep Dark Chocolate Fudge Cheesecake

SERVES 6 TO 8

Here's a chocolate fudge cheesecake that's so rich you'll need a glass of milk to wash it down!

Tip

Make sure the chocolate is cooled to room temperature after melting; otherwise you'll get strange chunks in your batter.

Variations

Use white chips in place of the semisweet for a black and white cheesecake.

To make this filling in a mixer instead of a food processor, follow the method for filling in Step 2 of Blue Ribbon Cheesecake (page 159), beating in melted chocolate in place of lemon juice. Proceed with Step 4.

- Preheat oven to 325°F (160°C)
- 6-inch (15 cm) cheesecake pan, or springform pan with 3-inch (7.5 cm) sides, lined with parchment paper

Crust

7	chocolate sandwich cookies (about 3 oz/90 g)	7
2 tbsp	unsalted butter, melted	25 mL

Filling

4 oz	unsweetened chocolate, melted and cooled	125 g
2	packages (each 8 oz/250 g) cream cheese, softened	2
¾ cup	granulated sugar	175 mL
2	eggs	2
1 tsp	vanilla extract	5 mL
¼ cup	semisweet chocolate chips	50 mL

1. *Crust:* In a food processor fitted with metal blade, process cookies until finely ground, about 20 seconds. You should have ¾ cup (175 mL). Transfer to a bowl and mix in butter. Press into bottom of cheesecake pan and freeze until filling is ready.
2. *Filling:* In a microwave-safe bowl, microwave chocolate on Medium (50%), stirring every 30 seconds, until soft and almost melted, 1 to 1½ minutes. Stir until completely melted and smooth. Let cool slightly.
3. In clean food processor work bowl fitted with metal blade, process cream cheese and sugar until smooth, about 20 seconds. With motor running, add melted chocolate, eggs and vanilla through the feed tube and process until blended.
4. Pour over frozen crust, smoothing out to sides of pan. Sprinkle chocolate chips over top. Bake in preheated oven until it starts to pull away from sides of pan and center has a slight jiggle to it, 35 to 45 minutes. Let cool on a wire rack for 2 hours. Cover with plastic wrap and refrigerate for at least 2 hours before serving.

3. Pour over frozen crust, smoothing out to sides of pan. Bake until the top is light brown and center has a slight jiggle to it, 45 to 55 minutes. Let cool on the counter for 10 minutes (do not turn the oven off). The cake will sink slightly.
4. *Topping:* In a bowl, combine sour cream, sugar, peanut butter, lemon juice and vanilla. Pour into center of cake and spread to edges. Sprinkle with chocolate. Bake for 5 minutes more. Let cool for 2 hours. Cover with plastic wrap and refrigerate for at least 6 hours before serving.

Chocolate Espresso Swirl Cheesecake

SERVES 10 TO 12

Chocolate with a light espresso swirled in the cake has just a hint of coffee flavor.

Tip

Cool melted chocolate to room temperature before adding the cheesecake batter or the chocolate will stiffen up and you will have to start all over.

Variation

Add 2 tbsp (25 mL) rum or coffee liqueur with the coffee for a little kick.

- Preheat oven to 350°F (180°C)
- 9-inch (23 cm) cheesecake pan, ungreased, or springform pan with 3-inch (7.5 cm) sides, greased

Crust

1½ cups	chocolate sandwich cookie crumbs	375 mL
¼ cup	unsalted butter, melted	50 mL

Filling

4	packages (each 8 oz/250 g) cream cheese, softened	4
1½ cups	granulated sugar	375 mL
½ cup	sour cream	125 mL
4	eggs	4
1 tbsp	instant coffee powder or granules	15 mL
1 tbsp	hot water	15 mL
1 tsp	vanilla extract	5 mL
3 oz	bittersweet chocolate, melted and cooled (see Melting Chocolate, page 250)	90 g

Decoration

½ cup	whipping (35%) cream	125 mL
2 tbsp	granulated sugar	25 mL

1. *Crust:* In a bowl, combine cookie crumbs and butter. Press into bottom of cheesecake pan and freeze.
2. *Filling:* In a mixer bowl fitted with paddle attachment, beat cream cheese and sugar until very smooth, for 3 minutes. Add sour cream. Add eggs, one at a time, beating after each addition. In a small bowl, dissolve coffee powder in hot water. With mixer running, pour coffee in a steady stream into the batter. Add vanilla. Stir 1 cup (250 mL) batter into melted chocolate and set aside. Pour remaining batter over frozen crust, smoothing out to sides of pan.

3. Using a spoon, drop six large puddles of melted chocolate mixture on top of batter. Using a small knife, drag through the puddles in spiral motions to create a marbling effect. Bake in preheated oven until top is light brown and center has a slight jiggle to it, 45 to 55 minutes. Let cool on a wire rack for 2 hours. Cover with plastic wrap and refrigerate for at least 6 hours before decorating or serving.
4. *Decoration:* In a well-chilled bowl, whip cream until soft peaks form. With the mixer still running, sprinkle sugar into cream and continue whipping until firm peaks form. Ice top of cake with whipped cream or pipe rosettes around top of cake, if desired.

French Apple Cheesecake

SERVES 10 TO 12

This cheesecake is rich with fresh apples and a topping just like a French apple pie.

Tip

You can prepare this cheesecake and freeze, including the topping, up to 3 weeks prior to serving. To freeze, I keep my cheesecakes in the pan and cover with plastic wrap, then foil. To use, place the wrapped cheesecake into the refrigerator a day prior to use.

Variation

Use the topping in the filling of the cheesecake instead of the top. Just blend it into the batter and bake as directed.

- Preheat oven to 350°F (180°C)
- 9-inch (23 cm) cheesecake pan, ungreased, or springform pan with 3-inch (7.5 cm) sides, greased
- Blending fork

Crust

1¼ cups	graham cracker crumbs	300 mL
3 tbsp	unsalted butter, melted	45 mL

Filling

3	packages (each 8 oz/250 g) cream cheese, softened	3
1 cup	sour cream	250 mL
1 cup	packed light brown sugar	250 mL
¼ cup	liquid honey	50 mL
4	eggs	4
1 tbsp	vanilla extract	15 mL
1 tsp	freshly squeezed lemon juice	5 mL
1 tsp	ground cinnamon	5 mL
½ tsp	freshly grated nutmeg	2 mL
¼ tsp	ground cloves	1 mL

Topping

3 tbsp	cold unsalted butter, cut into cubes	45 mL
¼ cup	all-purpose flour	50 mL
¼ cup	packed light brown sugar	50 mL
½ tsp	ground cinnamon	2 mL
¼ tsp	ground cloves	1 mL
1	medium baking apple, such as Granny Smith or Pippin, peeled and sliced into 12 thin slices	1

Decoration

½ cup	confectioner's (icing) sugar	125 mL
2 tbsp	unsalted butter, melted	25 mL
2 tbsp	hot water	25 mL

1. *Crust:* In a bowl, combine graham cracker crumbs and butter. Press into bottom of cheesecake pan and freeze.

2. *Filling:* In a mixer bowl fitted with paddle attachment, beat cream cheese, sour cream, brown sugar and honey until very smooth, for 3 minutes. Add eggs, one at a time, beating after each addition. Mix in vanilla and lemon juice. Beat in cinnamon, nutmeg and cloves. Pour over frozen crust, smoothing out to sides of pan.
3. *Topping:* In a bowl, using a blending fork or two knives, cut butter into flour as if making a piecrust. Add brown sugar, cinnamon and cloves. Toss apples with this mixture. Arrange apple mixture in a spiral over batter. Bake in preheated oven until apples are light brown and cake is slightly firm in center, 60 to 75 minutes. Let cool on a wire rack for 2 hours. Cover with plastic wrap and refrigerate for at least 6 hours before decorating or serving.
4. *Decoration:* In a small bowl, whisk sugar with butter and hot water. Drizzle on top of chilled cake.

Lemon Soufflé Cheesecake

SERVES 10 TO 12

While dining in Los Angeles at Ciudad, I had a wonderful cheesecake that was so light and airy, I had to create my own version in homage to Chefs Milliken and Feniger.

Tip

Save extra egg yolks in a small bowl in the refrigerator for up to 2 days by covering in water and sealing tightly with plastic wrap. To freeze, sprinkle salt or sugar over the yolks in water.

- Preheat oven to 325°F (160°C)
- 9-inch (23 cm) cheesecake pan, ungreased, or springform pan with 3-inch (7.5 cm) sides, greased

Crust

1½ cups	butter cookie crumbs	375 mL
¼ cup	unsalted butter, melted	50 mL

Filling

4	packages (each 8 oz/250 g) cream cheese, softened	4
½ cup	sour cream	125 mL
1½ cups	granulated sugar	375 mL
4	egg yolks	4
1 tbsp	freshly grated lemon zest	15 mL
3 tbsp	freshly squeezed lemon juice	45 mL
1½ tsp	vanilla extract	7 mL
6	egg whites	6
¼ tsp	cream of tartar	1 mL

Decoration

¼ cup	confectioner's (icing) sugar	50 mL

1. *Crust:* In a bowl, combine cookie crumbs and butter. Press into bottom of cheesecake pan and freeze.
2. *Filling:* In a mixer bowl fitted with paddle attachment, beat cream cheese, sour cream and sugar until very smooth, for 3 minutes. Add eggs yolks, one at a time, beating after each addition. Beat in lemon zest, juice and vanilla. Set aside. In a clean mixer bowl fitted with whip attachment, whip egg whites and cream of tartar on low speed for 1 minute. Increase speed to medium-high and whip until stiff peaks form, but not dry. Fold into cream cheese mixture carefully so as not to deflate the mixture.
3. Pour over frozen crust, smoothing out to sides of pan. Bake in preheated oven until top is light brown and center has a slight jiggle to it, 45 to 55 minutes. Let cool on a wire rack for 2 hours. Cover with plastic wrap and refrigerate for at least 6 hours before decorating or serving.
4. *Decoration:* Dust top of chilled cake with a sprinkling of confectioner's sugar using a sugar dredger or flour sifter.

Milk Chocolate Cheesecake

SERVES 10 TO 12

A sweet milk chocolate layer is paired with a rich vanilla layer.

Tip

Be careful not to blend the two cheesecake batters. If you do, swirl the chocolate into the vanilla and call it a Milk Chocolate Swirl Cheesecake.

Variation

Dust cocoa powder on top instead of shaved chocolate.

- Preheat oven to 350°F (180°C)
- 9-inch (23 cm) cheesecake pan, ungreased, or springform pan with 3-inch (7.5 cm) sides, greased

Crust

1½ cups	chocolate sandwich cookie crumbs	375 mL
¼ cup	unsalted butter, melted	50 mL

Filling

4	packages (each 8 oz/250 g) cream cheese, softened	4
1¼ cups	granulated sugar	300 mL
4	eggs	4
1 cup	sour cream	250 mL
1 tbsp	vanilla extract	15 mL
4 oz	milk chocolate, melted and cooled	125 g

Decoration

	Classic Whipped Cream (see recipe, page 239)	
¼ cup	shaved chocolate	50 mL

1. *Crust:* In a bowl, combine cookie crumbs and butter. Press into bottom of cheesecake pan and freeze.
2. *Filling:* In a mixer bowl fitted with paddle attachment, beat cream cheese and sugar until very smooth, for 3 minutes. Add eggs, one at a time, beating after each addition. Mix in sour cream and vanilla.
3. Divide batter in half. Stir cooled milk chocolate into one portion and pour over frozen crust, smoothing out to sides of pan. Pour remaining batter evenly over chocolate portion. Bake in preheated oven until top is light brown and center has a slight jiggle to it, 55 to 65 minutes. Let cool on a wire rack for 2 hours. Cover with plastic wrap and refrigerate for at least 6 hours before decorating or serving.
4. *Decoration:* Ice top of cake with Classic Whipped Cream or pipe rosettes around top of cake, if desired. Top with chocolate shavings.

New York–Style Cheesecake

SERVES 10 TO 12

In my first pastry job, I made a New York–style cheesecake. I never knew what it meant until I stepped into a deli in Manhattan, a Mecca for cheesecake fans.

Tip

Save leftover egg whites by freezing them for up to 6 months. Freeze them in an ice-cube tray. When frozen, pop them out and place cubes in plastic freezer bags.

Variation

You can replace the lemon and orange zest with 1 tsp (5 mL) rum extract for a different taste.

- Preheat oven to 500°F (260°C)
- 9-inch (23 cm) cheesecake pan, ungreased, or springform pan with 3-inch (7.5 cm) sides, greased

Crust

1½ cups	graham cracker crumbs	375 mL
¼ cup	unsalted butter, melted	50 mL

Filling

5	packages (each 8 oz/250 g) cream cheese, softened	5
1¼ cups	granulated sugar	300 mL
3 tbsp	all-purpose flour	45 mL
1½ tsp	freshly grated lemon zest	7 mL
1½ tsp	freshly grated orange zest	7 mL
5	eggs	5
2	egg yolks	2
1 tsp	vanilla extract	5 mL
¼ cup	whipping (35%) cream	50 mL

1. *Crust:* In a bowl, combine graham cracker crumbs and butter. Press into bottom of cheesecake pan and freeze.
2. *Filling:* In a mixer bowl fitted with paddle attachment, beat cream cheese and sugar until very smooth, for 3 minutes. Mix in flour, lemon and orange zest. Add eggs and egg yolks, one at a time, beating after each addition. Mix in vanilla and cream.
3. Pour over frozen crust, smoothing out to sides of pan. Bake for only 10 minutes at 500°F (260°C); reduce heat to 200°F (100°C). Bake for an additional 60 minutes. The top should be puffy like a soufflé with a light golden color. Let cool on a wire rack for 2 hours. Cover with plastic wrap and refrigerate for at least 6 hours before serving.

Toasted Pecan Cheesecake

SERVES 10 TO 12

When I was teaching in Whistler during the spring one year a student announced that this cheesecake should be proclaimed a national treasure.

Tip

Store raw nuts in the freezer and toast them right before using.

- Preheat oven to 350°F (180°C)
- 9-inch (23 cm) cheesecake pan, ungreased, or springform pan with 3-inch (7.5 cm) sides, greased

Crust

1½ cups	pecans, toasted and coarsely ground (see Tip, page 36)	375 mL
¼ cup	all-purpose flour	50 mL
¼ cup	unsalted butter, melted	50 mL

Filling

3	packages (each 8 oz/250 g) cream cheese, softened	3
1 cup	plain yogurt	250 mL
1¼ cups	granulated sugar	300 mL
4	eggs	4
1 cup	toasted chopped pecans	250 mL
1 tsp	vanilla extract	5 mL

Decoration

	Classic Whipped Cream (see recipe, page 239), optional	
¼ cup	toasted chopped pecans	50 mL

1. *Crust:* In a bowl, combine pecans, flour and butter. Press into bottom of cheesecake pan and freeze.
2. *Filling:* In a mixer bowl fitted with paddle attachment, beat cream cheese, yogurt and sugar until very smooth, for 3 minutes. Add eggs, one at a time, beating after each addition. Fold in pecans and vanilla by hand.
3. Pour over frozen crust, smoothing out to sides of pan. Bake in preheated oven until top is light brown and center has a slight jiggle to it, 45 to 55 minutes. Let cool on a wire rack for 2 hours. Cover with plastic wrap and refrigerate for at least 6 hours before decorating or serving.
4. *Decoration:* Ice top of cake with Classic Whipped Cream, if desired. Sprinkle with chopped pecans.

Tri-Berry Cheesecake

SERVES 10 TO 12

I love berries! If there is a fresh berry on a dessert menu, I'll choose it over anything but chocolate. They are nature's candies — packed with flavor and beauty.

Variations

Use all of one berry or two of the varieties if all three aren't available.

Spread 1 cup (250 mL) berry preserves on top.

- Preheat oven to 350°F (180°C)
- 9-inch (23 cm) cheesecake pan, ungreased, or springform pan with 3-inch (7.5 cm) sides, greased

Crust

1¼ cups	sugar cookie crumbs	300 mL
3 tbsp	unsalted butter, melted	45 mL

Filling

4	packages (each 8 oz/250 g) cream cheese, softened	4
1 cup	sour cream	250 mL
1 cup	granulated sugar	250 mL
3	eggs	3
2	egg yolks	2
¼ cup	all-purpose flour	50 mL
2½ tbsp	freshly squeezed lemon juice	32 mL
1 tbsp	vanilla extract	15 mL
½ cup	strawberries, crushed slightly	125 mL
½ cup	raspberries, cut into quarters	125 mL
½ cup	blackberries, cut into quarters	125 mL

Decoration

½ cup	strawberries, sliced	125 mL
½ cup	raspberries, whole	125 mL
½ cup	blackberries, whole	125 mL
2 tbsp	port wine	25 mL

1. *Crust:* In a bowl, combine cookie crumbs and butter. Press into bottom of cheesecake pan and freeze.
2. *Filling:* In a mixer bowl fitted with paddle attachment, beat cream cheese, sour cream and sugar until very smooth, for 3 minutes. Add eggs and egg yolks, one at a time, beating after each addition. Mix in flour, lemon juice and vanilla. Fold in berries by hand.
3. Pour over frozen crust, smoothing out to sides of pan. Bake in preheated oven until top is light brown and center has a slight jiggle to it, 55 to 65 minutes. Let cool on a wire rack for 2 hours. Cover with plastic wrap and refrigerate for at least 6 hours before decorating or serving.
4. *Decoration:* In a bowl, combine berries and port. Garnish each individual piece with a spoonful.

Banana Cake

SERVES 8 TO 10

A banana cake is so easy to make. I use all of my ripe bananas to make this very moist cake.

Tip

Decorate with any of the following icings:

- Buttercream Frosting (page 224)
- Cream Cheese Icing (page 226)
- French Buttercream Frosting (page 227)
- Seven-Minute Frosting (page 239)
- Whipped Cream Cheese Frosting (page 235)

- Preheat oven to 325°F (160°C)
- Two 9-inch (23 cm) round cake pans, sprayed with nonstick spray

3 cups	cake flour	750 mL
1 tsp	baking soda	5 mL
½ tsp	salt	2 mL
½ tsp	baking powder	2 mL
1 cup	unsalted butter, softened	250 mL
2 cups	granulated sugar	500 mL
3	eggs	3
1½ cups	mashed ripe bananas (about 4 large)	375 mL
6 tbsp	buttermilk	90 mL
2 tsp	vanilla extract	10 mL
½ cup	chopped pecans	125 mL

1. In a large bowl, whisk together flour, baking soda, salt and baking powder. Set aside.
2. In a mixer bowl fitted with paddle attachment, beat butter and sugar until creamy, about 2 minutes. Beat in eggs, one at a time, beating well after each addition. Add bananas, buttermilk and vanilla and mix until blended. Using a wooden spoon, gradually stir in flour mixture just until incorporated. Fold in pecans.
3. Divide batter evenly between prepared pans. Bake in preheated oven until a toothpick inserted into center comes out clean, 40 to 50 minutes. Let cool in pans on a wire rack for 10 minutes before transferring to rack to cool completely.
4. For best results for decorating, wrap cake layers in plastic wrap and freeze for 1 to 2 days. Decorate with any of the icings at left or one of your favorites.

Carrot Cake

SERVES 10 TO 12

Popularized in the 1970s, this moist cake is still going strong. I still have not found a carrot cake as moist as this one.

Tip

Decorate with any of the following icings:

- Buttercream Frosting (page 224)
- Cream Cheese Icing (page 226)
- French Buttercream Frosting (page 227)
- Island Frosting (page 231)
- Seven-Minute Frosting (page 239)
- Whipped Cream Cheese Frosting (page 235)

- Preheat oven to 375°F (190°C)
- Two 9-inch (23 cm) round cake pans, sprayed with nonstick spray

1¼ cups	all-purpose flour	300 mL
1¼ tsp	baking soda	6 mL
¼ tsp	salt	1 mL
¼ tsp	ground cinnamon	1 mL
⅛ tsp	freshly grated nutmeg	0.5 mL
1¼ cups	granulated sugar	300 mL
2	eggs	2
⅓ cup	vegetable oil	75 mL
1 tsp	vanilla extract	5 mL
⅔ cup	crushed pineapple, drained	150 mL
¼ cup	flaked sweetened coconut	50 mL
¼ cup	chopped pecans	50 mL
1 cup	shredded carrots	250 mL

1. In a bowl, whisk together flour, baking soda, salt, cinnamon and nutmeg. Set aside.
2. In a mixer bowl fitted with paddle attachment, combine sugar, eggs, oil and vanilla until well blended, for 2 minutes. Add pineapple, coconut and pecans and mix for 1 minute. Using a wooden spoon, gradually stir in flour mixture just until incorporated. Stir in carrots.
3. Divide batter evenly between prepared pans. Bake in preheated oven until a toothpick inserted into center comes out clean, 28 to 32 minutes. Let cool in pan on a wire rack for 10 minutes before transferring to rack to cool completely.
4. For best results for decorating, wrap cake layers in plastic wrap and freeze for 1 to 2 days. Decorate with any of the icings at left or one of your favorites.

Marble Layer Cake

SERVES 10 TO 12

If you love both chocolate and white cakes, this one will satisfy all your needs in one luscious cake.

Tip

Decorate with any of the following icings:

- Bittersweet Fudge Frosting (page 233)
- Buttercream Frosting (page 224)
- Chocolate Cream Cheese Icing (page 225)
- French Buttercream Frosting (page 227)
- French Chocolate Buttercream Frosting (page 229)
- Milk Chocolate Frosting (page 232)

- Preheat oven to 350°F (180°C)
- Two 9-inch (23 cm) round cake pans, sprayed with nonstick spray

4 cups	cake flour	1 L
1 tbsp	baking powder	15 mL
½ tsp	salt	2 mL
1¼ cups	cold water, divided	300 mL
1 tbsp	vanilla extract	15 mL
1¼ cups	unsalted butter, softened	300 mL
2 cups	granulated sugar	500 mL
6	egg whites	6
⅓ cup	unsweetened Dutch-process cocoa powder, sifted	75 mL
	Old-Fashioned Chocolate Fudge Frosting (page 233), optional	

1. In a large bowl, whisk together flour, baking powder and salt. In a small bowl, stir together ½ cup (250 mL) of the water and vanilla. Set both aside.
2. In a mixer bowl fitted with paddle attachment, cream butter and sugar until light and fluffy, about 3 minutes. Add egg whites, one at a time, beating for 1 minute between each addition. Using a wooden spoon, stir in flour mixture alternating with water mixture, making three additions of flour and two of water, just until blended.
3. Transfer about 1½ cups (375 mL) of batter to another small bowl. Blend in remaining water and cocoa powder.
4. Divide white batter evenly between prepared pans. Using a spoon, drop six large puddles of chocolate batter over top of each pan of white batter. Using a small knife, drag through puddles in a spiral motion to create a marbling effect. Bake in preheated oven until a toothpick inserted into center comes out clean, 22 to 28 minutes. Let cool in pans on a wire rack for 10 minutes before transferring to rack to cool completely.
5. For best results for decorating, wrap cake layers in plastic wrap and freeze for 1 to 2 days. Decorate with Old-Fashioned Chocolate Fudge Frosting or any of the icings at left.

Hummingbird Cake

SERVES 10 TO 12

The original recipe for this cake was first published in the 1970s in Southern Living. *It is a very similar to a moist carrot cake without carrots.*

Tip

Decorate with any of the following icings:

- Buttercream Frosting (page 224)
- Cream Cheese Icing (page 226)
- French Buttercream Frosting (page 227)
- Island Frosting (page 231)
- Seven-Minute Frosting (page 239)
- Whipped Cream Cheese Frosting (page 235)

- Preheat oven to 325°F (160°C)
- Two 9-inch (23 cm) round cake pans, sprayed with nonstick spray

3 cups	all-purpose flour	750 mL
1 tsp	ground cinnamon	5 mL
1 tsp	baking soda	5 mL
1 tsp	salt	5 mL
½ tsp	freshly grated nutmeg	2 mL
1¼ cups	vegetable oil	300 mL
2 cups	granulated sugar	500 mL
3	eggs	3
2 cups	very ripe bananas, mashed (about 6)	500 mL
1	can (8 oz/227 mL) crushed pineapple, drained	1
½ cup	chopped pecans	125 mL
1½ tsp	vanilla extract	7 mL

1. In a bowl, whisk together flour, cinnamon, baking soda, salt and nutmeg. Set aside.
2. In a mixer bowl fitted with paddle attachment, beat oil and sugar until smooth, about 2 minutes. Add eggs, one at a time, and beat until light, about 2 minutes. Add bananas, pineapple, pecans and vanilla. Stir in flour mixture in three additions just until blended.
3. Divide batter evenly between prepared pans. Bake in preheated oven until a toothpick inserted into center comes out clean, 45 to 50 minutes. Let cool in pans on a wire rack for 10 minutes before transferring to rack to cool completely.
4. For best results for decorating, wrap cake layers in plastic wrap and freeze for 1 to 2 days. Decorate with any of the icings at left or one of your favorites.

Orange Crunch Cake

SERVES 10 TO 12

This cake can stand on its own without any glaze or icing. But if you must, go all out.

Tip

Decorate with any of the following icings:

- Buttercream Frosting (page 224)
- French Buttercream Frosting (page 227)
- Orange Crunch Icing (page 234)

- Preheat oven to 350°F (180°C)
- Two 9-inch (23 cm) round cake pans, sprayed with nonstick spray

2 cups	cake flour	500 mL
1⅓ cups	granulated sugar	325 mL
2 tsp	baking soda	10 mL
¾ tsp	salt	4 mL
⅔ cup	vegetable shortening	150 mL
1 tbsp	grated orange zest	15 mL
⅓ cup	freshly squeezed orange juice	75 mL
⅓ cup	water	75 mL
2	eggs	2
2 tbsp	freshly squeezed lemon juice	25 mL
½ cup	almond slices, toasted	125 mL

1. In a mixer bowl fitted with paddle attachment, combine cake flour, sugar, baking soda and salt until blended, for 30 seconds. Add shortening, orange zest and juice, water and eggs and mix until well blended, for 2 minutes. Add lemon juice just until incorporated. Fold in almonds.
2. Divide batter evenly between prepared pans. Bake in preheated oven until a toothpick inserted into center comes out clean, 30 to 34 minutes. Let cool in pans on a wire rack for 10 minutes before transferring to rack to cool completely.
3. For best results for decorating, wrap cakes in plastic wrap and freeze for 1 to 2 days. Decorate with any of the icings at left or one of your favorites.

Rich Chocolate Chip Fudge Cake

SERVES 10 TO 12

You can never have too much chocolate in a cake.

Tip

Decorate with any of the following icings:

- Buttercream Frosting (page 224)
- Chocolate Cream Cheese Icing (page 225)
- French Buttercream Frosting (page 227)
- French Chocolate Buttercream Frosting (page 229)
- Milk Chocolate Frosting (page 232)
- Old-Fashioned Chocolate Fudge Frosting (page 233)

- Preheat oven to 350°F (180°C)
- Two 9-inch (23 cm) round cake pans, sprayed with nonstick spray
- Digital instant-read thermometer

1 cup	unsweetened Dutch-process cocoa powder, sifted	250 mL
1½ cups	milk, preferably whole, heated to 120°F (49°C)	375 mL
3	eggs	3
½ tsp	vanilla extract	2 mL
3 cups	cake flour	750 mL
2 cups	packed light brown sugar	500 mL
2¼ tsp	baking powder	11 mL
¾ tsp	baking soda	4 mL
½ tsp	salt	2 mL
1 cup	unsalted butter, softened	250 mL
1 cup	semisweet chocolate chips	250 mL
2 tbsp	all-purpose flour	25 mL

1. In a bowl, dissolve cocoa powder and milk, whisking until smooth. Let cool slightly, about 2 minutes. Whisk in eggs and vanilla. Set aside.
2. In a mixer bowl fitted with paddle attachment, combine cake flour, brown sugar, baking powder, baking soda and salt on low speed until blended, for 30 seconds. Add butter and mix until incorporated. Gradually add cocoa mixture in four additions, mixing until dry ingredients are moistened. Increase speed to medium-high and beat for 1½ minutes.
3. In a small bowl, coat chocolate chips with all-purpose flour. Fold into batter by hand.
4. Divide batter evenly between prepared pans. Bake in preheated oven until toothpick inserted into center comes out clean, 28 to 34 minutes. Let cool in pans on a wire rack for 10 minutes before transferring to rack to cool completely.
5. For best results for decorating, wrap cakes in plastic wrap and freeze layers for 1 to 2 days. Decorate with any of the icings at left or one of your favorites.

Strawberry Layer Cake

SERVES 12 TO 14

Light pink and perfect for a little girl's birthday party.

Tip

Decorate with any of the following icings:

- Buttercream Frosting (page 224)
- Seven-Minute Frosting (page 239)
- Whipped Cream Cheese Frosting (page 235)

- Preheat oven to 350°F (180°C)
- Two 9-inch (23 cm) round cake pans, sprayed with nonstick spray

2½ cups	cake flour	625 mL
1¼ tsp	baking powder	6 mL
1 tsp	salt	5 mL
½ tsp	baking soda	2 mL
¾ cup	unsalted butter, softened	175 mL
1½ cups	granulated sugar	375 mL
¾ cup	strawberry preserves	175 mL
4	eggs	4
1 tsp	vanilla extract	5 mL
4	drops liquid red food coloring	4
½ cup	buttermilk	125 mL

1. In bowl, whisk together cake flour, baking powder, salt and baking soda. Set aside.
2. In a mixer bowl fitted with paddle attachment, cream butter, sugar and preserves until fluffy, for 3 minutes. Add eggs, one at a time, beating well between each addition. Beat in vanilla and food coloring. Using a wooden spoon, stir in flour mixture alternating with buttermilk, making three additions of flour and two of buttermilk, just until blended.
3. Divide batter equally between prepared pans. Bake in preheated oven until a toothpick inserted into center comes out clean, 22 to 28 minutes. Let cool in pans on a wire rack for 10 minutes before transferring to rack to cool completely.
4. For best results for decorating, wrap cakes in plastic wrap and freeze for 1 to 2 days. Decorate with any of the icings at left or one of your favorites.

Tart Lemon Cake

SERVES 12 TO 14

I live in California — the citrus capital of the world. When lemons are in season this is the perfect cake to make.

Tip

Decorate with either of the following icings:

- Buttercream Frosting (page 224)
- Fresh Lemon Frosting (page 230)

- Preheat oven to 350°F (180°C)
- Two 9-inch (23 cm) round cake pans, sprayed with nonstick spray

2 cups	cake flour	500 mL
2 cups	all-purpose flour	500 mL
1½ tsp	baking soda	7 mL
1 tsp	salt	5 mL
1 cup	milk, preferably whole	250 mL
2 tsp	grated lemon zest	10 mL
¼ cup	freshly squeezed lemon juice	50 mL
1 cup	unsalted butter, softened	250 mL
2 cups	granulated sugar	500 mL
4	eggs	4

1. In a large bowl, whisk together cake flour, all-purpose flour, baking soda and salt. In another bowl, combine milk, lemon zest and juice. Set both aside.
2. In a mixer bowl fitted with paddle attachment, cream butter and sugar until light and fluffy, for 3 minutes. Add eggs, one at a time, beating well between each addition. Using a wooden spoon, stir in flour mixture alternating with milk mixture, making three additions of flour and two of milk just until blended.
3. Divide batter equally between prepared pans. Bake in preheated oven until light brown and a toothpick inserted into center comes out clean, 32 to 35 minutes. Let cool in pans on a wire rack for 10 minutes before transferring to rack to cool completely.
4. For best results for decorating, wrap cakes in plastic wrap and freeze for 1 to 2 days. Decorate with any of the icings at left or one of your favorites.

White Layer Cake

SERVES 10 TO 12

When you need a simply wonderful white cake this one does the trick.

Tip

Decorate with any of the following icings:

- Buttercream Frosting (page 224)
- Chocolate Cream Cheese Icing (page 225)
- French Chocolate Buttercream Frosting (page 229)
- Fresh Lemon Frosting (page 230)
- Milk Chocolate Frosting (page 232)
- White Cherry Buttercream Frosting (page 240)

- Preheat oven to 350°F (180°C)
- Two 9-inch (23 cm) round cake pans, sprayed with nonstick spray

4½ cups	cake flour	1.125 L
1 tbsp	baking powder	15 mL
½ tsp	salt	2 mL
1 cup	cold water	250 mL
1 tbsp	vanilla extract	15 mL
1¼ cups	unsalted butter, softened	300 mL
2 cups	granulated sugar	500 mL
6	egg whites	6

1. In a large bowl, whisk together flour, baking powder and salt. In a small bowl, stir together water and vanilla. Set both aside.
2. In a mixer bowl fitted with paddle attachment, cream butter and sugar until light and fluffy, about 3 minutes. Add egg whites, one at a time, beating for 1 minute between each addition. Using a wooden spoon, stir in flour mixture alternating with water mixture, making three additions of flour and two of water, just until blended.
3. Divide batter equally between prepared pans. Bake in preheated oven until a toothpick inserted into center comes out clean, 22 to 28 minutes. Let cool in pans on a wire rack for 10 minutes before transferring to rack to cool completely.
4. For best results for decorating, wrap cakes in plastic wrap and freeze for 1 to 2 days. Decorate with any of the icings at left or one of your favorites.

Red Velvet Cake

SERVES 10 TO 12

This cake has made a comeback. It is a rich red color, making it great for Valentine's Day or your anniversary.

Tip

Decorate with any of the following icings:

- Buttercream Frosting (page 224)
- Cream Cheese Icing (page 226)
- French Buttercream Frosting (page 227)
- Fresh Lemon Frosting (page 230)
- Milk Chocolate Frosting (page 232)
- Seven-Minute Frosting (page 239)

- Preheat oven to 350°F (180°C)
- Two 9-inch (23 cm) round cake pans, sprayed with nonstick spray

2½ cups	cake flour	625 mL
1 tsp	salt	5 mL
1 cup	unsalted butter, softened	250 mL
1½ cups	granulated sugar	375 mL
2	eggs	2
3 tbsp	unsweetened Dutch-process cocoa powder	45 mL
1 oz	liquid red food coloring	30 mL
1 tsp	vanilla extract	5 mL
1 cup	buttermilk	250 mL
1 tsp	apple cider vinegar	5 mL
1 tsp	baking soda	5 mL

1. In a bowl, sift cake flour and salt together two times. Set aside.
2. In a mixer bowl fitted with paddle attachment, cream butter and sugar until light and fluffy, for 3 minutes. Add eggs, one at a time, beating well between each addition.
3. In a small bowl, combine cocoa powder, food coloring and vanilla. Beat into butter mixture. Using a wooden spoon, stir in flour mixture alternating with buttermilk, making three additions of flour and two of buttermilk just until blended.
4. In another small bowl, combine vinegar and baking soda. As soon as mixture starts to bubble, fold into batter by hand.
5. Divide batter evenly between prepared pans. Bake in preheated oven until a toothpick inserted into center comes out clean, 22 to 26 minutes. Let cool in pans on a wire rack for 10 minutes before transferring to rack to cool completely.
6. For best results for decorating, wrap cakes in plastic wrap and freeze for 1 to 2 days. Decorate with any of the icings at left or one of your favorites.

Yellow Cake

SERVES 10 TO 12

This cake is quick to make and moist. I like to use it as a base when I make English Trifle. It also makes a nice layer cake.

Tip

Decorate with any of the following icings:

- Buttercream Frosting (page 224)
- Chocolate Cream Cheese Icing (page 225)
- French Chocolate Buttercream Frosting (page 229)
- Fresh Lemon Frosting (page 230)
- Milk Chocolate Frosting (page 232)

- Preheat 350°F (180°C)
- Two 9-inch (23 cm) round cake pans, sprayed with nonstick spray

3½ cups	cake flour	875 mL
4 tsp	baking powder	20 mL
½ tsp	salt	2 mL
1 cup	cold water	250 mL
1 tbsp	vanilla extract	15 mL
1½ cup	unsalted butter, softened	375 mL
2 cups	granulated sugar	500 mL
5	eggs	5

1. In a bowl, whisk together flour, baking powder and salt. In a small bowl, stir together water and vanilla. Set both aside.
2. In a mixer bowl fitted with paddle attachment, cream butter and sugar until light and fluffy, for 2 minutes. Add eggs, one at a time, beating well between each addition. Using a wooden spoon, stir in flour mixture alternating with water mixture, making three additions of flour and two of water, just until blended.
3. Divide batter equally between prepared pans. Bake in preheated oven until light brown and a toothpick inserted into center comes out clean, 28 to 36 minutes. Let cool in pans on a wire rack for 10 minutes before transferring to rack to cool completely.
4. For best results for decorating, wrap cakes in plastic wrap and freeze for 1 to 2 days. Decorate with any of the icings at left or one of your favorites.

Almond Raspberry Pound Cake

SERVES 10 TO 12

Almonds and raspberries make this cake a flavorful tea cake for a wedding shower or Sunday brunch.

- Preheat oven to 325°F (160°C)
- 10-inch (4 L) tube pan, sprayed with nonstick spray

3 cups	all-purpose flour	750 mL
½ tsp	baking soda	2 mL
1 cup	unsalted butter, softened	250 mL
3 cups	granulated sugar	750 mL
1 cup	sour cream	250 mL
1 tsp	vanilla extract	5 mL
1 tsp	almond extract	5 mL
6	eggs, beaten	6
1 cup	crushed raspberries	250 mL
2 tsp	confectioner's (icing) sugar	10 mL

1. In a bowl, whisk together flour and baking soda. Set aside.
2. In a mixer bowl fitted with paddle attachment, cream butter and sugar until light and fluffy, for 2 minutes. Add sour cream, vanilla and almond extracts and mix just until incorporated. Using a wooden spoon, stir in flour mixture alternating with eggs, making three additions of flour and two of eggs, just until blended. Fold in raspberries.
3. Spread batter into prepared pan. Bake in preheated oven until light brown and a toothpick inserted into center comes out clean, 70 to 80 minutes. Let cool in pan on a wire rack for 10 minutes before transferring to rack to cool completely. Dust with confectioner's sugar just before serving.

Apple Spice Cake

SERVES 10 TO 12

Richly laced with apples and spices. You will love this if you love apple pie.

- Preheat oven to 325°F (160°C)
- 10-inch (4 L) tube pan, sprayed with nonstick spray

3 cups	all-purpose flour	750 mL
1 tsp	ground cinnamon	5 mL
½ tsp	freshly grated nutmeg	2 mL
½ tsp	baking soda	2 mL
¼ tsp	ground ginger	1 mL
1 cup	unsalted butter, softened	250 mL
3 cups	granulated sugar	750 mL
1 cup	sour cream	250 mL
6	eggs, beaten	6
1 tsp	vanilla extract	5 mL
2	large baking apples, such as Pippin or Granny Smith, peeled and chopped	2

1. In large bowl, whisk together flour, cinnamon, nutmeg, baking soda and ginger. Set aside.
2. In a mixer bowl fitted with paddle attachment, cream butter and sugar until light and fluffy, for 2 minutes. Add sour cream and mix just until incorporated. Using a wooden spoon, stir in flour mixture alternating with eggs, making three additions of flour and two of eggs just until blended. Fold in vanilla and apples.
3. Pour batter into prepared pan. Bake in preheated oven until a toothpick inserted into center comes out clean, 70 to 80 minutes. Let cool in pan on a wire rack for 10 minutes before transferring to rack to cool completely.

Banana Sour Cream Pound Cake

MAKES 2 LOAVES, EACH SERVES 8 TO 10

The riper your bananas, the moister this cake will be.

Tip

Wrap cooled loaf in plastic wrap and then in foil and freeze for up to 3 months.

- Preheat oven to 325°F (160°C)
- Two 9-by 5-inch (2 L) metal loaf pans, sprayed with nonstick spray

3 cups	all-purpose flour	750 mL
1/4 tsp	baking soda	1 mL
1 cup	unsalted butter, softened	250 mL
3 cups	granulated sugar	750 mL
6	eggs	6
1 cup	sour cream	250 mL
1 tsp	vanilla extract	5 mL
1 cup	mashed ripe bananas (about 3)	250 mL

1. In a large bowl, whisk together flour and soda. Set aside.
2. In a mixer bowl fitted with paddle attachment, cream butter and sugar until light and fluffy, for 3 minutes. Add eggs, one at a time, beating well between each addition. Add sour cream and vanilla and mix until incorporated. Using a wooden spoon, gradually stir in flour mixture just until incorporated. Fold in bananas.
3. Divide batter equally between prepared pans. Bake in preheated oven until a toothpick inserted into center comes out clean, 38 to 45 minutes. Let cool in pans on a wire rack for 10 minutes before transferring to rack to cool completely.

Chocolate Génoise

SERVES 8 TO 10

A sponge cake, Génoise cakes are a base for many French cake desserts. This cake is a little dry on its own, so you need to make sure you use the liqueur to brush the cake before decorating.

Tips

Decorate with either of the following icings:

- French Buttercream Frosting (page 227)
- French Chocolate Buttercream Frosting (page 229).

Choose a liqueur that suits the flavor of the frosting you plan to use. If you use either of the buttercream frostings suggested here, a hazelnut, coffee-flavored or rum liqueur would work.

Variation

For a basic French Génoise, omit cocoa powder and increase cake flour to 2 cups (500 mL).

- Preheat oven to 375°F (190°C)
- 9-inch (23 cm) round cake pan, sprayed with nonstick spray

8	eggs	8
1¼ cups	granulated sugar	300 mL
1½ cups	cake flour	375 mL
½ cup	unsweetened Dutch-process cocoa powder	125 mL
2 tbsp	liqueur (see Tips, left and page 246)	25 mL

1. Fill a large saucepan (make sure your mixer bowl fits on top) with water and bring to a boil. In a mixer bowl, whisk together eggs and sugar. Place bowl on top of saucepan, creating a double boiler. Reduce heat and cook over simmering water, whisking constantly, until sugar has dissolved, for 2 minutes. Place bowl on mixer with whip attachment and beat on high until very pale and tripled in volume, about 15 minutes.
2. In a bowl, sift together flour and cocoa powder. After egg mixture has tripled, gradually fold in flour mixture by hand.
3. Pour batter into prepared pan. Bake in preheated oven until cake springs back when lightly touched in center or a toothpick inserted into center comes out clean, 18 to 24 minutes. Let cool in pan on a wire rack for 10 minutes before transferring to rack to cool completely. Brush cooled cake with liqueur.
4. For best results for decorating, wrap cake in plastic wrap and freeze for 1 to 2 days. Decorate with any of the icings at left or one of your favorites.

Chocolate Pudding Cake

SERVES 8 TO 10

Here's a rich pudding cake that makes its own thick chocolate sauce.

Tip

To reheat, cover baking pan with foil and heat in 350°F (180°C) oven until center is hot, 12 to 18 minutes.

- Preheat oven to 350°F (180°C)
- 9-inch (2.5 L) square baking pan, sprayed with nonstick spray
- Digital instant-read thermometer

Cake Batter

1 cup	all-purpose flour	250 mL
3/4 cup	granulated sugar	175 mL
2 tbsp	unsweetened Dutch-processed cocoa powder, sifted	25 mL
2 tsp	baking powder	10 mL
1/4 tsp	salt	1 mL
1/2 cup	milk, preferably whole	125 mL
3 tbsp	unsalted butter, melted	45 mL
1 tsp	vanilla extract	5 mL

Topping

1/2 cup	granulated sugar	125 mL
1/2 cup	packed brown sugar	125 mL
1/4 cup	unsweetened Dutch-processed cocoa powder, sifted	50 mL
1/2 cup	milk, preferably whole	125 mL
1/2 cup	hot water (120°F/49°C)	125 mL

1. *Cake Batter:* In a bowl, whisk together flour, sugar, cocoa powder, baking powder and salt. Stir in milk, butter and vanilla until incorporated. Pour into prepared pan. Set aside.
2. *Topping:* In a small bowl, combine granulated sugar, brown sugar and cocoa powder. Sprinkle over cake batter. Carefully pour milk and hot water over top (do not stir). Bake in preheated oven until firm-looking on top (a toothpick inserted into center will come out just a little moist), 40 to 45 minutes. Let stand for 10 to 15 minutes before serving.

Coconut Pound Cake

SERVES 10 TO 12

I'm usually not a big fan of coconut, but after tasting my friend Randy Gooch's cake I had to get the recipe. He works at the Pentagon and takes this cake into work.

- Preheat oven to 350°F (180°C)
- 10-inch (4 L) tube pan, sprayed with nonstick spray

Cake

3 cups	all-purpose flour	750 mL
1 tsp	baking powder	5 mL
½ tsp	salt	2 mL
1 cup	unsalted butter, softened	250 mL
⅔ cup	vegetable shortening	150 mL
3 cups	granulated sugar	750 mL
5	eggs	5
1 cup	coconut milk	250 mL
1 tsp	vanilla extract	5 mL
1 cup	sweetened flaked coconut	250 mL

Glaze

1 cup	granulated sugar	250 mL
½ cup	water	125 mL
1 tsp	coconut flavoring	5 mL

1. *Cake:* In a bowl, whisk together flour, baking powder and salt. Set aside.
2. In a mixer bowl fitted with paddle attachment, cream butter, shortening and sugar until pale yellow, about 6 minutes. Add eggs, one at a time, beating well between each addition. Using a wooden spoon, stir in flour mixture alternating with coconut milk, making three additions of flour and two of coconut milk, just until blended. Fold in vanilla and coconut.
3. Pour batter into prepared pan. Bake in preheated oven until golden brown and a toothpick inserted into center of cake comes out clean, 45 to 55 minutes. Let cool in pan on a wire rack for 10 minutes before transferring to rack.
4. *Glaze:* In a small saucepan, combine sugar and water and bring to a low boil over medium heat, about 5 minutes. Remove from heat, add coconut flavoring and drizzle over warm cake. Let cool completely.

Fresh Strawberry Pound Cake

MAKES 2 LOAVES, EACH SERVES 8 TO 10

Perfect for a breakfast or tea in early spring when the first berries are in season.

- Preheat oven to 350°F (180°C)
- Two 9-by 5-inch (2 L) metal loaf pans, sprayed with nonstick spray

3 cups	all-purpose flour	750 mL
2 tsp	ground cinnamon	10 mL
1 tsp	baking soda	5 mL
1 tsp	salt	5 mL
2 cups	granulated sugar	500 mL
4	eggs	4
2 cups	sliced fresh strawberries (about 12 oz/375 g)	500 mL
1¼ cups	vegetable oil	300 mL
1¼ cups	toasted chopped pecans	300 mL

1. In a large bowl, whisk together flour, cinnamon, baking soda and salt. Set aside.
2. In a mixer bowl fitted with paddle attachment, mix sugar, eggs, strawberries, oil and pecans on low speed until well blended, for 3 minutes. Using a wooden spoon, gradually stir in flour mixture until blended.
3. Divide batter evenly between prepared pans. Bake in preheated oven until a toothpick inserted into center comes out clean, 60 to 75 minutes. Let cool in pans on a wire rack for 10 minutes before transferring to rack to cool completely.

Ginger Pound Cake

SERVES 8 TO 10

Light ginger flavor in this moist pound cake makes it perfect for dessert after an Asian meal.

- Preheat oven to 325°F (160°C)
- 10-inch (4 L) tube pan, sprayed with nonstick spray

2 cups	all-purpose flour	500 mL
1 tbsp	ground ginger	15 mL
½ tsp	salt	2 mL
1 cup	unsalted butter, softened	250 mL
1⅔ cups	granulated sugar	400 mL
5	eggs	5
½ tsp	vanilla extract	2 mL
	Ginger Whipped Cream (see Variation, page 239)	

1. In bowl, whisk together flour, ginger and salt. Set aside.
2. In a mixer bowl fitted with paddle attachment, beat butter until very light, for 3 minutes. With mixer running, slowly sprinkle in sugar. Add eggs, one at a time, beating well between each addition. Beat in vanilla. Using a wooden spoon, gradually stir in flour mixture by spoonfuls until batter is smooth.
3. Spread batter into prepared pan. Bake in preheated oven until light brown and a toothpick inserted into center of cake comes out clean, 35 to 40 minutes. Let cool in pan on a wire rack for 10 minutes before transferring to rack to cool completely. Serve with Ginger Whipped Cream.

Hazelnut Génoise

SERVES 8 TO 10

A nutty French cake. It pairs perfectly with French Chocolate Buttercream Frosting (see recipe, page 229).

Tips

Decorate with either of the following icings:

- French Buttercream Frosting (page 227)
- Fresh Lemon Frosting (page 230)

Choose a liqueur that suits the flavor of the frosting you plan to use. For liqueur suggestions, see page 246.

- Preheat oven to 375°F (190°C)
- 9-inch (23 cm) round cake pan, sprayed with nonstick spray

8	eggs	8
1¼ cups	granulated sugar	300 mL
1 tsp	vanilla extract	5 mL
1 cup	cake flour	250 mL
1 cup	hazelnut flour	250 mL
2 tbsp	hazelnut-flavored liqueur (see Tips, left)	25 mL

1. Fill a large saucepan, (make sure your mixer bowl fits on top) with water and bring to a boil. In a mixer bowl, whisk together eggs and sugar. Place bowl on top of saucepan, creating a double boiler. Reduce heat and cook over simmering water, whisking constantly, until sugar has dissolved, for 2 minutes. Whisk in vanilla. Place bowl on mixer with whip attachment and beat on high until tripled in volume, about 15 minutes.
2. In a small bowl, sift together cake and hazelnut flours. After egg mixture has tripled, gradually fold in flour mixture by hand.
3. Pour batter into prepared pan. Bake in preheated oven until cake springs back when lightly touched in center or a toothpick inserted into center comes out clean, 18 to 24 minutes. Let cool in pan on a wire rack for 10 minutes before transferring to rack to cool completely. Brush cooled cake with liqueur.
4. For best results for decorating, wrap cake in plastic wrap and freeze for 1 to 2 days. Decorate with any of the icings at left or one of your favorites.

Lemon Citrus-Glazed Pound Cake

SERVES 10 TO 12

Pucker up. This is a lip-smacking cake for any time of year.

Tip

If you wait until cake has cooled too much before glazing, you will have to poke holes with a skewer to allow glaze to soak into cake.

Variation

I like to cut this cake into slices and sandwich with Fresh Lemon Curd (page 284) and then top with a dollop of Classic Whipped Cream (page 239).

- Preheat oven to 350°F (180°C)
- 10-inch (4 L) tube pan, sprayed with nonstick spray

Cake

3 cups	all-purpose flour	750 mL
2 tsp	baking powder	10 mL
½ tsp	salt	2 mL
1 cup	unsalted butter, softened	250 mL
2 cups	granulated sugar	500 mL
4	eggs	4
1 tbsp	grated lemon zest	15 mL
1 tsp	vanilla extract	5 mL
1 cup	milk, preferably whole	250 mL

Glaze

⅓ cup	freshly squeezed lemon juice	75 mL
⅓ cup	granulated sugar	75 mL
2 tbsp	unsalted butter, softened	25 mL

1. *Cake:* In a bowl, whisk together flour, baking powder and salt. Set aside.
2. In a mixer bowl fitted with paddle attachment, cream butter and sugar until light and fluffy, for 2 minutes. Add eggs, one at a time, beating well between each addition. Beat in lemon zest and vanilla. Using a wooden spoon, stir in flour mixture alternating with milk, making three additions of flour and two of milk just until blended.
3. Spread batter into prepared pan. Bake in preheated oven until a toothpick inserted into center comes out clean, 40 to 45 minutes. Let cool in pan on a wire rack for 10 minutes before transferring to rack.
4. *Glaze:* In a small saucepan over medium heat, cook lemon juice, sugar and butter, stirring often, until butter is completely melted and sugar has dissolved, about 3 minutes. Pour over warm cake. Let cool completely.

Marble Swirl Pound Cake

SERVES 12 TO 14

You get two flavors and a great-looking pound cake in this marble cake.

- Preheat oven to 350°F (180°C)
- 10-inch (4 L) tube pan, sprayed with nonstick spray

3½ cups	cake flour	825 mL
1½ tsp	baking powder	7 mL
¼ tsp	salt	1 mL
1 cup	unsalted butter, softened	250 mL
2 cups	granulated sugar	500 mL
4	eggs	4
2 tsp	vanilla extract	10 mL
1¼ cups	milk, preferably whole, divided	300 mL
⅓ cup	unsweetened Dutch-processed cocoa powder, sifted	75 mL

1. In a bowl, combine flour, baking powder and salt. Set aside.
2. In a mixer bowl fitted with paddle attachment, cream butter and sugar until light and fluffy, for 2 minutes. Add eggs, one at a time, beating well between each addition. Beat in vanilla. Add flour mixture alternating with 1 cup (250 mL) of the milk, making three additions of flour and two of milk, mixing on low speed just until blended.
3. Transfer 1½ cups (375 mL) of the batter to a bowl. Whisk in remaining milk and cocoa powder until smooth.
4. Drop large spoonfuls of vanilla batter into prepared pan alternating with chocolate batter. With a large spoon, cut and twist through batters to create a marbled effect. Bake in preheated oven until a toothpick inserted in the center comes out clean, about 60 minutes. Let cool in pan on a wire rack for 10 minutes before transferring to rack to cool completely.

Moist Key Lime Pound Cake with Lime Syrup

SERVES 10 TO 12

This will make you think of the Florida Keys every time you bake this cake, even in winter.

- Preheat oven to 350°F (180°C)
- 10-inch (4 L) tube pan, sprayed with nonstick spray

Cake

3 cups	all purpose flour	750 mL
2 tsp	baking powder	10 mL
½ tsp	salt	2 mL
1 cup	unsalted butter, softened	250 mL
2 cups	granulated sugar	500 mL
4	eggs	4
2 tsp	grated lime zest, preferably Key lime	10 mL
1 cup	milk, preferably whole	250 mL

Lime Syrup

⅓ cup	Key lime juice, freshly squeezed or bottled (see Sources, page 442)	75 mL
¾ cup	granulated sugar	175 mL
2 tbsp	unsalted butter, softened	25 mL

1. *Cake:* In a large bowl, whisk together flour, baking powder and salt. Set aside.
2. In a mixer bowl fitted with paddle attachment, cream butter and sugar until light and fluffy, for 3 minutes. Beat in eggs, one at a time, beating well after each addition. Beat in lime zest. Using a wooden spoon, stir in flour mixture alternating with milk, making three additions of flour and two of milk just until blended.
3. Spread into prepared pan. Bake in preheated oven until light brown on top and a toothpick inserted into center of cake comes out clean, 45 to 50 minutes. Let cool in pan on a wire rack for 10 minutes before transferring to rack.
4. *Lime Syrup:* In a small saucepan over low heat, cook lime juice, sugar and butter, stirring often, until lightly boiling, about 4 minutes. Brush over warm cake. Let cool completely.

Pistachio Cream Cake with Sherry

SERVES 10 TO 12

When given a choice of wedding cakes, the groom invariably picks this one.

Tip

If you wait until the cake has cooled too much before glazing, you'll have to poke holes in the cake with a skewer so the glaze can soak into cake.

- Preheat oven to 350°F (180°C)
- 10-inch (4 L) tube pan, sprayed with nonstick spray

Cake

½ cup	chopped pistachios, divided	125 mL
3 cups	all-purpose flour	750 mL
1	box (4-serving size) instant pistachio pudding mix	1
2 tsp	baking powder	10 mL
½ tsp	salt	2 mL
1 cup	unsalted butter, softened	250 mL
2 cups	granulated sugar	500 mL
4	eggs	4
1 cup	milk, preferably whole	250 mL

Glaze

⅓ cup	cream sherry	75 mL
⅓ cup	granulated sugar	75 mL
2 tbsp	unsalted butter, softened	25 mL

1. *Cake:* Sprinkle ¼ cup (50 mL) of the pistachios into bottom of prepared pan. Set aside.
2. In a large bowl, whisk together flour, pudding mix, baking powder and salt. Set aside.
3. In a mixer bowl fitted with paddle attachment, cream butter and sugar until light and fluffy, for 2 minutes. Add eggs, one at a time, beating well between each addition. Using a wooden spoon, stir in flour mixture alternating with milk, making three additions of flour and two of milk, just until blended. Fold in remaining pistachios.
4. Spread batter over pistachios in pan. Bake in preheated oven until a toothpick inserted into center comes out clean, 40 to 45 minutes. Let cool in pan on a wire rack for 10 minutes before transferring to rack.
5. *Glaze:* In a small saucepan over medium heat, heat sherry, sugar and butter, stirring, until butter is completely melted and sugar has dissolved, about 3 minutes. Pour over warm cake.

Orange Chiffon Cake

SERVES 10 TO 12

Chiffon cakes are soft and moist. They are a cross between a layer cake and an angel food cake and are simple to make as long as all of your ingredients are measured out ahead of time.

Tips

Make sure the tube pan is free of all oil or grease to allow the cake to get maximum lift in the oven. And be sure to thoroughly wash and dry mixer bowl and whip, making sure they are free of all oil, before beating whites.

Top with Classic Whipped Cream (page 239).

- Preheat oven to 325°F (160°C)
- 10-inch (4 L) tube pan, ungreased

2¼ cups	cake flour	550 mL
1 tbsp	baking powder	15 mL
½ tsp	salt	2 mL
6	eggs, separated	6
1	egg	1
1⅓ cups	superfine sugar, divided	325 mL
½ cup	vegetable oil, preferably safflower	125 mL
1 tbsp	vanilla extract	15 mL
1 tsp	orange oil	5 mL
¾ cup	cold water	175 mL
¼ tsp	cream of tartar	1 mL

1. In a large bowl, sift together cake flour, baking powder and salt three times. Set aside.
2. In a mixer bowl fitted with whip attachment, beat egg yolks and egg until thick and pale yellow, about 6 minutes. With mixer running, gradually spoon in 1 cup (250 mL) of the superfine sugar, 1 tbsp (15 mL) at a time, beating until mixture is pale yellow and thick. This should take 4 to 5 minutes total. With mixer running, in a steady stream, pour in oil, vanilla extract and orange oil.
3. Using a wooden spoon, stir in flour mixture alternating with water, making three additions of flour and two of water just until blended. Set aside.
4. In a clean mixer bowl fitted with whip attachment, whip egg whites with cream of tartar on low speed until frothy, about 2 minutes. Increase speed to high and continue beating until peaks just start to form. With mixer running, gradually sprinkle in remaining sugar and whip until soft peaks form.
5. Using a rubber spatula, gently stir about one-quarter of egg whites into batter. Fold in remaining whites, just until incorporated.
6. Pour batter into pan. Bake in preheated oven until golden brown and springy to touch, 60 to 70 minutes. Invert pan, balancing on tube, and let cake cool completely. The cake should fall out of pan when cool. If it needs a little help, run a rubber spatula around the sides of pan to loosen.

Perfect Angel Food Cake

SERVES 8 TO 10

So many feel that angel food is hard to make, but it really is a simple cake. Try it when you have extra egg whites. This really is a perfect nonfat dessert when paired with fresh berries.

Tip

Glaze with either of the following glazes:

- Espresso Chocolate Glaze (page 226)
- Lemon Glaze (page 230)

- Preheat oven to 375°F (190°C)
- 10-inch (4 L) tube pan, ungreased

1 cup	cake flour	250 mL
1½ cups	granulated sugar, divided	375 mL
12	egg whites, very cold (about 1¼ cups/300 mL)	12
1½ tsp	cream of tartar	7 mL
1½ tsp	vanilla extract	7 mL
1 tsp	almond extract	5 mL
½ tsp	salt	2 mL

1. Make sure all tools, including tube pan, mixer and whip attachment, are free of any oil, very clean and dry. If any traces of oil are on any of your tools your cake will not work.
2. Sift cake flour together with ¾ cup (175 mL) of the granulated sugar. Set aside.
3. In a mixer bowl fitted with whip attachment, whip egg whites, cream of tartar, vanilla and almond extracts and salt on high speed until soft peaks form, about 4 minutes. With mixer running, gradually sprinkle in remaining sugar, beating until stiff, glossy peaks form. Using a rubber spatula, gradually fold in flour mixture just until incorporated.
4. Pour batter into pan, smoothing top and gently removing any large bubbles. Bake in preheated oven until golden brown and top springs back when lightly touched, 40 to 45 minutes. Invert pan, balancing on tube, and let cake cool completely. The cake should fall out of pan when cool. If it needs a little help, run a rubber spatula around the sides of pan to loosen.
5. Glaze cake with either of the glazes at left.

Pineapple Upside-Down Cake

SERVES 10 TO 12

I have never tasted anything so moist or flavorful. You should eat it a little warm.

- Preheat oven to 350°F (180°C)
- 10-inch (25 cm) round cake pan, bottom lined with parchment and sides sprayed with nonstick spray

7	pineapple slices, drained	7
2⁄3 cup	unsalted butter, softened, divided	150 mL
2 cups	granulated sugar, divided	500 mL
2⁄3 cup	packed brown sugar	150 mL
3 cups	cake flour	750 mL
1 1⁄2 tsp	baking powder	7 mL
1 tsp	salt	5 mL
3⁄4 cup	milk, preferably whole	175 mL
1 1⁄2 tbsp	dark rum	22 mL
1 1⁄2 tsp	vanilla extract	7 mL
2	eggs	2
7	maraschino cherries, drained	7

1. Arrange pineapple slices in a single layer around bottom of prepared pan. Set aside.
2. In a small saucepan over medium heat, melt 1⁄3 cup (75 mL) of the butter, 1⁄2 cup (125 mL) of the granulated sugar and the brown sugar, stirring, until butter melts. Smooth evenly over pineapple. Set aside.
3. In a bowl, whisk together cake flour, baking powder and salt. In another bowl, whisk together milk, rum and vanilla. Set both aside.
4. In a mixer bowl fitted with paddle attachment, cream remaining butter and remaining granulated sugar until light and fluffy, for 3 minutes. Add eggs, one at a time, beating well after each addition. Using a wooden spoon, stir in flour mixture alternating with milk mixture, making three additions of flour and two of milk, just until incorporated.
5. Carefully pour batter over pineapple mixture. Bake in preheated oven until light brown and a toothpick inserted into center comes out clean, 50 to 55 minutes. Let cool in pan on a wire rack for 20 minutes before inverting onto a serving plate.
6. Peel off parchment. Place a maraschino cherry in cavity of each pineapple. Let cool slightly before cutting.

Pumpkin Chocolate Chip Pound Cake

SERVES 14 TO 16

This cake can be served as a breakfast bread or for afternoon tea.

Tip
Wrap cooled loaf in plastic wrap and then in foil and freeze for up to 3 months.

- Preheat oven to 350°F (180°C)
- Two 9-by 5-inch (2 L) metal loaf pans, sprayed with nonstick spray

2¾ cups	all-purpose flour	675 mL
2 tsp	baking powder	10 mL
1 tsp	baking soda	5 mL
1 tsp	ground cinnamon	5 mL
½ tsp	salt	2 mL
½ tsp	freshly grated nutmeg	2 mL
¼ tsp	ground cloves	1 mL
¼ tsp	ground allspice	1 mL
¼ tsp	ground ginger	1 mL
1 cup	unsalted butter, softened	250 mL
1 cup	granulated sugar	250 mL
1 cup	packed brown sugar	250 mL
4	eggs	4
1 cup	pumpkin purée (not pie filling)	250 mL
6 oz	bittersweet chocolate, cut into chunks	175 g

1. In a bowl, whisk together flour, baking powder, baking soda, cinnamon, salt, nutmeg, cloves, allspice and ginger. Set aside.
2. In a mixer bowl fitted with paddle attachment, cream butter, granulated and brown sugars until light and fluffy, for 3 minutes. Add eggs, one at a time, beating well between each addition. Beat in pumpkin. Using a wooden spoon, gradually stir in flour mixture just until blended. Fold in chocolate.
3. Divide batter evenly between prepared loaf pans. Bake in preheated oven until a toothpick inserted into center comes out clean, 40 to 50 minutes. Let cool in pan on a wire rack for 10 minutes before transferring to rack to cool completely.

Pumpkin Coffee Cake

SERVES 10 TO 12

This is a perfect autumn cake for a party. You can bake it on the weekend and freeze it to serve the following week.

- Preheat oven to 350°F (180°C)
- 10-inch (4 L) tube pan, sprayed with nonstick spray

2½ cups	all-purpose flour	625 mL
1 tsp	baking powder	5 mL
1 tsp	freshly grated nutmeg	5 mL
1 tsp	ground cinnamon	5 mL
1 tsp	ground allspice	5 mL
1 tsp	ground cloves	5 mL
¼ tsp	salt	1 mL
2½ cups	granulated sugar	625 mL
1 cup	vegetable oil	250 mL
3	eggs	3
1¾ cups	pumpkin purée (not pie filling)	425 mL
1 tsp	vanilla extract	5 mL
½ cup	toasted chopped pecans	125 mL
½ cup	coffee-flavored liqueur	125 mL

1. In a bowl, whisk together flour, baking powder, nutmeg, cinnamon, allspice, cloves and salt. Set aside.
2. In a mixer bowl fitted with paddle attachment, blend sugar, oil, eggs, pumpkin and vanilla until smooth, for 2 minutes. Using a wooden spoon, gradually stir in flour mixture, just until blended. Fold in pecans.
3. Pour batter into prepared pan. Bake in preheated oven until a toothpick inserted into center comes out clean, about 60 minutes. Let cool in pan on a wire rack for 10 minutes before transferring to rack. While still warm, brush with liqueur. Let cool completely.

Raspberry Citrus Pound Cake

SERVES 10 TO 12

This is a moist raspberry pound cake with a hint of orange flavor. It is best served warm.

- Preheat oven to 350°F (180°C)
- 10-inch (4 L) tube pan, sprayed with nonstick spray

3 cups	all-purpose flour	750 mL
2 tsp	baking powder	10 mL
½ tsp	salt	2 mL
1 cup	unsalted butter, softened	250 mL
2 cups	granulated sugar	500 mL
4	eggs	4
1 cup	whipping (35%) cream	250 mL
1 tbsp	grated orange zest	15 mL
½ cup	raspberries, crushed	125 mL

1. In a large bowl, whisk together flour, baking powder and salt. Set aside.
2. In a mixer bowl fitted with paddle attachment, cream butter and sugar until light and fluffy, for 2 minutes. Add eggs, one at a time, beating well between each addition. Using a wooden spoon, stir in flour mixture alternating with cream, making three additions of flour and two of cream, just until blended. Fold in zest and raspberries.
3. Spread batter into prepared pan. Bake in preheated oven until light brown and a toothpick inserted into center comes out clean, 55 to 65 minutes. Let cool in pan on a wire rack for 10 minutes before transferring to rack to cool completely.

Rich Dense Pound Cake

SERVES 6 TO 8

This pound cake is great topped with berries and softly whipped cream.

- Preheat oven to 325°F (160°C)
- 9-by 5-inch (2 L) loaf pan, sprayed with nonstick spray

2 cups	all-purpose flour	500 mL
½ tsp	salt	2 mL
1 cup	unsalted butter, softened	250 mL
1⅔ cups	granulated sugar	400 mL
5	eggs	5
2 tsp	vanilla extract	10 mL

1. In a bowl, whisk together flour and salt. Set aside.
2. In a mixer bowl fitted with paddle attachment, cream butter and sugar until light and fluffy, for 3 minutes. Add eggs, one at a time, beating well between each addition. Beat in vanilla. Using a wooden spoon, gradually stir in flour mixture, just until blended.
3. Spread batter into prepared pan. Bake in preheated oven until light brown and a toothpick inserted into center comes out clean, 35 to 45 minutes. Let cool in pan on a wire rack for 10 minutes before transferring to rack to cool completely. Serve with Classic Whipped Cream (page 239).

Chocolate Cupcakes

MAKES 24 CUPCAKES

Rich chocolate cupcakes are perfect for a child's birthday party.

Tip

Decorate with any of the following icings:

- Chocolate Ganache (page 241)
- Espresso Chocolate Glaze (page 226)
- Milk Chocolate Frosting (page 232)
- Old-Fashioned Chocolate Fudge Frosting (page 233)

Variation

Dark Chocolate Coffee Cupcakes: Add ¼ cup (50 mL) coffee-flavored liqueur with vanilla in Step 2.

- Preheat oven to 350°F (180°C)
- Two 12-cup muffin tins, lined with paper liners or sprayed with nonstick spray

2 cups	all-purpose flour	500 mL
1 tsp	baking soda	5 mL
¾ tsp	salt	4 mL
1 cup	unsalted butter, softened	250 mL
1 cup	packed brown sugar	250 mL
1 cup	granulated sugar	250 mL
4	eggs	4
6 oz	unsweetened chocolate, melted and cooled (see Melting Chocolate, page 250)	175 g
1 tsp	vanilla extract	5 mL
1 cup	buttermilk	250 mL

1. In a bowl, whisk together flour, baking soda and salt. Set aside.
2. In a mixer bowl fitted with paddle attachment, cream butter, brown and granulated sugars until light and fluffy, about 2 minutes. Add eggs, one at a time, beating well between each addition. Beat in melted chocolate and vanilla. Using a wooden spoon, stir in flour mixture alternating with buttermilk, making three additions of flour and two of buttermilk, just until blended.
3. Scoop batter evenly into prepared muffin tins. Bake in preheated oven until a toothpick inserted into center comes out clean, 18 to 22 minutes. Let cool in tin on a wire rack for 10 minutes before transferring to rack to cool completely.
4. Decorate cooled cupcakes with any of the icings at left.

Devil's Food Chocolate Cupcakes

MAKES 30 CUPCAKES

These are my favorite cupcakes, especially when crowned with Chocolate Ganache.

Tips

This amount of batter will make 30 cupcakes so you'll have to bake the batter in batches. Let the muffin tin cool completely between batches.

Decorate with any of the following icings:

- Chocolate Ganache (page 241)
- Espresso Chocolate Glaze (page 226)
- Milk Chocolate Frosting (page 232)
- Old-Fashioned Chocolate Fudge Frosting (page 233)

- Preheat oven to 350°F (180°C)
- Two 12-cup muffin tins, lined with paper liners or sprayed with nonstick spray

2 cups	all-purpose flour	500 mL
1 cup	unsweetened Dutch-process cocoa powder, sifted	250 mL
1½ tsp	baking soda	7 mL
½ tsp	salt	2 mL
¾ cup	unsalted butter, softened	175 mL
1½ cups	packed brown sugar	375 mL
½ cup	granulated sugar	125 mL
3	eggs	3
2 tsp	vanilla extract	10 mL
1½ cups	buttermilk	375 mL

1. In a bowl, whisk together flour, cocoa powder, baking soda and salt. Set aside.
2. In a mixer bowl fitted with paddle attachment, cream butter, brown and granulated sugars until light and fluffy, about 2 minutes. Add eggs, one at a time, beating well between each addition. Beat in vanilla. Using a wooden spoon, stir in flour mixture alternating with buttermilk, making three additions of flour and two of buttermilk, just until blended.
3. Scoop batter evenly into prepared muffin tins. Bake in preheated oven until a toothpick inserted into center comes out clean, 20 to 25 minutes. Let cool in tin on a wire rack for 10 minutes before transferring to rack to cool completely.
4. Decorate cooled cupcakes with any of the icings at left.

Pineapple Upside-Down Cupcakes

MAKES 24 CUPCAKES

These cupcakes are small versions of the famous Pineapple Upside-Down Cake.

- Preheat oven to 325°F (160°C)
- Two 12-cup muffin tins, sprayed with nonstick spray (do not use paper liners as they will stick)

2⁄3 cup	unsalted butter, softened, divided	150 mL
2 cups	granulated sugar, divided	500 mL
2⁄3 cup	packed brown sugar	150 mL
1	can (8 oz/227 mL) crushed pineapple, drained	1
1⁄4 cup	chopped drained maraschino cherries	50 mL
3 cups	cake flour	750 mL
1 1⁄2 tsp	baking powder	7 mL
1 tsp	salt	5 mL
3⁄4 cup	milk, preferably whole	175 mL
1 1⁄2 tbsp	dark rum	22 mL
1 1⁄2 tsp	vanilla extract	7 mL
2	eggs	2

1. In a small saucepan over medium heat, melt 1⁄3 cup (75 mL) of the butter, 1⁄2 cup (125 mL) of the granulated sugar and the brown sugar, stirring, until butter melts. Stir in pineapple and cherries. Set aside.
2. In a bowl, whisk together cake flour, baking powder and salt. In another bowl, whisk together milk, rum and vanilla. Set both aside.
3. In a mixer bowl fitted with paddle attachment, cream remaining butter and remaining granulated sugar until light and fluffy, about 3 minutes. Add eggs, one at a time, beating well between each addition. Using a wooden spoons, stir in flour mixture alternating with milk mixture, making three additions of flour and two of milk, just until blended.
4. Divide pineapple mixture evenly into prepared tins. Scoop batter evenly over top. Bake in preheated oven until light brown and a toothpick inserted into center comes out clean, 18 to 20 minutes. Let cool in tin on a wire rack for 20 minutes. Cut tops if they have a dome and then invert cupcakes onto a platter.

Simple Vanilla Cupcakes

MAKES 24 CUPCAKES

These are simple cupcakes until you frost them. Turn them into a glamorous treat with one (or more) of the suggested toppings.

Tip

Decorate with any of the following icings:

- Chocolate Cream Cheese Icing (page 225)
- Espresso Chocolate Glaze (page 226)
- Fresh Lemon Frosting (page 230)
- Milk Chocolate Frosting (page 232)
- White Cherry Buttercream Frosting (page 240)

- Preheat oven to 350°F (180°C)
- Two 12-cup muffin tins, lined with paper liners or sprayed with nonstick spray

2¾ cups	all-purpose flour	675 mL
2½ tsp	baking powder	12 mL
¾ tsp	salt	4 mL
1 cup	unsalted butter, softened	250 mL
2 cups	granulated sugar	500 mL
4	eggs	4
1 tsp	vanilla extract	5 mL
1 cup	milk, preferably whole	250 mL

1. In a bowl, combine flour, baking powder and salt. Set aside.
2. In a mixer bowl fitted with paddle attachment, cream butter and sugar until light and fluffy, about 2 minutes. Add eggs, one at a time, beating well between each addition. Beat in vanilla. Using a wooden spoon, stir in flour mixture alternating with milk, making three additions of flour and two of milk, just until blended.
3. Scoop batter evenly into prepared muffin tins. Bake in preheated oven until a toothpick inserted into center comes out clean, 20 to 25 minutes. Let cool in tin on a wire rack for 10 minutes before transferring to rack to cool completely.
4. Decorate cooled cupcakes with any of the icings at left.

Lemon Cupcakes

MAKES 12 CUPCAKES

Light and tart. I like to fill these cupcakes with Fresh Lemon Curd (page 284).

Tip

Decorate with either of the following icings:

- French Buttercream Frosting (page 227)
- Fresh Lemon Frosting (page 230)

- Preheat oven to 350°F (180°C)
- One 12-cup muffin tin, lined with paper liners or sprayed with nonstick spray

1½ cups	all-purpose flour	375 mL
1½ tsp	baking powder	7 mL
¼ tsp	salt	1 mL
1 cup	granulated sugar	250 mL
½ cup	unsalted butter, melted and cooled	125 mL
2	eggs	2
2 tsp	grated lemon zest	10 mL
¼ tsp	lemon extract (see page 14)	1 mL
½ cup	milk, preferably whole	125 mL

1. In a bowl, whisk together flour, baking powder and salt. Set aside.
2. In a large bowl, whisk together sugar, butter, eggs, lemon zest and lemon extract. Using a wooden spoon, stir in flour mixture alternating with milk, making three additions of flour and two of milk, just until blended.
3. Scoop batter evenly into prepared tin. Bake in preheated oven until a toothpick inserted into center comes out clean, 18 to 22 minutes. Let cool in tin on a wire rack for 10 minutes before transferring to rack to cool completely.
4. Decorate cooled cupcakes with any of the icings at left.

Yellow Cupcakes

MAKES 24 CUPCAKES

Rich with sour cream and butter. Try these for your next kids' party.

Tip

Decorate with any of the following icings:

- Buttercream Frosting (page 224)
- Chocolate Cream Cheese Icing (page 225)
- Milk Chocolate Frosting (page 232)
- White Cherry Buttercream Frosting (page 240)

- Preheat oven to 350°F (180°C)
- Two 12-cup muffin tins, lined with paper liners or sprayed with nonstick spray

3 cups	all-purpose flour	750 mL
1 tbsp	baking soda	15 mL
1 tsp	salt	5 mL
1 cup	unsalted butter, softened	250 mL
2 cups	granulated sugar	500 mL
2	eggs	2
4	egg yolks	4
1 cup	sour cream	250 mL
2½ tsp	vanilla extract	12 mL

1. In a bowl, whisk together flour, baking soda and salt. Set aside.
2. In a mixer bowl fitted with paddle attachment, cream butter and sugar until light and fluffy, about 2 minutes. Add eggs and egg yolks, one at a time, beating well between each addition. Beat in sour cream and vanilla on low speed. Using a wooden spoon, gradually stir in flour mixture just until blended.
3. Scoop batter evenly into prepared muffin tins. Bake in preheated oven until a toothpick inserted into center comes out clean, 20 to 25 minutes. Let cool in tin on a wire rack for 10 minutes before transferring to rack to cool completely.
4. Decorate cooled cupcakes with any of the icings at left.

French Sponge Jelly Roll

SERVES 8 TO 10

I love the rich flavor of this jelly roll. You can dress it up with any type of filling or frosting.

Variations

Chocolate Jelly Roll: Replace all-purpose flour with unsweetened Dutch-process cocoa powder.

Yellow Jelly Roll: Replace all-purpose flour with cake flour and increase egg yolks to 6.

Petit Fours: Do not roll baked cake. Cut into quarters and layer with about 2 cups (500 mL) frosting divided between layers, leaving top plain. Cut into 2-inch (5 cm) squares and place on a wire rack; pour Petit Four Glaze (page 223) on top.

- Preheat oven to 400°F (200°C)
- 17-by 11-inch (43 by 28 cm) rimmed baking sheet, lined with parchment paper

⅓ cup	cornstarch	75 mL
⅓ cup	all-purpose flour	75 mL
5	eggs, separated	5
1 tsp	vanilla extract	5 mL
½ tsp	salt	2 mL
⅓ cup	granulated sugar	75 mL
	Confectioner's (icing) sugar	

1. In a bowl, sift together cornstarch and flour three times. Set aside.
2. In another bowl, whisk together egg yolks and vanilla. Set aside.
3. In a mixer bowl fitted with whip attachment, beat egg whites and salt on medium-high speed until frothy, about 3 minutes. With mixer running, gradually sprinkle in granulated sugar and continue to whip until stiff, glossy peaks form, about 5 minutes.
4. Using a rubber spatula, fold about one-quarter of egg whites into egg yolk mixture. Pour yolk mixture over remaining whites; fold carefully, trying not to deflate mixture. Sprinkle cornstarch mixture over top and fold together just until incorporated.
5. Using an offset spatula, spread batter evenly onto prepared pan. Bake in preheated oven until light brown and top springs back when lightly touched, 12 to 14 minutes.
6. Dust a clean, lint-free towel liberally with confectioner's sugar. Turn cake over onto towel. Peel off parchment paper. Starting at one short end, roll cake up in towel and let rest in towel on a wire rack until completely cool, about 20 minutes. Unroll cake and fill it with about ½ cup (125 mL) of desired filling, such as berry preserves or frosting. Roll up carefully and transfer to a platter. If desired, decorate outside with 1 cup (250 mL) of frosting, such as French Buttercream Frosting (page 227), Fresh Lemon Frosting (page 230), Milk Chocolate Frosting (page 232).

French Chocolate Buttercream and Fresh Lemon Frosting

Frostings, Glazes & More

Frostings, Icings and Glazes

What's the difference? A frosting and icing are the same thing with a different name. Most Americans use the word "frosting," while Europeans tend to use "icing." Glazes are what the name implies — light sugar coatings, sometimes see-through, for cakes and breads.

Decorating Cakes

Most home bakers try to do too much in one day. Bake your cake layers and decorate the whole thing an hour before the birthday party. I do not know why people think that if cake is not made that day, it's not fresh. I worked at a bakery where every customer would ask, "Is that fresh?" Our set answer was, "We bake fresh daily." Now, we did bake fresh daily — but we didn't tell the customers what.

It's tricky to create a perfect-looking and -tasting cake if you attempt to bake and decorate it all in one day. So plan your cake baking. Day 1: Bake cake layers and freeze them. Day 2: Make frosting or icing and decorate cake layers right out of freezer. They will be much easier to decorate than when freshly baked and soft. By the time you cut the cake it will be the perfect temperature.

The amount of frosting or icing you'll need for decorating will depend on how thick you like it and how much detail you want to add. As a general guideline, you'll need 2 to 3 cups (500 to 750 mL) to fill and frost one 9-inch (23 cm) two-layer cake. You'll need about 2 cups (500 mL) to decorate 12 cupcakes.

Icing Cakes

1. With a spatula and using a good amount of frosting, start plastering it on sides of the layers, all the way around the cake.

2. Then smooth the frosting with spatula around the entire cake.
3. You can then use a cake comb or the edge of a serrated knife to design the sides.

4. Now take an offset spatula and smooth the edges into center of cake. You may need more frosting.

Glazing Cakes

Every holiday season a few or more of those intricate-design tube cake pans come onto the market. I think I have all of them. I am a nut for a three-dimensional cake pan. I see so many people just sprinkle sugar on top. You can do so much more with a poured glaze. Most chocolate glazes need to be warm so they pour and adhere to the cake. To avoid a mess in the kitchen, and also to save the glaze for another use, follow these easy steps:

1. Take a baking sheet and place on counter.
2. Place a cooling rack on the top of the sheet, making sure it fits without overhang.
3. Invert cooling rack on the top of cake in the pan. Invert cake and pan onto the rack so the top of the cake is now the bottom. Place rack and cake on baking sheet. Remove cake pan.
4. Now you can glaze your cake. All of the excess glaze will fall onto the baking sheet. If sheet is clean you can scrape the glaze up and reuse or save for another use.

Brown Sugar Meringue Icing

MAKES ABOUT 2 CUPS (500 ML)

For a rich meringue to top pies or a cake, try this icing.

Tips

Make sure your mixer bowl and whip are clean and free of any grease or oil to be sure the egg whites will whip properly.

Caution: This recipe contains uncooked egg whites. If the food safety is a concern for you, use pasteurized egg whites or avoid this recipe.

- Blowtorch

3	egg whites	3
1½ cups	packed brown sugar, sifted	375 mL
½ cup	sweetened flaked coconut	125 mL

1. In a mixer bowl fitted with whip attachment, whip egg whites on medium-high speed to soft peaks, about 4 minutes. With mixer running on low speed, gradually add brown sugar by spoonfuls into whites. Increase speed to high and whip until stiff peaks form. Fold in coconut by hand.
2. Spread meringue on item you are icing. Using a blowtorch, brown meringue to desired brownness.

Uses

- Key Lime Pie (page 132)
- Lemon Curd Tarts (page 144)
- Lemon Meringue Pie (page 133)

Petit Four Glaze

MAKES ABOUT 1 CUP (250 ML)

Simple and perfect to glaze little cakes for a brunch.

Tip

Tint only with pastel colors. Darker colors on cakes and petit fours tend to look unreal and inedible.

2 cups	confectioner's (icing) sugar	500 mL
2 tbsp	water	25 mL
2 tbsp	light corn syrup	25 mL
½ tsp	almond extract	2 mL

1. In a saucepan, melt confectioner's sugar, water, corn syrup and almond extract over medium heat, whisking until smooth and well blended, about 3 minutes. If necessary, add hot water, a few drops at a time, until proper pouring consistency.

Uses

- Petit Fours (Variations, page 219)

Buttercream Frosting

MAKES ABOUT 2 CUPS (500 ML)

The food processor makes the creamiest and smoothest frostings! You don't even have to sift the confectioner's sugar.

Tips

If you would like to use this as a glaze you can add additional milk to thin the texture.

For a stiffer frosting add additional confectioner's sugar after adding milk.

Variations

Add 1 cup (250 mL) toasted sweetened coconut flaked for a flavorful frosting.

Use the same amount of vanilla in place of almond extract for a vanilla buttercream.

½ cup	unsalted butter, softened, cut into cubes	125 mL
3½ cups	confectioner's (icing) sugar	875 mL
¼ cup	milk, preferably whole	50 mL
2 tsp	almond extract	10 mL

1. In work bowl of a food processor fitted with metal blade, process butter until smooth, about 30 seconds. Scrape down bowl. Add confectioner's sugar and process until it just begins to gather, about 15 seconds. With motor running, drizzle milk and almond extract through the feed tube and process until smooth, about 30 seconds.

Uses

- Banana Cake (page 176)
- Carrot Cake (page 177)
- Hummingbird Cake (page 180)
- Marble Layer Cake (page 178)
- Orange Crunch Cake (page 181)
- Red Velvet Cake (page 186)
- Rich Chocolate Chip Fudge Cake (page 182)
- Strawberry Layer Cake (page 183)
- Tart Lemon Cake (page 184)
- White Layer Cake (page 185)
- Yellow Cake (page 187)
- Yellow Cupcakes (page 218)

Chocolate Cream Cheese Icing

MAKES ABOUT 2 CUPS (500 ML)

This is the richest icing I know. Use high-quality chocolate for best results.

6 oz	unsweetened chocolate, chopped	175 g
4 oz	bittersweet chocolate, chopped	125 g
4 oz	cream cheese, softened	125 g
2 cups	confectioner's (icing) sugar	500 mL
1/4 cup	milk, preferably whole	50 mL
1 1/2 tbsp	unsalted butter, softened	22 mL
1 tsp	vanilla extract	5 mL

1. In a heatproof bowl set over a saucepan of simmering water, melt unsweetened and bittersweet chocolate, stirring until smooth. Let cool slightly.
2. In work bowl of a food processor fitted with metal blade, process cream cheese and melted chocolates for 10 seconds. Add confectioner's sugar and process for another 15 seconds. With motor running, add milk, butter and vanilla through feed tube and process until smooth, about 45 seconds.
3. Transfer to a bowl. If icing is too loose, chill in the refrigerator until firm enough to spread.

Uses

- Marble Layer Cake (page 178)
- Rich Chocolate Chip Fudge Cake (page 182)
- Simple Vanilla Cupcakes (page 215)
- White Layer Cake (page 185)
- Yellow Cake (page 187)
- Yellow Cupcakes (page 218)

Cream Cheese Icing

MAKES ABOUT 3 CUPS (750 ML)

This rich icing has so many uses (see suggestions, below right).

1	package cream cheese (8 oz/250 g), softened	1
½ cup	unsalted butter, softened	125 mL
1 tsp	vanilla extract	5 mL
2 lbs	confectioner's (icing) sugar (about 8 cups/2 L), sifted	1 kg

1. In a mixer bowl fitted with paddle attachment, beat cream cheese and butter until smooth, about 5 minutes. Beat in vanilla. Gradually add confectioner's sugar, mixing on low speed until it gathers, about 2 minutes. Increase speed and beat until very fluffy, for 4 minutes. If icing is too stiff add a few drops of water.

Uses

- Banana Cake (page 176)
- Carrot Cake (page 177)
- Hummingbird Cake (page 180)
- Red Velvet Cake (page 186)

Espresso Chocolate Glaze

MAKES ABOUT 2 CUPS (500 ML)

This milk chocolate glaze turns very dark and glossy when you use it on cakes.

¾ cup	whipping (35%) cream	175 mL
3 tbsp	instant espresso powder	45 mL
1 tbsp	light corn syrup	15 mL
10 oz	milk chocolate, chopped	300 g

1. In a saucepan, bring cream to a boil over medium heat, about 4 minutes. Add espresso powder, corn syrup and milk chocolate. Remove from heat and stir until completely melted and smooth. Let cool slightly.
2. Pour over cooled cake or dip each cupcake into the glaze.

Uses

- Chocolate Cupcakes (page 212)
- Devil's Food Chocolate Cupcakes (page 213)
- Perfect Angel Food Cake (page 205)
- Simple Vanilla Cupcakes (page 215)

French Buttercream Frosting

MAKES ABOUT 2 CUPS (500 ML)

Light and creamy like whipped cream, yet sturdy enough to make detailed decorations.

Tips

If you overcook the sugar and add it to egg mixture you may have crunchy caramelized bits. If this happens, just add ½ cup (125 mL) chopped nuts into finished buttercream so you will not be able to tell if it is nuts or sugar.

If the sugar overcooks to the point it is dark in color, add 2 oz (60 g) cooled melted unsweetened chocolate after the butter and make it chocolate buttercream.

If your buttercream is still runny after the last step, it is likely you added the butter before the mixture was fully cool. To firm it up, place entire bowl with whip into refrigerator for 5 minutes, then re-whip.

- Candy thermometer or digital instant-read thermometer

1 cup	granulated sugar	250 mL
6 tbsp	water	90 mL
2	eggs	2
1 cup	unsalted butter, softened, cut into small pieces	250 mL

1. In a saucepan, cook sugar and water over medium heat, stirring until sugar is dissolved. Boil gently, without stirring, until temperature reaches 242°F (117°C) on a thermometer. Check to make sure sugar granules are not clinging to sides of pan. If there are, gently brush off with a wet pastry brush.
2. Meanwhile, in a mixer bowl fitted with whip attachment, beat eggs on high speed just until foamy.
3. Remove sugar syrup from heat, reduce mixer speed to low and gradually pour in syrup in a steady stream. Try not to pour syrup onto the whip as this will spray sugar onto sides of bowl and it will harden. After all sugar mixture has been added, increase speed to high and whip until mixture cools to room temperature, about 20 minutes. You can test this by touching bottom half of bowl.
4. With mixer running, add butter, a couple of pieces at a time, whipping until butter is incorporated and buttercream is fluffy and creamy, about 4 minutes.

Uses

- Banana Cake (page 176)
- Chocolate Jelly Roll (Variations, page 219)
- French Sponge Jelly Roll (page 219)
- Hazelnut Génoise (page 198)
- Hummingbird Cake (page 180)
- Lemon Cupcakes (page 216)
- Marble Layer Cake (page 178)
- Orange Crunch Cake (page 181)
- Red Velvet Cake (page 186)
- Rich Chocolate Chip Fudge Cake (page 182)
- Spring Easter Lemon Cake (page 412)

French Chocolate Buttercream Frosting

MAKES ABOUT 2 CUPS (500 ML)

This is not a rich chocolate frosting but more like a light chocolate whipped cream with the advantage of being more suited to detailed decorations.

Tips

If you overcook the sugar and add it to egg mixture you may have crunchy caramelized bits. If this happens, just add 1/2 cup (125 mL) chopped nuts into finished buttercream so you will not be able to tell if it is nuts or sugar.

If your buttercream is still runny after adding butter, it is likely you added the butter before the mixture was fully cool. To firm it up, place entire bowl with whip into refrigerator for 5 minutes, then re-whip.

Make sure that melted chocolate is completely cooled but still fluid before adding; otherwise it will warm up buttercream too much and make is soft.

- Candy thermometer or digital instant-read thermometer

1 cup	granulated sugar	250 mL
6 tbsp	water	90 mL
3	eggs	3
1 cup	unsalted butter, softened	250 mL
2 oz	unsweetened chocolate, melted and cooled (see Melting Chocolate, page 250)	60 g

1. In a saucepan, cook sugar and water over medium heat, stirring until sugar is dissolved. Boil gently, without stirring, until temperature reaches 242°F (117°C) on a thermometer. Check to make sure sugar granules are not clinging to sides of pan. If there are, gently brush off with a wet pastry brush.
2. Meanwhile, in a mixer bowl fitted with whip attachment, beat eggs on high speed just until foamy.
3. Remove sugar syrup from heat, reduce mixer speed to low and gradually pour in syrup in a steady stream. Try not to pour syrup onto the whip as this will spray sugar onto sides of bowl and it will harden. After all sugar mixture has been added, increase speed to high and whip until mixture cools to room temperature, about 20 minutes. You can test this by touching bottom half of bowl.
4. With mixer running, add butter, a couple of pieces at a time, whipping until butter is incorporated and buttercream is fluffy and creamy, about 4 minutes. Fold cooled chocolate into buttercream.

Uses

- Buche de Noël (Yule Log) (page 403)
- Christmas Raspberry Cake (page 405)
- Hazelnut Génoise (page 198)
- Marble Layer Cake (page 178)
- Rich Chocolate Chip Fudge Cake (page 182)
- White Layer Cake (page 185)
- Yellow Cake (page 187)

Fresh Lemon Frosting

MAKES ABOUT 3 CUPS (750 ML)

Tart yet fresh, this lemon frosting will make any citrus lover pucker up!

Tip

Frosting can be stored, covered, at room temperature for up to 48 hours. If you refrigerate frosting, let it stand at room temperature for 20 minutes. Whip again in mixer until light and fluffy.

⅓ cup	unsalted butter, softened	75 mL
2 tsp	grated lemon zest	10 mL
¼ cup	freshly squeezed lemon juice	50 mL
1½ tsp	vanilla extract	7 mL
4½ cups	confectioner's (icing) sugar, sifted	1.125 L

1. In a mixer bowl fitted with paddle attachment, cream butter until light and fluffy, about 4 minutes.
2. Add lemon zest and juice and vanilla and mix on low speed until incorporated, about 2 minutes. Gradually add confectioner's sugar, mixing on low speed, until it starts to blend into butter, about 2 minutes. Increase speed to high and whip until fluffy and light, about 4 minutes.

Uses

- Chocolate Jelly Roll (Variations, page 219)
- French Sponge Jelly Roll (page 219)
- Hazelnut Génoise (page 198)
- Lemon Cupcakes (page 216)
- Simple Vanilla Cupcakes (page 215)
- Tart Lemon Cake (page 184)
- White Layer Cake (page 185)
- Yellow Cake (page 187)

Lemon Glaze

MAKES ABOUT 2 CUPS (500 ML)

This glaze can jazz up cupcakes, cakes or muffins.

3 cups	confectioner's (icing) sugar	750 mL
2 tsp	grated lemon zest	10 mL
5 tbsp	freshly squeezed lemon juice	75 mL

1. In a medium bowl, whisk together sugar, lemon zest and juice until smooth.

Uses

- Lemon Cupcakes (page 216)
- Perfect Angel Food Cake (page 205)
- The Perfect Blueberry Muffins (page 350)

Island Frosting

MAKES ABOUT 2 CUPS (500 ML)

I use this frosting when the flavor of a cake calls for cream cheese with tropical-island flair.

1	package (8 oz/250 g) cream cheese, softened	1
¼ cup	unsalted butter, softened	50 mL
2 cups	confectioner's (icing) sugar, sifted	500 mL
1 tsp	vanilla extract	5 mL
½ cup	chopped pecans, toasted	125 mL
½ cup	sweetened flaked coconut, toasted	125 mL

1. In a mixer bowl fitted with paddle attachment, beat cream cheese and butter until smooth, for 3 minutes. Gradually add confectioner's sugar, mixing on low speed until it gathers, about 2 minutes. Increase speed to high and whip until fluffy, about 3 minutes. Fold in vanilla, pecans and coconut by hand.

Uses

- Carrot Cake (page 177)
- Hummingbird Cake (page 180)

Milk Chocolate Frosting

MAKES ABOUT 3 CUPS (750 ML)

Sweet chocolate icing — the perfect addition to chocolate, white or yellow cake layers.

Tip

Frosting can be stored, covered, at room temperature for up to 48 hours. If you refrigerate frosting, let it stand at room temperature for 20 minutes. Whip again in mixer until light and fluffy.

⅓ cup	unsalted butter, softened	75 mL
1½ tsp	vanilla extract	7 mL
4½ cups	confectioner's (icing) sugar	1.125 L
6 oz	milk chocolate, melted and cooled (see Melting Chocolate, page 250)	175 g

1. In a mixer bowl fitted with paddle attachment, cream butter and vanilla until light and fluffy, about 4 minutes.
2. Gradually add confectioner's sugar, mixing on low speed, until it starts to blend into butter, about 2 minutes. Increase speed to high and whip until fluffy and light, about 4 minutes. Decrease speed to low and drizzle in cooled milk chocolate. Increase speed to high and whip until fully blended, about 3 minutes.

Uses

- Chocolate Cupcakes (page 212)
- Chocolate Jelly Roll (Variation, page 219)
- Devil's Food Chocolate Cupcakes (page 213)
- French Sponge Jelly Roll (page 219)
- Marble Layer Cake (page 178)
- Red Velvet Cake (page 186)
- Rich Chocolate Chip Fudge Cake (page 182)
- Simple Vanilla Cupcakes (page 215)
- White Layer Cake (page 185)
- Yellow Cupcakes (page 218)

Old-Fashioned Chocolate Fudge Frosting

MAKES ABOUT 3 CUPS (750 ML)

My favorite cake includes this frosting and dark chocolate layers.

Tip

Frosting can be stored, covered, at room temperature for up to 48 hours. If you refrigerate frosting, let it stand at room temperature for 20 minutes. Whip again in mixer until light and fluffy.

1/3 cup	unsalted butter, softened	75 mL
1 1/2 tsp	vanilla extract	7 mL
1/2 tsp	chocolate extract	2 mL
4 1/2 cups	confectioner's (icing) sugar	1.125 L
10 oz	bittersweet chocolate, melted and cooled (see Melting Chocolate, page 250)	300 g

1. In a mixer bowl fitted with paddle attachment, cream butter, vanilla and chocolate extracts until light and fluffy, about 4 minutes.
2. Gradually add confectioner's sugar, mixing on low speed until it starts to blend into butter, about 2 minutes. Increase speed to high and whip until fluffy and light, about 4 minutes. Decrease speed to low and drizzle in cooled bittersweet chocolate. Increase speed to high and whip until fully blended, about 3 minutes.

Bittersweet Fudge Frosting

MAKES ABOUT 2 1/4 CUPS (550 ML)

When it's my birthday, the only cake I still want my Mom to make is a chocolate one with this frosting!

4 oz	bittersweet chocolate, chopped	125 g
1/2 cup	unsalted butter, softened, cut into cubes	125 mL
4 cups	confectioner's (icing) sugar	1 L
1 tsp	rum extract	5 mL

1. In a heatproof bowl set over a saucepan of simmering water, melt chocolate, stirring until smooth. Let cool slightly.
2. In work bowl of a food processor fitted with metal blade, process butter until smooth, about 30 seconds. Scrape down bowl. Add confectioner's sugar and process until it just begins to gather, about 15 seconds. With motor running, add chocolate and rum extract through the feed tube and process until smooth, about 30 seconds.

Orange Crunch Icing

MAKES ABOUT 2½ CUPS (625 ML)

This icing adds a zesty orange flavor to chocolate or vanilla cakes.

- Baking sheets, lined with parchment paper or Silpat
- Candy thermometer or digital instant-read thermometer

1½ cups	granulated sugar, divided	375 mL
6 tbsp	water	90 mL
2	eggs	2
1 cup	unsalted butter, softened	250 mL
1 tbsp	grated orange zest	15 mL
2 cups	sliced almonds	500 mL
1	egg white, beaten	1

1. In a saucepan, cook 1 cup (250 mL) of the sugar and water over medium heat, stirring until sugar is dissolved. Boil gently, without stirring, until temperature reaches 242°F (117°C) on a thermometer. Check to make sure sugar granules are not clinging to sides of pan. If there are, gently brush off with a wet pastry brush.
2. Meanwhile, in a mixer bowl fitted with whip attachment, beat eggs on high speed just until foamy.
3. Remove sugar syrup from heat, reduce mixer speed to low and gradually pour in syrup in a steady stream. Try not to pour syrup onto the whip as this will spray sugar onto sides of bowl and it will harden. After all sugar mixture has been added, increase speed to high and whip until mixture cools to room temperature, about 20 minutes. You can test this by touching bottom half of bowl.
4. With mixer running, add butter, a few pieces at a time, whipping until butter is incorporated and buttercream is fluffy and creamy, 4 minutes. Fold in orange zest by hand. Set aside.
5. Meanwhile, preheat oven to 350°F (180°C). In a bowl, combine almonds, egg white and remaining ½ cup (125 mL) sugar. Toss to coat evenly. Spread onto prepared baking sheet in a single layer. Bake in preheated oven until golden, 8 to 10 minutes, stirring almonds once or twice to bake evenly. Let cool completely. Fold into orange buttercream.

Uses

- Orange Crunch Cake (page 181)
- White Layer Cake (page 185)

Royal Icing

MAKES ABOUT 2 CUPS (500 ML)

Use this to create hard icing on gingerbread men and iced cookies.

Tip

Caution: This recipe contains uncooked egg whites. If the food safety is a concern for you, substitute pasteurized egg whites or replace whites with 2 tbsp (25 mL) meringue powder and ¼ cup (50 mL) additional water.

2	egg whites	2
4 cups	confectioner's (icing) sugar, sifted	1 L
5 tbsp	water	75 mL

1. In a mixer bowl fitted with whip attachment, whip egg whites, confectioner's sugar, and water on high speed until stiff peaks form, 7 to 10 minutes.
2. Cover icing bowl with a damp cloth immediately after whipping and while using, to prevent icing from drying.
3. *To store:* Place a wet paper towel on top of icing and place an airtight lid on top. Using a spoon, stir icing before use. If icing is too firm, stir in a few drops of water to loosen it.
4. *To color:* You can color icing with cake decorating colors. Use bold colors, as colors fade quickly as the icing dries.

Uses

- Gingerbread People (page 422)

Whipped Cream Cheese Frosting

MAKES ABOUT 4 CUPS (1 L)

This is a perfect whipped cream for icing cakes and pastry when you need to have it sit on a table for a while. Extra fat from cream cheese helps keep its shape.

6 oz	cream cheese, softened	175 g
2 tbsp	milk, preferably whole	25 mL
4 cups	whipping (35%) cream	1 L
1⅓ cups	confectioner's (icing) sugar	325 mL

1. In a mixer bowl fitted with whip attachment, beat cream cheese and milk until smooth, for 4 minutes. Gradually pour in whipping cream and sugar, mixing until blended. Beat on high speed until soft peaks form, about 6 minutes.

Uses

- Any cheesecake to use as decoration
- Banana Cake (page 176)
- Carrot Cake (page 177)
- Hummingbird Cake (page 180)
- Strawberry Layer Cake (page 183)

Meringues

There are three types of meringues, named for the country where each one originated: French, Swiss and Italian. Meringue is whipped foam of egg whites and sugar. It is how you introduce these ingredients and the heat that differentiates the meringues.

French Meringue

MAKES ABOUT 2 CUPS (500 ML)

This version is made by whipping raw egg whites with sugar.It has little stability and should be served soon after making.

8	egg whites	8
2 tsp	cream of tartar	10 mL
1 cup	granulated sugar	250 mL

1. In a mixer bowl fitted with whip attachment, whip egg whites and cream of tartar until frothy, about 4 minutes.
2. Gradually add sugar in a steady stream, mixing until incorporated. Increase speed to high and whip until stiff peaks form. For browning, see Tips, page 133.

Uses

- Lemon Meringue Pie (page 133)

Swiss Meringue

MAKES ABOUT 2 CUPS (500 ML)

Made by cooking raw egg whites and sugar and then whipping to incorporate air. It holds up very well and once dry is stable at room temperature.

- Candy thermometer or digital instant-read thermometer

1 cup	granulated sugar	250 mL
4	egg whites	4

1. In a mixer bowl set over a saucepan of simmering water, whisk together sugar and egg whites. Cook, whisking constantly, until temperature reaches 130°F (54°C) on a thermometer. Place bowl on mixer fitted with whip attachment and whip on high speed until stiff peaks form, about 5 minutes. For browning, see Tips, page 133.

Uses

- Angel Pie (page 293)

Italian Meringue

MAKES ABOUT 2 CUPS (500 ML)

Made by pouring boiling sugar syrup while whipping air into egg whites. After it dries completely it is very stable for many uses.

- Candy thermometer or digital instant-read thermometer

1⅓ cups	granulated sugar	325 mL
½ cup	water	125 mL
5	egg whites	5
¼ tsp	cream of tartar	1 mL
⅛ tsp	salt	0.5 mL

1. In a saucepan, heat sugar and water over medium-high heat, without stirring, until temperature reaches 234°F (112°C) on a thermometer.
2. Meanwhile, in a mixer bowl fitted with whip attachment, whip egg whites on low speed until foamy, about 1 minute. Add cream of tartar and salt and gradually increase speed to high. Beat until soft peaks form, about 3 minutes.
3. Remove sugar syrup from heat, reduce mixer speed to low and gradually drizzle in syrup in a steady stream. Try not to pour syrup onto the whip as this will spray sugar onto sides of bowl and it will harden. Increase speed to high and whip until mixture cools to room temperature and stiff peaks form, about 20 minutes. For browning, see Tip, page 133.

Uses

- Baked Alaska (page 295)

Seven-Minute Frosting

MAKES ABOUT 2 CUPS (500 ML)

This frosting was made famous in the 1950s. With the revolutionary new electric mixers, it would only take seven minutes of mixing to create a perfect light frosting.

Variation

Beat 3 oz (90 g) unsweetened chocolate, melted and cooled, with vanilla.

- Hand-held electric mixer

1½ cups	granulated sugar	375 mL
¼ tsp	cream of tartar	1 mL
⅛ tsp	salt	0.5 mL
⅓ cup	water	75 mL
2	egg whites	2
1½ tsp	vanilla extract	7 mL

1. In the top of a double boiler or a heatproof bowl, using hand-held electric mixer, whip sugar, cream of tartar, salt, water and egg whites on high speed for 1 minute. Place over saucepan of boiling water over medium heat, being sure that boiling water does not touch bottom of top pan. Beat on high speed until very light and fluffy, for 7 minutes. Beat in vanilla. Let cool.

Uses

- Banana Cake (page 176)
- Carrot Cake (page 177)
- Hummingbird Cake (page 180)
- Red Velvet Cake (page 186)
- Strawberry Layer Cake (page 183)

Classic Whipped Cream

MAKES ABOUT 1 CUP (250 ML)

Use this classic topping on almost any cheesecake or cake.

Variation

Ginger Whipped Cream: Add ½ tsp (2 mL) ground ginger to the cream after the sugar.

½ cup	whipping (35%) cream	125 mL
2 tbsp	granulated sugar	25 mL

1. In a well-chilled mixer bowl fitted with whip attachment or with a hand-held mixer, whip cream on medium-high speed until soft peaks form. With mixer running, sprinkle sugar into cream and continue whipping until firm peaks form.

White Cherry Buttercream Frosting

MAKES ABOUT 3 CUPS (750 ML)

This frosting makes any cake look completed when iced.

¾ cup	unsalted butter, softened	175 mL
1½ lbs	confectioner's (icing) sugar (6 cups/1.5 L)	750 g
¼ cup	drained maraschino cherries, finely chopped	50 mL
2 tsp	vanilla extract	10 mL
2 to 5	drops hot water, optional	2 to 5

1. In a mixer bowl fitted with paddle attachment, cream butter until fluffy, for 3 minutes. Gradually add confectioner's sugar, mixing on low speed until it gathers, about 4 minutes. Increase speed to high and beat until fluffy, about 3 minutes. Beat in cherries and vanilla. If frosting is too thick, add a few drops of hot water to thin it out.

Uses

- Simple Vanilla Cupcakes (page 215)
- White Layer Cake (page 185)

Banana Crème Crêpe Filling

MAKES ABOUT 2 CUPS (500 ML)

Crêpes filled with bananas are a treat for everyone.

1 cup	whipping (35%) cream	250 mL
2 tbsp	rum	25 mL
1	package (8 oz/250 g) cream cheese, softened	1
¼ cup	confectioner's (icing) sugar	50 mL
4	ripe bananas, thinly sliced	4

1. In a mixer bowl fitted with whip attachment, whip cream until soft peaks form, about 3 minutes. Fold in rum.
2. In another bowl, blend together cream cheese and confectioner's sugar until smooth. Stir in bananas. Fold whipped cream into banana mixture.

Uses

- Dessert Crêpes (page 301)

Chocolate Ganache

MAKES ABOUT 2 CUPS (500 ML)

This is one of the most useful items in a pastry kitchen other than a mixer! You can use it for icing a cake, dipping strawberries, molding into truffles and more.

8 oz	semisweet chocolate, finely chopped	250 g
1½ tsp	unsalted butter	7 mL
1 cup	whipping (35%) cream	250 mL

1. Place chocolate and butter in a large heatproof bowl. Set aside.
2. In a saucepan, bring cream to a full boil over medium heat, without stirring, about 4 minutes. Once it starts to climb up sides of pan, remove from heat and pour over chocolate. Let stand for 2 minutes, undisturbed. Whisk mixture until chocolate is completely melted and ganache is smooth. (If chocolate does not melt after adding hot cream, place bowl over a saucepan of hot, not boiling, water and heat, stirring, until melted.)

Fresh Raspberry Sauce

MAKES ABOUT 2 CUPS (500 ML)

This sauce is a staple in all pastry kitchens as well as my own. You can create many desserts with it. Fold into whipped cream for a mousse, use as a topping on ice cream or drizzle on warm chocolate brownies.

Tip

You can use frozen berries that have been individually quick frozen and not packed in sugar syrup. Just make sure you thaw out the berries before using.

2½ cups	fresh raspberries	625 mL
½ cup	granulated sugar	125 mL
2 tbsp	cornstarch	25 mL
¼ cup	cold water	50 mL
¼ cup	raspberry liqueur	50 mL
2 tsp	freshly squeezed lemon juice	10 mL

1. In a saucepan, heat berries and sugar over medium heat until they begin to boil, 3 to 5 minutes.
2. Remove from heat and using a fine mesh strainer, strain seeds from the mixture. (You can keep the seeds in, if you desire.) Return juice to heat and bring to a boil.
3. Meanwhile, in a small bowl, blend cornstarch and cold water to make a milky substance. Pour into boiling juice and whisk to incorporate. Heat until berry juice is no longer cloudy, the color is ruby red and thickened. Remove from heat. Add raspberry liqueur and lemon juice and whisk to incorporate. Let cool completely before storing in a covered container in the refrigerator for up to 1 week.

French Pastry Cream

MAKES ABOUT 3 CUPS (750 ML)

The essence of vanilla will fill your home with sweet smells. This is a staple in a pastry kitchen.

Tip

Whole (homogenized) milk is essential for this recipe. Lower-fat milk will not give the desired smooth, velvety texture and is likely to curdle.

Variations

Mocha: Dilute 1 tbsp (15 mL) instant coffee granules in 1 tsp (5 mL) of hot water and whisk into hot pastry cream.

Raspberry: Whisk in 2 tbsp (25 mL) of raspberry liqueur to hot pastry cream.

Rum: Whisk in 2 tbsp (25 mL) of rum to hot pastry cream.

Chocolate: Whisk in 2 oz (60 g) finely chopped unsweetened chocolate to hot pastry cream.

Vanilla Bean: Replace extract with 1 vanilla bean, split and scraped; add seeds and pod to milk in Step 1. Remove pod at end of Step 3.

1¾ cups + 2 tbsp	whole milk, divided	450 mL
1 tsp	vanilla extract	5 mL
1 cup	granulated sugar	250 mL
2 tbsp	cornstarch	25 mL
5	eggs	5

1. In a heavy saucepan, bring 1½ cups (375 mL) of the milk and vanilla to a boil over medium heat.
2. In a large bowl, whisk together sugar and cornstarch. Set aside.
3. In another bowl, whisk together remaining milk and eggs. Gradually pour into sugar mixture, whisking until blended. Gradually pour egg mixture into saucepan, whisking until blended. Cook over medium heat, whisking constantly, until it thickens and coats the back of a spoon, about 10 minutes. Transfer to a bowl, cover surface directly with plastic wrap and let cool completely.
4. *To store:* Pour hot pastry cream onto a rimmed baking sheet (to cool faster), place plastic wrap directly on the surface and let cool to room temperature. Transfer to an airtight container and refrigerate for up to 2 days.

Port Wine Berry Sauce

MAKES ABOUT 3 CUPS (750 ML)

Such an easy sauce, and so tasty too! Serve on top of the Tri-Berry Cheesecake for an added berry punch *(see recipe, page 175)**.*

Tip

To make superfine sugar, sometimes called instant-dissolving or berry sugar, from granulated sugar, place the amount called for into a food processor and process for 2 minutes.

1½ lbs	fresh berries, such as strawberries, raspberries, blackberries and/or blueberries (about 6 cup/1.5 L)	750 g
½ cup	superfine sugar (see Tip, left)	125 mL
¼ cup	aged port	50 mL

1. Place berries in a large bowl. Pour sugar and port on top and toss. Let stand for 30 minutes or for up to 1 day prior to use for flavors to develop. Keep in the refrigerator until needed. The berry sauce will keep as long as the berries are fresh, for 1 to 4 days.

Vanilla Cinnamon Sauce

MAKES ABOUT 2 CUPS (500 ML)

This sauce can be used on top of a cake, apple strudel or torte or to dip fruits with fondue.

Tips

To make sure ice cream is good quality, the container should feel heavy for its size and cream should be the first ingredient listed.

This recipe doubles easily for a party.

¼ cup	unsalted butter, softened	50 mL
1 cup	good-quality vanilla ice cream (see Tip, left)	250 mL
1 cup	packed brown sugar	250 mL
½ cup	confectioner's (icing) sugar	125 mL
1½ tsp	ground cinnamon	7 mL
¼ cup	dark rum	50 mL

1. In a saucepan, melt butter and vanilla ice cream over low heat. Add brown sugar, confectioner's sugar and cinnamon and cook, whisking, until smooth. Whisk in rum. Serve warm.

Tiger Swirl Fudge

Confections

Fudges

Confections

Confections

When I retire, I may think about opening a confectionery. When I walk the streets of Belgium and Paris I gaze at the windows full of candies, confections and truffles and imagine the wonderful flavors waiting to be enjoyed. Some of us cannot have the most expensive car, house or toys — but we can all eat a high-quality chocolate confection once in a while.

A colleague, Alice Medrich of the famed Cocolat of San Francisco, brought truffles to America in the form of two-bite-size confections. Another colleague, Elaine Gonzalez, introduced the masses to tempering chocolate with her perfect timing and technique. In this chapter I will teach you the art of making fine confections just like these professionals do.

I think many home cooks do not try sugar-based confections because they think it's a hard technique to master and they are timid and afraid of failing. And truthfully, sometimes the candy gods are not with us and your sugar will harden unexpectedly while you're cooking it. But think about it — it's only sugar and, sometimes, water. Unlike cakes, with candy making you don't have too much invested in ingredients, so go ahead and try it!

Confection Ingredients

SUGARS

Look for only cane sugars, as beet sugars have larger sugar crystals and produce grainy syrups.

CHOCOLATES

I tend to use Belgian, French and some artisanal American chocolates. Be sure to use the specific type of chocolate called for in the recipes. For more on chocolates, see page 14.

LIQUEURS

Watch your measurements on liqueurs — even one extra spoonful can result in a curdled confection. Check out the "pastry liqueurs," below, for the liqueurs that work best.

PASTRY (SWEET) LIQUEURS

You can change the flavors in buttercreams, cakes and confections by exchanging the liqueur called for in the recipe with another. Make sure you use the same amount called for. You can also substitute any liquor called for in a recipe with the same amount of a liqueur. Try to stay away from Schnapps as the flavors become watered down in baking after cooking. Here's a sampling of liqueurs that work best in sweets:

- Amaretto (made from apricot pits, not almonds)
- Chambord (black raspberry)
- Cointreau (tangerine/orange flavor)
- Cream sherry (a thick, sweet, fortified aged wine)
- Frangelico (hazelnut flavor)
- Grand Marnier (orange flavor)
- Irish Cream (creamy mint flavor)
- Kahlua (coffee flavor)
- Kirsch (cherry flavor)
- Rum
- Sambuca (light anise flavor)
- Tia Maria (rum-based coffee liqueur)

Tools

It is very important to use high-quality tools for candy making.

SUGAR POT

You sometimes see copper pots in a candy-making supply store, but copper isn't necessarily the best for making perfect candies (though it does conduct heat best). I did purchase one on my first trip to Paris in 1992, but I have yet to use it. Instead, I use a heavy-bottomed 4-quart (3.7 L) stainless saucepan (mine is All-Clad). The heavy bottom is what is most important in candy making.

CANDY THERMOMETERS

I have seen little thermometers with a paper gauge inside a glass tube with mercury that rises to tell you the temperature. I'm not sure how accurate these are; instead I suggest a digital instant-read thermometer. I use the same type that I use for meat, in fact. I can get accurate readings within 1°F (0.17°C). Make sure you calibrate your thermometer occasionally. Test it by placing in a container of boiling water; if you are at sea level the thermometer should read 212°F (100°C).

CHOCOLATE CHIPPER

This looks like an ice pick with six prongs and chops large blocks of chocolate more easily than using a knife (which gets dull from chopping chocolate).

HEATPROOF SPATULAS

Wooden spoons absorb moisture and flavors from other foods that can ruin delicate foods. So use a spatula made from heatproof rubber or silicone to stir chocolates and confections.

DOUBLE BOILER

I don't own a double boiler per se. I make my own using a heatproof stainless steel bowl set over a 4-quart (3.7 L) saucepan that is about half-full of boiling water. Make sure the bottom of the bowl sits snugly on top of the pan and doesn't touch the water. Most commercial double boilers have a "lip" and you can lose about 3 oz (90 g) of chocolate because it clings to the lip. It is impossible to clean it out with a spatula and it's too far down to lick it out. So I say, make your own.

KITCHEN TIMER

An electronic digital timer is the best method to keep track of the precise boiling times that are important in candy making.

Sugar Stages

Unlike a bulky thermometer that just has a printed gauge that says hard ball, soft ball, etc., for the stages of the cooked syrup, you

Temperature	Stage	When dropped into ice water
223°F–234°F (106°C–112°C)	Thread	Syrup forms a soft thread.
234°F–240°F (112°C–116°C)	Soft Ball	Syrup forms a soft ball that flattens upon removal from water.
242°F–248°F (117°C–120°C)	Firm Ball	Syrup forms a firm ball that does not flatten upon removal from water.
250°F–265°F (121°C–129°C)	Hard Ball	Syrup forms a hard ball that is hard enough to hold its shape yet is pliable.
270°F–290°F (132°C–143°C)	Soft Crack	Syrup separates into threads that are hard yet still pliable. You will also notice the color changing to amber.
300°F–310°F (150°C–154°C)	Hard Crack	Syrup separates into threads that are hard and brittle. You will also notice the color changing to light brown.

can view a digital thermometer to the exact degree. See page 246 for a chart about sugar stages. Sometimes you want a soft texture, such as for fudge, sometimes a harder, such as for caramel.

If your thermometer stops working — you dropped it off the counter, for example — you can do a manual test to determine the sugar stage instead. Set out a glass of ice-cold water beside the stove. When you think the candy may be close to the right temperature, drop a spoonful of your boiling liquid into the water. Wait a few seconds and check the hardened syrup. When the hot syrup does what the chart says, the candy has reached the temperature that corresponds with the described stage.

Fudge

Because of the chemistry involved in fudge and confection making, I recommend making only a single batch at a time. If you need more than one recipe yields, make additional batches separately. It may seem more time-consuming, but doubling recipes can lead to disaster.

Humid conditions also affect candy making. I suggest you stay away from making a batch of fudge or confections on a humid day.

STORING FUDGE

My grandmother made fudge every year. She would make two kinds: dark chocolate, with and without walnuts. After the fudge was completely cool, she would wrap each piece in plastic wrap, being sure to cover all sides. Have you ever seen those fudge counters in tourist areas? They usually have an array of flavors, all open to the air. When they give you a sample, it's generally dried out and brittle. Good fudge shouldn't be treated this way! As soon as you cut a pan of fudge, the candy is exposed to air, which dries it out. That's why you should do what my grandmother was wise to do back in 1955. Wrap it well.

Never refrigerate your fudge to cool it or it will loose its sheen and become dry. Be sure to let it cool slowly at room temperature for the best texture. When wrapped properly, fudge should keep at room temperature for up to 1 month.

Tempering Chocolate

Walking the exhibit floor at a bakery convention in Las Vegas with one of my favorite chocolate goddesses, Elaine Gonzalez, we came upon a French-speaking chef who was going to create something with chocolate. He started to temper it — 20 minutes passed, then 45. I looked at Elaine and said, "You know, you should step in and show him how Americans do it." She said she wouldn't dare, and by the time we left the show, the chocolate still wasn't in temper. With the French there is only one way to do something, the classic way, and never another.

I think home confectioners are afraid of tempering chocolate because of the old, drawn-out methods. Here I will show you a method similar to Elaine's. It's much easier and faster than the traditional way.

Have you ever had a chocolate candy bar that had melted so you put it in the refrigerator or freezer? Later, when you unwrap it, you see a white powdery substance on the chocolate, and it looks old. It's fine — it's just out of temper.

What is tempering?
The stabilization of cocoa butter crystals in chocolate.

Why do we have to temper chocolate?
To make a bar of chocolate "snap" rather than crumble when you break it. It also makes the

coating on a truffle look wonderful, helps chocolate set faster and creates a glossy sheen on chocolate garnishes.

How can I tell if my chocolate is not in temper? You get a bloom (white streaks) on the chocolate.

Chocolate manufacturers always send their chocolate bars into market properly tempered. But when you want to change the shape and use chocolate to make confections, you'll need to melt it, and that will take it out of temper. Look at the chocolate block you are going to temper. Does it shine? Is there any "blooming" effect? Then you're set to go. If there is a bloom, the chocolate may have encountered temperatures that were too warm during shipping or storage. If you have bloom on your chocolate you will have to temper it using chunks of tempered chocolate (without any bloom) to cool down the melted chocolate.

If you have a truffle or bon bon that has bloomed you cannot save the candy. It is still edible but not very good-looking. I suggest you roll it in sifted unsweetened cocoa powder to hide the bloom.

When do I need to use tempered chocolate? If you are making a candy that you want to have a shine and perfect-looking coating you will need to temper the chocolate. Dark chocolates are much easier to temper than white chocolate or milk chocolate, as the latter two have so many milk solids. For your first try, I suggest you use dark chocolate.

DARK CHOCOLATE TEMPERING

You'll need a digital thermometer and a large heatproof bowl that fits snugly on top of a saucepan to act as a double boiler.

Start with 1½ lbs (750 g) of dark (semisweet or bittersweet) chocolate. After dipping your candies, any extra tempered chocolate can be cooled and stored in an airtight container at cool room temperature to be used another time.

1. Finely chop 1 lb (500 g) of the chocolate and place in heatproof bowl. Cut remaining 8 oz (250 g) into 3 chunks; set aside. Bring water to a boil in saucepan. Remove from heat and place bowl of chopped chocolate on top, making sure the bottom of the bowl doesn't touch the water. Let stand, allowing the steam to melt the chocolate. When the temperature reaches 115°F (46°C) on a thermometer, remove bowl from saucepan. Using a spatula, stir chocolate until it cools to 100°F (38°C). Add the reserved chunks to the melted chocolate, folding them into the chocolate over and over until bowl feels cool. When the temperature drops below 90°F (32°C), it is time to test the chocolate. Remove any larger pieces of unmelted chocolate from the melted chocolate and save them to melt for a later project.
2. *To test if chocolate is in temper*: Smear a thin patch of chocolate on a sheet of parchment paper and place in refrigerator for 5 minutes. It should be dry to the touch and glossy-looking. If not, stir a 3 oz (90 g) chunk of tempered chocolate into the bowl of melted chocolate to cool it down a bit more. Repeat the test again.

WHITE AND MILK CHOCOLATE TEMPERING

The same method as above, but you only need to warm the chocolate to 110°F (43°C) and then cool it to 88°F (31°C).

Melting Chocolate

The word "chocolate" puts a smile on most people's faces. It brings pleasure to the senses: the decadent aroma, and the flavor, of course, and the velvety texture as it melts in your mouth. High-quality chocolate is one of the only ingredients that melts at body temperature (98.6°F/37°C), giving us that unparalleled experience.

Because of chocolate's delicate nature, I never use the microwave to melt my chocolate, as just a few seconds too long can scorch it and then it is ruined. Chocolate and butter are the most expensive ingredients in candy making, so you can't afford failure. Plus, I enjoy watching the chocolate melt and smelling the aroma wafting from the bowl. I do melt small quantities of unsweetened chocolate in the microwave, however, as it does not have sugars and milk solids to burn.

Have you ever tried to melt milk or white chocolate over a double boiler and it did not melt, it just became harder? You burned and dried it out. If chocolate melts at body temperature, why do we need a double boiler over boiling water at 212°F (100°C)? Here's how you should melt chocolates:

MILK AND WHITE CHOCOLATE

Finely chop chocolate and place in a heatproof stainless steel bowl that fits snugly on the top of a saucepan. Bring water to a boil in saucepan. Remove from heat and place bowl of chopped chocolate on top, making sure the bottom of the bowl doesn't touch the water. Let stand, allowing the steam to melt the chocolate. When it is almost melted, stir until smooth. The finer you chop the chocolate, the faster it will melt.

DARK CHOCOLATE (SEMISWEET AND BITTERSWEET)

Finely chop chocolate and place in a heatproof stainless steel bowl that fits snugly on the top of a saucepan. Bring water to a boil in saucepan. Reduce heat to lowest possible setting so that the water just ripples. Place bowl of chopped chocolate on top. When it is almost melted, stir until smooth. The finer you chop the chocolate, the faster it will melt.

Packaging Confections

Nothing makes your confections "pop" more than packaging. For a number of years, I would package my French Bittersweet Truffles in black boxes with bright red or gold ribbon and the candy cups were always gold. The presentation made a dramatic statement. Yours should too. Check Sources on page 442 to help find your own look.

Storing Candies

If I am not packaging my confections for gifts, I tend to keep my truffles and bon bons in an airtight container in the refrigerator until about an hour prior to serving to my guests. I never refrigerate fudge since the moisture from the refrigerator causes it to soften. Most candies will keep for several weeks. I tend to make chocolates for gift giving and holiday parties about 3 weeks before I need them.

Black and White Fudge

MAKES 48 PIECES

Chunks of white chocolate in a dark chocolate fudge make a great contrast — visually and in taste.

- 13-by 9-inch (3 L) metal baking pan, lined with foil, then parchment paper

18 oz	bittersweet chocolate, finely chopped	540 g
6 oz	milk chocolate, finely chopped	175 g
1¾ cups	marshmallow cream (fluff) (7 oz/198 g)	425 mL
4½ cups	granulated sugar	1.125 L
1⅔ cups	evaporated milk	400 mL
2 tbsp	unsalted butter, softened	25 mL
½ tsp	salt	2 mL
1 tbsp	vanilla extract	15 mL
8 oz	white chocolate, cut into chunks	250 g

1. In a mixer bowl fitted with paddle attachment, combine bittersweet chocolate, milk chocolate and marshmallow cream. Set aside.
2. In a saucepan, combine sugar, evaporated milk, butter and salt. Bring to a boil over medium heat, stirring constantly, about 4 minutes. Reduce heat to medium-low and cook, stirring constantly, and adjusting heat as necessary to keep mixture boiling steadily, for exactly 6 minutes. Remove from heat and gradually pour boiling syrup into chocolate mixture, mixing on low speed until chocolate is melted, about 2 minutes. Stir in vanilla and white chocolate chunks.
3. Pour into prepared pan, smoothing top. Let cool completely at room temperature until firm before cutting, about 2 hours. See storage information on page 248.

Chocolate Peanut Butter Fudge

MAKES 48 PIECES

The rich combination of chocolate and peanuts makes this fudge taste just like a candy bar.

- 13-by 9-inch (3 L) metal baking pan, lined with foil, then parchment paper

18 oz	bittersweet chocolate, finely chopped	540 g
1 cup	creamy peanut butter	250 mL
1¾ cups	marshmallow cream (fluff) (7 oz/198 g)	425 mL
4½ cups	granulated sugar	1.125 L
1⅔ cups	evaporated milk	400 mL
2 tbsp	unsalted butter, softened	25 mL
½ tsp	salt	2 mL
1 tbsp	vanilla extract	15 mL
1½ cups	chopped roasted peanuts (8 oz/250 g)	375 mL

1. In a mixer bowl fitted with paddle attachment, combine chocolate, peanut butter and marshmallow cream. Set aside.
2. In a saucepan, combine sugar, evaporated milk, butter and salt. Bring to a boil over medium heat, stirring constantly, about 4 minutes. Reduce heat to medium-low and cook, stirring constantly, and adjusting heat as necessary to keep mixture boiling steadily, for exactly 6 minutes. Remove from heat and pour boiling syrup into chocolate mixture, mixing on low speed until chocolate is melted, about 2 minutes. Stir in vanilla and peanuts.
3. Pour into prepared pan, smoothing top. Let cool completely at room temperature until firm before cutting, about 2 hours. See storage information on page 248.

Five-Minute Fudge

MAKES 16 PIECES

Really, this fudge takes less than five minutes to make, but no one will ever guess since it tastes so good.

- 8-inch (2 L) square baking pan, lined with foil, then parchment paper

12 oz	semisweet chocolate, cut into small pieces	375 g
1 cup	butterscotch chips (6 oz/175 g)	250 mL
1¾ cups + 2 tbsp	evaporated milk	450 mL
1 tsp	vanilla extract	5 mL

1. In a microwave-safe bowl, combine chocolate, butterscotch chips and evaporated milk. Microwave on High for 2 minutes or until it looks like it is just starting to melt. Stir in vanilla, stirring until mixture is melted and smooth.
2. Pour into prepared pan, smoothing top. Let cool completely at room temperature until set before cutting, about 1 hour. See storage information on page 248.

Milk Chocolate Fudge

MAKES 16 TO 18 PIECES

This fudge is slightly sweeter than a fudge made with dark chocolate but not quite as rich in flavor. It's perfect for milk chocolate fans.

- 9-inch (2.5 L) square baking pan, lined with foil, then parchment paper

1½ cups	granulated sugar	375 mL
⅔ cup	evaporated milk	150 mL
2 tbsp	unsalted butter, softened	25 mL
¼ tsp	salt	1 mL
2 cups	miniature marshmallows	500 mL
12 oz	milk chocolate, finely chopped	375 g
½ cup	toasted chopped pecans	125 mL
1 tsp	vanilla extract	5 mL

1. In a saucepan, combine sugar, evaporated milk, butter and salt. Bring to a full boil over medium heat, stirring constantly, 4 to 5 minutes. Remove from heat. Add marshmallows, chocolate, pecans and vanilla. Stir vigorously for 1 minute or until chocolate and marshmallows are completely melted.
2. Pour into prepared pan, smoothing top. Let cool completely at room temperature until firm before cutting, about 2 hours. See storage information on page 248.

Mocha Fudge

MAKES 16 PIECES

A hint of coffee in this rich fudge makes it a perfect addition to coffee time.

- Candy thermometer or digital instant-read thermometer
- 9-inch (2.5 L) square baking pan, lined with foil, then parchment paper

12 oz	semisweet chocolate, finely chopped	375 g
1 cup	marshmallow cream (fluff)	250 mL
½ cup	chopped toasted pecans	125 mL
2 tsp	instant espresso powder	10 mL
½ tsp	vanilla extract	2 mL
2 cups	granulated sugar	500 mL
¾ cup	evaporated milk	175 mL
¼ cup	unsalted butter	50 mL
⅛ tsp	salt	0.5 mL

1. In a bowl, combine chocolate, marshmallow cream, pecans, espresso powder and vanilla. Set aside.
2. In a saucepan, combine sugar, evaporated milk, butter and salt. Bring to a boil over medium heat, stirring constantly, just until sugar is completely dissolved, about 4 minutes. Cook, without stirring, until mixture reaches 236°F (113°C) on a thermometer, or Soft Ball stage. Remove from heat and immediately pour over chocolate mixture. Let stand for 2 minutes. Stir until melted and smooth.
3. Pour into prepared pan, smoothing top. Let cool completely at room temperature until firm before cutting, about 2 hours. See storage information on page 248.

Peppermint Fudge

MAKES 48 PIECES

A creamy chocolate fudge studded with peppermints adds a festive touch to a sweet tray.

- 13-by 9-inch (3 L) metal baking pan, lined with foil, then parchment paper

12 oz	bittersweet chocolate, finely chopped	375 g
12 oz	semisweet chocolate, finely chopped	375 g
1¾ cups	marshmallow cream (fluff) (7 oz/198 g)	425 mL
4½ cups	granulated sugar	1.125 L
1⅔ cups	evaporated milk	400 mL
2 tbsp	unsalted butter, softened	25 mL
½ tsp	salt	2 mL
1 tbsp	vanilla extract	15 mL
1 tsp	peppermint extract	5 mL
1 cup	chopped peppermint candies	250 mL

1. In a mixer bowl fitted with paddle attachment, combine bittersweet chocolate, semisweet chocolate and marshmallow cream. Set aside.
2. In a saucepan, combine sugar, evaporated milk, butter and salt. Bring to a boil over medium heat, stirring constantly, about 4 minutes. Reduce heat to medium-low and cook, stirring constantly, and adjusting heat as necessary to keep mixture boiling steadily, for exactly 6 minutes. Remove from heat and pour boiling syrup into chocolate mixture, mixing on low speed until chocolate is melted, about 2 minutes. Stir in vanilla and peppermint extracts and candies.
3. Pour into prepared pan, smoothing top. Let cool completely at room temperature until firm before cutting, about 2 hours. See storage information on page 248.

Rocky Road Chocolate Fudge

MAKES 18 PIECES

I'm not sure which came first, rocky road ice cream or fudge — regardless, they are both a decadent combination of chocolate, nuts and marshmallows.

- 9-inch (2.5 L) square pan, lined with foil, then parchment paper

1½ cups	granulated sugar	375 mL
⅔ cup	evaporated milk	150 mL
2 tbsp	unsalted butter, softened	25 mL
¼ tsp	salt	1 mL
2 cups	miniature marshmallows	500 mL
12 oz	semisweet chocolate, finely chopped	375 g
1 tsp	vanilla extract	5 mL
½ cup	toasted chopped walnuts	125 mL
½ cup	large marshmallows, cut in quarters	125 mL

1. In a saucepan, combine sugar, evaporated milk, butter and salt. Bring to a full boil over medium heat, stirring constantly, 4 to 5 minutes. Remove from heat and add miniature marshmallows, chocolate and vanilla. Stir vigorously for 1 minute or until chocolate and marshmallows are completely melted. Fold in quartered marshmallows and walnuts.
2. Pour into prepared pan, smoothing top. Let cool completely at room temperature until firm before cutting, about 2 hours. See storage information on page 248.

Tiger Swirl Fudge

MAKES 24 PIECES

This is the simplest fudge recipe I know.

- 17-by 11-inch (43 by 28 cm) rimmed baking sheet, lined with parchment paper

2 lbs	white chocolate, finely chopped	1 kg
½ cup	creamy peanut butter	125 mL
4 oz	bittersweet chocolate, finely chopped	125 g

1. In a bowl set over a saucepan of steaming, not boiling, water, melt white chocolate. Add peanut butter, stirring until blended and creamy. Pour onto prepared baking sheet. Smooth with offset spatula to edges of baking sheet.
2. In same bowl, set over lightly simmering water, melt bittersweet chocolate. Drizzle over white chocolate. Using the tip of a knife, swirl chocolates to create a marble effect. Refrigerate (this is an exception to the refrigeration rule) until firm, for 30 minutes. Break into pieces. Wrap carefully in plastic wrap and place in an airtight container and store in the refrigerator for up to 2 weeks.

Ohio Buckeyes

MAKES ABOUT 72 CANDIES

The state of Ohio treasures its own peanut butter candies called Buckeyes. You can find them in every store along Ohio highways, and now you can make them at home.

- #70 disher or scoop
- Baking sheet, lined with parchment paper or Silpat

2½ cups	creamy peanut butter (1 lb/500 g)	625 mL
1 cup	unsalted butter, softened	250 mL
5¼ cups	confectioner's (icing) sugar	1.3 L
12 oz	semisweet chocolate, finely chopped	375 g

1. In a mixer bowl fitted with paddle attachment, beat peanut butter, butter and sugar on low speed until blended and smooth, about 4 minutes. Scoop into balls, placing on prepared baking sheet. Refrigerate until firm, for 20 minutes.
2. Meanwhile, in a heatproof bowl set over a saucepan of hot, not boiling water, melt semisweet chocolate. Stir until smooth. Let cool slightly.
3. With a toothpick, pick up each ball and dip bottom two-thirds into melted chocolate. Place on prepared baking sheet. Let cool until set and dry. See storage information on page 250.

Academy Dark Truffles

MAKES ABOUT 5 LBS (2.5 KG), ABOUT 48 TRUFFLES

Rich chocolate scented with orange and almond liqueurs create a south-of-France favorite.

Tips

If time is a factor, you can stop after Step 2 and refrigerate for up to 3 weeks before proceeding with Step 3.

These truffles work best with a chocolate made of 70% cocoa liquor. A lower percentage chocolate may cause the filling to be a softer texture, making it tricky to shape.

- #100 disher or scoop
- Baking sheets, lined with parchment paper or Silpats

3¾ lbs	bittersweet chocolate, finely chopped, divided (see Tips, left)	1.875 kg
¾ cup	unsalted butter, softened	175 mL
¼ cup	orange-flavored liqueur	50 mL
¼ cup	almond-flavored liqueur	50 mL
1 tsp	vanilla extract	5 mL
2 cups	whipping (35%) cream	500 mL
¼ cup	unsweetened Dutch-process cocoa powder	50 mL

1. In a large bowl, combine 2¾ lbs (1.375 kg) bittersweet chocolate, butter, orange liqueur, almond liqueur and vanilla. Set aside.
2. In a saucepan, bring cream to a boil over medium heat. Pour over chocolate. Stir until chocolate is completely melted and mixture is smooth. Transfer truffle filling to a shallow dish and let cool at room temperature for 1 hour. Cover and refrigerate until firm, about 2 hours or overnight.
3. Temper remaining 1 lb (500 g) bittersweet chocolate according to directions on page 249. Let cool slightly.
4. Sift cocoa powder into a shallow dish. Scoop truffle filling into balls, placing on a prepared baking sheet. Roll each ball in cocoa powder, shaking off excess.
5. Dip each ball into tempered chocolate. Place on a clean prepared baking sheet. Let cool until set and dry. See storage information on page 250.

Beer Nuts

MAKES ABOUT 4½ CUPS (1.125 L)

Sweet, salty and crunchy, these are great for a topping on ice cream or in a dish at a party.

- Rimmed baking sheet, lined with parchment paper or Silpat

4½ cups	raw peanuts	1.125 L
2 cups	granulated sugar	500 mL
1 cup	water	250 mL
½ tsp	salt	2 mL
½ tsp	coarse salt	2 mL

1. In a saucepan, combine peanuts, sugar, water and salt. Bring to a boil over medium-high heat. Reduce heat and boil gently until all liquid is absorbed, 25 to 30 minutes.
2. Preheat oven to 300°F (150°C).
3. Spread peanuts on prepared baking sheet and sprinkle with coarse salt. Bake in preheated oven for exactly 20 minutes. Let cool completely on pan on a rack. Store in an airtight container at room temperature for up to 2 weeks.

Candied Almonds

MAKES ABOUT 1 CUP (250 ML)

I use these almonds as garnish on cakes, toppings for ice creams and just to snack on.

- Preheat oven to 400°F (200°C)
- Rimmed baking sheet, lined with parchment paper or Silpat

1 cup	sliced almonds	250 mL
2	egg whites, beaten	2
½ cup	granulated sugar	125 mL

1. In a large bowl, toss almonds with egg whites until evenly coated. Sprinkle with sugar and toss to coat. Spread out on prepared baking sheet in a single layer.
2. Bake in preheated oven until light brown, about 5 minutes. Stir and bake until almonds are an even light brown color, another 5 minutes. Let cool completely on pan on a rack. They will get crunchy as they dry. Store in an airtight container at room temperature for up to 2 weeks.

Caramel Turtles

MAKES 36 CANDIES

A nice platter of turtles will delight old and young.

- Baking sheet, lined with parchment paper or Silpat

12 oz	soft caramels	375 g
3 tbsp	whipping (35%) cream	45 mL
2 cups	pecan halves	500 mL
6 oz	semisweet chocolate, finely chopped	175 g

1. In a heatproof bowl set over a saucepan of simmering water, combine caramels and cream. Heat until caramels are melted. Stir until mixture is smooth. Let cool for 5 minutes.
2. On prepared baking sheet, arrange pecan halves in groups of three. Spoon about a teaspoon (5 mL) of melted caramel over each trio of nuts, trying to keep tops of pecans exposed. Let stand until set, for 30 minutes.
3. Meanwhile, temper semisweet chocolate according to directions on page 249. Drop a spoonful of tempered chocolate over caramel. Let stand until set, for 30 minutes. Store in an airtight container at room temperature for 2 weeks.

Chocolate Raspberry Bon Bons

MAKES ABOUT 36 CANDIES

A fresh raspberry is the center star of each of these tasty bon bons. They need to be eaten the day they are made, but that likely won't be a problem.

- #70 disher or scoop
- Baking sheet, ungreased

1½ cups	confectioner's (icing) sugar	375 mL
2 tbsp	unsweetened Dutch-process cocoa powder	25 mL
1½ cups	chocolate cookie crumbs	375 mL
1½ cups	coarsely ground pecans	375 mL
6 tbsp	liquid honey	90 mL
2 tbsp	raspberry-flavored liqueur	25 mL
36	fresh raspberries (approx.)	36

1. In a large bowl, sift together confectioner's sugar and cocoa. Stir in cookie crumbs, pecans, honey and raspberry liqueur, mixing until evenly moistened and sticking together.
2. Scoop mixture and wrap around a raspberry, placing on a baking sheet. Let stand until set and dry, for about 15 minutes. Cover and refrigerate for up to 6 hours.

Chocolate Rum Bon Bons

MAKES ABOUT 24 CANDIES

Make these about one week before you are going to eat them to allow the flavors to develop.

- #70 disher or scoop
- Baking sheet, ungreased

1 cup	confectioner's (icing) sugar	250 mL
2 tbsp	unsweetened Dutch-process cocoa powder	25 mL
1 cup	chocolate cookie crumbs	250 mL
1 cup	finely chopped pecans	250 mL
1⁄4 cup	corn syrup	50 mL
2 tbsp	pure maple syrup	25 mL
2 tbsp	rum	25 mL
1⁄2 cup	finely chopped toasted pecans	125 mL

1. In a large bowl, sift together confectioner's sugar and cocoa. Stir in cookie crumbs, untoasted pecans, corn syrup, maple syrup and rum, mixing until evenly moistened and sticking together.
2. Place toasted pecans in a shallow dish. Scoop mixture into balls and roll in toasted pecans. Place on a baking sheet and let air-dry for 1 hour. Transfer to an airtight container and store at room temperature for at least 1 week or for up to 3 weeks.

Cinnamon Truffles

MAKES ABOUT 24 TRUFFLES

A version of these rich candies is a staple in confection shops across France.

Tip

These truffles work best with a chocolate made of 70% cocoa liquor. A lower percentage chocolate may cause the filling to be a softer texture, making it tricky to shape.

- #100 disher or scoop
- Baking sheets, lined with parchment paper or Silpats

2 lbs	bittersweet chocolate, finely chopped, divided (see Tip, left)	1 kg
1 tbsp	unsalted butter, softened	15 mL
1 tbsp	ground cinnamon, divided	15 mL
2 cups	whipping (35%) cream	500 mL
½ cup	unsweetened Dutch-process cocoa powder, sifted	125 mL

1. In a bowl, combine 1 lb (500 g) of the chocolate, butter and 2 tsp (10 mL) of the cinnamon. Set aside.
2. In a saucepan, bring cream to a boil over medium heat, about 6 minutes. Pour over chocolate mixture. Stir until chocolate is completely melted and mixture is smooth. Transfer truffle filling to a shallow dish and let cool at room temperature for 1 hour. Cover and refrigerate until firm, about 2 hours or overnight.
3. Temper remaining 1 lb (500 g) chocolate according to directions on page 249.
4. In a shallow dish, combine remaining cinnamon and cocoa powder. Scoop truffle filling into balls, placing on a prepared baking sheet. Dip each ball into tempered chocolate, then roll wet truffle in cocoa mixture. Place on a clean prepared baking sheet. Let cool until set and dry. See storage information on page 250.

Raspberry Truffles

MAKES ABOUT 24 TRUFFLES

A wonderful raspberry flavor is hidden inside this dark, rich truffle.

- #100 disher or scoop
- Baking sheets, lined with parchment paper or Silpats

1 lb	semisweet chocolate, finely chopped	500 g
2 tsp	unsalted butter, softened	10 mL
1 tsp	raspberry-flavored liqueur	5 mL
3/4 cup	whipping (35%) cream	175 mL
1/4 cup	raspberry preserves or jam	50 mL
1 lb	bittersweet chocolate, finely chopped	500 g
2 tsp	red-colored coarse sugar	10 mL

1. In a bowl, combine semisweet chocolate, butter and raspberry liqueur. Set aside.
2. In a saucepan, bring cream to a boil over medium heat, about 6 minutes. Pour over chocolate mixture. Stir until chocolate is completely melted and mixture is smooth. Fold in preserves. Transfer truffle filling to a shallow dish and let cool at room temperature for 1 hour. Cover and refrigerate until firm, about 2 hours or overnight.
3. Temper bittersweet chocolate according to directions on page 249.
4. Scoop truffle filling into balls, placing on a prepared baking sheet. Dip each ball into tempered chocolate. Place on prepared baking sheet. Sprinkle red sugar on top while chocolate is still wet. Let cool until set and dry. Store in an airtight container in the refrigerator for up to 1 week.

English Toffee

MAKES ABOUT 1½ LBS (750 G)

If you can boil water you can make this toffee. It is that simple.

- Candy thermometer or digital instant-read thermometer
- Rimmed baking sheet, brushed with 2 tbsp (25 mL) melted butter

1½ cups	unsalted butter, softened	375 mL
2 cups	granulated sugar	500 mL
2 tbsp	water	25 mL
⅛ tsp	salt	0.5 mL
6 oz	semisweet chocolate, finely chopped	175 g
1 cup	ground toasted pecans	250 mL

1. In a heavy saucepan, melt butter over low heat, about 3 minutes. Add sugar, water and salt and cook, stirring, just until sugar is dissolved. Increase heat to medium-high and boil gently until temperature reaches 290°F (143°C) on a thermometer (Soft Crack stage). Immediately pour on prepared baking sheet, smoothing to edges. Set aside.
2. In a heatproof bowl set over a saucepan of gently simmering water, melt chocolate. Stir until smooth. Using an offset spatula, spread evenly over toffee. Sprinkle with nuts while chocolate is still wet.
3. Let cool on baking sheet until toffee is set and hard. Break it into pieces. Store in a tin, layered between waxed paper, at room temperature for up to 2 weeks.

Fast Peanut Brittle

MAKES ABOUT 1 LB (500 G)

Now that the novelty has worn off, many of us seem to only use the microwave to make popcorn and reheat drinks. Here is a fast and easy recipe from my good friend Randy Gooch of Virginia that takes advantage of the speedy microwave.

Tip

Do not double this recipe.

Variations

You can use macadamia or raw peanuts.

- Rimmed baking sheet, greased or lined with Silpat

1 cup	unsalted Spanish peanuts	250 mL
1 cup	granulated sugar	250 mL
½ cup	light corn syrup	125 mL
⅛ tsp	salt	0.5 mL
1 tsp	vanilla extract	5 mL
1 tsp	unsalted butter, softened	5 mL
1 tsp	baking soda	5 mL

1. In an 8-cup (2 L) glass measuring bowl with a handle, combine peanuts, sugar, syrup and salt. Microwave on High for 4 minutes. Stir well. Cook until it starts to turn a very light brown, 3 to 4 minutes longer. Watch closely to ensure it does not burn. Carefully add vanilla and butter (it will bubble up), stirring until butter is completely melted. Cook for another 2 minutes. Carefully add baking soda, stirring constantly until mixture is light and foamy.
2. Immediately pour mixture onto prepared baking sheet. Using an offset spatula, spread as thinly as possible. Let cool completely until set and hard, about 30 minutes. Break into bite-size pieces.

French Bittersweet Truffles

MAKES 24 TRUFFLES

This truffle recipe was such a big hit with family and friends, it snowballed into my tradition of making pounds and pounds of truffles each year for the holidays.

- #100 disher or scoop
- Baking sheets, lined with parchment paper or Silpats

1½ lbs	bittersweet chocolate, finely chopped, divided	750 g
8 oz	semisweet chocolate, finely chopped	250 g
1½ tsp	unsalted butter, softened	7 mL
2 tsp	rum	10 mL
1½ cups	whipping (35%) cream	375 mL

1. In a medium bowl, combine 8 oz (250 g) of the bittersweet chocolate, semisweet chocolate, butter and rum. Set aside.
2. In a saucepan, bring cream to a boil over medium heat. Pour over chocolate mixture. Stir until chocolate is completely melted and mixture is smooth. Transfer truffle filling to shallow dish and let cool at room temperature for 1 hour. Cover and refrigerate until firm, about 2 hours or overnight.
3. Temper remaining 1 lb (500 g) bittersweet chocolate according to directions on page 249.
4. Scoop truffle filling into balls, placing on a prepared baking sheet. Dip each ball into tempered chocolate. Place on prepared baking sheet. Let cool until set and dry. See storage information on page 250.

Lemon Champagne Macadamia Bon Bons

MAKES ABOUT 48 CANDIES

Once, I gave a box of these to my dental assistant, Cookie. She ate one and left the remainder at her bedside. The next morning they were all gone. She had gotten up during the night, and without realizing it, she ate them while half-asleep. This is a lesson to remember: keep these in the fridge!

- #70 disher or scoop
- Baking sheets, lined with parchment paper or Silpats

¾ cup	unsalted butter, softened	175 mL
6 cups	confectioner's (icing) sugar	1.5 L
1 tbsp	grated lemon zest	15 mL
⅓ cup	Champagne or sparkling wine (use an inexpensive brand)	75 mL
1 lb	white chocolate, finely chopped	500 g
1½ cups	finely chopped macadamia nuts	375 mL

1. In a mixer bowl fitted with paddle attachment, beat butter, sugar and lemon zest until combined. With mixer running on low speed, slowly pour in Champagne in a steady stream, just until it starts to hold together. (You may not need all of it.) Increase speed to high and beat until fluffy, for 5 minutes. Refrigerate until fairly firm, for 15 minutes.
2. Meanwhile, in a heatproof bowl set over a saucepan of steaming water, melt white chocolate. Stir until smooth. Let cool slightly.
3. Place nuts in a shallow dish. Scoop lemon mixture into balls, placing on a prepared baking sheet. Dip each ball in white chocolate and then roll in nuts. Place on prepared baking sheet. Let cool until set and dry. See storage information on page 250.

Raspberry Marshmallows

MAKES ABOUT 48 MARSHMALLOWS

Nothing is as light and airy as these delicate marshmallows and the hint of raspberry flavor makes them an extra-special treat.

Tips

It is helpful to have a stand mixer as well as an electric hand-held mixer for this recipe. You can use the hand-held mixer to whip the egg whites without having to clean the bowl from the gelatin mixture first.

Raspberry oil is available at specialty baking supply stores (see Sources, page 442).

Caution: This recipe contains uncooked egg whites. If the food safety is a concern for you, use pasteurized egg whites or avoid this recipe.

- Candy thermometer or digital instant-read thermometer
- 13-by 9-inch (3 L) metal baking pan, sprayed with a nonstick spray and dusted with 1⁄4 cup (50 mL) confectioner's (icing) sugar

3 1⁄2	envelopes (each 1⁄4 oz/7 g) powdered unflavored gelatin	3 1⁄2
1⁄2 cup	cold water	125 mL
2 cups	granulated sugar	500 mL
1⁄2 cup	light corn syrup	125 mL
1⁄2 cup	hot water (about 115°F/46°C)	125 mL
1⁄4 tsp	salt	1 mL
2	egg whites	2
1 tsp	vanilla extract	5 mL
3	drops raspberry oil (see Tips, left)	3
1⁄2 cup	confectioner's (icing) sugar, divided	125 mL

1. In a mixer bowl fitted with whip attachment, dissolve gelatin in cold water. Set aside.
2. In a saucepan, combine granulated sugar, corn syrup, hot water and salt. Cook over low heat, stirring just until sugar is dissolved. Increase heat to medium and boil, without stirring, until temperature reaches 240°F (116°C) on a thermometer (Soft Ball stage), about 12 minutes. Pour over gelatin mixture. Beat on high speed until white, thick and nearly tripled in volume, about 6 minutes.
3. In a clean mixer bowl, whip egg whites on high speed until soft peaks form. Fold in vanilla and raspberry oil. Add to sugar mixture and mix on low speed just until blended.
4. Pour mixture into prepared baking pan, smoothing to edges. Sift 1⁄4 cup (50 mL) confectioner's sugar evenly over top. Chill, uncovered, until firm, about 3 hours.

5. *To unmold:* Run a thin knife around edges of pan and invert pan onto large cutting board. Lift up one corner of inverted pan and, using fingers, loosen marshmallow and let it drop onto cutting board. Remove pan. Using a large knife, trim edges off marshmallow and cut marshmallows into roughly 1-inch (2.5 cm) cubes. Sift remaining ¼ cup (50 mL) confectioner's sugar into a large bowl and add marshmallows in batches, tossing to evenly coat. Serve immediately or transfer to an airtight container and store at a cool room temperature for up to 2 weeks.

1 cup
3/4
1/2

Pecan Pralines

MAKES ABOUT 24 CANDIES

Pralines are famous in New Orleans and a staple candy of the French Quarter.

Tip

An accurate thermometer is important for this recipe. The manual test for sugar stages doesn't work for the temperatures required to make perfect pralines.

- Baking sheet, lined with parchment paper or Silpat
- Candy thermometer or digital instant-read thermometer

1½ cups	granulated sugar	375 mL
1 cup	packed brown sugar	250 mL
1 cup	buttermilk	250 mL
1 tsp	baking soda	5 mL
¼ tsp	salt	1 mL
2 cups	pecan halves	500 mL
¼ cup	unsalted butter	50 mL

1. In a saucepan, combine sugars, buttermilk, soda and salt. Cook over low heat, stirring until sugar dissolves. Increase heat to medium and boil gently, stirring constantly, until temperature reaches 220°F (104°C) on a thermometer. Stir in pecans and butter and continue to boil, without stirring, until temperature reaches 230°F (110°C).
2. Remove from heat and let stand for exactly 5 minutes. Using a wooden spoon, beat until creamy, about 4 minutes. Drop candy in 24 piles on prepared baking sheet. Let cool completely. When cool, wrap each piece in plastic wrap. Store wrapped candies in an airtight container at room temperature for up to 1 month.

Rocky Cashews

MAKES 32 PIECES

An updated rocky road candy with rich cashews.

- 13-by 9-inch (3 L) metal baking pan lined with foil, then parchment paper

2 lbs	milk chocolate, finely chopped	1 kg
2 cups	toasted chopped cashews	500 mL
24	large marshmallows, cut in quarters	24

1. In a heatproof bowl set over a saucepan of steaming water, melt milk chocolate. Stir until smooth.
2. Pour about half of chocolate into bottom of prepared pan. Sprinkle nuts and marshmallows on top of melted chocolate. Gently pour remaining chocolate over marshmallows and nuts, covering as evenly as possible. Let set until firm, about 1 hour. Cut into pieces. See storage information on page 250.

White Chocolate Truffles

MAKES ABOUT 36 TRUFFLES

Sweet white chocolate truffles look great on a pastry table when presented along with a few dark chocolate ones.

- #100 disher or scoop
- Baking sheets, lined with parchment paper or Silpats

1 lb	white chocolate, finely chopped, divided	500 g
2½ cups	confectioner's (icing) sugar	625 mL
6 tbsp	unsalted butter, softened	90 mL
2 tbsp	white rum	25 mL

1. In a heatproof bowl set over a saucepan of steaming water, melt 6 oz (175 g) of the white chocolate. Stir until smooth. Let cool slightly.
2. In a mixer bowl fitted with paddle attachment, beat confectioner's sugar and butter on medium-high speed until creamy and light, about 4 minutes. Add melted white chocolate, mixing until incorporated. Fold in rum. Set aside.
3. In a heatproof bowl set over a saucepan of steaming water, melt remaining 10 oz (300 g) white chocolate. Stir until smooth. Let cool slightly.
4. Scoop truffle filling into balls, placing on prepared baking sheet. Dip each ball into melted chocolate. Place on prepared baking sheets. Let cool until set and dry. See storage information on page 250.

White Ginger Truffles

MAKES ABOUT 36 TRUFFLES

Ginger balances sweet white chocolate in this truffle for a refreshing taste.

Tip

If ginger nibs are not available, use finely chopped candied ginger instead.

- #100 disher or scoop
- Baking sheets, lined with parchment paper or silpats

1 lb	white chocolate, finely chopped, divided	500 g
2½ cups	confectioner's (icing) sugar	625 mL
6 tbsp	unsalted butter, softened	90 mL
2 tsp	finely chopped candied ginger	10 mL
¼ cup	ginger nibs (see Tip, left)	50 mL

1. In a heatproof bowl set over a saucepan of steaming water, melt 6 oz (175 g) of the white chocolate. Stir until smooth. Let cool slightly.
2. In a mixer bowl fitted with paddle attachment, blend confectioner's sugar and butter on medium-high speed until creamy and light, about 4 minutes. Add melted white chocolate, mixing until incorporated. Fold in candied ginger. Set aside.
3. In a heatproof bowl set over a saucepan of steaming water, melt remaining 10 oz (300 g) white chocolate. Stir until smooth. Let cool slightly.
4. Scoop truffle filling into balls, placing on prepared baking sheet. Dip each ball into melted chocolate. Place on prepared baking sheets. Place one ginger nib on each truffle for decoration while chocolate is still wet. Let cool until set and dry. See storage information on page 250.

English Trifle

Grand Finales

Puddings & Custards

Desserts

Banana Toasted Pecan Pudding

SERVES 6

This has a multitude of uses. It's lovely on its own or you can try one of the options to turn it into a different dessert.

1 cup	granulated sugar	250 mL
1/2 cup	all-purpose flour	125 mL
1 tsp	salt	5 mL
2 cups	whole milk	500 mL
4	egg yolks	4
4	ripe bananas, smashed	4
1/2 cup	toasted chopped pecans	125 mL
1 tbsp	unsalted butter, softened	15 mL
1 tsp	vanilla extract	5 mL

1. In a large saucepan, combine sugar, flour and salt. Whisk in milk until incorporated. Cook over medium heat, whisking constantly, until thick, about 7 minutes. Remove from heat.
2. In a small bowl, whisk egg yolks. Gradually whisk in about 1/4 cup (50 mL) hot milk mixture in a thin, steady stream. Whisk egg mixture back into saucepan. Cook over low heat, stirring until thickened, about 3 minutes. Remove from heat. Fold in bananas, pecans, butter and vanilla until butter is melted. Transfer to a container and let cool slightly at room temperature. Cover and refrigerate until chilled or for up to 24 hours.

Uses

- *Cream Pie:* Fill pre-baked Flaky Pie Pastry Crust (Variations, page 115) with pudding. Top with Classic Whipped Cream (page 239).
- *Cake Filling:* Recipe yields enough to fill two cakes.
- *Trifle:* Use this pudding to replace French Pastry Cream in English Trifle (page 303).
- *Banana Pecan Mousse:* Fold one recipe of Classic Whipped Cream (page 239) into pudding.

Caramel Custard (Flan)

SERVES 12

It seems as though every country has a baked cream custard dessert it calls its own. Here is a fast and simple caramel custard.

- Preheat oven to 375°F (190°C)
- Twelve 6-oz (175 mL) custard cups
- Roasting pan

¾ cup	dark corn syrup	175 mL
4 cups	whipping (35%) cream	1 L
6	eggs	6
½ cup	granulated sugar	125 mL
2 tsp	vanilla extract	10 mL

1. Divide corn syrup between custard cups. Set aside.
2. In a saucepan, scald cream over medium heat just until steaming and bubbles form around the edge, about 3 minutes. Remove from heat.
3. In a bowl, whisk together eggs and granulated sugar until blended. Gradually whisk in about ½ cup (125 mL) of hot cream in a thin, steady stream. Whisk egg mixture back into saucepan. Cook over medium heat, whisking constantly, until slightly thickened, for 2 minutes.
4. Divide custard among cups on top of corn syrup. Place cups into roasting pan and pour in hot water about halfway up sides of cups. Bake in preheated oven until a knife inserted into center comes out clean, 32 to 40 minutes. Remove cups from water and let cool slightly. Or cover and refrigerate for up to 2 days.
5. To serve, run a knife around the edge of custard, being careful not to cut into custard. Invert a small dessert plate onto cup and flip over to invert custard onto plate. Lift off cup. Syrup will flow over the baked custard.

Chocolate Crème Brûlée

SERVES 12

I always say that crème brûlée was invented as a way to use day-old custards. Sprinkle sugar on top, broil and you have a new dessert.

- Preheat oven to 375°F (190°C)
- Twelve 4-oz (125 mL) shallow crème brûlée dishes
- Roasting pan
- Blowtorch or broiler

4 cups	whipping (35%) cream	1 L
8 oz	bittersweet chocolate, chopped	250 g
6	eggs	6
½ cup	granulated sugar	125 mL
1 tsp	rum	5 mL
¼ cup	packed brown sugar	50 mL

1. In a saucepan, scald cream over medium heat just until steaming and bubbles form around the edge, about 3 minutes. Remove from heat. Add chopped chocolate and stir until melted.
2. In a bowl, whisk together eggs and granulated sugar until blended. Gradually whisk in about ½ cup (125 mL) of the hot cream in a thin, steady stream. Whisk egg mixture back into saucepan. Whisk in rum. Divide among dishes, filling about three-quarters full. Place dishes into roasting pan and pour in hot water about halfway up sides of dishes. Bake in preheated oven until a knife inserted into center comes out clean, 28 to 34 minutes.
3. Remove dishes from water and let cool completely at room temperature. Cover and refrigerate until chilled, about 2 hours or for up to 2 days.
4. Preheat broiler, if using.
5. Press brown sugar through a fine mesh strainer, sprinkling evenly on top of chilled custards. Using a blowtorch or boiler, brown sugar just until bubbling, 1 to 2 minutes. Serve immediately.

Chocolate Custards

SERVES 12

As a child I loved anything chocolate for dessert, but my favorite was chocolate custard.

- Preheat oven to 375°F (190°C)
- Twelve 4-oz (125 mL) custard cups
- Roasting pan

2 cups	whipping (35%) cream	500 mL
2 cups	half-and-half (10%) cream	500 mL
8 oz	bittersweet chocolate, chopped	250 g
7	eggs	7
½ cup	granulated sugar	125 mL
1 tsp	vanilla extract	5 mL

1. In a saucepan, scald whipping cream and half-and-half cream over medium heat just until steaming and bubbles form around the edge, about 3 minutes. Remove from heat. Add chopped chocolate and stir until melted.
2. In a bowl, whisk together eggs and sugar until blended. Gradually whisk in about ½ cup (125 mL) of the hot cream in a thin, steady stream. Whisk egg mixture back into saucepan. Whisk in vanilla. Divide among custard cups, filling about three-quarters full. Place cups into roasting pan and pour in hot water about halfway up sides of cups. Bake in preheated oven until a knife inserted into center comes out clean, 28 to 34 minutes.
3. Remove cups from water and let cool completely at room temperature. Cover and refrigerate until chilled, for 2 hours or for up to 2 days. Serve cold.

White Chocolate Caramel Crème Brûlée

SERVES 12

This creamy dessert has a surprise hint of caramel inside.

- Preheat oven to 375°F (190°C)
- Twelve 4-oz (125 mL) shallow crème brûlée dishes
- Roasting pan
- Blowtorch or broiler

4 cups	whipping (35%) cream	1 L
8 oz	white chocolate, chopped	250 g
6	eggs	6
3/4 cup	granulated sugar, divided	175 mL
2 tsp	vanilla extract	10 mL
4 oz	soft caramels, cut into pieces	125 g

1. In a saucepan, scald cream over medium heat just until steaming and bubbles form around the edge, about 3 minutes. Remove from heat. Add white chocolate and stir until melted.
2. In a bowl, whisk together eggs, 1/2 cup (125 mL) of the sugar and vanilla until blended. Gradually whisk in about 1/2 cup (125 mL) of the hot cream mixture in a thin steady stream. Whisk egg mixture back into saucepan.
3. Divide caramels among dishes. Divide custard mixture over caramels.
4. Place dishes into roasting pan and pour in hot water about halfway up sides of dishes. Bake in preheated oven, until a knife inserted into center comes out clean, 30 to 40 minutes. Remove dishes from water and let cool completely at room temperature. Cover and refrigerate until chilled, for 2 hours or for up 2 days.
5. Preheat broiler, if using.
6. Sprinkle remaining 1/4 cup (50 mL) sugar evenly on top of each chilled custard. Using a blowtorch or boiler, brown sugar just until bubbling, about 3 minutes. Serve immediately.

Fresh Lemon Curd

MAKES 2 CUPS (500 ML)

This is the most useful fruit item in a pastry kitchen. My sister Monica is addicted to Lemon Curd Tarts (see recipe, page 144).

Variation

You can use Meyer lemon or tangerine juice if you like.

10	egg yolks	10
¾ cup	granulated sugar	175 mL
¾ cup	freshly squeezed lemon juice	175 mL
½ cup	unsalted butter, softened, cut into pieces	125 mL

1. In a large heatproof glass or nonreactive metal bowl, whisk egg yolks for 2 minutes. Gradually sprinkle sugar over egg yolks while whisking. Whisk in lemon juice. Place on top of a saucepan of simmering water over medium heat, making sure bowl does not touch the water. Cook, whisking constantly, until mixture is thickened and coats the back of a spoon, about 7 minutes.
2. Remove bowl from saucepan and whisk in butter, a few pieces at a time. Transfer to a cool bowl and place plastic wrap directly on the surface of curd. Let cool completely at room temperature. Cover and refrigerate until chilled, about 2 hours or for up to 2 days.

Uses

- Use as filling for a cake such as White Layer Cake (page 185).
- Fill Cream Puffs (page 312).
- Spread on top of a cooled cheesecake.

Milk Chocolate Macadamia Pudding

SERVES 6

Warm pudding on a snowy night brings warmth to all.

1 cup	granulated sugar	250 mL
½ cup	all-purpose flour	125 mL
1 tsp	salt	5 mL
2 cups	whole milk	500 mL
5	egg yolks	5
6 oz	milk chocolate, chopped	175 g
½ cup	macadamia nuts, chopped and toasted	125 mL
1 tbsp	unsalted butter, softened	15 mL
1 tsp	dark rum	5 mL

1. In a large saucepan, whisk together sugar, flour and salt. Gradually whisk in milk until incorporated. Cook over medium heat, whisking constantly, until thickened, about 7 minutes. Remove from heat.
2. In a small bowl, whisk egg yolks. Gradually whisk in about ¼ cup (50 mL) of the hot milk mixture in a thin, steady stream. Whisk egg mixture back into saucepan. Cook over low heat, whisking constantly, until thickened, for about 3 minutes. Remove from heat. Add milk chocolate and stir until melted. Fold in macadamia nuts, butter and rum until butter is melted. Pour into serving dishes or a container. Let cool at room temperature. Serve warm or cover and refrigerate until chilled, about 2 hours or for up to 2 days.

Uses

- *Cream Pie:* Fill pre-baked Chocolate Pie Pastry Dough (page 116) with pudding. Top with Classic Whipped Cream (page 239).
- *Cake Filling:* Recipe yields enough to fill two cakes.
- *Trifle:* Substitute this pudding for French Pastry Cream in English Trifle (page 303).
- *Milk Chocolate Macadamia Mousse:* Fold one recipe of Classic Whipped Cream (page 239) into pudding.

Pumpkin Bread Pudding

SERVES 12

Fall spices make this bread pudding a favorite for an easy dessert.

- Preheat oven to 350°F (180°C)
- 13-by 9-inch (3 L) metal baking pan, sprayed with nonstick spray

1 lb	day-old white bread, cut into cubes	500 g
5 cups	whole milk	1.25 L
1 cup	pumpkin purée (not pie filling)	250 mL
1 cup	granulated sugar	250 mL
½ cup	unsalted butter, melted	125 mL
2 tbsp	ground cinnamon	25 mL
2 tsp	vanilla extract	10 mL
½ tsp	freshly grated nutmeg	2 mL
½ tsp	salt	2 mL
¼ tsp	ground ginger	1 mL
10	eggs	10
	Ginger Whipped Cream (see Variation, page 239)	

1. Place bread in prepared baking pan. Set aside.
2. In a saucepan, scald milk over medium heat just until steaming and bubbles form around the edge, about 5 minutes.
3. In a large bowl, whisk together pumpkin, sugar, butter, cinnamon, vanilla, nutmeg, salt and ginger. Whisk in eggs, one at a time, until incorporated. Gradually whisk in scalded milk in a thin, steady stream. Pour over dry bread, pressing down to soak bread completely.
4. Bake in preheated oven until a knife inserted into center comes out clean, 32 to 38 minutes. Serve warm with Ginger Whipped Cream.

Pumpkin Spice Custards

SERVES 12

This was a holiday favorite on the Mike and Maty Show that I did on ABC. The combination of spices with pumpkin and the smooth texture of custard will leave your taste buds craving more.

Tip

If you can only find a 28 oz (796 mL) can of pumpkin purée, that is fine for this recipe.

- Preheat oven to 375°F (190°C)
- Twelve 6-oz (175 mL) custard cups
- Roasting pan

2 cups	whipping (35%) cream	500 mL
1	can (29 oz/824 g) pumpkin purée (not pie filling)	1
1½ cups	packed light brown sugar	375 mL
6	eggs	6
2 tsp	ground cinnamon	10 mL
1 tsp	freshly grated nutmeg	5 mL
1 tsp	ground ginger	5 mL

1. In a saucepan, scald cream over medium heat just until steaming and bubbles form around the edge, about 2 minutes.
2. In a large bowl, whisk together pumpkin, brown sugar, eggs, cinnamon, nutmeg and ginger. Gradually whisk in scalded cream in a thin, steady stream.
3. Divide among custard cups, filling about three-quarters full. Place cups into roasting pan and pour in hot water about halfway up sides of cups. Bake in preheated oven until a knife inserted in center comes out clean, 38 to 45 minutes. Remove cups from water, let cool slightly at room temperature and serve warm. Or cover and refrigerate until chilled, for 2 hours or for up to 2 days. Serve cold.

Vanilla Bean Custards

SERVES 12

These custards are great when you need a simple dessert to finish off a meal.

Variation

Berry or Nut Custards: Divide up to ½ cup (125 mL) of fresh berries or toasted nuts among the cups prior to filling with custard mixture.

- Preheat oven to 375°F (190°C)
- Twelve 4-oz (125 mL) custard cups
- Roasting pan

4 cups	whipping (35%) cream	1 L
½ cup	granulated sugar	125 mL
5	eggs	5
2	egg yolks	2
1 tbsp	vanilla bean paste	15 mL

1. In a saucepan, scald cream over medium heat just until steaming and bubbles form around the edge, about 3 minutes.
2. In a bowl, whisk sugar with eggs and egg yolks until blended. Gradually whisk in about ½ cup (125 mL) of the scalded cream in a thin, steady stream. Whisk egg mixture back into saucepan. Whisk in vanilla paste.
3. Divide among custard cups, filling about three-quarters full. Place cups into roasting pan and pour in hot water about half way up sides of cups. Bake in preheated oven until a knife inserted into center comes out clean, 28 to 34 minutes.
4. Remove cups from water and let cool completely at room temperature. Cover and refrigerate until chilled, for 2 hours or for up to 2 days. Serve cold.

Almond Praline

MAKES 1 CUP (250 ML)

This praline is used in pastry creams and whipped creams to create nutty fillings.

- Baking sheet, lined with parchment paper or Silpat

1⁄3 cup	water	75 mL
1⁄3 cup	superfine sugar (see Tip, page 243)	75 mL
1 cup	toasted sliced almonds	250 mL

1. In a saucepan, bring water and sugar to a boil over medium heat, stirring until sugar is dissolved. Boil gently until light brown, about 8 minutes. Stir in toasted almonds until coated. Pour onto prepared baking sheet, spreading into a single layer. Let cool completely.
2. Break almond candy into chunks and place in a food processor fitted with metal blade. Pulse until finely ground.

Uses

- Paris Brest (page 313)
- Filling for any cake if mixed with French Pastry Cream (page 242) or Classic Whipped Cream (page 239)

Bananas Foster

MAKES 6 SERVINGS

Made famous by Brennan's Restaurant in New Orleans in the 1950s. It is still served up today at their "typical" New Orleans breakfast. This is my version.

6	scoops vanilla ice cream	6
1/4 cup	unsalted butter	50 mL
3/4 cup	packed dark brown sugar	175 mL
1/2 cup	banana-flavored liqueur	125 mL
1 tsp	vanilla extract	5 mL
3	bananas, quartered	3
1/2 cup	light rum	125 mL
1/2 tsp	ground cinnamon	2 mL

1. Place ice cream in individual serving dishes and freeze.
2. In a large skillet, melt butter over medium heat. Add brown sugar and cook, stirring, until it forms a thick paste. Add banana liqueur and vanilla and cook, stirring well, until heated through, for 3 minutes.
3. Add bananas and cook, basting bananas with butter mixture until coated and hot, about 2 minutes. Add rum and ignite with a match. Carefully sprinkle with cinnamon and cook, shaking pan gently, until flames go out, about 3 minutes. Spoon bananas and sauce over ice cream. Serve immediately.

Almond Raspberry Charlotte

SERVES 14 TO 16

This dessert is so rich you only need a small piece for satisfaction.

Tip

To make almond meal, place 1½ cups (375 mL) whole blanched almonds and 2 tbsp (25 mL) of all-purpose flour into a food processor fitted with metal blade and process until finely ground, about 2 minutes. Flour prevents the almonds from turning into almond butter.

- 4-cup (1 L) charlotte mold or tall, round soufflé dish

1	recipe French Sponge Jelly Roll, unrolled (see recipe, page 219)	1
2 tbsp	raspberry-flavored liqueur	25 mL
2 cups	confectioner's (icing) sugar	500 mL
1½ cups	almond meal or ground almonds (see Tip, left)	375 mL
1 cup	whipping (35%) cream	250 mL
1 cup	unsalted butter, softened	250 mL
1¼ cups	raspberries	300 mL
1	recipe Fresh Raspberry Sauce (see recipe, page 241)	1

1. Cut a strip of the jelly roll to fit the height and circumference of dish. Fit around inside of dish. Cut a circle of cake and fit in bottom of dish. Brush cake with liqueur. Set aside. (Reserve any remaining cake for another use.)
2. In a food processor fitted with metal blade, process confectioner's sugar and almond meal for 2 minutes. Set aside.
3. In a chilled mixer bowl fitted with whip attachment, whip cream to soft peaks. Transfer to another bowl and set aside.
4. In same mixer bowl fitted with paddle attachment, beat butter until fluffy, for 2 minutes. Gradually add almond mixture, mixing on low speed just until incorporated. Fold in raspberries and whipped cream. Spoon carefully into cake-lined dish. Cover and refrigerate for 2 hours or for up to 2 days.
5. To un-mold, place a serving plate on top of mold and flip over to invert Charlotte onto plate. The Charlotte should pop out of the mold easily. Cut Charlotte into wedges and serve with raspberry sauce on top.

Angel Pie

SERVES 10 TO 12

Light as angel wings, this flavorful pie can be made into any flavor you like with fresh fruits or berries.

Tips

I suggest you avoid making meringues in humid weather. Humidity causes them to get soggy quite quickly.

Do not refrigerate meringue shells, as they will get soggy.

- Preheat oven to 200°F (100°C)
- Two 9-inch (23 cm) pie plates, bottoms lined with parchment

1	recipe Swiss Meringue (see recipe, page 236)	1
1	recipe French Pastry Cream (see recipe, page 242)	1
6 cups	fresh fruit, sliced if necessary (berries, kiwi, bananas, etc)	1.5 L

1. Divide meringue between pie plates. Spread evenly, smoothing over bottom and up sides, creating a well. Bake in preheated oven until light brown, about 1 hour. Let cool completely in pie plates on a rack, about 45 minutes. Meringue shells can be covered with foil or plastic wrap and stored at room temperature for up to 3 days.
2. Spoon half of pastry cream into each meringue shell. Top with prepared fruit. Serve as soon as possible.

Apple Triangle Puffs

MAKES 24 PUFFS

Tart apples encased in puff pastry are simple and full of flavor.

Tips

If you have a smaller package of puff pastry, the pastry may be thinner but will still work.

You can prepare apple puffs ahead. Place unbaked puffs in plastic bags and freeze for up to 1 month. Bake from frozen, increasing baking time by about 2 minutes.

- Preheat oven to 425°F (220°C)
- Baking sheets, lined with parchment paper or Silpats
- Pizza cutter

1	package (18 oz/540 g) puff pastry, thawed	1
¾ cup	granulated sugar	175 mL
2 tbsp	all-purpose flour	25 mL
1 tbsp	ground cinnamon	15 mL
½ tsp	freshly grated nutmeg	2 mL
3	large baking apples (see Apples, page 15), peeled, cored and diced	3
1 tbsp	unsalted butter, melted	15 mL

1. Working with one half of pastry, on a lightly floured surface, roll out to a 12-by 6-inch (30 by 15 cm) rectangle. Using a pizza cutter, cut each sheet in half lengthwise, then in half crosswise to make 4 pieces. Cut crosswise two more times on each side of center cut, creating 12 rectangles that are 3 by 2 inches (7.5 by 5 cm). Repeat with remaining pastry. Set aside.
2. In a large bowl, combine sugar, flour, cinnamon and nutmeg. Add apples and toss to evenly coat.
3. Place 2 tbsp (25 mL) of apple mixture in center of each rectangle of pastry. Working with one rectangle at a time, bring two opposite corners together to create a triangle. Press edges to seal. If pastry seems dry, lightly brush edges with water before folding to ensure a good seal. Place on prepared baking sheets, about 2 inches (5 cm) apart. Brush tops with melted butter. Repeat with remaining pastry and filling to make 24 puffs. Bake in preheated oven until light brown, 14 to 18 minutes. Serve hot.

Baked Alaska

SERVES 12 TO 14

Baked Alaska originated at Delmonico's Restaurant in New York City in 1876, and was created in honor of the newly acquired territory of Alaska.

Tip

If you have room in your freezer you may prepare dessert through to Step 4. Cover and freeze for up to 1 day. Proceed with Step 5 just before serving.

- Blowtorch or broiler
- Two 9-by 5-inch (2 L) loaf pans, lined with parchment paper

2 quarts	vanilla ice cream or desired flavor, slightly softened, divided	2 L
1	recipe French Sponge Jelly Roll (see recipe, page 219), unrolled	1
1	recipe Italian Meringue (see recipe, page 238)	1

1. Spread half of ice cream into each prepared loaf pan. Freeze overnight.
2. Cut two pieces of French Sponge Jelly Roll to fit as base for ice cream loaf. Place each on a heatproof serving platter. (Reserve any remaining cake for another use.)
3. Un-mold ice cream and place one loaf on each piece of cake.
4. Dollop meringue on top of ice cream, smoothing and making sure all ice cream and cake are covered.
5. Preheat broiler, if using.
6. Using a blowtorch or broiler, brown meringue to desired brownness. Serve immediately.

Baked Maple Apples

SERVES 6 TO 8

To gain the full flavor of this dessert, you must use real maple syrup. It is worth the cost for terrific flavor.

- Preheat oven to 375°F (190°C)
- 9-inch (2.5 L) square baking pan

6 to 8	large baking apples (see Apples, page 15), cored	6 to 8
⅓ cup	raisins	75 mL
2 tsp	ground cinnamon	10 mL
1 tsp	freshly grated nutmeg	5 mL
1 cup	pure maple syrup	250 mL
½ cup	hot water	125 mL
1 cup	whipping (35%) cream, at room temperature	250 mL
3 tbsp	rum	45 mL

1. Place apples into baking pan. Set aside.
2. In a small bowl, combine raisins, cinnamon and nutmeg. Fill cored apples evenly with raisin mixture. Pour maple syrup evenly into center of apples. Pour water into pan around apples. Bake in preheated oven, basting every 10 minutes, until fork-tender, 45 to 50 minutes.
3. Using a slotted spoon, transfer apples to individual serving bowls. Pour liquid from pan into saucepan and set over medium heat. Whisk cream and rum into saucepan and cook until heated, about 3 minutes. Pour sauce on top of each apple.

Banoffee Pie

SERVES 10 TO 12

On my first trip to London I tasted this incredible dessert. They call it pie, but it is made in a cheesecake pan. Try a little taste of merry old England next time you entertain.

Tip

You can bake tart pastry up to 2 days before assembly. Cover with foil and store at room temperature.

- Preheat oven to 375°F (190°C)
- 9-inch (23 cm) cheesecake pan or springform pan

½	recipe Buttery Tart Pastry Dough (see recipe, page 120)	½
1	can (14 oz/396 g or 300 mL) sweetened condensed milk	1
2 cups	whipping (35%) cream	500 mL
½ cup	granulated sugar	125 mL
2	bananas	2

1. On a lightly floured surface, roll out tart dough to a circle and fit into bottom of cheesecake pan. Bake in preheated oven until light brown, 20 to 22 minutes. Set aside and let cool.
2. In a heatproof bowl set over a saucepan of lightly simmering water, heat sweetened condensed milk, stirring occasionally, until light caramel in color and thick, 60 to 70 minutes. Check water periodically and add more as necessary to keep the level of water just below the bottom of the bowl.
3. Meanwhile, in a chilled mixer bowl fitted with whip attachment, whip cream on low speed until starting to thicken, about 3 minutes. Sprinkle in sugar. Increase speed to high and whip until firm peaks form. Set aside.
4. Pour about half of caramelized sweetened condensed milk on top of baked pastry base. Slice one banana and arrange evenly on top. Fold remaining caramelized sweetened condensed milk into half of whipped cream. Spread on top of bananas, smoothing to sides. Slice remaining banana and arrange on top of cream. Top with remaining whipped cream, smoothing top. Cover with plastic wrap. Refrigerate for 2 hours or for up to 1 day. Remove from pan just before serving.

Best Berry Frozen Cake

SERVES 12

Bright pink and perfect for a child's party.

- 9-inch (23 cm) cheesecake pan or springform pan, lined with parchment paper

1	recipe French Sponge Jelly Roll (see recipe, page 219), unrolled	1
3 cups	assorted berries (strawberries, raspberries, blackberries), sliced if necessary	750 mL
2 quarts	berry-flavored ice cream, slightly softened, divided	2 L
2/3 cup	chopped toasted almonds	150 mL

1. Using cake bottom as a template, cut two 9-inch (23 cm) rounds out of French Sponge Jelly Roll cake. (Reserve any remaining cake for another use.)
2. Place one cake round in bottom of prepared cake pan. Top with 1 cup (250 mL) of the berries. Spread half of ice cream evenly over berries. Sprinkle 1 cup (250 mL) of berries over ice cream. Place second cake round on top of berries and spread with remaining ice cream. Top with remaining berries.
3. Cover and freeze for at least 24 hours or for up to 2 weeks. Sprinkle with almonds before serving.

Birthday Ice Cream Cake

SERVES 12

This wonderful cake doesn't have to only be served for a birthday; for other occasions you can call it Decadent Chocolate Ice Cream Cake.

Variation

For a festive look, shave chocolate curls on top of cake just before serving.

- 9-inch (23 cm) cheesecake pan or springform pan, lined with parchment paper

1 cup	whipping (35%) cream	250 mL
6 oz	bittersweet chocolate, chopped	175 g
1	recipe Chocolate Jelly Roll (see Variations, page 219), unrolled	1
2 quarts	chocolate chunk or chip ice cream, slightly softened, divided	1 L

1. In a saucepan, bring cream to a full boil over medium heat, about 4 minutes. Remove from heat. Add chocolate and stir until melted and smooth. Transfer to a shallow bowl and let cool.
2. Using cake bottom as a template, cut two 9-inch (23 cm) rounds out of Chocolate Jelly Roll cake. (Reserve any remaining cake for another use.)
3. Place one cake round in bottom of prepared cake pan. Pour about one-third of chocolate sauce on top of cake. Spread half of ice cream evenly over cake. Place second cake round on ice cream. Spread half of remaining sauce on cake and spread with remaining ice cream. Drizzle top with remaining sauce.
4. Cover and freeze for at least 24 hours or for up to 2 weeks.

Dessert Crêpes

MAKES ABOUT 16 TO 20 CRÊPES

With practice and confidence you will be a master crêpe maker in no time! Try making these a few days before you are going to serve them so you can rest assured that your dessert will be wonderful!

Tips

After cooling crêpes, you can then place them into a resealable freezer bag in a layered stack and refrigerate for up to 2 days or freeze for up to 1 month. If frozen, thaw in refrigerator overnight before using.

If you are using crêpes for a savory dish, when cooking, flip crêpe over and brown slightly on second side.

- 8-inch (20 cm) nonstick skillet or crêpe pan
- Nonstick cooking spray

2 cups	all-purpose flour	500 mL
1⁄8 tsp	salt	0.5 mL
4	eggs, beaten	4
2 1⁄2 cups	whole milk, divided	625 mL
2 tbsp	unsalted butter, melted and cooled	25 mL

1. In a bowl, sift together flour and salt. Make a well in center of flour and add eggs and 1⁄2 cup (125 mL) of the milk. Using a whisk, beat well, working in all of the flour. Gradually beat in remaining milk, beating until bubbles form on top of batter. Stir in butter.
2. Heat pan over high heat. Coat evenly with nonstick spray. Pour 2 to 3 tbsp (25 to 45 mL) of batter into hot pan, quickly tilting pan so batter covers bottom of pan thinly and evenly as you pour batter. Cook until underside has released from bottom of pan and top is no longer shiny, about 1 minute. Do not flip to other side. Slide out of pan onto a plate, layering with parchment or paper towel between each crêpe. Repeat with remaining batter, reheating pan and spraying between each crêpe.

Uses

- Banana Crème Crêpe Filling (page 240)

Dr. Darren's Lemon Dessert

SERVES 10 TO 12

When my friend Darren and I get together we seem to talk food. Years back he was my sous chef when I was invited to bake for the Chefs' Holidays event at Yosemite's Ahwahnee Hotel. I just had to include his famous Kansas City Lemon Dessert.

Tip
If one of the meringue cake layers breaks, use it on the bottom.

- Preheat oven to 500°F (260°C)
- Two 9-inch (23 cm) round cake pans, lined with parchment paper and sides sprayed with nonstick spray

Meringue Cake Base

9	egg whites	9
2 tsp	cream of tartar	5 mL
2½ cups	granulated sugar	625 mL
1 tsp	vanilla extract	5 mL

Lemon Filling

9	egg yolks, beaten	9
1⅛ cups	granulated sugar	275 mL
3 tbsp	grated lemon zest	45 mL
1⅛ cups	freshly squeezed lemon juice	275 mL
1½ cups	whipping (35%) cream	375 mL
2 tbsp	confectioner's (icing) sugar	25 mL

1. *Meringue Cake Base:* In a mixer bowl fitted with whip attachment, whip egg whites with cream of tartar until frothy, about 3 minutes. With mixer running, gradually add sugar. Increase speed to high and whip until stiff glossy peaks form. Divide meringue into prepared pans, smoothing tops. Place in preheated oven. Turn oven off. Let pans stand in oven for 8 to 10 hours or overnight to dry completely.
2. *Lemon Filling:* In heavy saucepan, whisk together egg yolks, granulated sugar, lemon zest and juice. Cook over medium heat, whisking constantly, until it starts to boil, about 3 minutes. Reduce heat to low and cook, stirring constantly, until thickened, about 2 minutes. Transfer to a cool bowl and let cool completely, about 30 minutes.
3. Meanwhile, in a chilled mixer bowl fitted with whip attachment, whip cream until soft peaks form, about 5 minutes. Fold into cooled lemon filling.
4. To assemble, run a knife around edge of meringues and remove from pans. Peel off paper. Place one meringue cake layer on a serving platter, smooth side up. Cover with lemon filling. Gently place second layer on top with smooth side up. Dust with confectioner's sugar.

English Trifle

SERVES 12 TO 16

Originally this was a dessert that used up day-old bread or cake.

Tip

You can make this ahead. Cover and refrigerate for up to 2 days. Decorate just before serving.

- 10-cup (2.5 L) clear glass trifle bowl

½	recipe Yellow Cake, cut into slices (see recipe, page 187)	½
½ cup	cream sherry	125 mL
1 cup	strawberry preserves	250 mL
1	recipe French Pastry Cream (see recipe, page 242)	1
4 cups	fresh berries (raspberries, strawberries, etc.)	1 L
2	kiwis, peeled and sliced	2
2	recipes Classic Whipped Cream (see recipe, page 239)	2
2	sprigs fresh mint	2

1. Brush cake slices with ¼ cup (50 mL) of the sherry. Line bottom of bowl with about one-third of cake slices. Smooth ½ cup (125 mL) strawberry preserves over cake. Top with half of pastry cream. Reserve some of best-looking berries for top. Arrange about half of remaining berries and kiwis on top of pastry cream, placing some of berries against sides of bowl so you can see layers. Sprinkle with 2 tbsp (25 mL) sherry. Spread about one-third of whipped cream on top of berries.
2. Top with half of remaining cake slices. Repeat with remaining preserves, pastry cream, berries and kiwis and half of remaining whipped cream. Sprinkle with remaining sherry. Top with remaining cake. Spread with remaining whipped cream. Decorate with reserved berries and mint leaves.

French Apple Tarte Tatin

SERVES 8 TO 10

This is a time-consuming dessert to make but well worth the effort. It is best if you use a cast-iron pan.

- Preheat oven to 375°F (190°C)
- 10-inch (25 cm) cast-iron skillet or other ovenproof skillet (including handle)

½ cup	unsalted butter, softened	125 mL
1 cup	granulated sugar	250 mL
10	tart baking apples (see Apples, page 15), peeled, cored and halved	10
½	package (18 oz/540 g) puff pastry, thawed and cold	½
	Ginger Whipped Cream (see Variation, page 239)	

1. In skillet, melt butter over medium heat. Sprinkle sugar evenly over melted butter. Arrange apple halves, rounded sides all facing the same way, nestling tightly together in a spiral around pan and filling the center. Increase heat to high and cook, without stirring, but shaking pan gently occasionally, until juices and sugar turn a deep caramelized brown, about 12 minutes.
2. Carefully turn each apple over to coat other side. Cook for 5 minutes longer. Remove from heat.
3. On a lightly floured surface, roll out pastry to a 12-inch (30 cm) circle. Place on top of apples, folding any excess pastry on top
4. Bake in preheated oven until pastry puffs and is light brown, 25 to 30 minutes. Let cool in pan for 10 minutes, invert serving platter onto skillet and flip over to invert tart onto platter. Using tongs, replace any apples that may have moved or stuck to pan. Serve hot with Ginger Whipped Cream.

Fresh Peach Puffs

MAKES 36 PUFFS

Puffy peach desserts are easy when you use prepared puff pastry.

Tips

Thaw puff pastry according to package directions. To make sure it is thawed, take dough out of packaging and pick up one side of dough to make sure it is limp and not still frozen.

You can prepare puffs ahead. Place unbaked puffs in plastic bags and freeze for up to 1 month. Bake from frozen, increasing baking time by about 2 minutes.

- Preheat oven to 425°F (220°C)
- Baking sheets, lined with parchment paper or Silpats
- Pizza cutter

1	package (18 oz/540 g) puff pastry, thawed	1
½ cup	granulated sugar	125 mL
2 tbsp	cornstarch	25 mL
½ tsp	ground cinnamon	2 mL
¼ tsp	ground nutmeg	1 mL
2 cups	chopped peeled fresh peaches	500 mL
1 tbsp	freshly squeezed lemon juice	15 mL
2 tbsp	unsalted butter, melted	25 mL

1. Working with one half of pastry, on a lightly floured surface, roll out to a 12-by 6-inch (30 by 15 cm) rectangle. Using a pizza cutter, cut into thirds lengthwise, then in half crosswise to make 6 pieces. Cut crosswise two more times on each side of center cut, creating eighteen 2-inch (5 cm) squares. Repeat with remaining pastry. Set aside.
2. In a large bowl, combine sugar, cornstarch, cinnamon and nutmeg. Add peaches and lemon juice and toss to evenly coat.
3. Place 2 tbsp (25 mL) of peach mixture in center of each square of pastry. Working with one square at a time, starting with two opposite corners, fold into the center and press to seal over the peach filling. Repeat with third and fourth corners, meeting over top first one to resemble an envelope, and press to seal edges. If pastry seems dry, lightly brush edges with water before folding to ensure a good seal. Place on prepared baking sheets, at least 2 inches (5 cm) apart. Brush top with melted butter. Repeat with remaining pastry and filling to make 36 puffs. Bake in preheated oven until light brown, 14 to 18 minutes. Serve hot.

Boston Cream Pie

SERVES 8 TO 10

This is nothing close to a pie; rather, it is a cake dessert. It was invented in 1856 by Chef Sanzian for opening day at the Parker House Hotel in Boston.

1	recipe White Layer Cake (see recipe, page 185), baked and cooled completely	1
½	recipe French Pastry Cream (see recipe, page 242), cooled	½
1	recipe Chocolate Ganache (see recipe, page 241), slightly warm	1

1. Place one cake layer on a platter. Top with pastry cream, smoothing to sides without going too close to edge. Place second cake layer on top of pastry cream. Pour ganache over top, drizzling evenly so it will coat top and flow over sides of cake.
2. Serve immediately or refrigerate for up to 2 hours.

Honey Baklava

MAKES 24 PIECES

Years ago, when I was a chef at Disney, a supervisor was moving departments and I was asked to make baklava, a favorite of his as a child, to honor him. I had never made the Greek pastry before, so I went to a Greek bakery and researched the recipe. He told me this version was better then his grandmother's.

Tip

When working with phyllo dough, keep sheets covered and moist at all times. It only takes about 2 minutes for sheets to dry out once exposed to air, making them brittle.

- Preheat oven to 300°F (150°C)
- 13-by 9-inch (3 L) metal baking pan, buttered well

4 cups	chopped pecans	1 L
½ cup	granulated sugar	125 mL
1 tsp	ground cinnamon	5 mL
½ tsp	freshly grated nutmeg	2 mL
¼ tsp	ground allspice	1 mL
1 lb	phyllo pastry dough, thawed if frozen	500 g
2 cups	unsalted butter, melted	500 mL
1½ cups	honey	375 mL

1. In a large bowl, combine pecans, sugar, cinnamon, nutmeg and allspice. Set aside.
2. Place phyllo dough on top of a damp towel. Place another damp towel on top while using dough (see Tip, left).
3. Place one sheet of phyllo in bottom of prepared pan, brush with butter, add another sheet on top, brush with butter. Repeat until you have 6 sheets of stacked phyllo. Sprinkle with 1 cup (250 mL) nut mixture.
4. Repeat layering three more times. Layer 6 more sheets on top, buttering between each sheet.
5. Using a sharp paring knife, score halfway through layers in four straight rows lengthwise. Score diagonally across pan five times to make six rows of diamonds. Bake in preheated oven until golden brown, 75 to 85 minutes.
6. About 5 minutes before baklava is finished baking, in a small saucepan over medium heat, bring honey almost to a boil, about 3 minutes. Spoon hot honey over baklava. Let cool in pan at room temperature for at least 1 hour before cutting along scored lines into diamonds.

Peach Melba Ice Cream Cake

SERVES 12

The classic dessert was named for the Australian singer Nellie Melba in 1894. Melba toast was also named after the singer. This frozen dessert is my version of the honor.

- 9-inch (23 cm) cheesecake pan or springform pan, lined with parchment paper

1	recipe French Sponge Jelly Roll (see recipe, page 219), unrolled	1
3½ cups	thinly sliced peaches	875 mL
2 tbsp	freshly squeezed lemon juice	25 mL
2 quarts	peach or vanilla ice cream, slightly softened, divided	2 L
1 cup	grenadine syrup	250 mL
⅔ cup	chopped toasted almonds	150 mL

1. Using bottom of pan as a template, cut two 9-inch (23 cm) rounds out of French Sponge Jelly Roll cake. (Reserve any remaining cake for another use.)
2. In a large bowl, sprinkle peaches with lemon juice and toss gently to coat.
3. Place one cake round in bottom of prepared cake pan. Top with 1 cup (250 mL) of the peaches. Spread half of ice cream evenly over cake. Arrange 1 cup (250 mL) of the peaches over ice cream. Place second cake round on top of peaches and spread with remaining ice cream. Top with remaining peach slices in a spiral fashion.
4. Cover and freeze overnight or for up to 24 hours. Cut cake into 12 servings and place on dessert plates. Pour grenadine evenly over each serving and sprinkle with almonds.

Raspberry Soufflés

SERVES 8

Soufflés are actually simple to make. You don't have to worry about making yours between your courses since they can be assembled ahead of time and the results are impressive. Your guests will never know this version is low in fat!

Tip

Make sure straight-sided soufflé dishes or ramekins are completely clean and dry. Very carefully brush the sides lightly and evenly with melted butter, making sure not to create "pools" of melted butter. Spoon granulated sugar into dishes to dust them completely, then shake out excess. Prepared dishes can be placed on a baking sheet and refrigerated up to 1 day ahead of filling.

- Preheat oven to 375°F (190°C)
- Candy thermometer or digital instant-read thermometer
- Eight 3-oz (90 mL) ramekins, buttered and coated with granulated sugar (See Tip, left)
- Roasting pan

1¼ cups	raspberries	300 mL
⅓ cup	granulated sugar	75 mL
2 tbsp	water	25 mL
4	egg whites	4
¼ cup	raspberry-flavored liqueur	50 mL

1. In a small saucepan, cook raspberries on low heat until reduced to 1 cup (250 mL). Set aside.
2. In another small saucepan, cook granulated sugar and water over medium heat, stirring, until sugar dissolves. Boil until temperature reaches 225°F (107°C) on a thermometer. Pour into raspberries, stirring to combine. Bring to a boil over medium-high heat. Boil until temperature reaches 242°F (117°C).
3. Meanwhile, in a mixer bowl fitted with whip attachment, whip egg whites to soft peaks, about 4 minutes. With mixer running on low speed, pour in raspberry mixture in a thin, steady stream. Beat in liqueur.
4. Divide among prepared ramekins, smoothing tops. Soufflés can be covered loosely and refrigerated before baking for up to 2 hours.
5. Place ramekins into roasting pan and pour in hot water about halfway up sides of ramekins. Bake in preheated oven until top is dry-looking, 18 to 22 minutes. Serve immediately.

Strawberries Flambé

MAKES 6 SERVINGS

In Jackson, Mississippi, I was asked to do a quick segment using strawberries on a morning TV show. On morning shows you generally get less than 3 minutes to create a complete dessert. I came up with this the night before my segment and it was a hit!

¼ cup	unsalted butter	50 mL
¾ cup	granulated sugar	175 mL
6 cups	strawberries, stemmed and halved	1.5 L
½ cup	orange-flavored liqueur	125 mL

1. In a large skillet, melt butter over medium heat. Add sugar, stirring until it forms a thick paste. Add strawberries. Cook, basting strawberries with sugar mixture, until sugar turns a bright red, about 2 minutes. Add liqueur and ignite with a match. Cook until flames go out, about 2 minutes. Serve immediately.

Uses

- Topping for Dessert Crêpes (page 301)
- Filling for Orange Chiffon Cake (page 204)

Pâte à Choux (Cream Puff Dough)

This is a versatile dough to make a variety of pastries, from cream puffs to éclairs.

- Preheat oven to 500°F (260°C)
- Pastry bag, fitted with round or star tip
- Baking sheets, lined with parchment paper or Silpats

1 cup	water	250 mL
1/2 cup	unsalted butter, softened	125 mL
1/2 tsp	salt	2 mL
1 1/4 cups	cake flour	300 mL
4	eggs	4

1. In a saucepan, cook water, butter and salt over medium heat until boiling, about 4 minutes. Remove from heat and stir in flour until blended well. Return to heat and cook, stirring vigorously, for 2 minutes. Add eggs, one at a time, mixing well between additions.
2. Spoon dough into pastry bag fitted with appropriate tip and follow instructions for desired shape (see below and right).
3. Bake in preheated oven until pastry puffs up, about 5 minutes. Reduce oven temperature to 450°F (230°C), prop door of oven open with handle of a wooden spoon to help steam escape and bake until golden brown (see shapes for baking times). Let cool completely on pan on a wire rack.

Cream Puffs

Great for a party for an elegant dessert.

- *Shape:* Round. Form with a large pastry tip. Dough should be size of a silver dollar. You can also use a #30 disher or scoop.
- *Exterior:* Prior to baking, brush with 1 tbsp (15 mL) melted butter, sprinkle with 1/4 cup (50 mL) sliced almonds.
- *Baking time:* 18 to 20 minutes.
- *To fill:* Cut baked shells in half; fill with Classic Whipped Cream (page 239). Dust with confectioner's (icing) sugar. Makes about 24.

Éclairs

Pair with cream puffs for a French pastry table.

- *Shape:* Long tube. Pipe a 3-inch (7.5 cm) long "tube" of pastry from a large round tip.
- *Exterior:* Prior to baking, brush with 1 beaten egg.
- *Baking time:* 20 to 25 minutes.
- *To fill:* Cut éclair shells in half lengthwise, keeping top on

like a "hinge." Fill with French Pastry Cream (vanilla, mocha or chocolate variations, page 242).

- *Garnish:* Dip in Chocolate Ganache (page 241). Makes about 18.

Cream Puff Swans

I have made these for many wedding showers.

- *Shape:* Each swan requires two different shapes. For the body, using a large star tip, pipe a "teardrop" body shape, about 2-inches (5 cm) long. For the neck, using a #3 writing tip, pipe "question mark" shape about 2 inches (5 cm) long. Pipe all of the body shapes onto one prepared baking sheet and the neck shapes onto another. Do not mix shapes on one pan.
- *Baking time:* Bake the neck shapes about 5 minutes and the body shapes about 22 minutes.
- *To assemble:* Cut "teardrop" body piece in half crosswise into top and bottom. Place the bottom on a plate. Cut top piece in half lengthwise to form two wings. Fill bottom with Classic Whipped Cream (page 239). Stick wings into cream. Place neck piece in cream at front of body. Dust with confectioner's (icing) sugar. Makes about 18.

Paris Brest

This dessert was created in 1891 to celebrate a bicycle race from Paris to Brest, France.

- *Shape:* Using a large round tip, pipe an 8-inch (20 cm) round "donut."
- *Exterior:* Prior to baking, brush with 1 beaten egg, sprinkle with ¼ cup (50 mL) sliced almonds.
- *Baking time:* 22 to 26 minutes.
- *To fill:* Cut ring in half crosswise into top and bottom. Place bottom on a platter and fill with French Pastry Cream (page 242) that has been mixed with Almond Praline (page 289). Replace top pastry. Dust with confectioner's sugar. Serves 12 to 14.

Profiteroles

Mini cream puffs are delightful when filled with ice cream or whipped cream.

- *Shape:* Round. Form with a large round tip. Dough should be size of a quarter. You can also use a #70 disher or scoop.
- *Baking time:* 10 to 12 minutes.
- *To fill:* Cut baked shells in half; fill with mini scoops of Classic Whipped Cream (page 239) and replace with top. Drizzle with Chocolate Ganache (page 241). Makes about 36.

Jumbo Cinnamon Rolls

Breakfast Breads

Breakfast Rolls

Muffins

Scones & Biscuits

Coffee Cakes, Donuts & Shortcakes

Breakfast Breads

In hotels in many countries, breakfast breads are served as your first meal and included in the cost of your room. They are a cultural staple. Breakfast breads are easy to make at home and they last frozen for a good amount of time. You can whip up a few batches of muffins, scones or coffee cakes for a brunch in no time.

Yeast Facts and Usage

Yeast is a one-cell, live fungus that increases by division when it comes in contact with sugar, starches and moisture, producing alcohol fermentation and carbon dioxide that leavens and lightens dough. It needs a warm room temperature of about 70°F to 90°F (21°C to 32°C) along with moisture and sugar or starch to grow. Fermentation is also called "rising," as dough literally grows at this point. The time it takes a yeast dough to rise depends, among other things, upon the richness of dough, the manner in which yeast was introduced and the room temperature.

Most commonly, recipes specify to let yeast doughs rise until doubled in volume. An easy way to determine this is to use a large, clear bucket with measurements printed on the side as your rising bowl. These buckets are available at restaurant supply stores. I have also seen them called "rising buckets." They are very handy since you can see the amount the dough has risen clearly. For example, if the dough reaches the 2-inch (5 cm) mark to start with, I know it needs to rise to the 4-inch (10 cm) mark.

There are three main types of yeast available.

ACTIVE DRY YEAST

These are dried granules of yeast, which are usually dissolved in liquid before adding to flour. It comes in tri-fold foil packets, in jars or in bulk. It is usually found with baking supply ingredients in regular grocery stores.

QUICK-RISING (INSTANT) DRY YEAST

These are smaller dried granules of yeast formulated to decrease the time required for rising. This type was originally made for the baking industry to increase production and is now available for home use. It is packaged the same way as active dry yeast (see left). I prefer it because it makes baking yeast breads faster with the same success as the slower-acting active dry yeast.

FRESH CAKE YEAST

This is found in small cakes, often in the deli section in some grocery stores or specialty stores. It must be kept refrigerated and has a short life span. It can be frozen for 2 to 3 months. One 0.6-oz (17 g) package can be substituted for one package of dry yeast.

If you purchase dry yeast in tri-fold packets, keep in mind that it is three separate packages, not one. If you purchase yeast in bulk or jars use, 1 tbsp (15 mL) yeast for each ¼-oz (7 g) package called for in the recipe.

THREE THINGS THAT WILL KILL YEAST.

1. Water temperature was too hot. Use a thermometer to check the water temperature before adding to yeast.
2. Direct contact with a salt product. Sugar enhances yeast growth but salt kills the yeast if it has not had a proper time to react with the activating ingredients before salt is added.
3. Old age. Check package expiry date before you start.

Tips for Perfect Muffins

To have a perfect muffin, follow guidelines below for ease and great-tasting muffins.

1. Measure all ingredients correctly (see page 6).
2. When combining the wet and dry ingredients, stir carefully just enough to "moisten" the dry ingredients. Overmixing causes gluten to develop, thus toughening batter. Overmixed muffins will have tunnels inside and low or peaked domes on top.
3. To test muffins for doneness, insert a toothpick into center and it should come out clean. Also, the sides should start to pull away from pan.
4. Store cooled muffins in an airtight container and keep in a cool, dry place for up to 2 days.
5. To reheat muffins, wrap muffins in foil and heat in a 400°F (200°C) oven for 10 minutes.
6. Paper liners vs. spraying or greasing tins: Most muffins can be baked with or without paper liners.

Tips for Perfect Scones and Biscuits

To make tender, fluffy scones and biscuits and to avoid making hockey pucks, I suggest these tips.

1. After flour has been introduced to your wet ingredients, stir only enough to blend ingredients. Do not overmix.
2. Place scones close together on baking sheets to keep the heat only on top of scones and not around each scone, keeping the sides tender.
3. To reheat scones, wrap scones in foil and heat in a 400°F (200°C) oven for 10 minutes.

Tips for Making Sweet Roll Shapes

POCKETS

Place a dollop of preserves in center of dough square. Take opposite corners of dough and press together in the air. Then press into preserves so preserves show on both sides of dough.

BEAR CLAWS

After rolling dough into serving piece, use a pizza wheel to cut "claws" about 1 inch (2.5 cm) inward. Brush with egg wash. Sprinkle with almond slices.

Note: Use a pizza cutter because it rolls, while and a knife may "rip" the dough.

PINWHEELS

1. Using a pizza cutter and working with one square at a time, make a cut from each corner of square to center of dough square without cutting all way through.

2. Each side of dough has a "triangle" look. There is a left and a right point. Starting at one point (right or left) fold that point all way around and press it into center.

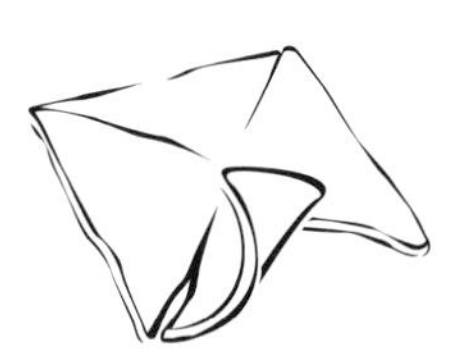

3. Repeat with all four points.

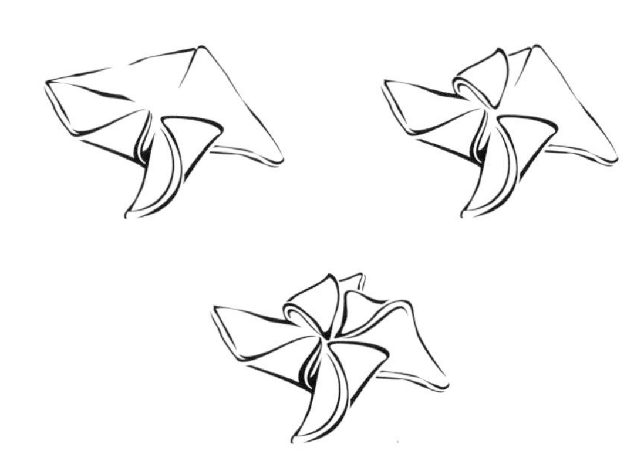

4. Brush dough with egg as directed in recipe and then place preserves into center of each pinwheel.

Sweet Roll Dough

MAKES 1 BATCH DOUGH

This dough is the base for all of the yeast breakfast rolls in this chapter.

Tips

Be sure you use regular Jell-O brand instant pudding mix, not a sugar-free one. The pudding mix is imperative for the taste and texture of the dough.

You may double the recipe and use one 4-serving size box of pudding mix. You'll need a 5-qt (4.7 L) mixer to make a double batch.

I prefer the paddle attachment for dough, but you can use the dough hook if you prefer.

- Stand mixer with paddle attachment

1/4 cup	warm water (110°F/42°C)	50 mL
1	package (1/4 oz/7 g) quick-rising (instant) dry yeast	1
1 tbsp	granulated sugar	15 mL
1/4 cup	instant vanilla pudding mix (see Tips, left)	50 mL
1 cup	whole milk	250 mL
1/4 cup	unsalted butter, melted	50 mL
1	egg, beaten	1
4 cups	all-purpose flour (approx.)	1 L
1/2 tsp	salt	2 mL

1. In a small bowl, whisk water, yeast and sugar until dissolved. Let stand until it starts to foam, about 5 minutes.
2. In mixer bowl, whisk together pudding mix, milk, butter and egg. Stir in yeast mixture. Place on mixer fitted with paddle attachment.
3. Add 3 cups (750 mL) of the flour and salt to bowl on top of liquid. Beat on low speed until dough starts to clean sides of bowl, adding up to 1 cup (250 mL) additional flour to make a soft, not sticky dough. Increase speed to medium and knead dough for 2 minutes.
4. Remove dough from mixer bowl and turn dough out onto a floured work surface. Knead by hand until smooth and elastic, about 2 minutes. Place in a very large oiled bowl, turning to coat dough with oil. Cover and let rise in a warm, draft-free place until doubled in bulk, 30 to 40 minutes. Punch down dough. Proceed as directed in recipe.

After shaping, any of these breakfast yeast breads can be covered and refrigerated for up to 24 hours prior to baking them. If you are going to need more time, freeze shaped rolls for up to 1 month. Thaw in refrigerator for 12 hours, then bake as directed.

Bear Claws

MAKES ABOUT 12 BEAR CLAWS

The first time I discovered bear claws was when I worked at Dick's Bakery in San Jose, California. I was in charge of making the filling. We didn't use a recipe there, since we used up day-old cakes and made them by look and feel. I designed this recipe for you to try at home.

Tip

You can use any day-old baked goods in place of the pound cake, such as cake donuts, cakes or muffins.

- Baking sheet, lined with parchment paper or Silpats

1	recipe Sweet Roll Dough (see recipe, page 319)	1
12 oz	pound cake, broken into chunks (about 2 cups/500 mL)	375 g
2 tbsp	honey	25 mL
1 tsp	almond extract	5 mL
1 tsp	ground cinnamon	5 mL
½ tsp	ground nutmeg	2 mL
1	egg, beaten	1
1 cup	sliced almonds	250 mL
	Breakfast Roll Cream Cheese Drizzle (see Variation, page 328)	

1. On a floured surface, roll half of dough out to an 18-by 9-inch (45 by 23 cm) rectangle. Set aside.
2. In a food processor fitted with metal blade, process pound cake, honey, almond extract, cinnamon and nutmeg until smooth, about 20 seconds.
3. If mixture is pliable, roll half into a long log and distribute it along one long side of the dough, about 2 inches (5 cm) from edge. (If filling is not pliable, spoon onto dough.) Fold dough over so mixture is in center.
4. With palm of your hand, press dough down so it is flat and filling is enclosed, pressing edge to seal. Cut crosswise into 3-inch (7.5 cm) pieces. On each piece, make small cuts at the seam side like "fingers," about 2-inches (5 cm) long (see illustration, page 317). Brush top of each bear claw with beaten egg and sprinkle with almonds. Place on prepared baking sheet, at least 2 inches (5 cm) apart. Cover with a towel and let rise for 20 minutes. Repeat with remaining dough and filling.
5. Meanwhile, preheat oven to 375°F (190°C).
6. Bake in preheated oven, one sheet at a time, until light brown, 18 to 22 minutes. Let cool completely on pans on a rack. Decorate with Breakfast Roll Cream Cheese Drizzle.

Pecan Sticky Buns

MAKES ABOUT 18 BUNS

These are like cinnamon rolls but with a crunchy, sugary pecan topping.

- 13-by 9-inch (3 L) metal baking pan, lined with foil, then lined with parchment paper

Topping

1 cup	packed brown sugar	250 mL
1/4 cup	unsalted butter, softened	50 mL
1 tbsp	vanilla extract	15 mL
1 cup	pecan halves, chopped	250 mL

Filling

1	recipe Sweet Roll Dough (see recipe, page 319)	1
1/4 cup	unsalted butter, melted	50 mL
3/4 cup	packed brown sugar	175 mL
1 tbsp	ground cinnamon	15 mL
1/2 tsp	ground nutmeg	2 mL
	Breakfast Roll Cream Cheese Icing (see recipe, page 328)	

1. *Topping:* In a mixer bowl fitted with paddle attachment, beat brown sugar, butter, vanilla and pecans for 3 minutes. Sprinkle over bottom of prepared baking pan. Set aside.
2. *Filling:* On a floured surface, roll Sweet Roll Dough out to an 18-inch (45 cm) square. Brush with melted butter. Sprinkle evenly with brown sugar, cinnamon and nutmeg, leaving a 1-inch (2.5 cm) border along the edge closest to you with only butter.
3. Starting with the side farthest from you, roll dough toward you jelly-roll style. If some areas are thin or thick you can jiggle the dough to make it uniform. Pinch edge to seal seam. With seam down, cut dough crosswise into 1-inch (2.5 cm) thick slices to make about 18 rolls. Place rolls cut-side up and touching each other in prepared pan. Cover with a towel and let rise for 20 minutes.
4. Meanwhile, preheat oven to 375°F (190°C).
5. Bake in preheated oven until light brown, 18 to 24 minutes. Smear with Breakfast Roll Cream Cheese Icing while still hot. Serve warm.

Cream Cheese Pockets

MAKES 36 POCKETS

The creamy cheese filling in these pockets is like having a bite of cheesecake for breakfast.

Tip

The cream cheese mixture can be covered and refrigerated for up to 2 days before filling pockets.

Variation

You can use 2 tsp (10 mL) of a berry preserve to add a splash of contrasting color to some of the pockets instead of the cream cheese filling. A jelly will not work; be sure it is a thick preserve or jam.

- Preheat oven to 350°F (180°C)
- Baking sheets, lined with parchment paper or Silpats
- Pizza cutter

4 oz	cream cheese, softened	125 g
1	egg yolk	1
½ cup	confectioner's (icing) sugar, sifted	125 mL
1	recipe Sweet Roll Dough (see recipe, page 319)	1
	Breakfast Roll Cream Cheese Drizzle (see Variation, page 328)	

1. In a mixer bowl fitted with paddle attachment, beat cream cheese, egg yolk and confectioner's sugar until smooth, about 2 minutes. Set aside.
2. On a floured surface, roll half of Sweet Roll Dough out to an 18-by 9-inch (45 by 23 cm) rectangle. Using a pizza cutter, cut dough lengthwise into three strips. Cut crosswise into six strips to make eighteen 3-inch (7.5 cm) squares.
3. Place about 2 tsp (10 mL) of cream cheese filling into center of each square. Working with one square at a time, starting with two opposite corners, bring toward center in the air above the filling. Pinch together and press down into filling, leaving remaining two corners flat (see illustration, page 317). Repeat with remaining squares and filling.
4. Place on prepared baking sheets, at least 2 inches (5 cm) apart. Bake in preheated oven until light brown, 12 to 16 minutes. Let cool completely on pan on a rack. Repeat with remaining half of dough and filling. Decorate with Breakfast Roll Cream Cheese Drizzle.

Jumbo Cinnamon Rolls

MAKES ABOUT 18 ROLLS

These are the cinnamon rolls that launched my television career. Take them to work and see what they do for you.

Tip

Some people recommend using dental floss to cut dough but I prefer a thin blade knife, as floss may fray into dough and leave fragments.

Variations

Orange Macadamia Rolls: Replace butter with ½ cup (125 mL) orange marmalade and omit cinnamon. Sprinkle 1 cup (250 mL) chopped macadamia nuts with sugar and spices.

Sprinkle up to 1 cup (250 mL) of any type of chocolate chips, chunks or nuts that you prefer with brown sugar and spices.

- 13-by 9-inch (3 L) baking pan, lined with foil, then lined with parchment paper

1	recipe Sweet Roll Dough (see recipe, page 319)	1
2 tbsp	unsalted butter, melted	25 mL
¾ cup	packed brown sugar	175 mL
1 tbsp	ground cinnamon	15 mL
½ tsp	ground nutmeg	2 mL
	Breakfast Roll Cream Cheese Icing (see recipe, page 328)	

1. On a floured surface, roll Sweet Roll Dough out to an 18-inch (45 cm) square. Brush with melted butter. Sprinkle evenly with brown sugar, cinnamon and nutmeg, leaving a 1-inch (2.5 cm) border along the edge closest to you with only butter.
2. Starting with the side farthest from you, roll dough toward you jelly-roll style. If some areas are thin or thick you can jiggle the dough to make it uniform. Pinch edge to seal seam. With seam down, cut dough crosswise into 1-inch (2.5 cm) thick slices to make about 18 rolls.
3. Place rolls cut-side up and touching each other in prepared baking pan. Cover with a towel and let rise for 20 minutes.
4. Meanwhile, preheat oven to 375°F (190°C).
5. Bake in preheated oven until light brown, 18 to 24 minutes. Smear with Breakfast Roll Cream Cheese Icing while still hot. Serve warm.

Monkey Bread

SERVES 12

I am not sure where this name came from, but in some places it is called "pull-apart" bread. Regardless of what you call it, it is fun for kids to pull pieces of the sweet bread off and eat them.

Tip

If you try to release bread too soon or after it has cooled, the bread may stick or come out in small pieces. Set a timer and release the bread from the pan after exactly 15 minutes.

- Preheat oven to 375°F (190°C)
- 10-inch (4 L) tube pan, sprayed with nonstick spray

1	recipe Sweet Roll Dough (see recipe, page 319)	1
2 tbsp	unsalted butter, melted	25 mL
3/4 cup	granulated sugar	175 mL
1 tbsp	ground cinnamon	15 mL
1 tsp	ground nutmeg	5 mL
	Breakfast Roll Cream Cheese Drizzle (see Variation, page 328)	

1. Cut dough into small bite-size pieces. Place in a large bowl, pour melted butter on top and toss with your hands to coat. Add sugar, cinnamon and nutmeg and toss to evenly coat. Place dough mixture into prepared tube pan. Press down slightly. Cover with plastic wrap and let rise in a warm, draft-free place until it rises to top of pan, about 20 minutes.
2. Bake in preheated oven until light brown, 24 to 28 minutes. Let cool in pan on a rack for 15 minutes. Invert onto a rack and remove pan. Let cool completely. Decorate with Breakfast Roll Cream Cheese Icing.

Strawberry Pinwheels

MAKES ABOUT 36 PINWHEELS

My students go crazy when they learn how to make this simple Danish.

Tip

Make sure you use thick preserves or jams. A jelly will bleed out of Danish.

Variation

Use any berry preserve or use a combination of different preserves.

- Preheat oven to 350°F (180°C)
- Baking sheets, lined with parchment paper or Silpats
- Pizza cutter

1	recipe Sweet Roll Dough (see recipe, page 319)	1
1	egg, beaten	1
½ cup	strawberry preserves (approx.)	125 mL
	Breakfast Roll Cream Cheese Drizzle (see Variation, page 328)	

1. On a floured surface, roll half of Sweet Roll Dough out to an 18-by 9-inch (45 by 23 cm) rectangle. Using a pizza cutter, cut dough lengthwise into three strips. Cut crosswise into six strips to make eighteen 3-inch (7.5 cm) squares. Working with one square at a time, make a cut from each corner of square to center of square without cutting all the way through (see illustrations, page 318).
2. Each side of dough has a "triangle" look. There is a left and a right point. Starting at one point (right or left), fold that point all the way around and press it into center. Repeat with all four points.
3. Place on prepared baking sheets, at least 2 inches (5 cm) apart. Brush dough with beaten egg. Spoon about ½ tsp (2 mL) of preserves in center of each pinwheel. Bake in preheated oven until light brown, 12 to 16 minutes. Let cool completely on pan on a rack. Repeat with remaining dough, egg and preserves. Decorate with Breakfast Roll Cream Cheese Drizzle.

Breakfast Roll Cream Cheese Icing

MAKES ABOUT 2 CUPS (500 ML)

This is a finishing touch for all breakfast rolls.

Variation

Breakfast Roll Cream Cheese Drizzle: For a thinner icing, add an extra 1½ tbsp (22 mL) milk to icing.

4 oz	cream cheese, softened	125 g
⅓ cup	unsalted butter, softened	75 mL
1 tsp	vanilla extract	5 mL
1½ cups	confectioner's (icing) sugar, sifted	375 mL
1 tbsp	milk	15 mL

1. In a mixer bowl fitted with paddle attachment, whip cream cheese and butter until smooth, for 3 minutes. Gradually add vanilla, confectioner's sugar and milk, mixing on low speed until it starts to cream together, about 3 minutes. Increase speed and beat until light and fluffy, for 2 minutes.

Uses

Icing

- Christmas Tree Cinnamon Rolls (page 414)
- Jumbo Cinnamon Rolls (page 324)
- Pecan Praline Mini-Muffins (page 344)
- Pecan Sticky Buns (page 322)

Drizzle

- Bear Claws (page 320)
- Cream Cheese Pockets (page 323)
- Monkey Bread (page 325)
- Strawberry Pinwheels (page 326)

Almond Apricot Muffins

MAKES 12 MUFFINS

Rich flavor with nutty almonds make this a perfect muffin for brunch or breakfast.

Variation

Substitute pecans for the almonds if you like.

Substitute 1/4 cup (50 mL) finely chopped dried apricots for the fresh.

- Preheat oven to 375°F (190°C)
- One 12-cup muffin tin, lined with paper liners or sprayed with nonstick spray

2 1/2 cups	cake flour	625 mL
2 1/2 tsp	baking powder	12 mL
1/2 tsp	salt	2 mL
1/2 tsp	ground cardamom	2 mL
1/2 cup	unsalted butter, softened	125 mL
1 cup	granulated sugar	250 mL
2	eggs	2
3/4 cup	whipping (35%) cream	175 mL
1 tsp	vanilla extract	5 mL
1/2 tsp	almond extract	2 mL
1/2 cup	finely chopped fresh apricots	125 mL
1/2 cup	almonds, chopped	125 mL

1. In a bowl, whisk together flour, baking powder, salt and cardamom. Set aside.
2. In a mixer bowl fitted with paddle attachment, cream butter and sugar until fluffy, for 2 minutes. Beat in eggs, cream, vanilla and almond extracts. Using a wooden spoon, stir in flour mixture just until moistened. Fold in apricots and almonds.
3. Scoop into prepared muffin tin. Bake in preheated oven, until a toothpick inserted into center comes out clean, 15 to 18 minutes. Let cool in tin on a wire rack for 10 minutes. Transfer to rack to cool completely.

Banana Bran Muffins

MAKES 12 MUFFINS

These muffins are full of flavor and stay moist for days.

Tip

Use the ripest banana to get optimal flavor.

Variation

Try ½ cup (125 mL) of chopped prunes (dried plums) in place of pecans.

- Preheat oven to 350°F (180°C)
- One 12-cup muffin tin, lined with paper liners or sprayed with nonstick spray

1 cup	all-purpose flour	250 mL
⅓ cup	granulated sugar	75 mL
2 tsp	baking powder	10 mL
½ tsp	salt	2 mL
½ tsp	ground cinnamon	2 mL
1 cup	oat bran	250 mL
1 cup	milk	250 mL
1	very ripe large banana, mashed	1
1	egg	1
3 tbsp	vegetable oil	45 mL
1 cup	pecan halves, chopped	250 mL

1. In a small bowl, whisk together flour, sugar, baking powder, salt and cinnamon. Set aside.
2. In a large bowl, whisk together bran, milk, banana, egg and oil. Let stand for 5 minutes. Using a wooden spoon, stir in flour mixture just until moistened. Fold in pecans.
3. Scoop into prepared muffin tin. Bake in preheated oven until a toothpick inserted into center comes out clean, 18 to 22 minutes. Let cool in tin on a wire rack for 10 minutes. Transfer to rack to cool completely.

Banana Chocolate Chip Muffins

MAKES 12 MUFFINS

Filled with taste and moisture, these muffins freeze nicely.

Variation

Replace semisweet chips with white chocolate chips for a sweeter muffin.

- Preheat oven to 400°F (200°C)
- One 12-cup muffin tin, lined with paper liners or sprayed with nonstick spray

2 cups	all-purpose flour	500 mL
1 tbsp	baking powder	15 mL
1/2 tsp	salt	2 mL
1/4 cup	unsalted butter, softened	50 mL
3/4 cup	packed brown sugar	175 mL
1	egg	1
1 cup	buttermilk	250 mL
2	very ripe large bananas, chopped	2
1 cup	semisweet chocolate chips	250 mL

1. In a bowl, whisk together flour, baking powder and salt. Set aside.
2. In a mixer bowl fitted with paddle attachment, cream butter and brown sugar until fluffy, for 2 minutes. Beat in egg and buttermilk. Using a wooden spoon, stir in flour mixture just until moistened. Fold in bananas and chocolate chips.
3. Scoop into prepared muffin tin. Bake in preheated oven until light brown and a toothpick inserted into center comes out clean, 20 to 24 minutes. Let cool in tin on a wire rack for 10 minutes. Transfer to rack to cool completely.

Banana Oatmeal Pecan Chip Muffins

MAKES 12 MUFFINS

Rich pecans and sweet chocolate make these muffins like a dessert for breakfast!

- Preheat oven to 400°F (200°C)
- One 12-cup muffin tin, lined with paper liners or sprayed with nonstick spray

1 cup	old-fashioned rolled oats	250 mL
1 cup	all-purpose flour	250 mL
1 tbsp	baking powder	15 mL
1½ tsp	ground cinnamon	7 mL
½ tsp	ground nutmeg	2 mL
½ tsp	salt	2 mL
½ tsp	ground allspice	2 mL
¼ cup	unsalted butter, softened	50 mL
¾ cup	packed brown sugar	175 mL
1	egg	1
1 cup	buttermilk	250 mL
2	very ripe bananas, chopped	2
1 cup	semisweet chocolate chips	250 mL
½ cup	pecan halves, chopped	125 mL

1. In a bowl, whisk together oats, flour, baking powder, cinnamon, nutmeg, salt and allspice. Set aside.
2. In a mixer bowl fitted with paddle attachment, cream butter and brown sugar until fluffy, for 2 minutes. Beat in egg and buttermilk. Using a wooden spoon, stir in flour mixture just until moistened. Fold in bananas, chocolate chips and pecans.
3. Scoop into prepared muffin tin. Bake in preheated oven until light brown and a toothpick inserted into center comes out clean, 20 to 24 minutes. Let cool in tin on a wire rack for 10 minutes. Transfer to rack to cool completely.

Citrus Muffins

MAKES 12 MUFFINS

Orange and lemon zests unite to make this a flavor-packed muffin.

Tip

Make sure when you are zesting citrus fruits you only zest the outer colored part of the skin, as the white pith is bitter.

Variation

Stir 1/4 cup (50 mL) of chopped candied citrus into batter after flour mixture.

- Preheat oven to 375°F (190°C)
- One 12-cup muffin tins, lined with paper liners or sprayed with nonstick spray

2 1/2 cups	cake flour	625 mL
2 1/2 tsp	baking powder	12 mL
1/2 tsp	salt	2 mL
1/2 cup	vegetable shortening or unsalted butter, softened	125 mL
1 cup	granulated sugar	250 mL
1 tbsp	grated orange zest	15 mL
1 tbsp	grated lemon zest	15 mL
3/4 cup	milk, preferably whole	175 mL
2	eggs	2
1 tsp	vanilla extract	5 mL

1. In a bowl, whisk together flour, baking powder and salt. Set aside.
2. In a mixer bowl fitted with paddle attachment, cream shortening and sugar until fluffy, for 2 minutes. Beat in orange and lemon zests, milk, eggs and vanilla. Using a wooden spoon, stir in flour mixture just until moistened.
3. Scoop into prepared muffin tin. Bake in preheated oven until light brown and a toothpick inserted into center comes out clean, 14 to 18 minutes. Let cool in tin on a wire rack for 10 minutes. Transfer to rack to cool completely.

Cranberry Almond Muffins

MAKES 12 MUFFINS

I like to make these muffins in fall as soon as I see the first bag of fresh cranberries in the markets.

Tip

If using frozen berries, keep them frozen until you are ready to fold into batter.

Variation

Substitute 1 cup (250 mL) of raisins or dried cranberries in place of fresh or frozen cranberries.

- Preheat oven to 375°F (190°C)
- One 12-cup muffin tin, lined with paper liners or sprayed with nonstick spray

2½ cups	cake flour	625 mL
2½ tsp	baking powder	12 mL
½ tsp	salt	2 mL
½ cup	vegetable shortening or unsalted butter, softened	125 mL
1 cup	granulated sugar	250 mL
2	eggs	2
¾ cup	milk, preferably whole	175 mL
1 tsp	vanilla extract	5 mL
1 cup	cranberries, fresh or frozen (see Tip, left)	250 mL
½ cup	almonds, chopped	125 mL

1. In a bowl, whisk together flour, baking powder and salt. Set aside.
2. In a mixer bowl fitted with paddle attachment, cream shortening and sugar until light and fluffy, for 2 minutes. Beat in eggs, milk and vanilla. Using a wooden spoon, stir in flour mixture just until moistened. Fold in cranberries and almonds.
3. Scoop into prepared muffin tin. Bake in preheated oven until light brown and a toothpick inserted into center comes out clean, 12 to 18 minutes. Let cool in tin on a wire rack for 10 minutes. Transfer to rack to cool completely.

Double Chocolate Raspberry Muffins

MAKES 24 MUFFINS

Two chocolates with sweet fresh raspberries make a rich breakfast muffin that anyone would be proud to serve.

Tip

These muffins are a dark color, so start checking for doneness after 15 minutes and be sure not to overbake them.

Variation

Try finely chopped strawberries in place of raspberries.

- Preheat oven to 400°F (200°C)
- Two 12-cup muffin tins, lined with paper liners or sprayed with nonstick spray

3½ cups	all-purpose flour	875 mL
½ cup	unsweetened Dutch-process cocoa powder	125 mL
1 tbsp	baking soda	15 mL
2 tsp	salt	10 mL
2 cups	milk, preferably whole	500 mL
1 cup	unsalted butter, melted	250 mL
4	eggs, beaten	4
¾ cup	granulated sugar	175 mL
2 tsp	vanilla extract	10 mL
1 cup	semisweet chocolate chips	250 mL
1 cup	fresh raspberries	250 mL
2 tsp	all-purpose flour	10 mL

1. In a large bowl, whisk together 3½ cups (875 mL) flour, cocoa powder, baking soda and salt. Set aside.
2. In another large bowl, whisk together milk, butter, eggs, sugar and vanilla until blended. Using a wooden spoon, stir in flour mixture just until moistened.
3. In another bowl, combine chocolate chips, raspberries and 2 tsp (10 mL) flour. Gently fold into batter.
4. Scoop into prepared muffin tins. Bake in preheated oven until a toothpick inserted into center comes out clean, 15 to 20 minutes. Let cool in tin on a wire rack for 10 minutes. Transfer to rack to cool completely.

Honey Bran Muffins

MAKES 24 MUFFINS

These muffins are rich and dense because there is no flour in the recipe. They are sticky and flavorful.

Variation

Honey Blueberry Bran Muffins: Add 1 cup (250 mL) frozen blueberries to batter.

- Preheat oven to 375°F (190°C)
- Two 12-cup muffin tins, lined with paper liners or sprayed with nonstick spray

4 cups	oat bran	1 L
½ cup	packed light brown sugar	125 mL
1 tbsp	baking powder	15 mL
1 tsp	salt	5 mL
2 cups	milk	500 mL
4	eggs	4
½ cup	honey	125 mL
¼ cup	vegetable oil	50 mL

1. In a large bowl, whisk together oat bran, brown sugar, baking powder and salt.
2. In another bowl, whisk together milk, eggs, honey and oil until blended. Pour over dry ingredients and, using a wooden spoon, stir just until moistened.
3. Scoop into prepared muffin tins. Bake in preheated oven until golden brown and a toothpick inserted into center comes out clean, 18 to 22 minutes. Let cool in tin on a wire rack for 10 minutes. Transfer to rack to cool completely.

Lemon Poppy Seed Muffins

MAKES 24 MUFFINS

Lemon and poppy seeds always pair well together. And are once again perfect here for these light, cake-like muffins.

Tip

Be sure to glaze the muffins while hot. If you let muffins cool the glaze will not soak into them.

Variation

Orange Poppy Seed Muffins: Substitute orange zest and juice for the lemon.

- Preheat oven to 350°F (180°C)
- Two 12-cup muffin tins, lined with paper liners or sprayed with nonstick spray

6 tbsp	whipping (35%) cream	90 mL
6	eggs	6
2 tsp	vanilla extract	10 mL
3½ cups	cake flour	875 mL
1½ cups	granulated sugar	375 mL
2 tbsp	grated lemon zest	25 mL
1 tbsp	poppy seeds	15 mL
2 tsp	baking powder	10 mL
½ tsp	salt	2 mL
1½ cups	unsalted butter, softened, cut into cubes	375 mL

Glaze

½ cup	granulated sugar	125 mL
½ cup	freshly squeezed lemon juice	125 mL
6 tbsp	unsalted butter, softened	90 mL

1. In a bowl, whisk together cream, eggs and vanilla until blended. Set aside.
2. In a mixer bowl fitted with paddle attachment, combine flour, sugar, lemon zest, poppy seeds, baking powder and salt on low speed. With mixer running, gradually add butter cubes, mixing until it starts to look crumbly. Pour in cream mixture and, using a fork, mix just until moistened.
3. Scoop into prepared muffin tins. Bake in preheated oven until golden and a toothpick inserted into center comes out clean, 18 to 22 minutes.
4. *Glaze:* Meanwhile, in a small saucepan, melt sugar, lemon juice and butter over low heat, stirring, until sugar is dissolved, for about 3 minutes. Spoon hot glaze on top of hot muffins. Let cool in tin on a wire rack for 10 minutes. Transfer to rack to cool completely.

Maple Muffins

MAKES 24 MUFFINS

Rich real maple syrup makes these muffins full of flavor.

- Preheat oven to 400°F (200°C)
- Two 12-cup muffin tins, lined with paper liners or sprayed with nonstick spray

3 cups	all-purpose flour	750 mL
½ cup	old-fashioned rolled oats	125 mL
1 tbsp	baking powder	15 mL
1 tsp	salt	5 mL
½ cup	vegetable shortening or unsalted butter, softened	125 mL
½ cup	packed light brown sugar	125 mL
2	eggs	2
1 cup	milk, preferably whole	250 mL
1 cup	pure maple syrup	250 mL

1. In a large bowl, whisk together flour, oats, baking powder and salt. Set aside.
2. In a mixer bowl fitted with paddle attachment, cream shortening and brown sugar until fluffy, for 2 minutes. Beat in eggs, milk and syrup. Using a wooden spoon, stir in flour mixture just until moistened.
3. Scoop into prepared muffin tins. Bake in preheated oven until light brown and a toothpick inserted into center comes out clean, 18 to 22 minutes. Let cool in tin on a wire rack for 10 minutes. Transfer to rack to cool completely.

Oat Berry Muffins

MAKES 12 MUFFINS

The sweetness of berries complements the nutty flavor of oats.

Tip

If using frozen berries, keep them frozen until you are ready to add them to the batter to prevent the color from tinting the batter.

Variation

You can use one type of berry, but I enjoy a multi-colored muffin you get with using a mixture of varieties.

- Preheat oven to 400°F (200°C)
- One 12-cup muffin tin, lined with paper liners or sprayed with nonstick spray

1 cup	all-purpose flour	250 mL
1 cup	old-fashioned rolled oats	250 mL
1 tbsp	baking powder	15 mL
1⁄2 tsp	salt	2 mL
1⁄4 cup	unsalted butter, softened	50 mL
3⁄4 cup	packed brown sugar	175 mL
1	egg	1
1 cup	buttermilk	250 mL
1 cup	mixed berries, frozen or fresh	250 mL

1. In a bowl, whisk together flour, oats, baking powder and salt. Set aside.
2. In a mixer bowl fitted with paddle attachment, cream butter and brown sugar until fluffy, for 2 minutes. Beat in egg and buttermilk. Using a wooden spoon, stir in flour mixture just until moistened. Fold in berries.
3. Scoop into prepared muffin tin. Bake in preheated oven until light brown and a toothpick inserted into center comes out clean, 20 to 24 minutes. Let cool in tin on a wire rack for 10 minutes. Transfer to rack to cool completely.

Orange Muffins

MAKES 12 MUFFINS

Tart orange flavor is baked into sweet muffins and accented with an orange glaze.

- Preheat oven to 375°F (190°C)
- One 12-cup muffin tin, lined with paper liners or sprayed with nonstick spray

2½ cups	cake flour	625 mL
2½ tsp	baking powder	12 mL
½ tsp	salt	2 mL
½ cup	unsalted butter, softened	125 mL
1 cup	granulated sugar	250 mL
1 tbsp	grated orange zest	15 mL
2	eggs	2
¾ cup	whipping (35%) cream	175 mL
1 tsp	vanilla extract	5 mL
½ tsp	orange extract	2 mL
Glaze		
¼ cup	frozen orange juice concentrate	50 mL
¼ cup	granulated sugar	50 mL
2 tbsp	unsalted butter, softened	25 mL

1. In a bowl, whisk together flour, baking powder and salt. Set aside.
2. In a mixer bowl fitted with paddle attachment, cream butter and sugar until fluffy, for 2 minutes. Beat in orange zest, eggs, cream, vanilla and orange extract. Using a wooden spoon, stir in flour mixture just until moistened.
3. Scoop into prepared muffin tin. Bake in preheated oven until light brown and a toothpick inserted into center comes out clean, 14 to 18 minutes.
4. *Glaze:* Meanwhile, in a small saucepan, melt orange juice concentrate, sugar and butter over low heat, stirring, until bubbling, about 2 minutes. Brush hot glaze on hot muffins. Let cool in tin on a wire rack for 10 minutes. Transfer to rack to cool completely.

Apple Spice Muffins

MAKES 12 MUFFINS

Just like a piece of apple pie, all in a muffin for breakfast.

Tip

Make sure apples are chopped fine or your muffins will be very crunchy.

Variation

Substitute fresh pears in place of apples.

- Preheat oven to 375°F (190°C)
- One 12-cup muffin tin, lined with paper liners or sprayed with nonstick spray

2½ cups	cake flour	625 mL
2½ tsp	baking powder	12 mL
½ tsp	salt	7 mL
½ cup	vegetable shortening or unsalted butter, softened	125 mL
1 cup	granulated sugar	250 mL
2	eggs	2
¾ cup	milk, preferably whole	175 mL
1 tsp	vanilla extract	5 mL
1½ cups	finely chopped apples	375 mL
2 tsp	ground cinnamon	10 mL
1 tsp	ground nutmeg	5 mL

1. In a bowl, whisk together flour, baking powder and salt. Set aside.
2. In a mixer bowl fitted with paddle attachment, cream shortening and sugar until fluffy, for 2 minutes. Beat in eggs, milk and vanilla. Using a wooden spoon, stir in flour mixture just until moistened. Fold in apples, cinnamon and nutmeg.
3. Scoop into prepared muffin tin. Bake in preheated oven until a toothpick inserted into center comes out clean, 15 to 18 minutes. Let cool in tins on a wire rack for 10 minutes. Transfer to rack to cool completely.

Pecan Praline Mini-Muffins

MAKES
24 MINI-MUFFINS

These muffins are adapted from a recipe from the Cookin' Cajun Cooking School in New Orleans. This is a perfect mini-muffin for snacking.

Tips

This unusual recipe will only work in mini-muffin tins.

It is important to use a flour-based nonstick spray to make sure they don't stick in the tin. Do not use paper liners.

Variation

Make these extra special for a brunch by adding a swirl of Breakfast Roll Cream Cheese Icing (page 328) on top.

- Preheat oven to 350°F (180°C)
- One 24-cup mini-muffin tin, sprayed with flour-based nonstick spray (see Tips, left)

1 cup	packed light brown sugar	250 mL
1 cup	chopped toasted pecans	250 mL
1/2 cup	all-purpose flour	125 mL
2/3 cup	unsalted butter, melted	150 mL
2	eggs, beaten	2

1. In a bowl, whisk together brown sugar, pecans, flour, butter and eggs just until incorporated.
2. Scoop into prepared muffin tin. Bake in preheated oven until light brown and crunchy looking and a toothpick inserted into center comes out clean, 18 to 20 minutes. Let cool in tin on a wire rack for 10 minutes. Transfer to rack to cool completely.

Perfect Bran Muffins

MAKES 12 MUFFINS

A great source of fiber and nutrients.

Tip

Make sure you wait the entire 5 minutes for bran to soak up buttermilk or the muffins will be very dry.

Variation

You can add ½ cup (125 mL) of fresh berries such as raspberries, blackberries, etc. with the raisins.

- Preheat oven to 375°F (190°C)
- One 12-cup muffin tin, lined with paper liners or sprayed with nonstick spray

1½ cups	natural wheat bran	375 mL
1 cup	buttermilk	250 mL
1 cup	all-purpose flour	250 mL
1 tsp	baking soda	5 mL
1 tsp	baking powder	5 mL
½ tsp	salt	2 mL
1	egg	1
⅔ cup	packed brown sugar	150 mL
⅓ cup	vegetable oil	75 mL
½ tsp	vanilla extract	2 mL
½ cup	golden raisins	125 mL

1. In a bowl, soak bran with buttermilk for 5 minutes. In another bowl, whisk together flour, baking soda, baking powder and salt. Set aside.
2. In a large bowl, whisk together egg, brown sugar, oil and vanilla until blended. Add bran mixture and flour mixture and, using a wooden spoon, stir just until moistened. Fold in raisins.
3. Scoop into prepared muffin tin. Bake in preheated oven until firm to the touch and a toothpick inserted into center comes out clean, 15 to 20 minutes. Let cool in tin on a wire rack for 10 minutes. Transfer to rack to cool completely.

Pineapple Macadamia Nut Muffins

MAKES 12 MUFFINS

Flavors full of the Hawaiian Islands. All you need to do is to put on your grass skirt!

- Preheat oven to 400°F (200°C)
- One 12-cup muffin tin, lined with paper liners or sprayed with nonstick spray

1 cup	all-purpose flour	250 mL
1 cup	old-fashioned rolled oats	250 mL
1 tbsp	baking powder	15 mL
1½ tsp	ground cinnamon	7 mL
½ tsp	salt	2 mL
½ tsp	ground nutmeg	2 mL
½ tsp	ground allspice	2 mL
¼ cup	unsalted butter, softened	50 mL
¾ cup	packed light brown sugar	175 mL
1	egg	1
1 cup	buttermilk	250 mL
½ cup	crushed pineapple	125 mL
½ cup	macadamia nuts, chopped and toasted	125 mL

1. In a bowl, whisk together flour, oats, baking powder, cinnamon, salt, nutmeg and allspice. Set aside.
2. In a mixer bowl fitted with paddle attachment, cream butter and brown sugar until fluffy, for 2 minutes. Beat in egg and buttermilk. Using a wooden spoon, stir in flour mixture just until moistened. Fold in pineapple and nuts.
3. Scoop into prepared muffin tin. Bake in preheated oven until light brown and a toothpick inserted into center comes out clean, 20 to 25 minutes. Let cool in tin on a wire rack for 10 minutes. Transfer to rack to cool completely.

Sour Cream Blackberry Muffins

MAKES 12 MUFFINS

Sometimes I will have some extra sour cream in the fridge so I like to use it in muffins — it makes them very moist.

Tip

If using frozen berries, keep them frozen until you are ready to add them to the batter to prevent the color from tinting the batter.

Variation

Substitute raspberries or chopped strawberries in place of blackberries.

- Preheat oven to 375°F (190°C)
- One 12-cup muffin tin, lined with paper liners or sprayed with nonstick spray

2½ cups	cake flour	625 mL
2½ tsp	baking powder	12 mL
½ tsp	salt	2 mL
½ cup	vegetable shortening or unsalted butter, softened	125 mL
1 cup	granulated sugar	250 mL
2	eggs	2
½ cup	milk, preferably whole	125 mL
¼ cup	sour cream (not fat-free)	50 mL
1 tsp	vanilla extract	5 mL
1 cup	blackberries, fresh or frozen	250 mL

1. In a bowl, whisk together flour, baking powder and salt. Set aside.
2. In a mixer bowl fitted with paddle attachment, cream shortening and sugar until fluffy, for 2 minutes. Beat in eggs, milk, sour cream and vanilla. Using a wooden spoon, stir in flour mixture just until moistened. Fold in blackberries.
3. Scoop into prepared muffin tin. Bake in preheated oven until light brown and a toothpick inserted into center comes out clean, 22 to 26 minutes. Let cool in tin on a wire rack for 10 minutes. Transfer to rack to cool completely.

Strawberry Muffins

MAKES 12 MUFFINS

These muffins are a must when fresh strawberries are in season. When the berries are at their peak, make a double batch of these muffins and freeze half.

Tip

Be sure to cut the berries into small pieces so they get evenly dispersed in the batter.

Variation

Add ½ tsp (2 mL) of almond extract with the vanilla.

- Preheat oven to 375°F (190°C)
- One 12-cup muffin tin, lined with paper liners or sprayed with nonstick spray

2 cups	all-purpose flour	500 mL
2½ tsp	baking powder	12 mL
½ tsp	salt	2 mL
½ cup	unsalted butter, softened	125 mL
1 cup	granulated sugar	250 mL
2	eggs	2
¾ cup	whipping (35%) cream	175 mL
1 tsp	vanilla extract	5 mL
1 cup	finely chopped strawberries	250 mL

1. In a bowl, whisk together flour, baking powder and salt. Set aside.
2. In a mixer bowl fitted with paddle attachment, cream butter and sugar until fluffy, for 2 minutes. Beat in eggs, cream and vanilla. Using a wooden spoon, stir in flour mixture just until moistened. Fold in strawberries.
3. Scoop into prepared muffin tin. Bake in preheated oven until light brown and a toothpick inserted into center comes out clean, 22 to 26 minutes. Let cool in tin on a wire rack for 10 minutes. Transfer to rack to cool completely.

White Chocolate Key Lime Muffins

MAKES 18 SMALL MUFFINS

Refreshing citrus with a hit of sweet white chocolate make these muffins quite a treat for brunch or afternoon tea.

Tip

If you don't have fresh Key limes you can use bottled Key lime juice (see Sources, page 442) and regular lime zest.

- Preheat oven to 350°F (180°C)
- Two 12-cup muffin tins, lined with paper liners or sprayed with nonstick spray

1¾ cups	all-purpose flour	425 mL
2 tsp	baking powder	10 mL
½ tsp	salt	2 mL
6 tbsp	unsalted butter, softened	90 mL
½ cup	granulated sugar	125 mL
2	eggs	2
⅔ cup	buttermilk	150 mL
1½ tsp	grated Key lime zest	7 mL
1 tbsp	Key lime juice	15 mL
6 oz	white chocolate, cut into chunks	175 g
Glaze		
1 cup	confectioner's (icing) sugar	250 mL
2 tbsp	Key lime juice	25 mL

1. In a bowl, whisk together flour, baking powder and salt. Set aside.
2. In a mixer bowl fitted with paddle attachment, cream butter and sugar until fluffy, for 2 minutes. Beat in eggs, buttermilk and lime zest and juice. Using a wooden spoon, stir in flour mixture just until moistened. Fold in white chocolate chunks.
3. Scoop into 18 cups of prepared muffin tins, filling each about halfway. Bake in preheated oven until a toothpick inserted into center comes out clean, 18 to 24 minutes.
4. *Glaze:* Meanwhile, in a small bowl, whisk together confectioner's sugar and lime juice until smooth. Spoon glaze on top of hot muffins. Let cool in tin on a wire rack for 10 minutes. Transfer to rack to cool completely.

The Perfect Blueberry Muffins

MAKES 12 MUFFINS

These muffins turn out perfect every time. Your guests will think you bought them — until they taste them!

Tip

If your berries are frozen, make sure you keep them frozen until you are ready to add them to the batter or they will start to defrost and turn your batter a purple-blue color.

Variation

Make a richer muffin by using whipping (35%) cream instead of milk.

- Preheat oven to 375°F (190°C)
- One 12-cup muffin tin, lined with paper liners or sprayed with nonstick spray

2½ cups	cake flour	625 mL
2½ tsp	baking powder	12 mL
½ tsp	salt	2 mL
½ cup	vegetable shortening or unsalted butter, softened	125 mL
1 cup	granulated sugar	250 mL
2	eggs	2
¾ cup	milk, preferably whole	175 mL
1 tsp	vanilla extract	5 mL
1 cup	blueberries, fresh or frozen	250 mL

1. In a bowl, whisk together flour, baking powder and salt. Set aside.
2. In a mixer bowl fitted with paddle attachment, cream shortening and sugar until fluffy, for 2 minutes. Beat in eggs, milk and vanilla. Using a wooden spoon, stir in flour mixture just until moistened. Fold in blueberries.
3. Scoop into prepared muffin tin. Bake in preheated oven until light brown and a toothpick inserted into center comes out clean, 22 to 26 minutes. Let cool in tin on a wire rack for 10 minutes. Transfer to rack to cool completely.

Apple Oatmeal Scones

MAKES 18 SCONES

Just like a comforting bowl of oatmeal with apple chunks, all baked into a tender scone.

- Preheat oven to 425°F (220°C)
- Baking sheet, lined with parchment paper or a Silpat
- Pizza cutter

3 cups	all-purpose flour	750 mL
1 cup	quick-cooking rolled oats	250 mL
2⁄3 cup	granulated sugar	150 mL
1 tbsp	baking powder	15 mL
1 tsp	salt	5 mL
1 tsp	ground cinnamon	5 mL
1⁄2 tsp	ground nutmeg	2 mL
1⁄2 cup	cold unsalted butter, cut into chunks	125 mL
2	eggs, beaten, divided	2
1 1⁄2 cups	whipping (35%) cream	375 mL
1 tbsp	vanilla extract	15 mL
1	baking apple (see Apples, page 15), finely chopped	1

Mixer Method

1. In a mixer bowl fitted with paddle attachment, beat flour, oats, sugar, baking powder, salt, cinnamon and nutmeg on low speed until blended, for 2 minutes. With mixer running, gradually drop in chunks of butter, mixing until it resembles coarse crumbs, about 2 minutes. Set 1 tbsp (15 mL) of the beaten egg aside. Whisk together remaining egg, cream and vanilla. Pour over dry ingredients and, using a fork, stir just until dough starts to bind together.
2. Turn dough out onto a lightly floured work surface and knead in apple pieces. Continue to knead dough just until it holds together, about 6 times. Shape into a ball and pat into a 10-inch (25 cm) circle. Place on prepared baking sheet.
3. Using a pizza cutter or sharp knife, cut into 18 wedges. Do not separate wedges. Brush top with reserved egg. Bake in preheated oven until light brown, 18 to 22 minutes. Serve warm.

Food Processor Method

1. In work bowl fitted with metal blade, process flour, oats, sugar, baking powder, salt, cinnamon and nutmeg until combined, about 10 seconds. Add butter chunks around work bowl; pulse until mixture resembles coarse crumbs, about 10 times. Set 1 tbsp (15 mL) of the beaten egg aside. With motor running, add remaining egg, cream and vanilla through feed tube and process just until mixture starts to gather. If dough is tacky, refrigerate for 5 minutes. Proceed with Step 2 at left.

Apple Pecan Scones

MAKES 18 SCONES

Fall is time for pecans, apples and cinnamon. They are all combined in this scone.

- Preheat oven to 425°F (220°C)
- Baking sheet, lined with parchment paper or Silpat
- Pizza cutter

4 cups	all-purpose flour	1 L
2/3 cup	granulated sugar	150 mL
1 tbsp	baking powder	15 mL
1 tsp	salt	5 mL
1 tsp	ground cinnamon	5 mL
1/2 tsp	ground nutmeg	2 mL
1/2 cup	cold unsalted butter, cut into chunks	125 mL
2	eggs, beaten, divided	2
1 1/2 cups	whipping (35%) cream	375 mL
1 tbsp	vanilla extract	15 mL
1	baking apple (see Apples, page 15), finely chopped	1
1/4 cup	chopped pecans	50 mL

Mixer Method

1. In a mixer bowl fitted with paddle attachment, beat flour, sugar, baking powder, salt, cinnamon and nutmeg on low speed until blended, for 2 minutes. With mixer running, gradually drop in chunks of butter, mixing until it resembles coarse crumbs. Set 1 tbsp (15 mL) of the beaten egg aside. Whisk together remaining egg, cream and vanilla. Pour over dry ingredients and using a fork, stir just until dough starts to bind together.
2. Turn dough out onto a lightly floured work surface and knead in apple pieces and pecans. Continue to knead dough just until it holds together, about 6 times. Shape into a ball and pat into a 10-inch (25 cm) circle. Place on prepared baking sheet.
3. Using a pizza cutter or sharp knife, cut into 18 wedges. Do not separate wedges. Brush top with reserved egg. Bake in preheated oven until light brown, 18 to 22 minutes. Serve warm.

Food Processor Method

1. In work bowl fitted with metal blade, process flour, sugar, baking powder, salt, cinnamon and nutmeg until combined, about 10 seconds. Add butter chunks around work bowl; pulse until mixture resembles coarse crumbs, about 10 times. Set 1 tbsp (15 mL) of the beaten egg aside. With motor running, add reserved egg, cream and vanilla through feed tube and process just until mixture starts to gather. If dough is tacky, refrigerate for 5 minutes. Proceed with Step 2 at left.

Blueberry Lemon Scones

MAKES 12 SCONES

My sister Patty loves to eat these scones in the springtime with cream cheese.

- Preheat oven to 425°F (220°C)
- Baking sheet, lined with parchment paper or Silpat
- Pizza cutter

1½ cups	all-purpose flour	375 mL
1¼ cups	cake flour	300 mL
3 tbsp	granulated sugar	45 mL
1 tbsp	baking powder	15 mL
1 tsp	salt	5 mL
2 tsp	grated lemon zest	10 mL
6 tbsp	cold vegetable shortening or unsalted butter, cut into chunks	90 mL
2	eggs, beaten, divided	2
¾ cup	whipping (35%) cream	175 mL
1 tbsp	freshly squeezed lemon juice	15 mL
½ cup	blueberries, fresh or frozen	125 mL

Mixer Method

1. In a mixer bowl fitted with paddle attachment, beat flours, sugar, baking powder, salt and lemon zest on low speed until blended, for 2 minutes. With mixer running, drop in chunks of shortening, mixing until it resembles coarse crumbs. Set 1 tbsp (15 mL) of beaten egg aside. Whisk together remaining egg, cream and juice. Pour over dry ingredients and, using a fork, stir just until dough starts to bind together.
2. Turn dough out onto a lightly floured work surface and knead in blueberries. Continue to knead dough just until it holds together, about 6 times. Shape into a ball and pat into a 10-inch (25 cm) circle. Place on prepared baking sheet.
3. Using a pizza cutter, cut into 12 wedges. Do not separate wedges. Brush top with reserved egg. Bake in preheated oven until light brown, 18 to 22 minutes. Serve warm.

Food Processor Method

1. In work bowl fitted with metal blade, process flours, sugar, baking powder, salt and zest until combined, about 10 seconds. Add shortening chunks around work bowl; pulse until mixture resembles coarse crumbs, about 10 times. Set 1 tbsp (15 mL) of the beaten egg aside. With motor running, add remaining egg, cream and lemon juice through feed tube and process just until mixture starts to gather. If dough is tacky, refrigerate for 5 minutes. Proceed with Step 2 above.

Cherry Sour Cream Scones

MAKES 12 SCONES

I have used fresh and canned cherries for these scones, without my guests knowing if they were fresh or not.

- Preheat oven to 425°F (220°C)
- Baking sheet, lined with parchment paper or Silpat
- Pizza cutter

2 cups	all-purpose flour	500 mL
3 tbsp	granulated sugar	45 mL
2 tsp	baking powder	10 mL
½ tsp	baking soda	2 mL
½ tsp	salt	2 mL
6 tbsp	cold unsalted butter, cut into chunks	90 mL
1	egg, beaten, divided	1
1 cup	sour cream	250 mL
1 tsp	vanilla extract	5 mL
½ cup	fresh or canned sour cherries, pitted and drained	125 mL

Mixer Method

1. In a mixer bowl fitted with paddle attachment, beat flour, sugar, baking powder, baking soda and salt on low speed until blended, for 2 minutes. With mixer running, drop in chunks of butter, mixing until it resembles coarse crumbs. Set 1 tbsp (15 mL) of the beaten egg aside. Whisk together remaining egg, sour cream and vanilla. Pour over dry ingredients and using a fork, stir just until dough starts to bind together.
2. Turn dough out onto a lightly floured work surface and knead in cherries. Continue to knead dough just until it holds together, about 6 times. Shape into a ball and pat into a 10-inch (25 cm) circle. Place on prepared baking sheet.
3. Using a pizza cutter or sharp knife, cut into 12 wedges. Do not separate wedges. Brush with reserved egg. Bake in preheated oven until light brown, 18 to 22 minutes. Serve warm.

Food Processor Method

1. In work bowl fitted with metal blade, process flour, sugar, baking powder, baking soda and salt until combined, about 10 seconds. Add butter chunks around work bowl; pulse until mixture resembles coarse crumbs, about 10 times. Set 1 tbsp (15 mL) of the beaten egg aside. With motor running, add remaining egg, sour cream and vanilla through feed tube and process just until mixture starts to gather. If dough is tacky, refrigerate for 5 minutes. Proceed with Step 2 above.

Citrus Scones

MAKES 16 SCONES

In my opinion, the perfect scone contains essences of citrus.

Tip

Grate the citrus zest one day and then juice the fruit the next so its walls have broken down and release more juice.

Variation

Add about 1/4 cup (50 mL) chopped dried apricots to the dough for a fruity taste.

- Preheat oven to 425°F (220°C)
- Baking sheet, lined with parchment paper or Silpat
- Pizza cutter

4 cups	dry biscuit mix, such as Bisquick or other dry biscuit mix	1 L
1/3 cup	packed light brown sugar	75 mL
2/3 cup	whipping (35%) cream	150 mL
2	eggs, beaten	2
	Grated zest of 1 lemon	
	Grated zest of 1 orange	
1 tbsp	granulated sugar	15 mL

1. In a large bowl, mix together biscuit mix, brown sugar, cream, eggs and lemon and orange zests until well combined.
2. Turn dough out onto a work surface that has been lightly dusted with biscuit mix. Knead just until dough holds together, about 12 times. Shape into a ball and pat into a 10-inch (25 cm) circle. Place on prepared baking sheet.
3. Using a pizza cutter or sharp knife, cut into 16 wedges. Do not separate wedges. Brush with 1 tbsp (15 mL) water and sprinkle with sugar. Bake in preheated oven until light brown, 18 to 22 minutes. Serve warm.

Apricot Buttermilk Scones

MAKES 12 SCONES

While in London I noticed a scone and tea shop. I stopped in and enjoyed an apricot buttermilk scone. They were great, but these are better.

- Preheat oven to 425°F (220°C)
- Baking sheet, lined with parchment paper or Silpat
- Pizza cutter

½ cup	dried apricots, finely chopped	125 mL
¼ cup	water	75 mL
2½ cups	all-purpose flour	625 mL
2 tbsp	granulated sugar	25 mL
2 tsp	baking powder	10 mL
½ tsp	salt	2 mL
½ cup	cold unsalted butter, cut into chunks	125 mL
1	egg, beaten, divided	1
¾ cup	buttermilk	175 mL

Mixer Method

1. In a small saucepan, bring apricots and water to a simmer over medium heat, about 4 minutes. Remove from heat and set aside.
2. In a mixer bowl fitted with paddle attachment, beat flour, baking powder, sugar and salt on low speed until blended, for 2 minutes. With mixer running, gradually drop in chunks of butter, mixing until it resembles coarse crumbs. Set 1 tbsp (15 mL) of the beaten egg aside. Whisk together remaining egg and buttermilk. Pour over dry ingredients and, using a fork, stir just until dough starts to bind together.
3. Turn dough out onto a lightly floured work surface. Drain apricots and knead into dough. Continue to knead dough just until it holds together, about 6 times. Shape into a ball and pat into a 10-inch (25 cm) circle. Place on prepared baking sheet.
4. Using a pizza cutter or sharp knife, cut into 12 wedges. Do not separate wedges. Brush top with reserved egg. Bake in preheated oven until light brown, 18 to 22 minutes. Serve warm.

Food Processor Method

1. In a small saucepan, bring apricots and water to a simmer over medium heat, about 4 minutes. Remove from heat and set aside.
2. In work bowl fitted with metal blade, process all-purpose flour, baking powder, sugar and salt until combined, about 10 seconds. Add butter chunks around work bowl; pulse until mixture resembles coarse crumbs, about 10 times. Set 1 tbsp (15 mL) of the beaten egg aside. With motor running, add remaining egg and the buttermilk through feed tube and process just until mixture starts to gather. If dough is tacky, refrigerate for 5 minutes. Proceed with step 3 at left.

Cranberry Orange English Scones

MAKES 12 SCONES

True English-style scones should have a tender, heavy crumb and a slightly crusty top.

- Preheat oven to 425°F (220°C)
- Baking sheet, lined with parchment paper or Silpat
- Pizza cutter

1½ cups	all-purpose flour	375 mL
1¼ cups	cake flour	300 mL
3 tbsp	granulated sugar	45 mL
1 tbsp	baking powder	15 mL
1 tsp	salt	5 mL
1½ tsp	grated orange zest	7 mL
6 tbsp	cold unsalted butter, cut into chunks	90 mL
2	eggs, beaten, divided	2
¾ cup	milk, preferably whole	175 mL
1 tbsp	frozen orange juice concentrate, thawed	15 mL
½ cup	dried cranberries	125 mL

Mixer Method

1. In a mixer bowl fitted with paddle attachment, beat all-purpose flour, cake flour, sugar, baking powder, salt and orange zest on low speed until blended, for 2 minutes. With mixer running, drop in chunks of butter, mixing until it resembles coarse crumbs. Set 1 tbsp (15 mL) of the beaten egg aside. Whisk together remaining egg, milk and orange juice concentrate. Pour over dry ingredients and, using a fork, stir just until dough starts to bind together.
2. Turn dough out onto a lightly floured work surface and knead in cranberries. Continue to knead dough just until it holds together, about 6 times. Shape into a ball and pat into a 10-inch (25 cm) circle. Place on prepared baking sheet.
3. Using a pizza cutter or sharp knife, cut into 12 wedges. Do not separate wedges. Brush with reserved egg. Bake in preheated oven until light brown, 18 to 22 minutes. Serve warm.

Food Processor Method

(See page 363.)

Fresh Blueberry Ginger Scones

MAKES 12 SCONES

Tart blueberries and ginger make a perfect balance of flavors.

- Preheat oven to 425°F (220°C)
- Baking sheet, lined with parchment paper or Silpat
- Pizza cutter

3 cups	all-purpose flour	750 mL
3 tbsp	granulated sugar	45 mL
1 tbsp	baking powder	15 mL
1 tsp	salt	5 mL
1 tsp	grated lemon zest	5 mL
½ tsp	ground ginger	2 mL
6 tbsp	cold unsalted butter, cut into chunks	90 mL
2	eggs, beaten, divided	2
¾ cup	milk, preferably whole	175 mL
¼ cup	fresh blueberries	50 mL

Mixer Method

1. In a mixer bowl fitted with paddle attachment, beat flour, sugar, baking powder, salt, lemon zest and ginger on low speed until blended, for 2 minutes. With mixer running, drop in chunks of butter, mixing until it resembles coarse crumbs. Set 1 tbsp (15 mL) of the beaten egg aside. Whisk together remaining egg and milk. Pour over dry ingredients and, using a fork, stir just until dough starts to bind together.
2. Turn dough out onto a lightly floured work surface and knead in blueberries. Continue to knead dough just until it holds together, about 6 times. Shape into a ball and pat into a 10-inch (25 cm) circle. Place on prepared baking sheet.
3. Using a pizza cutter or sharp knife, cut into 12 wedges. Do not separate wedges. Brush with reserved egg. Bake in preheated oven until light brown, 18 to 22 minutes. Serve warm.

Food Processor Method

1. In work bowl fitted with metal blade, process flour, sugar, baking powder, salt, lemon zest and ginger until combined, about 10 seconds. Add butter chunks around work bowl; pulse until mixture resembles coarse crumbs, about 10 times. Set 1 tbsp (15 mL) of the beaten egg aside. With motor running, add remaining egg and milk through feed tube and process just until mixture starts to gather. If dough is tacky, refrigerate for 5 minutes. Proceed with Step 2 above.

Fresh Raspberry Scones

MAKES 12 SCONES

These scones are full of red raspberries that turn them a light pink. Perfect for Valentine's Day or a baby shower.

- Preheat oven to 425°F (220°C)
- Baking sheet, lined with parchment paper or Silpat
- Pizza cutter

3 cups	all-purpose flour	750 mL
3 tbsp	granulated sugar	45 mL
1 tbsp	baking powder	15 mL
1 tsp	salt	5 mL
6 tbsp	cold vegetable shortening or unsalted butter, cut into chunks	90 mL
2	eggs, beaten, divided	2
¾ cup	milk, preferably whole	175 mL
½ cup	raspberries, cut into small pieces	125 mL

Mixer Method

1. In a mixer bowl fitted with paddle attachment, beat flour, sugar, baking powder and salt on low speed until blended, for 2 minutes. With mixer running, drop in chunks of shortening, mixing until it resembles coarse crumbs. Set 1 tbsp (15 mL) of the beaten egg aside. Whisk together remaining egg and milk. Pour over dry ingredients and, using a fork, stir just until dough starts to bind together.
2. Turn dough out onto a lightly floured work surface and knead in raspberries. Continue to knead dough just until it holds together, about 6 times. Shape into a ball and pat into a 10-inch (25 cm) circle. Place on prepared baking sheet.
3. Using a pizza cutter or sharp knife, cut into 12 wedges. Do not separate wedges. Brush with reserved egg. Bake in preheated oven until light brown, 18 to 22 minutes. Serve warm.

Food Processor Method

1. In work bowl fitted with metal blade, process flour, sugar, baking powder and salt until combined, about 10 seconds. Add shortening chunks around work bowl; pulse until mixture resembles coarse crumbs, about 10 times. Set 1 tbsp (15 mL) of the beaten egg aside. With motor running, add remaining egg and milk through feed tube and process just until mixture starts to gather. If dough is tacky, refrigerate for 5 minutes. Proceed with Step 2 above.

Island Scones

MAKES 24 SCONES

This tasty scone is full of tropical flavors.

Tips

Serve with pineapple jam or honey.

If you like drier scones, place on parchment- or Silpat-lined baking sheets, leaving 2 inches (5 cm) in between wedges. This way the air will bake all sides of the scone.

- Preheat oven to 425°F (220°C)
- 2 baking sheets, lined with parchment paper or Silpat
- Blending fork
- Pizza cutter

5 cups	dry biscuit mix, such as Bisquick or other dry biscuit mix	1.25 L
½ cup	granulated sugar	125 mL
½ cup	cold unsalted butter	125 mL
1 cup	flaked sweetened coconut, optional	250 mL
1 cup	chopped macadamia nuts, optional	250 mL
1	can (14 oz/398 mL) crushed pineapple, drained	1
½ cup	whipping (35%) cream	125 mL
2	eggs, beaten	2
1 tsp	rum flavoring	5 mL
1 tbsp	granulated sugar, divided	15 mL

1. In a large bowl, mix together biscuit mix and ½ cup (125 mL) sugar. With a blending fork or two knives, cut butter into dough until crumbly. Stir in coconut and nuts, if using, pineapple, cream, eggs and rum flavoring until well combined.
2. Turn dough out onto a work surface that has been lightly dusted with biscuit mix. Knead just until dough holds together, about 12 times. Divide dough in half and shape into 2 balls. Pat each into a 10-inch (25 cm) circle. Place on prepared baking sheets.
3. Using a pizza cutter or sharp knife, cut each into 12 wedges. Do not separate wedges. Brush each circle with 1 tbsp (15 mL) water and sprinkle with ½ tbsp (7 mL) sugar. Bake in preheated oven until light brown, 18 to 22 minutes, rotating pans in oven halfway as necessary for even browning. Serve warm.

White Chocolate Pecan Scones

MAKES 18 SCONES

Nutty scones with a hit of sweet chocolate.

- Preheat oven to 425°F (220°C)
- Baking sheet, lined with parchment paper or Silpat
- Pizza cutter

4 cups	all-purpose flour	1 L
2⁄3 cup	granulated sugar	150 mL
1 tbsp	baking powder	15 mL
1 tsp	salt	5 mL
1⁄2 cup	cold unsalted butter, cut into chunks	125 mL
2	eggs, beaten, divided	2
1 1⁄2 cups	whipping (35%) cream	375 mL
1 tbsp	vanilla extract	15 mL
2 cups	white chocolate chips	500 mL
1 cup	pecans, chopped and toasted	250 mL

Mixer Method

1. In a mixer bowl fitted with paddle attachment, beat flour, sugar, baking powder and salt on low speed until blended, for 2 minutes. With mixer running, drop in chunks of butter, mixing until it resembles coarse crumbs. Set 1 tbsp (15 mL) of the beaten egg aside. Whisk together remaining egg, cream and vanilla. Pour over dry ingredients and, using a fork, stir just until dough starts to bind together.
2. Turn dough out onto a lightly floured work surface and knead in chocolate chips and pecans. Continue to knead dough just until it holds together, about 6 times. Shape into a ball and pat into a 10-inch (25 cm) circle. Place on prepared baking sheet.
3. Using a pizza cutter, cut into 18 wedges. Do not separate wedges. Brush with reserved egg. Bake in preheated oven until light brown, 18 to 22 minutes. Serve warm.

Food Processor Method

1. In work bowl fitted with metal blade, process flour, sugar, baking powder and salt until combined, about 10 seconds. Add butter chunks around work bowl; pulse until mixture resembles coarse crumbs, about 10 times. Set 1 tbsp (15 mL) of the beaten egg aside.With motor running, add remaining egg, cream and vanilla through feed tube and process just until mixture starts to gather. If dough is tacky, refrigerate for 5 minutes. Proceed with Step 2 above.

Lemon Currant Scones

MAKES 12 SCONES

These scones are filled with sweet currants.

Variations

Lemon Zest Scones: Omit currants and hot water and increase lemon zest to 1 tbsp (15 mL).

Substitute milk for cream, if you like a lighter scone.

- Preheat oven to 425°F (220°C)
- Baking sheet, lined with parchment paper or Silpat
- Pizza cutter

½ cup	currants	125 mL
¼ cup	hot water	50 mL
1½ cups	all-purpose flour	375 mL
1¼ cups	cake flour	300 mL
3 tbsp	granulated sugar	45 mL
1 tbsp	baking powder	15 mL
1 tsp	salt	5 mL
2 tsp	grated lemon zest	10 mL
6 tbsp	cold vegetable shortening or unsalted butter, cut into chunks	90 mL
2	eggs, beaten, divided	2
¾ cup	whipping (35%) cream	175 mL
1 tbsp	freshly squeezed lemon juice	15 mL

Mixer Method

1. In a small saucepan, bring currants and water to a simmer over medium heat, about 4 minutes. Set aside.
2. In a mixer bowl fitted with paddle attachment, beat all-purpose flour, cake flour, sugar, baking powder, salt and lemon zest on low speed until blended, for 2 minutes. With mixer running, drop in chunks of shortening, mixing until it resembles coarse crumbs. Set 1 tbsp (15 mL) of the beaten egg aside. Whisk together remaining egg, cream and lemon juice. Pour over dry ingredients and, using a fork, stir just until dough starts to bind together.
3. Turn dough out onto a lightly floured work surface. Drain currants and knead into dough. Continue to knead dough just until it holds together, about 6 times. Shape into a ball and pat into a 10-inch (25 cm) circle. Place on prepared baking sheet.
4. Using a pizza cutter or sharp knife, cut into 12 wedges. Do not separate wedges. Brush with reserved egg. Bake in preheated oven until light brown, 18 to 22 minutes. Serve warm.

Food Processor Method

1. In a small saucepan, bring currants and water to a simmer over medium heat, about 4 minutes. Set aside.
2. In work bowl fitted with metal blade, process all-purpose flour, cake flour, sugar, baking powder, salt and lemon zest until combined, about 10 seconds. Add shortening chunks around work bowl; pulse until mixture resembles coarse crumbs, about 10 times. Set 1 tbsp (15 mL) of the beaten egg aside. With motor running, add remaining egg, cream and lemon juice through feed tube and process just until mixture starts to gather. If dough is tacky, refrigerate for 5 minutes. Proceed with Step 3 at left.

Orange White Chocolate Scones

MAKES 12 SCONES

The sweet taste of chocolate and hint of citrus make this a perfect scone for spring.

- Preheat oven to 425°F (220°C)
- Baking sheet, lined with parchment paper or Silpat
- Pizza cutter

1½ cups	all-purpose flour	375 mL
1¼ cups	cake flour	300 mL
3 tbsp	granulated sugar	45 mL
1 tbsp	baking powder	15 mL
1 tsp	salt	5 mL
2 tsp	grated orange zest	10 mL
6 tbsp	cold vegetable shortening or unsalted butter, cut into chunks	90 mL
2	eggs, beaten, divided	2
¾ cup	milk, preferably whole	175 mL
1 tbsp	freshly squeezed orange juice	15 mL
1 cup	white chocolate chips	250 mL

Mixer Method

1. In a mixer bowl fitted with paddle attachment, beat all-purpose flour, cake flour, sugar, baking powder, salt and orange zest on low speed until blended, for 2 minutes. With mixer running, drop in chunks of shortening, mixing until it resembles coarse crumbs. Set 1 tbsp (15 mL) of the beaten egg aside. Whisk together remaining egg, milk and orange juice. Pour over dry ingredients and using a fork, stir just until dough starts to bind together.
2. Turn dough out onto a lightly floured work surface and knead in chocolate chips. Continue to knead dough just until it holds together, about 6 times. Shape into a ball and pat into a 10-inch (25 cm) circle. Place on prepared baking sheet.
3. Using a pizza cutter or sharp knife, cut into 12 wedges. Do not separate wedges. Brush with reserved egg. Bake in preheated oven until light brown, 18 to 22 minutes. Serve warm.

Food Processor Method

(See page 371.)

Peach Scones

MAKES 18 SCONES

Use fresh ripe peaches for these scones for the most flavor.

Tip

If the mixture seems a bit wet from the peaches you can add up to an additional ½ cup (125 mL) cake flour.

Variation

You may add up to ½ cup (125 mL) chopped pecans or walnuts to the scones with the peaches.

- Preheat oven to 425°F (220°C)
- Baking sheet, lined with parchment paper or Silpat

1	peach, pitted and quartered	1
3¼ cups	cake flour	800 mL
¼ cup	lightly packed brown sugar	50 mL
4 tsp	baking powder	20 mL
1 tsp	ground cinnamon	5 mL
1 tsp	salt	5 mL
6 tbsp	cold unsalted butter, cut into chunks	90 mL
2	eggs, beaten	2
¾ cup	milk, preferably whole	175 mL

Mixer Method

1. Finely chop peach. Set aside.
2. In a mixer bowl fitted with paddle attachment, beat flour, sugar, baking powder, cinnamon and salt on low speed until blended, for 2 minutes. With mixer running, drop in chunks of butter, mixing until it resembles coarse crumbs. Whisk together egg and milk. Pour over the dry ingredients and, using a fork, stir just until dough starts to bind together.
3. Turn dough out onto a lightly floured work surface and knead in peaches. Continue to knead dough just until it holds together, about 6 times. Shape into a ball and pat into a 10-inch (25 cm) circle. Place on prepared baking sheet.
4. Using a pizza cutter or sharp knife, cut into 18 wedges. Do not separate wedges. Bake in preheated oven until light brown, 18 to 22 minutes. Serve warm.

Food Processor Method

1. In work bowl fitted with metal blade, pulse peach quarters until coarsely chopped. Transfer to a bowl.
2. In same work bowl, process flour, sugar, baking powder, cinnamon and salt until combined, about 10 seconds. Add butter chunks around work bowl pulse until mixture resembles coarse crumbs, about 10 times. With motor running, add beaten egg and milk through feed tube and process just until mixture starts to gather. If dough is tacky, refrigerate for 5 minutes. Proceed with Step 3 above.

Pumpkin Raisin Scones

MAKES 12 SCONES

These scones have a beautiful orange color, just like fall leaves.

- Preheat oven to 425°F (220°C)
- Baking sheet, lined with parchment paper or Silpat
- Pizza cutter

1½ cups	all-purpose flour	375 mL
1¼ cups	cake flour	300 mL
3 tbsp	granulated sugar	45 mL
1 tbsp	baking powder	15 mL
1 tsp	salt	5 mL
1 tsp	ground cinnamon	5 mL
½ tsp	ground nutmeg	2 mL
¼ tsp	ground allspice	1 mL
¼ tsp	ground cloves	1 mL
6 tbsp	cold vegetable shortening or unsalted butter, cut into chunks	90 mL
2	eggs, beaten, divided	2
¼ cup	pumpkin purée (not pie filling)	50 mL
½ cup	milk, preferably whole	125 mL
1 tbsp	freshly squeezed lemon juice	15 mL
½ cup	golden raisins	125 mL

Mixer Method

1. In a mixer bowl fitted with paddle attachment, beat all-purpose flour, cake flour, sugar, baking powder, salt, cinnamon, nutmeg, allspice and cloves on low speed until blended, for 2 minutes. With mixer running, drop in chunks of shortening, mixing until it resembles coarse crumbs. Set 1 tbsp (15 mL) of the beaten egg aside. Whisk together remaining egg, pumpkin, milk and lemon juice. Pour over the dry ingredients and, using a fork, stir just until dough starts to bind together.
2. Turn dough out onto a lightly floured work surface and knead in raisins. Continue to knead dough just until it holds together, about 6 times. Shape into a ball and pat into a 10-inch (25 cm) circle. Place on prepared baking sheet.
3. Using a pizza cutter or sharp knife, cut into 12 wedges. Do not separate wedges. Brush with reserved egg. Bake in preheated oven until light brown, 18 to 22 minutes. Serve warm.

Food Processor Method

1. In work bowl fitted with metal blade, process all-purpose flour, cake flour, sugar, baking powder, salt, cinnamon, nutmeg, allspice and cloves until combined, about 10 seconds. Add butter chunks around work bowl; pulse until mixture resembles coarse crumbs, about 10 times. Set 1 tbsp (15 mL) of the beaten egg aside. With motor running, add remaining egg, pumpkin, milk and lemon juice through feed tube and process just until mixture starts to gather. If dough is tacky, refrigerate for 5 minutes. Proceed with Step 2 at left.

Old-Fashioned Buttermilk Biscuits

MAKES ABOUT 24 BISCUITS

Rich biscuits with a hint of buttermilk flavor.

- Preheat oven to 425°F (220°C)
- Baking sheet, lined with parchment paper or Silpat
- 2½ inch (6 cm) round biscuit cutter
- Blending fork

2½ cups	all-purpose flour	625 mL
3 tbsp	granulated sugar	45 mL
2 tbsp	baking powder	25 mL
¾ tsp	salt	4 mL
¾ tsp	cream of tartar	4 mL
¾ cup	cold vegetable shortening	175 mL
1 cup	buttermilk	250 mL
1	egg, beaten	1

1. In a large bowl, using a blending fork, combine flour, sugar, baking powder, salt and cream of tartar. Add shortening by spoonfuls, blending with fork until well mixed into dry ingredients and it resembles coarse meal. Add buttermilk all at once and stir just until dry ingredients are moistened.
2. Turn dough out onto a floured surface and knead a few times just until dough gathers. Pat down. Using a rolling pin, roll dough to about ½-inch (1 cm) thickness. Cut with biscuit cutter, re-rolling scraps (see Tip, page 377). Brush each biscuit with beaten egg. Place biscuits close to each other on prepared baking sheet. Bake in preheated oven until biscuits have risen and are light brown, 15 to 22 minutes. Serve warm.

Pecan Scones

MAKES 12 SCONES

Crunchy, nutty and full of flavor. Perfect when you do not want a fruit-based scone.

- Preheat oven to 425°F (220°C)
- Baking sheet, lined with parchment paper or Silpat
- Pizza cutter

2 cups	all-purpose flour	500 mL
1¼ cups	pecan flour	300 mL
3 tbsp	granulated sugar	45 mL
1 tbsp	baking powder	15 mL
1 tsp	salt	5 mL
6 tbsp	cold unsalted butter, cut into chunks	90 mL
2	eggs, beaten, divided	2
¾ cup	milk, preferably whole	175 mL
2 tsp	vanilla extract	10 mL
½ cup	chopped pecans	125 mL

Mixer Method

1. In a mixer bowl fitted with paddle attachment, beat all-purpose flour, pecan flour, sugar, baking powder and salt on low speed until blended, for 2 minutes. With mixer running, drop in chunks of butter, mixing until it resembles coarse crumbs. Add three-quarters of the beaten egg, milk and vanilla and mix on low speed just until dough starts to bind together.
2. Turn dough out onto a lightly floured work surface and knead in pecans. Continue to knead dough just until it holds together, about 6 times. Shape into a ball and pat into a 10-inch (25 cm) circle. Place on prepared baking sheet.
3. Using a pizza cutter or sharp knife, cut into 12 wedges. Do not separate wedges. Brush with remaining beaten egg. Bake in preheated oven until light brown, 12 to 16 minutes. Serve warm.

Food Processor Method

1. In work bowl fitted with metal blade, process all-purpose flour, pecan flour, sugar, baking powder and salt until combined, about 10 seconds. Add butter chunks around work bowl; pulse until mixture resembles coarse crumbs, about 10 times. With motor running, add three-quarters of the beaten egg, milk and vanilla through feed tube and process just until mixture starts to gather. If dough is tacky, refrigerate for 5 minutes. Proceed with Step 2 above.

Easy Baking Powder Biscuits

MAKES ABOUT 24 BISCUITS

Within 15 minutes you can have hot, flaky biscuits for any meal.

Tip

Try to get as many biscuits cut as possible the first time you roll the dough. Re-rolling too many times toughens the biscuits.

- Preheat oven to 425°F (220°C)
- Baking sheet, lined with parchment paper or Silpat
- 2½-inch (6 cm) round biscuit cutter
- Blending fork

1¼ cups	all-purpose flour	300 mL
1¼ cups	cake flour	300 mL
3 tbsp	granulated sugar	45 mL
2 tbsp	baking powder	25 mL
¾ tsp	salt	4 mL
¾ tsp	cream of tartar	4 mL
¾ cup	cold vegetable shortening	175 mL
1 cup	milk, preferably whole	250 mL

1. In a large bowl, using a blending fork, combine all-purpose flour, cake flour, sugar, baking powder, salt and cream of tartar. Add shortening by spoonfuls, blending with fork until well mixed into dry ingredients and it resembles coarse meal. Add milk all at once and stir just until dry ingredients are moistened.
2. Turn dough out onto a floured surface and knead a few times just until dough gathers. Pat down. Using a rolling pin, roll dough to about ½-inch (1 cm) thickness. Cut with biscuit cutter, re-rolling scraps (see Tip, left). Place biscuits close to each other on prepared baking sheet. Bake in preheated oven until biscuits have risen and are light brown, 15 to 22 minutes. Serve warm.

Hearty Butter Biscuits

MAKES ABOUT 24 BISCUITS

Most biscuits use lard or shortening as the fat. Here I use butter for rich flavor.

Tip

If you would like your biscuits to have a crispy crust, place biscuits about 2 inches (5 cm) apart on baking sheets. The air will flow around biscuits, creating a firm crust.

- Preheat oven to 425°F (220°C)
- Baking sheet, lined with parchment paper or Silpat
- 2½-inch (6 cm) round biscuit cutter
- Blending fork

2½ cups	all-purpose flour	625 mL
1 tbsp	baking powder	15 mL
1 tsp	granulated sugar	5 mL
¾ tsp	salt	4 mL
½ cup	cold unsalted butter, cut into small pieces	125 mL
¾ cup	milk, preferably whole	175 mL
1	egg, beaten	1

1. In a large bowl, using a blending fork, combine all-purpose flour, baking powder, sugar and salt. Add butter chunks and blend with fork until well mixed into dry ingredients and it resembles coarse meal. Add milk and egg all at once and stir just until dry ingredients are moistened.
2. Turn dough out onto a floured surface and knead a few times just until dough gathers. Pat down. Using a rolling pin, roll dough to about ½-inch (1 cm) thickness. Cut with biscuit cutter, re-rolling scraps (see Tip, page 377). Place biscuits close to each other on prepared baking sheet. Bake in preheated oven until biscuits have risen and are light brown, 15 to 22 minutes. Serve warm.

Pecan Cinnamon Biscuits

MAKES ABOUT 18 BISCUITS

This flavorful biscuit is perfect served on the side with an egg dish or topped with fresh fruit or a fruit compote for a dessert.

- Preheat oven to 425°F (220°C)
- Baking sheet, lined with parchment paper or Silpat
- 2½-inch (6 cm) round biscuit cutter
- Blending fork

2 cups	all-purpose flour	500 mL
2 tbsp	granulated sugar	25 mL
4 tsp	baking powder	20 mL
1 tsp	ground cinnamon	5 mL
½ tsp	salt	2 mL
½ cup	cold vegetable shortening	125 mL
¾ cup	milk, preferably whole	175 mL
¼ cup	pecans, chopped	50 mL

1. In a large bowl, using a blending fork, combine flour, sugar, baking powder, cinnamon and salt. Add shortening by spoonfuls, blending with fork until well mixed into dry ingredients and it resembles coarse meal. Add milk all at once and stir just until dry ingredients are moistened.
2. Turn dough out onto a floured surface and knead, adding pecans, a few times just until dough gathers. Pat down. Using a rolling pin, roll dough to about ½-inch (1 cm) thickness. Cut with biscuit cutter, re-rolling scraps (see Tip, page 377). Place biscuits close to each other on prepared baking sheet. Bake in preheated oven until biscuits have risen and are light brown, 15 to 22 minutes. Serve warm.

Strawberry Biscuits

MAKES ABOUT 12 BISCUITS

You don't have to use jam since the fruit is baked right in.

- Preheat oven to 425°F (220°C)
- Baking sheet, lined with parchment paper or Silpat
- 2½-inch (6 cm) round biscuit cutter
- Blending fork

2½ cups	all-purpose flour	625 mL
2 tbsp	granulated sugar	25 mL
4 tsp	baking powder	10 mL
½ tsp	salt	2 mL
½ cup	cold vegetable shortening	125 mL
¾ cup	whipping (35%) cream	175 mL
¼ cup	finely chopped strawberries	50 mL

1. In a large bowl, using a blending fork, combine flour, sugar, baking powder and salt. Add shortening by spoonfuls, blending until well mixed into dry ingredients and it resembles coarse meal. Add cream all at once and stir just until dry ingredients are moistened.
2. Turn dough out onto a floured surface and knead, adding strawberries, a few times just until dough gathers. Pat down. Using a rolling pin, roll dough to about ½-inch (1 cm) thickness. Cut with biscuit cutter, re-rolling scraps (see Tip, page 377). Place biscuits close to each other on prepared baking sheet. Bake in preheated oven until biscuits have risen and are light brown, 15 to 22 minutes. Serve warm.

Chocolate Shortcakes

Not your traditional shortcake, but rich and perfect with a fruit topping.

- Preheat oven to 400°F (200°F)
- 9-inch (23 cm) round cake pan, sprayed with nonstick spray
- Blending fork

1½ cups	all-purpose flour	375 mL
½ cup	unsweetened Dutch-processed cocoa powder	125 mL
3 tbsp	granulated sugar	45 mL
4 tsp	baking powder	20 mL
½ tsp	salt	2 mL
½ tsp	cream of tartar	2 mL
½ cup	cold unsalted butter, cut into chunks	125 mL
1	egg, beaten	1
⅓ cup	milk, preferably whole	75 mL
	Port Wine Berry Sauce (see recipe, page 243)	

1. In a large bowl, using a blending fork, blend flour, cocoa powder, sugar, baking powder, salt and cream of tartar. Add butter chunks and blend with fork until it resembles coarse meal. Whisk together egg and milk. Pour over dry ingredients all at once and stir just until dry ingredients are moistened.
2. Turn dough out onto a lightly floured work surface and knead 12 times. Pat into prepared baking pan. Bake in preheated oven until it puffs up a bit, 15 to 20 minutes. Let cool slightly in pan on a rack. Serve warm with Port Wine Berry Sauce.

Cinnamon Pecan Shortcakes

MAKES 12 SHORTCAKES

I enjoy these shortcakes topped with juicy sliced peaches.

- Preheat oven to 400°F (200°F)
- 9-inch (23 cm) round cake pan, sprayed with nonstick spray
- Blending fork

1½ cups	all-purpose flour	375 mL
½ cup	cake flour	125 mL
3 tbsp	granulated sugar	45 mL
4 tsp	baking powder	20 mL
2 tsp	ground cinnamon	10 mL
½ tsp	salt	2 mL
½ tsp	cream of tartar	2 mL
½ cup	cold unsalted butter, cut into chunks	125 mL
1	egg, beaten	1
⅓ cup	milk, preferably whole	75 mL
½ cup	pecans, chopped	125 mL

1. In a large bowl, using a blending fork, combine all-purpose flour, cake flour, sugar, baking powder, cinnamon, salt and cream of tartar. Add butter chunks and blend with fork until it resembles coarse meal. Whisk together beaten egg and milk. Pour over dry ingredients all at once and stir just until dry ingredients are moistened.
2. Turn dough out onto a lightly floured work surface. Knead, adding pecans, 12 times. Pat into prepared baking pan. Bake in preheated oven until light brown, about 15 to 20 minutes. Let cool slightly in pan on a rack. Serve warm.

Chocolate Cake Donuts

MAKES ABOUT 24 DONUTS

The donuts I look for first in a bakery case are the chocolate cake ones. Here is a recipe that I fell in love with and is so easy to make.

- 16-cup (4 L) saucepan or deep-fryer
- Candy/deep-fry thermometer
- 3-inch (7.5 cm) round donut cutter

3½ cups	all-purpose flour	875 mL
1 tbsp	baking powder	15 mL
1 tsp	baking soda	5 mL
½ tsp	salt	2 mL
1½ cups	granulated sugar	375 mL
2	eggs	2
4 tbsp	unsalted butter, softened	60 mL
3 oz	unsweetened chocolate, chopped	90 g
1 cup	buttermilk	250 mL
1½ tsp	vanilla extract	7 mL
	Vegetable oil for frying	
	Chocolate Ganache (see recipe, page 241)	

1. In a bowl, whisk together flour, baking powder, baking soda and salt. Set aside.
2. In a mixer bowl fitted with whip attachment, beat sugar and eggs until pale yellow, for 5 minutes.
3. Meanwhile, in a saucepan, melt butter and unsweetened chocolate over low heat, stirring constantly, about 2 minutes. Add to egg mixture and beat on high speed until blended. Beat in buttermilk and vanilla. Add flour mixture, mixing on low speed just until combined, about 4 minutes. Cover and refrigerate dough for 1 hour.
4. In a large saucepan, heat about 4-inches (10 cm) of oil over medium heat until temperature registers 360°F (185°C) on thermometer.
5. On a floured surface, roll dough to about ¼-inch (0.5 cm) thickness. If dough is tacky, dust with additional flour. Cut dough, with cutter, into 24 donuts, re-rolling scraps as necessary. Deep-fry in hot oil, 4 at a time, turning once, until done, 15 seconds per side. Using a slotted spoon, transfer to paper towels to absorb excess oil. Let cool on a wire rack. Repeat with remaining donuts, reheating oil and adjusting heat as necessary between batches.
6. Dip cooled donuts into slightly warm Chocolate Ganache.

Banana Rum Coffee Cake

SERVES 16

This rich and moist cake can be serve as a dessert or for a late brunch.

- Preheat oven to 325°F (160°C)
- Two 9-by 5-inch (2 L) loaf pans, sprayed with nonstick spray

4 cups	all-purpose flour	1 L
1 tsp	baking soda	5 mL
1 tsp	ground allspice	5 mL
½ tsp	salt	2 mL
1 cup	unsalted butter, softened	250 mL
3 cups	granulated sugar	750 mL
4	eggs	4
½ cup	buttermilk	125 mL
2 tbsp	freshly squeezed lemon juice	25 mL
2 tsp	vanilla extract	10 mL
5	ripe bananas, chopped	5
1½ cups	pecans, chopped and toasted	375 mL
¼ cup	dark rum	50 mL

1. In a large bowl, whisk together flour, baking soda, allspice and salt. Set aside.
2. In a mixer bowl fitted with paddle attachment, cream butter and sugar until light and fluffy, for 3 minutes. Beat in eggs, buttermilk, lemon juice and vanilla. Using a wooden spoon, gradually stir in dry ingredients just until moistened. Fold in bananas and pecans.
3. Divide batter evenly between prepared pans. Bake in preheated oven until a toothpick inserted into center comes out clean, 65 to 75 minutes. Let cool in pans on a wire rack for 10 minutes. Transfer to rack and brush with rum. Let cool completely.

Orange Yeast Donuts

MAKES ABOUT 32 DONUTS

Years ago when I was in pastry school we would make orange yeast donuts every day for students to purchase. I loved their simple orange flavor. Donuts are simple to make.

- 16-cup (4 L) saucepan or deep-fryer
- Candy/deep-fry thermometer
- 3-inch (7.5 cm) round donut cutter

2	packages (each 1/4 oz/7 g) quick-rising (instant) dry yeast	2
2 cups	milk, preferably whole, warmed to 110°F (43°C)	500 mL
1/2 cup	vegetable shortening	125 mL
1/4 cup	granulated sugar	50 mL
3 tbsp	grated orange zest	45 mL
2 tsp	salt	10 mL
3	egg whites	3
6 cups	all-purpose flour, divided	1.5 L
	Vegetable oil for frying	
1 cup	confectioner's (icing) sugar, sifted	250 mL
2 tbsp	ground cinnamon	25 mL

1. In a bowl, combine yeast and milk. Let stand in a warm place until it starts to bubble, about 5 minutes.
2. In a mixer bowl fitted with paddle attachment, cream shortening and sugar until fluffy, for 2 minutes. Beat in orange zest, salt and egg whites. Add yeast mixture and mix until blended. Add 4 1/2 cups (1.125 L) of the flour and mix on low speed for 5 minutes. With mixer running, gradually add enough of the remaining flour by spoonfuls until dough starts to pull away from sides of bowl. Turn dough out onto a lightly floured work surface. Knead until smooth and elastic, for about 3 minutes. Shape into a ball; place in an oiled bowl. Cover with plastic wrap and let rise in a warm, draft-free place until doubled in volume, 30 to 40 minutes.
3. In a large saucepan, heat about 4 inches (10 cm) of oil over medium heat until temperature reaches 360°F (185°C) on a thermometer.

4. On a floured surface, roll dough to about ¼-inch (0.5 cm) thickness. If dough is tacky, dust with additional flour. Cut dough, with cutter, into 24 donuts, re-rolling scraps as necessary. Deep-fry in hot oil, 4 at a time, turning once, until golden brown, 15 seconds per side. Using a slotted spoon, transfer to paper towels to absorb excess oil.
5. In a shallow bowl, combine confectioner's sugar and cinnamon. Roll hot donuts in sugar mixture to coat. Serve warm. Repeat with remaining donuts, reheating oil or adjusting heat as necessary between batches.

Pumpkin Nutmeg Donuts with Orange Glaze

MAKES ABOUT 26 DONUTS

Every fall when I teach in Ohio I cannot wait to get a taste of the pumpkin donuts from Bill's Donuts of Centerville. They are so light and flavorful. They inspired this recipe and I have added a glaze to go with them.

- 16-cup (4 L) saucepan or deep-fryer
- Candy/deep-fry thermometer
- 3-inch (7.5 cm) round donut cutter

4 cups	all-purpose flour (approx.)	1 L
2 tsp	baking powder	10 mL
1 tsp	baking soda	5 mL
1 tsp	ground nutmeg	5 mL
1 cup	granulated sugar	250 mL
1 cup	evaporated milk	250 mL
1 cup	pumpkin purée (not pie filling)	250 mL
2	eggs	2
2 tbsp	unsalted butter, melted	25 mL
1 tbsp	freshly squeezed orange juice	15 mL
	Vegetable oil for frying	

Glaze

3 cups	confectioner's (icing) sugar, sifted	750 mL
2 tbsp	frozen orange juice concentrate, thawed	25 mL
1 tbsp	evaporated milk	15 mL
1 tsp	grated orange zest	5 mL

1. In a large bowl, combine 4 cups (1 L) flour, baking powder, baking soda and nutmeg. Set aside.
2. In a mixer bowl fitted with paddle attachment, beat sugar, evaporated milk, pumpkin, eggs, melted butter and orange juice until blended, for 2 minutes. Gradually add flour mixture by spoonfuls, mixing on low speed until incorporated, about 3 minutes. If dough is too tacky and is sticking to sides, add just enough additional flour until dough starts to pull away from sides of bowl. Cover and refrigerate dough for 2 hours.

3. In a large saucepan, heat about 4-inches (10 cm) of oil over medium heat until temperature reaches 360°F (185°C) on a thermometer.
4. *Glaze:* In a mixer bowl fitted with whisk attachment, whip confectioner's sugar, orange juice concentrate, evaporated milk and orange zest until smooth, about 2 minutes. Set aside.
5. On a floured surface, roll dough to about 1⁄4-inch (0.5 cm) thickness. If dough is tacky, dust with additional flour. Cut dough with cutter, into 24 donuts, re-rolling scraps as necessary. Deep-fry in hot oil, 4 at a time, turning once, until golden brown, 15 seconds per side. Using a slotted spoon, transfer to paper towels to absorb excess oil. Glaze hot donuts and let cool slightly on rack. Repeat with remaining donuts, reheating oil or adjusting heat as necessary between batches. Serve warm.

Blueberry Coffee Cake

SERVES 8 TO 10

This coffee cake is so rich I dare you to eat more than one piece.

Tip

I try to only make this with fresh blueberries, as frozen ones color batter blue and it looks like you have added food coloring.

- Preheat oven to 375°F (190°C)
- 9-inch (23 cm) cheesecake pan or springform pan, sprayed with nonstick spray, bottom lined with parchment paper
- Blending fork

Topping

½ cup	granulated sugar	125 mL
½ cup	all-purpose flour	125 mL
½ tsp	ground cinnamon	2 mL
½ tsp	ground nutmeg	2 mL
¼ cup	unsalted butter, softened	50 mL

Cake

2 cups	all-purpose flour	500 mL
2½ tsp	baking powder	12 mL
¾ tsp	salt	4 mL
¼ cup	unsalted butter, softened	50 mL
¾ cup	granulated sugar	175 mL
1	egg	1
¾ cup	milk, preferably whole	175 mL
2 cups	fresh blueberries	500 mL

Glaze

½ cup	confectioner's (icing) sugar	125 mL
2 tsp	milk, preferably whole	10 mL
¼ tsp	almond extract	1 mL

1. *Topping:* In a bowl, using a blending fork, blend sugar, flour, cinnamon, nutmeg and butter until crumbly. Set aside.
2. *Cake:* In a bowl, whisk together flour, baking powder and salt. Set aside.
3. In a mixer bowl fitted with paddle attachment, cream butter and sugar until light and fluffy, for 2 minutes. Add egg and mix until blended. Using a wooden spoon, stir in flour mixture alternating with milk, making three additions of flour and two of milk, just until blended. Fold in blueberries.
4. Pour into prepared baking pan, smoothing top. Sprinkle with topping. Bake in preheated oven until top is light brown and a toothpick inserted into center comes out clean, 45 to 50 minutes. Let cool in pan on a wire rack for 20 minutes.
5. *Glaze:* In a small bowl, whisk sugar, milk and almond extract until smooth. Drizzle over cake. Serve warm.

Cherry Nut Coffee Cake

SERVES 8 TO 12

I always seem to have candied cherries left over after making fruitcake during the holidays. Here is a great use for them.

Tip

You can also bake this cake in two 8-by 4-inch (1.5 L) loaf pans. Reduce the baking time to 22 to 28 minutes.

Variation

Try using candied pineapple instead of cherries.

- Preheat oven to 350°F (180°C)
- 10-inch (3 L) Bundt pan, sprayed with nonstick spray

3 cups	dry biscuit mix, such as Bisquick or other dry biscuit mix	750 mL
1 cup	milk, preferably whole	250 mL
½ cup	granulated sugar	125 mL
⅓ cup	all-purpose flour	75 mL
1	egg, beaten	1
1 tsp	ground cinnamon	5 mL
½ tsp	almond extract	2 mL
1 cup	chopped candied cherries	250 mL
¾ cup	chopped almonds	175 mL

1. In a large bowl, mix together biscuit mix, milk, sugar, flour, egg, cinnamon and almond extract until well combined. Fold in cherries and almonds.
2. Spoon into prepared pan, smoothing top with a rubber spatula. Bake in preheated oven until a toothpick inserted into center comes out clean, 35 to 45 minutes. Let cool in pan on a wire rack for 20 minutes. Transfer to rack and let cool completely.

Raspberry Cream Cheese Coffee Cake

SERVES 12

When I was in New York City years back I came across a bakery in the East Village. They had a most remarkable berry cheese coffee cake. Here is my version.

Tip

Make sure your cream cheese and butter are softened before mixing or you will have chunks in your batter.

Variation

Try blackberries in place of raspberries.

- Preheat oven to 350°F (180°C)
- 13-by 9-inch (3 L) metal baking pan, lined with foil, then lined with parchment paper

Topping

¾ cup	old-fashioned rolled oats	175 mL
¼ cup	packed light brown sugar	50 mL
¼ cup	all-purpose flour	50 mL
¼ cup	chopped pecans	50 mL
¼ cup	unsalted butter, melted	50 mL

Cake

1¾ cups	all-purpose flour	425 mL
1 tsp	baking powder	5 mL
½ tsp	baking soda	2 mL
¼ tsp	salt	1 mL
1	package (8 oz/250 g) cream cheese, softened	1
½ cup	unsalted butter, softened	125 mL
1 cup	granulated sugar	250 mL
2	eggs	2
¼ cup	whipping (35%) cream	50 mL
½ tsp	vanilla extract	2 mL
1 cup	fresh raspberries, crushed	250 mL

1. *Topping:* In a bowl, combine oats, brown sugar, flour, pecans and butter until crumbly. Set aside.
2. *Cake:* In a bowl, whisk together flour, baking powder, baking soda and salt. Set aside.
3. In a mixer bowl fitted with paddle attachment, beat cream cheese, butter and sugar until fluffy, for 3 minutes. Add eggs, one at a time, beating well between each addition. Using a wooden spoon, stir in flour mixture alternating with cream making three additions of flour mixture and two of cream, just until blended. Beat in vanilla.
4. Spread batter into pan, smoothing top. Sprinkle raspberries on top. Sprinkle with topping. Bake in preheated oven until light brown and a toothpick inserted into center comes out clean, 30 to 35 minutes. Let cool in pan on a rack, about 30 minutes. Transfer to rack to cool completely.

Chocolate Chip Coffee Cake

SERVES 18 TO 24

This coffee cake is perfect for a bake sale or a brunch.

Variation

You can substitute ½ cup (125 mL) chopped pecans for chocolate chips.

- Preheat oven to 325°F (160°F)
- 13-by 9-inch (3 L) baking pan, lined with foil, then lined with parchment paper
- Blending fork

Streusel Topping

¼ cup	cake flour	50 mL
¼ cup	all-purpose flour	50 mL
¼ cup	granulated sugar	50 mL
2 tbsp	unsalted butter, softened	25 mL

Cake

2 cups	all-purpose flour	500 mL
1 tbsp	baking powder	15 mL
¼ tsp	salt	1 mL
1¾ cups	granulated sugar	425 mL
¾ cup	vegetable oil	175 mL
3	eggs	3
1 tsp	vanilla extract	5 mL
1 cup	milk, preferably whole	250 mL
½ cup	semisweet chocolate chips	125 mL
	Breakfast Roll Cream Cheese Drizzle (see Variation, page 328)	

1. *Streusel Topping:* In a bowl, using a blending fork, blend cake flour, all-purpose flour, sugar and butter until crumbly. Set aside.
2. *Cake:* In a bowl, whisk together flour, baking powder and salt. Set aside.
3. In a mixer bowl fitted with paddle attachment, beat sugar, oil, eggs and vanilla until well blended, for 2 minutes. Using a wooden spoon, stir in flour mixture alternating with milk, making three additions of flour and two of milk, just until combined.
4. Pour into prepared baking pan, smoothing top. Sprinkle with chocolate chips and streusel topping. Bake in preheated oven until a toothpick inserted into center comes out clean, 22 to 26 minutes. Let cool completely in pan on wire rack. Decorate with Breakfast Roll Cream Cheese Drizzle.

Cinnamon Nut Coffee Cake

SERVES 8 TO 10

I like how this coffee cake is packed with three kinds of nuts, making it full of flavor.

- Preheat oven to 375°F (190°C)
- 9-inch (23 cm) cheesecake pan or springform pan, sprayed with nonstick spray, bottom lined with parchment paper
- Blending fork

Topping

1/2 cup	granulated sugar	125 mL
1/2 cup	all-purpose flour	125 mL
1/2 tsp	ground cinnamon	2 mL
1/2 tsp	ground nutmeg	2 mL
1/4 cup	unsalted butter, softened	50 mL
1/4 cup	chopped pecans	50 mL

Cake

2 cups	all-purpose flour	500 mL
2 1/2 tsp	baking powder	12 mL
3/4 tsp	salt	4 mL
1/4 cup	unsalted butter, softened	50 mL
3/4 cup	granulated sugar	175 mL
1	egg	1
3/4 cup	milk, preferably whole	175 mL
1 cup	chopped macadamia nuts	250 mL
1/2 cup	chopped walnuts	125 mL

1. *Topping:* In a bowl, using a blending fork, blend sugar, flour, cinnamon, nutmeg, butter and pecans until crumbly. Set aside.
2. *Cake:* In a bowl, whisk together flour, baking powder and salt. Set aside.
3. In a mixer bowl fitted with paddle attachment, cream butter and sugar until light and fluffy, for 2 minutes. Add egg and mix until blended. Using a wooden spoon, stir in flour mixture alternating with milk, making three additions of flour and two of milk, just until blended. Fold in macadamia nuts and walnuts.
4. Pour into prepared baking pan, smoothing top. Sprinkle with topping. Bake in preheated oven until top is light brown and a toothpick inserted into center comes out clean, 45 to 50 minutes. Let cool completely in pan on a wire rack.

Cranberry Almond Coffee Cake

SERVES 18 TO 24

This coffee cake uses canned cranberries so you can make it any time of year.

- Preheat oven to 350°F (180°C)
- 13-by 9-inch (3 L) metal baking pan, lined with foil, then lined with parchment paper

2 cups	all-purpose flour	500 mL
1 tbsp	baking powder	15 mL
1/2 tsp	salt	2 mL
1 cup	unsalted butter, softened	250 mL
1 cup	granulated sugar	250 mL
2	eggs	2
1 cup	sour cream	250 mL
1/2 tsp	almond extract	2 mL
1 cup	canned whole cranberry sauce	250 mL
1 cup	sliced almonds	250 mL
1 cup	confectioner's (icing) sugar	250 mL
2 tbsp	milk, preferably whole	25 mL
1/2 tsp	vanilla extract	2 mL

1. In a bowl, whisk together flour, baking powder and salt. Set aside.
2. In a mixer bowl fitted with paddle attachment, cream butter and sugar until light and fluffy, for 3 minutes. Add eggs, one at a time, beating well between each addition. Using a wooden spoon, stir in flour mixture alternating with sour cream making three additions of flour mixture and two of sour cream, just until blended. Stir in almond extract.
3. Spread into prepared baking pan, smoothing top. Spread cranberry sauce evenly over batter. Sprinkle with almonds. Bake in preheated oven until a toothpick inserted into center comes out clean, 34 to 42 minutes. Let cool in pan on a wire rack until cool to the touch, about 45 minutes.
4. In a small bowl, whisk together confectioner's sugar, milk and vanilla until smooth. Drizzle on top of coffee cake. Let cool completely on a rack.

Lemon Cherry Coffee Cake

SERVES 12

Pucker up! This is a lip-smacking coffee cake.

Tip

You can also bake this cake in two 8-by 4-inch (1.5 L) loaf pans. Reduce baking time to 22 to 28 minutes.

Variation

Try using candied pineapple instead of cherries.

- Preheat oven to 350°F (180°C)
- 13-by 9-inch (3 L) baking pan, greased

4 cups	biscuit mix	1 L
2 cups	whipping (35%) cream	500 mL
½ cup	vegetable oil	125 mL
4	eggs	4
2	packages (each 4-serving size) lemon instant pudding mix	2
1 cup	finely chopped candied cherries	250 mL

1. In a large bowl, mix together biscuit mix, cream, oil, eggs and lemon pudding mix until well blended. Fold in cherries.
2. Spoon into prepared pan, smoothing top with a rubber spatula. Bake in preheated oven until a toothpick inserted into center comes out clean, 35 to 45 minutes. Let cool for 20 minutes before removing from pan.

Pecan Crown Breakfast Cake

SERVES 10 TO 12

My first pastry job was in Hollywood. At The Cake Walk, we were called "The Pastry Shop to The Stars." This cake is rich and full of pecans and was one of the shop specialties.

Tips

Make sure your cream cheese and butter are room temperature.

Do not toast your pecans before adding to batter or they will taste burnt.

Variation

Try black walnuts or regular walnuts in place of pecans.

- Preheat oven to 325°F (160°C)
- 10-inch (3 L) Bundt pan, sprayed with a nonstick spray

Topping

½ cup	chopped pecans	125 mL
2 tsp	granulated sugar	10 mL
1 tsp	ground cinnamon	5 mL

Cake

2⅔ cups	cake flour	650 mL
2 tsp	ground cinnamon	10 mL
1 tsp	ground nutmeg	5 mL
⅛ tsp	salt	0.5 mL
1½ cups	unsalted butter, softened	375 mL
1	package (8 oz/250 g) cream cheese, softened	1
3 cups	granulated sugar	750 mL
1 tbsp	freshly squeezed lemon juice	15 mL
2 tsp	vanilla extract	10 mL
6	eggs	6
¾ cup	chopped pecans	175 mL

1. *Topping:* In a small bowl, combine pecans, sugar and cinnamon. Sprinkle on bottom of prepared pan. Set aside.
2. *Cake:* In a bowl, whisk together flour, cinnamon, nutmeg and salt. Set aside.
3. In a mixer bowl fitted with paddle attachment, cream butter, cream cheese and sugar until fluffy, for 3 minutes. Add eggs, one at a time, beating well after each addition. Using a wooden spoon, gradually stir in flour mixture just until blended. Fold in pecans.
4. Spoon batter into prepared pan, smoothing top. Bake in preheated oven until a toothpick inserted into center comes out clean, 70 to 80 minutes. Let cool in pan on a wire rack for 10 minutes. Invert onto rack and let cool completely.

Sour Cream Chocolate Chunk Coffee Cake

SERVES 10 TO 12

This coffee cake is very moist. You can freeze half of cake to enjoy at a later date.

Tips

Make sure you use a large enough bowl for sour cream and baking soda, as it will start to bubble and rise in the bowl.

When freezing this cake, wrap cake in plastic wrap and then foil to seal cake completely. I like to use this within a month.

Variation

Use macadamia nuts in place of chocolate chunks.

- Preheat oven to 350°F (180°C)
- 10-inch (4 L) tube pan, sprayed with a nonstick spray

1¾ cups	sour cream	425 mL
1 tsp	baking soda	5 mL
3 cups	all-purpose flour	750 mL
1½ tsp	baking powder	7 mL
½ tsp	salt	2 mL
¾ cup	unsalted butter, softened	175 mL
1¾ cups	granulated sugar	425 mL
3	eggs	3
2 tsp	vanilla extract	10 mL
4 oz	semisweet chocolate, cut into chunks	125 g

1. In a bowl, combine sour cream and baking soda. In another bowl, whisk together flour, baking powder and salt. Set both aside.
2. In a mixer bowl fitted with paddle attachment, cream butter and sugar until light and fluffy, for 2 minutes. Add eggs, one at a time, beating well between each addition. Using a wooden spoon, stir in flour mixture alternating with sour cream mixture, making three additions of flour and two of sour cream, just until blended. Fold in chocolate chunks.
3. Spoon into prepared pan, smoothing top. Bake in preheated oven until a toothpick inserted into center comes out clean, 55 to 65 minutes. Let cool in pan on a wire rack for 10 minutes. Invert onto rack to cool completely.

Traditional Fruitcake

Holiday Favorites

Holiday Cakes, Pies & Pastry

Muffins, Quick Breads, Cookies & Candies

Holiday Cheesecakes

Holiday Favorites

When you think of holidays it brings you right to the season between Thanksgiving through to New Year's Day. We do seem to have an abundance of parties and family gathering in the last weeks of the year, more than at any other time.

I like to throw pastry parties instead of full-meal parties. A pastry party consists of just that — pastry and wine — red wine, if I am serving a heavy, chocolate-based pastry table. A full table of pastry delights the eye and the palate, as you'll know from the look of your guests when they see it. Make sure when you're having one of these parties you state it on the invitation, and also choose a time that would work, such as 2 p.m. or 7:30 p.m. These are not around a mealtime, thus justifying a pastry party.

Great reasons to have a pastry party

1. It costs less for a larger number of guests.
2. You don't have to serve everything from appetizers to desserts.
3. It also simplifies your drink choices — wine or Champagne.
4. You can serve more guests.
5. You can have two parties in one week. For the first party, all desserts can be whole, such as a whole cheesecake cut in slices; on the second night, you can arrange all your slices on trays.
6. You can bake and freeze almost everything weeks ahead. Decorate the pastries and display them just before your guests' arrival.
7. During the holidays, I especially like to have chocolate and port parties.

How many pastries should I make?

To calculate how many servings of dessert to make, multiply the number of guests by one and a half. That number is the total yield in servings you'll need of all the desserts combined. You do not want your pastry table to have one slice of a pastry left with two guests looking at it trying to decide who gets it!

HOLIDAY PASTRY PARTY

I like to make more than I really need. When having a party of 25 guests, I tend to make at least five different kinds of desserts. I would make one cheesecake, one layered cake, one type of bar or squares, one drop cookie and two pies or tarts. For every five additional guests, I would add one item.

WEDDING PARTY

So many overdo weddings and receptions. You have to have a cake and something to drink, so I'd focus on these. Have a great cake, but keep it simple. And the drink must be Champagne. Here in Southern California we have local wineries that produce Champagne-style sparkling wines that are flavorful and accompany wedding cakes very well. Most wineries will give a discount on cases. If you join their wine club, you can save even more.

SPRING BRUNCH

Make everything mini-size — muffins, scones, cinnamon rolls — and count on three pieces per person.

Buche de Noël (Yule Log)

SERVES 10 TO 12

This cake, which serves as an edible centerpiece, will delight every adult and child.

Variation

You can use fruit preserves instead of buttercream to fill log.

- Pastry bag, fitted with round tip
- Baking sheets, lined with parchment paper or Silpats

1	recipe Chocolate-Drizzled Meringue Cookie batter (see recipe, page 41)	1
4 oz	semisweet chocolate, melted and slightly cooled	125 g
1	recipe Chocolate Jelly Roll (see Variations, page 219)	1
1	recipe French Chocolate Buttercream Frosting (see recipe, page 229)	1
2 tbsp	confectioner's (icing) sugar	25 mL

1. Prepare Chocolate-Drizzled Meringue Cookie batter. Using a prepared bag fitted with a round tip pipe half of the cookie batter into one prepared baking sheet into small mounds to resemble mushroom caps. Pipe remaining batter on second prepared baking sheet to resemble mushroom stems. Follow recipe directions for drying. After drying and cooling completely, dip each mushroom cap into melted chocolate and affix a stem to cap. Place on a baking sheet and let cool completely until chocolate is set. (This will make plenty of extra mushrooms to decorate log and for you to eat.)
2. Spread inside of jelly roll with ¼ cup (50 mL) buttercream. Place on serving platter; cut one end of jelly roll at an angle and place slice on top of log to resemble a knot on the log. Spread outside of log with remaining buttercream. Using a fork, drag tines through buttercream so it looks like bark. Dust with confectioner's sugar. Place some of the meringue mushrooms around sides of log to decorate. Place remaining mushrooms on a seperate plate to serve immediately.

Cherry Almond Tart

SERVES 10 TO 12

Bright red cherries encased by the almond cream make this a delight for any holiday pastry table in spring or winter.

Tips

Make sure almond paste is cut into smaller pieces prior to placing into food processor.

To use up leftover dough, I like to add a little lemon zest and make small rounds the size of a large marble. Place on a lined baking sheet and bake in 350°F (180°C) oven until golden, for 8 to 10 minutes. Roll warm cookies in sugar.

- Preheat oven to 375°F (190°C)
- One 10-inch (25 cm), metal tart pan with removable bottom

1	recipe Buttery Tart Pastry Dough (see recipe, page 120)	1
7 oz	almond paste, cut into chunks	210 g
¾ cup	packed light brown sugar	175 mL
⅓ cup	unsalted butter, softened	75 mL
3	eggs	3
1 tsp	vanilla extract	5 mL
1 tsp	almond extract	5 mL
¾ cup	cake flour	175 mL
¾ cup	drained sour cherries (jarred or thawed frozen)	175 mL

1. Press dough into tart pan and set aside. (You will not need all of the dough. See Tips, left).
2. In a food processor fitted with metal blade, process almond paste and brown sugar until softened, about 30 seconds. Add butter and process until incorporated. With motor running, add eggs, vanilla and almond extracts through feed tube until well incorporated, about 20 seconds. Add flour and process until smooth, about 30 seconds.
3. Pour mixture into prepared tart shell. Arrange cherries on top. Bake in preheated oven until crust is light brown and filling is set, 45 to 60 minutes.

Christmas Raspberry Cake

SERVES 10 TO 12

The contrast of red raspberries and chocolate make for a great presentation.

- Pastry bag, fitted with star tip

1	recipe Rich Chocolate Chip Fudge Cake (see recipe, page 182)	1
2	recipes French Chocolate Buttercream Frosting (see recipe, page 229)	2
½ cup	raspberry preserves, divided	125 mL

1. Cut each cake layer in half (see Cutting a Cake to Make Two Layers, page 158).
2. Place half of buttercream into pastry bag. Set aside.
3. Place one cake layer cut-side up on serving platter. Spread with ¼ cup (50 mL) of remaining buttercream. Place another cake layer on top. With pastry bag, pipe a wall of buttercream around top edge of cake. Place ¼ cup (50 mL) of raspberry preserves into center of cake. Place third layer of cake on top. Spread with ¼ cup (50 mL) of buttercream. Place remaining cake layer on top, cut-side down. Decoratively pipe a wall of buttercream around top edge of cake. Spread remaining raspberry preserves into center of cake. Ice sides of cake with remaining buttercream. Serve immediately or refrigerate for up to 1 day.

Eggnog Custard Pie

SERVES 6 TO 8

Rich eggnog custard in a flaky pie crust makes a delightful holiday dessert.

Tip

It is easiest to pour the custard into the pie shell on the oven rack to prevent spillage. See page 109, Step 8, for instructions.

- Preheat oven to 350°F (180°C)
- 9-inch (23 cm) pie pan

1	recipe Flaky Pie Pastry Dough (see Variation, page 115), unbaked	1
1½ cups	whole milk	375 mL
1 cup	prepared eggnog	250 mL
4	eggs	4
½ cup	granulated sugar	125 mL
1 tbsp	dark rum	15 mL
⅛ tsp	salt	0.5 mL
¼ tsp	freshly grated nutmeg	1 mL

1. On a lightly floured surface, roll out dough and fit into bottom of pie pan. (To roll out dough, see page 110.)
2. In a saucepan, scald milk and eggnog over medium heat until bubbles start to form around sides of pan and a "skin" forms on top, about 3 minutes. Set aside.
3. In a large bowl, whisk eggs, sugar, rum and salt until blended. Gradually whisk in scalded milk mixture. Pour custard mixture into pie shell. Sprinkle top with nutmeg. Bake in preheated oven until knife inserted into center comes out clean, 35 to 40 minutes. Let cool completely on a wire rack for at least 2 hours before cutting.

Eggnog Pastry Cream

MAKES ABOUT 3 CUPS (750 ML)

This pastry cream is filled with essence of eggnog.

Tip

To store: Pour hot pastry cream onto a rimmed baking sheet (to cool faster), place plastic wrap directly on the surface and let cool to room temperature. Transfer to an airtight container and refrigerate for up to 2 days.

1¾ cups + 2 tbsp	prepared eggnog, divided	450 mL
1 tsp	vanilla extract	5 mL
1 cup	granulated sugar	250 mL
2 tbsp	cornstarch	25 mL
5	eggs	5
2 tsp	freshly grated nutmeg	10 mL

1. In saucepan, bring 1½ cups (375 mL) eggnog and vanilla to a boil over medium heat.
2. In a large bowl, whisk together sugar and cornstarch. Set aside.
3. In another bowl, whisk together remaining eggnog and eggs. Gradually pour into sugar mixture, whisking until blended. Gradually pour egg mixture into saucepan, whisking until blended. Cook over medium heat, whisking constantly, until it thickens, about 10 minutes. Add nutmeg. Transfer to a bowl, cover surface directly with plastic wrap and let cool completely.

Uses

- Christmas Raspberry Cake (page 405)
- Holiday Cranberry Tarts (page 410)
- Holiday English Trifle (page 411)

Chocolate Raspberry Linzer Torte

SERVES 10 TO 12

This is an elegant rich torte I like to serve after Christmas dinner.

Tips

After cooling completely, you can wrap tart in pan in plastic wrap, then foil, and freeze for up to 1 month. One hour prior to serving, place in 300°F (150°C) oven for 15 minutes or until heated thoroughly.

Make sure you use preserves. A jelly will not set up correctly.

- Preheat oven to 350°F (180°C)
- Blending fork
- One 10-inch (25 cm) metal tart pan with removable bottom

1¼ cups	unsweetened Dutch-processed cocoa powder	300 mL
1 cup	all-purpose flour	250 mL
1 cup	cold unsalted butter, cut into chunks	250 mL
1 cup	granulated sugar	250 mL
1¼ cups	chopped almonds	300 mL
1 tbsp	grated lemon zest	15 mL
2 tbsp	freshly squeezed lemon juice	25 mL
¼ tsp	ground cinnamon	1 mL
¼ tsp	freshly grated nutmeg	1 mL
¼ tsp	ground cloves	1 mL
4	egg yolks	4
1 cup	raspberry preserves	250 mL
1	egg, beaten	1
¼ cup	sliced almonds	50 mL
2 tbsp	confectioner's (icing) sugar	25 mL

1. In a food processor fitted with metal blade, pulse cocoa powder, flour and butter until it resembles coarse meal, about 15 times. Transfer to a large bowl and add granulated sugar, chopped almonds, lemon zest and juice, cinnamon, nutmeg, cloves and egg yolks, stir with blending fork until dough gathers.
2. Turn dough out onto a lightly floured surface and knead a few times. Place in a bowl and refrigerate until firm, about 30 minutes. Press half of dough into bottom and sides of tart pan. Spread raspberry preserves evenly over tart shell. Break remaining dough into small pieces and place randomly on top of preserves. Brush with beaten egg and sprinkle with sliced almonds.
3. Bake in preheated oven until pastry is dry-looking and raspberry preserves are bubbling slightly, 40 to 45 minutes. Let cool in pan on a rack. Remove from pan and dust with confectioner's sugar just before serving.

Holiday Cranberry Tarts

MAKES 12 TARTS

Make these as small individual tarts. They are impressive in small bites.

Tips

You can make each element ahead and then assemble and refrigerate tarts up to about 1 hour prior to serving.

You only need half a recipe of the pastry cream for these tarts. However, it is best to make the whole recipe at once.

- Preheat oven to 350°F (180°C)
- Twelve 3-inch (7.5 cm) tart pans
- Baking sheet

1	recipe Buttery Tart Pastry Dough (see recipe, page 120)	1
½	recipe Eggnog Pastry Cream (see recipe, page 407) (see Tips, left)	½
1	recipe Spiked Cranberries (see recipe below)	1

1. Press dough into tart pans and prick sides and bottom of tart shells. Place on a baking sheet. Bake in preheated oven until golden brown, 12 to 18 minutes. Let cool completely in pans on a wire rack.
2. Place 2 tbsp (25 mL) pastry cream in each baked shell. Top with cranberries.

Spiked Cranberries

MAKES 2 CUPS (500 ML)

You can eat these plain or use as a filling for tarts.

½ cup	frozen orange juice concentrate	125 mL
½ cup	water	125 mL
12 oz	fresh cranberries (about 3 cups/750 mL)	375 g
¼ cup	orange-flavored liqueur	50 mL

1. In a small saucepan, bring orange juice concentrate and water to a boil over medium heat, about 5 minutes. Add cranberries. Cook, stirring until sauce is thickened and cranberries are popping, about 10 minutes. Remove from heat and stir in liqueur.
2. Pour into a bowl and let cool completely. Cover and refrigerate for up to 1 week.

Uses

- Holiday Cranberry Tarts (above)

Holiday English Trifle

SERVES 12 TO 16

Red, green and chocolate — the perfect colors of the holiday season.

Tip

You can make this ahead. Cover and refrigerate for up to 2 days. Decorate just before serving.

Variation

For a different festive flavor, substitute Eggnog Pastry Cream (page 407) for the Chocolate French Pastry Cream.

- 10-cup (2.5 L) clear glass trifle bowl

½	recipe Rich Chocolate Chip Fudge Cake, cut into slices (see recipe, page 182)	½
½ cup	raspberry-flavored liqueur	125 mL
1 cup	raspberry preserves	250 mL
1	recipe Chocolate French Pastry Cream (see Variations, page 242)	1
4 cups	fresh raspberries	1 L
2	kiwis, peeled and sliced	2
2	recipes Classic Whipped Cream (see recipe, page 239)	2
2	sprigs fresh mint	2

1. Brush cake slices with ¼ cup (50 mL) liqueur. Line bottom of bowl with about one-third of cake slices. Smooth ½ cup (125 mL) raspberry preserves over cake. Top with half of pastry cream. Reserve some of the best-looking raspberries for top. Arrange about half of remaining berries and kiwis on top of pastry cream, placing some of berries against sides of bowl so you can see layers. Sprinkle with 2 tbsp (25 mL) liqueur. Spread about one-third of whipped cream on top of berries.
2. Top with half of remaining cake slices. Repeat with remaining preserves, pastry cream, raspberries and kiwis and half of remaining whipped cream. Sprinkle with remaining liqueur. Top with remaining cake. Spread with remaining whipped cream. Decorate with reserved raspberries and mint leaves.

Spring Easter Lemon Cake

MAKES 2 CAKES, SERVES 14 TO 16

I always think of lemons for spring. This cake makes you pucker up.

Tip

You only need half a recipe of the Fresh Lemon Curd for these cakes. It is best to make a whole recipe at once.

- Pastry bag, fitted with star tip

1	recipe Tart Lemon Cake (see recipe, page 184)	1
1	recipe French Buttercream Frosting (see recipe, page 227)	1
1 cup	sweetened flaked coconut	250 mL
4	drops pastel food coloring (pink or yellow, etc.)	4
½	recipe Fresh Lemon Curd (see recipe, page 284), chilled	½

1. Cut each cake layer in half horizontally into two layers. Set aside.
2. Place half of buttercream into prepared pastry bag. Set aside.
3. In a large plastic bag, combine coconut and food coloring, mixing and rubbing coloring into coconut. Set aside.
4. Place one of the cake layers cut-side up on a cake plate. Spread ¼ cup (50 mL) lemon curd on cake. Top with a second layer, cut-side down. Ice sides of cake with about half of the remaining buttercream. With piping bag, decoratively pipe a wall of buttercream around top edge of cake. Spread ¼ cup (50 mL) of lemon curd in center. Repeat with remaining cake, lemon curd and buttercream on another cake plate. Press colored coconut onto sides of each cake. Serve immediately or refrigerate for up to 1 day.

Traditional Fruitcake

MAKES THREE 1-LB (500 G) LOAVES

It's always a joke during holiday season that there is the one fruitcake in the world and it gets recycled over and over. Just to make sure you avoid a recycled cake, make your own this year. This recipe is one of my first that I created in culinary school.

Tips

I like to use only candied cherries and pineapple. Some of other mixed fruits are too bitter for my taste.

I normally don't age this cake; I like to make it and serve it right away. If you prefer, you can soak cheesecloth in the reserved liquid and wrap around the cooled cakes. Wrap in plastic wrap and then foil. Store in a cool, dry place for up to 6 months.

- Three 9-by 5-inch (2 L) loaf pans, sprayed with nonstick spray

2 lb	candied fruit (cherries, pineapple etc.), chopped if necessary	1 kg
1 lb	raisins	500 g
2 cups	brandy	500 mL
1 cup	orange-flavored liqueur	250 mL
⅓ cup	unsalted butter, softened	75 mL
⅓ cup	granulated sugar	75 mL
⅓ cup	packed dark brown sugar	75 mL
⅛ tsp	salt	0.5 mL
3	eggs	3
¼ cup	liquid honey	50 mL
1 tbsp	dark rum	15 mL
1 tsp	vanilla extract	5 mL
1½ cups	bread flour	375 mL
3 cups	chopped pecans	750 mL

1. In a large bowl, stir together candied fruit, raisins, brandy and orange liqueur. Cover and refrigerate for 3 weeks, stirring weekly.
2. In a mixer bowl fitted with paddle attachment, cream butter, granulated sugar, brown sugar and salt until fluffy, for 2 minutes. Add eggs one at a time, beating well between each addition. Add honey, rum and vanilla and mix until blended. Using a wooden spoon, gradually stir in bread flour just until incorporated.
3. Preheat oven to 350°F (180°C). Drain soaked fruit, reserving liquid. Fold fruit and pecans into batter. Divide batter equally between prepared pans, smoothing tops. Bake in preheated oven until top is light brown and firm when touched and a toothpick inserted into center comes out clean of cake batter (you may get some fruit particles adhering to the toothpick), 38 to 45 minutes. Let cool completely in pans on a wire rack. Brush tops of cooled cakes with reserved soaking liquid.

Christmas Tree Cinnamon Rolls

MAKES 18 ROLLS

A delightful breakfast treat for Christmas morning.

Tip

To prepare these to bake fresh on Christmas morning, after assembling the rolls in the shape of the tree, cover with plastic wrap and refrigerate overnight. In the morning, proceed with Step 2.

- Preheat oven to 375°F (190°C)
- Rimmed baking sheet, lined with parchment paper or Silpat

1	recipe Jumbo Cinnamon Rolls (see recipe, page 324)	1
1 cup	candied cherries (red and green), cut into small pieces, divided	250 mL
1	recipe Breakfast Roll Cream Cheese Icing (see recipe, page 328)	1

1. Prepare Jumbo Cinnamon Rolls as directed, adding three-quarters of the cherries on top of sugar and spices. Place rolls on prepared baking sheet in shape of a tree, starting with one roll at one short end of the baking sheet. Place two rolls touching the first one, creating a triangle. Then place three, then four, then five in rows. At this point you have a large triangle. Place two rolls in the centre at the wide end of the triangle and then last roll to create a small triangle for the trunk. Press remaining cherries into top of cinnamon rolls. Cover with a towel and let rise for 20 minutes.
2. Bake in preheated oven until light brown, 18 to 24 minutes. Smear with cream cheese icing while still hot. Serve warm.

Christmas Muffins

MAKES 12 MUFFINS

These muffins are full of color and holiday flavors.

- Preheat oven to 400°F (200°C)
- One 12-cup muffin tin, lined with paper liners or sprayed with nonstick spray

1 cup	all-purpose flour	250 mL
1 cup	old-fashioned rolled oats	250 mL
1 tbsp	baking powder	15 mL
1/4 cup	unsalted butter, softened	50 mL
3/4 cup	packed light brown sugar	175 mL
1	egg	1
1 cup	buttermilk	250 mL
1/2 cup	candied fruit, chopped	125 mL
1/2 cup	toasted chopped pecans	125 mL

1. In a bowl, whisk together flour, oats and baking powder. Set aside.
2. In a mixer bowl fitted with paddle attachment, cream butter and brown sugar until fluffy, for 2 minutes. Beat in egg and buttermilk. Using a wooden spoon, stir in flour mixture just until moistened. Fold in candied fruit and nuts.
3. Scoop into prepared muffin tin. Bake in preheated oven until light brown and a toothpick inserted into center comes out clean, 20 to 25 minutes. Let cool in tin for 10 minutes on a wire rack. Transfer to rack to cool completely.

Easter Muffins

MAKES 12 MUFFINS

Flavorful muffins for the springtime.

- Preheat oven to 400°F (200°C)
- One 12-cup muffin tin, lined with paper liners or sprayed with nonstick spray

2 cups	all-purpose flour	500 mL
1 tbsp	baking powder	15 mL
1/4 cup	unsalted butter, softened	50 mL
3/4 cup	packed light brown sugar	175 mL
1	egg	1
1 cup	buttermilk	250 mL
1/2 cup	sweetened flaked coconut	125 mL
1/2 cup	toasted chopped pecans	125 mL
1/2 cup	drained crushed pineapple	125 mL

1. In a bowl, whisk together flour and baking powder. Set aside.
2. In a mixer bowl fitted with paddle attachment, cream butter and brown sugar until fluffy, for 2 minutes. Beat in egg and buttermilk. Using a wooden spoon, stir in flour mixture just until moistened. Fold in coconut, pecans and pineapple.
3. Scoop into prepared muffin tin. Bake in preheated oven until light brown and a toothpick inserted into center comes out clean, 20 to 25 minutes. Let cool in tin for 10 minutes on a wire rack. Transfer to rack to cool completely.

Eggnog Cookies

MAKES 30 LARGE COOKIES

When you bite into one of these cookies it's just like drinking eggnog.

- Preheat oven to 350°F (180°C)
- Baking sheets, lined with parchment paper or Silpats
- #30 disher or scoop

3¼ cups	all-purpose flour	800 mL
1 tsp	baking powder	5 mL
1 tsp	baking soda	5 mL
½ tsp	salt	2 mL
½ tsp	freshly grated nutmeg	2 mL
1 cup	unsalted butter, softened	250 mL
1 cup	granulated sugar	250 mL
1	egg	1
1 cup	prepared eggnog	250 mL
Icing		
1½ cups	confectioner's (icing) sugar	375 mL
3 tbsp	prepared eggnog	45 mL
½ tsp	freshly grated nutmeg	2 mL

1. In a large bowl, whisk together flour, baking powder, baking soda, salt and nutmeg. Set aside.
2. In a mixer bowl fitted with paddle attachment, cream butter and sugar until fluffy, about 3 minutes. Beat in egg and eggnog. Using a wooden spoon, gradually stir in flour mixture until blended. Refrigerate dough for 15 minutes.
3. Using disher, scoop dough and place on prepared baking sheets, at least 2 inches (5 cm) apart. Press down with palm of your hand. Bake in preheated oven until light brown, 8 to 10 minutes. Let cool completely on baking sheets on a wire rack.
4. *Icing:* In a small bowl, whisk together confectioner's sugar and eggnog until smooth. Spread on top of cooled cookies and sprinkle nutmeg on top. Let dry before serving.

Fruitcake Cookies

MAKES ABOUT 18 LARGE COOKIES

Colorful and filled with dried fruits and nuts.

Tip

Make sure you take dough out of food processor or remove from mixer and add the fruit and nuts by hand or they will become pulverized and make the cookies very sticky.

- Preheat oven to 325°F (160°C)
- Baking sheets, lined with parchment paper or Silpats
- #24 disher or scoop

2¼ cups	all-purpose flour	550 mL
½ tsp	salt	2 mL
½ tsp	baking soda	2 mL
¾ cup	unsalted butter, melted and cooled	175 mL
1 cup	packed brown sugar	250 mL
1	egg	1
2 tsp	vanilla extract	10 mL
2 cups	chopped candied fruit	500 mL
1 cup	toasted chopped pecans	250 mL

Mixer Method

1. In a bowl, whisk together flour, salt and baking soda. Set aside.
2. In a mixer bowl fitted with paddle attachment, beat melted butter and brown sugar until creamy, for 3 minutes. Add egg and vanilla and mix until incorporated. Using a wooden spoon, gradually stir in flour mixture until blended. Fold in candied fruit and pecans. Refrigerate dough for 10 minutes.
3. Using disher, scoop dough onto prepared baking sheets, at least 2 inches (5 cm) apart. Press down with palm of your hand. Bake in preheated oven until light brown around the edges, 14 to 18 minutes.

Food Processor Method

1. In a medium bowl, whisk together flour, salt and baking soda. Set aside.
2. In work bowl fitted with metal blade, process melted butter and brown sugar for 15 seconds. With processor running, add egg and vanilla through feed tube and process for 10 seconds. Add flour mixture and process for 20 seconds, until blended. Transfer dough to a large bowl and fold in candied fruit and pecans by hand. Refrigerate dough for 20 minutes. Proceed with Step 3 above.

Hungarian Meringue Holiday Bars

MAKES 24 BARS

Katrina, a wonderful cook and baker, gave me this recipe to share with you. She takes many of my classes and we love to go to the Hollywood Bowl together.

- Preheat oven to 350°F (180°C)
- 13-by 9-inch (3 L) metal baking pan, lined with foil, then lined with parchment paper

1 cup	unsalted butter, softened	250 mL
1¼ cups	granulated sugar, divided	300 mL
2	egg yolks	2
½ tsp	salt	2 mL
2¼ cups	all-purpose flour	550 mL
1½ cups	seedless all-fruit raspberry jam	375 mL
3	egg whites	3
¾ cup	chopped walnuts	175 mL
¾ cup	sweetened flaked coconut	175 mL

1. In a mixer bowl fitted with paddle attachment, cream butter and ½ cup (125 mL) of the sugar until light and fluffy, about 3 minutes. Add egg yolks and salt and mix until incorporated. Using a wooden spoon, gradually stir in flour until blended. Pat dough evenly into bottom of prepared pan. Bake in preheated oven until light brown, 20 to 25 minutes. (Leave oven on.) While base is hot, spread raspberry jam on top. Set aside.
2. In clean mixer bowl fitted with whip attachment, beat egg whites on low speed until frothy, about 2 minutes. Increase speed to high and gradually add the remaining sugar, beating until soft peaks form, about 3 minutes. Fold in walnuts and coconut by hand. Spread evenly on top of jam. Bake until top is golden brown, 20 to 25 minutes. Let cool completely in pan on a wire rack. Cut into 24 bars.

Chocolate Cherry Mash Candies

MAKES ABOUT 100 CANDIES

Every Christmas season my two good friends, Darren and Gary, send my parents a box of these chocolates. Now you can make some to send to yours.

- Baking sheets, lined with parchment paper or Silpats
- #70 disher or scoop

Filling

1	recipe White Cherry Buttercream Frosting (see recipe, page 240)	1
¾ cup	sweetened condensed milk	175 mL
½ cup	unsalted butter, softened	125 mL
1 cup	finely chopped drained maraschino cherries (15 oz/430 g or 375 mL)	250 mL
2 lbs	confectioner's (icing) sugar	1 kg
½ tsp	liquid red food coloring	2 mL

Coating

12 oz	semisweet chocolate, finely chopped	375 g
12 oz	milk chocolate, finely chopped	375 g
2 cups	finely chopped peanuts	500 mL

1. *Filling:* In a mixer bowl fitted with paddle attachment, beat frosting, sweetened condensed milk and butter until fluffy, about 4 minutes. Add cherries, confectioner's sugar and food coloring and mix on low speed until smooth and creamy, about 3 minutes. Cover and refrigerate for 3 hours. Scoop filling onto prepared baking sheets. Refrigerate until all of filling has been scooped.
2. *Coating:* Temper semisweet and milk chocolates according to directions on page 249. Let cool slightly. In large bowl, combine tempered chocolates and peanuts. Dip each ball into chocolate mixture. Place on clean prepared baking sheets. Let cool until set and dry, about 10 minutes. See storage information, page 250.

Gingerbread People

MAKES ABOUT 36 COOKIES

The holidays would not be the same without gingerbread men and women. You can make these and before baking make a hole in the top part of the cookie and string them on a traditional tree!

Tips

Prior to baking, you can press raisins into dough for eyes. After baking, using Royal Icing as glue, place red hot candy for a mouth and pipe drops of icing for buttons.

To prepare cookies as tree decorations, before baking, use a straw to make a hole on top of the head area. While cookies are still hot, make sure hole is still open. Thread a ribbon through the hole after decorating cookies.

- Baking sheets, lined with parchment paper or Silpats
- Gingerbread people cookie cutters

4⅔ cups	all-purpose flour	1.15 L
1 tbsp	ground ginger	15 mL
1 tbsp	ground cinnamon	15 mL
1 tsp	baking soda	5 mL
½ tsp	ground cloves	2 mL
½ tsp	salt	2 mL
1½ cups	unsalted butter, softened	375 mL
1 cup	packed dark brown sugar	250 mL
1 cup	light (fancy) molasses	250 mL
2	eggs	2
	Royal Icing (see recipe, page 235)	

1. In a large bowl, whisk together flour, ginger, cinnamon, soda, cloves and salt. Set aside.
2. In a mixer bowl fitted with paddle attachment, beat butter, brown sugar and molasses until creamy, for 4 minutes. Add eggs, one at a time, beating well between each addition. Using a wooden spoon, gradually stir in flour mixture until well combined. Divide dough into two disks and wrap in plastic wrap. Refrigerate to firm up for about 30 minutes.
3. Preheat oven to 375°F (190°C).
4. On a floured surface, roll out one disk of dough at a time to ⅛- to ¼-inch (0.25 to 0.5 cm) thickness. Using cookie cutters, cut out gingerbread people, re-rolling scraps. Place cookies on prepared baking sheets, keeping similar-sized cookies together, at least 2 inches (5 cm) apart. Bake in preheated oven until lightly browned, 10 to 14 minutes. Let cool completely on pans on a wire rack.
5. Decorate cooled cookies with Royal Icing.

Heavenly Cherry Christmas Candies

MAKES ABOUT 96 CANDIES

This makes a large batch of candies, enough for you to give as gifts.

Tips

You'll need about 8 oz (250 g) of each type of nuts. Make sure they are fresh.

To toast nuts, see page 13.

- Baking sheets, lined with parchment paper or Silpats
- #70 disher or scoop

2 lbs	milk chocolate, finely chopped	1 kg
1	can (14 oz/396 g or 300 mL) sweetened condensed milk	1
4 tbsp	unsalted butter, softened	60 mL
¼ cup	whipping (35%) cream	50 mL
1 tbsp	vanilla extract	15 mL
1 cup	finely chopped drained maraschino cherries (15 oz/430 g or 375 mL)	250 mL
2	bags (each 1 lb/500 g) large marshmallows, cut into quarters	2
2 cups	almonds, toasted and chopped	500 mL
2 cups	pecans, toasted and chopped	500 mL
2 cups	walnuts, toasted and chopped	500 mL

1. In a heavy saucepan, melt chocolate, sweetened condensed milk, butter and cream over low heat, stirring until melted and smooth, about 6 minutes. Remove from heat and stir in vanilla. Pour into a large bowl. Add cherries, marshmallows, almonds, pecans and walnuts and stir until evenly coated.
2. Scoop onto prepared baking sheets. Let cool completely on pan on wire racks. Wrap cooled candies individually in plastic wrap. Store in sealed container at a cool room temperature for up to 2 weeks.

Mom's Favorite Peanut Butter Fingers

MAKES ABOUT 65 CANDIES

Besides the Chocolate Cherry Mash Candies (see recipe, page 421), these are also in the box delivered yearly from my friends Darren and Gary to my folks.

Tip

Place in candy tin and store at a cool room temperature for up to 3 weeks.

- Baking sheets, lined with parchment paper or Silpats

2½ cups	peanut butter	625 mL
¾ cup	unsalted butter, melted	175 mL
3½ cups	confectioner's sugar, sifted (1 lb/500 g)	875 mL
3 cups	crisp rice cereal	750 mL
1½ lbs	semisweet or milk chocolate, finely chopped	750 g

1. In a large bowl, combine peanut butter, butter, confectioner's sugar and puffed rice cereal. Shape into 1½-by ½-inch (4 by 1 cm) logs. Place on prepared baking sheets. Refrigerate for 1 hour or until firm.
2. Meanwhile, temper chocolate according to directions on page 249. Dip each "finger" in tempered chocolate. Return to prepared baking sheets and let stand until set, about 20 minutes.

Rich Chocolate Pecan Caramels

MAKES ABOUT 48 CANDIES

When you mention caramels many people think of a rich, sinful confection, while others think of making a difficult candy. Here is an easy confection to create.

Tip

To prevent the candies from sticking to knife as you cut them, you may have to dip your knife into hot water after each cut.

- 13-by 9-inch (3 L) metal baking pan, lined with foil, then lined with parchment paper
- Candy thermometer or digital instant-read thermometer

1 cup	unsalted butter, softened	250 mL
2 oz	unsweetened chocolate, chopped	60 g
2¼ cups	granulated sugar	550 mL
1	can (14 oz/396 g or 300 mL) sweetened condensed milk	1
1 cup	light corn syrup	250 mL
1 tsp	vanilla extract	5 mL
¼ tsp	salt	1 mL
1 cup	chopped toasted pecans	250 mL

1. In a saucepan, melt butter and chocolate over low heat and stir until smooth. Add sugar, sweetened condensed milk and corn syrup. Increase heat to medium and cook, stirring occasionally, until temperature reaches 248°F (120°C) on thermometer (Firm Ball stage).
2. Remove from heat and let stand for exactly 5 minutes. Stir in vanilla, salt and pecans. Working quickly, spread evenly in prepared pan. Let cool completely in pan on a wire rack.
3. When completely cooled, transfer candy to a cutting board and cut into squares. Wrap each piece individually in plastic wrap. Store wrapped candies in a candy tin at a cool room temperature for up to 3 weeks.

Snowmen Marshmallows

MAKES 24 SNOWMEN

I love these snowmen as little treats for the kids.

Tips

It is helpful to have a stand mixer as well as an electric hand-held mixer for this recipe. You can use the hand-held mixer to whip the egg whites without having to clean the bowl from the gelatin mixture first.

These are best served the day they are made but can be carefully transferred to an airtight container and stored at a cool room temperature for up to 2 days.

Caution: This recipe contains uncooked egg whites. If the food safety is a concern for you, use pasteurized egg whites or avoid this recipe.

- Baking sheets, each dusted with 2 tbsp (25 mL) confectioner's (icing) sugar
- Candy thermometer or digital instant-read thermometer
- Pastry bag, fitted with large round tip

3½	envelopes (each ¼ oz/7 g) powdered unflavored gelatin	3½
½ cup	cold water	125 mL
2 cups	granulated sugar	500 mL
½ cup	light corn syrup	125 mL
½ cup	hot water (about 115°F/46°C)	125 mL
¼ tsp	salt	1 mL
2	egg whites	2
1 tsp	vanilla extract	5 mL
¼ cup	confectioner's (icing) sugar	50 mL
	Black food coloring	

1. In a mixer bowl fitted with whip attachment, dissolve gelatin in cold water. Set aside.
2. In a saucepan, combine granulated sugar, corn syrup, hot water and salt. Cook over low heat, stirring just until sugar is dissolved. Increase heat to medium and boil, without stirring, until temperature reaches 240°F (116°C) on thermometer (Soft Ball stage), about 12 minutes. Pour over gelatin mixture. Beat on high speed until white, thick and nearly tripled in volume, about 6 minutes.
3. In a clean mixer bowl, whip egg whites on high speed until soft peaks form. Fold in vanilla. Add to sugar mixture and mix on low speed just until blended.
4. Place a few scoops of marshmallow mixture into pastry bag at a time and refill as necessary. Pipe 24 rounds the size of large silver dollars on prepared baking sheets. Building snowmen vertically, pipe a second round on top, about the size of a quarter, then another on top, about the size of a dime.
5. With a toothpick dipped in black food coloring, dot the buttons and face of snowman.
6. Dust with confectioner's sugar. Let dry on baking sheets for about 30 minutes.

Christmas Cut-Up Cookies

MAKES ABOUT 36 COOKIES

Children love making cookies with different-shaped cookie cutters and decorating them.

Tip

The dough can be made ahead and refrigerated for up to 1 week before rolling and baking.

- Baking sheets, lined with parchment or Silpats
- Cookie cutters

4 cups	all-purpose flour	1 L
½ tsp	baking soda	2 mL
¼ tsp	ground cinnamon	1 mL
¼ tsp	ground allspice	1 mL
¼ tsp	ground ginger	1 mL
¼ tsp	ground mace	1 mL
1 cup	liquid honey	250 mL
2 tbsp	dark corn syrup	25 mL
½ cup	granulated sugar	125 mL
1	egg	1
	Royal Icing (see recipe, page 235) and colored sugars	

1. In a large bowl, whisk together flour, baking soda, cinnamon, allspice, ginger and mace. Set aside.
2. In a mixer bowl fitted with paddle attachment, beat honey, corn syrup, sugar and egg until well blended, about 2 minutes. Using a wooden spoon, stir in flour mixture just until dough holds together. Cover and refrigerate for 20 minutes.
3. Preheat oven to 350°F (180°C).
4. Working in batches, on a floured surface, roll dough out to ¼-inch (0.5 cm) thickness. Cut into desired shapes with cookie cutters, re-rolling scraps. Place on prepared baking sheets, keeping similar-sized cookies together, at least 2 inches (5 cm) apart. Bake until firm, 10 to 12 minutes. Let cool completely on pans on a wire rack.
5. Decorate cooled cookies with Royal Icing and colored sugars as desired.

4th of July Cheesecake

SERVES 18 TO 20

Here's an all-American cheesecake that you will be proud to serve at a picnic or summer gathering.

Tip

You can make the cheesecake weeks ahead and freeze it. Decorate the day of the event.

Variation

Substitute fresh cherries for the strawberries to keep the patriotic theme. Using all of one berry is delicious, but not as colorful.

- Preheat oven to 350°F (180°C)
- 10-inch (25 cm) cheesecake pan, ungreased, or springform pan with 3-inch (7.5 cm) sides, greased

Crust

2 cups	butter cookie crumbs	500 mL
1/3 cup	unsalted butter, melted	75 mL

Filling

6	packages (each 8 oz/250 g) cream cheese, softened	6
2 1/4 cups	granulated sugar	550 mL
6	eggs	6
1 cup	fresh strawberries, cut into quarters	250 mL
1/2 cup	fresh raspberries	125 mL
1/2 cup	fresh blueberries	125 mL
1 tbsp	vanilla extract	15 mL

Decoration

1/2 cup	whipping (35%) cream	125 mL
2 tbsp	granulated sugar	25 mL
1 cup	fresh strawberries, with tops cut off	250 mL
1/2 cup	fresh raspberries	125 mL
1/2 cup	fresh blueberries	125 mL

1. *Crust:* In a bowl, combine cookie crumbs and butter. Press into bottom of cheesecake pan and freeze.
2. *Filling:* In a mixer bowl fitted with paddle attachment, beat cream cheese and sugar until very smooth, for 5 minutes. Add eggs, one at a time, beating after each addition. Fold in strawberries, raspberries, blueberries and vanilla by hand.
3. Pour batter over frozen crust. Bake in preheated oven for 60 to 75 minutes or until the top is light brown and the center has a slight jiggle to it. Let cool on a rack for 2 hours. Cover with plastic wrap and refrigerate for at least 8 hours before decorating or serving.
4. *Decoration:* In a well-chilled mixer bowl, whip cream until soft peaks form. With the mixer still running, sprinkle sugar into cream and continue whipping until firm peaks form. Top entire cake with whipped cream. Place perfectly shaped strawberries around outside edge of cake, followed by a row of raspberries. Fill in the center with blueberries.

Autumn Festival Cheesecake

SERVES 18 TO 20

Full of warm harvest flavors, this cheesecake is great served on a cool autumn night or Halloween.

Tip

If the raisins are hard, you can plump them up in a little hot water. Cover them for 10 minutes, then drain and use.

- Preheat oven to 350°F (180°C)
- 10-inch (25 cm) cheesecake pan, ungreased, or springform pan with 3-inch (7.5 cm) sides, greased

Crust

1½ cups	graham cracker crumbs	375 mL
½ cup	pecans, toasted and ground	125 mL
⅓ cup	unsalted butter, melted	75 mL

Filling

6	packages (each 8 oz/250 g) cream cheese, softened	6
2¼ cups	granulated sugar	550 mL
6	eggs	6
1	medium baking apple, peeled and chopped fine	1
½ cup	golden raisins	125 mL
2 tbsp	grated orange zest	25 mL
1 tsp	each ground nutmeg and cinnamon	5 mL
½ tsp	each ground cloves and allspice	2 mL
2 tsp	vanilla extract	10 mL

Decoration

½ cup	whipping (35%) cream	125 mL
2 tbsp	granulated sugar	25 mL
¼ tsp	grated orange zest	1 mL
1 tsp	ground cinnamon	5 mL
½ tsp	ground nutmeg	2 mL

1. *Crust:* In a bowl, combine graham cracker crumbs, pecans and butter. Press into pan and freeze.
2. *Filling:* In a large mixer bowl fitted with paddle attachment, beat cream cheese and sugar on medium-high speed until very smooth, for 5 minutes. Add eggs, one at a time, beating after each addition. Fold in chopped apple, raisins, orange zest, nutmeg, cinnamon, cloves, allspice and vanilla by hand.
3. Pour over frozen crust. Bake for 60 to 75 minutes or until the top is light brown. Let cool on a rack for 2 hours. Cover and refrigerate for 8 hours before decorating or serving.
4. *Decoration:* In a well-chilled mixer bowl, whip cream on medium-high until soft peaks form. With mixer running, sprinkle in sugar and continue whipping until firm peaks form. Fold in zest, cinnamon and nutmeg. Spread on cake.

Christmas Cheesecake

SERVES 18 TO 20

Give in to the Christmas spirit of red and green everything by garnishing this cheesecake with raspberry preserves and a ring of sliced kiwi.

Tips

When choosing kiwis they should be firm like tomatoes with a little give when you hold one in the palm of your hand.

Preserves are best to use here rather than jellies or jams. They adhere to the cheesecake better because they are thicker and less runny.

Variation

Substitute strawberry preserves for the raspberry preserves.

- Preheat oven to 350°F (180°C)
- 10-inch (25 cm) cheesecake pan, ungreased, or springform pan with 3-inch (7.5 cm) sides, greased

Crust

2 cups	graham cracker crumbs	500 mL
1/4 cup	pecans, coarsely ground	50 mL
1/3 cup	unsalted butter, melted	75 mL

Filling

5	packages (each 8 oz/250 g) cream cheese, softened	5
2 1/4 cups	granulated sugar	550 mL
1 cup	sour cream	250 mL
6	eggs	6
1/3 cup	all-purpose flour	75 mL
1 tbsp	grated orange zest	15 mL
1 tbsp	grated lemon zest	15 mL
1 tsp	freshly squeezed lemon juice	5 mL
2 tsp	vanilla extract	10 mL

Decoration

1/2 cup	whipping (35%) cream	125 mL
2 tbsp	granulated sugar	25 mL
2/3 cup	raspberry preserves	150 mL
2	kiwis, peeled and sliced thin	2

1. *Crust:* In a bowl, combine graham cracker crumbs, pecans and butter. Press into cheesecake pan and freeze.
2. *Filling:* In a large mixer bowl fitted with paddle attachment, beat cream cheese, sugar and sour cream on medium-high speed until very smooth, for 5 minutes. Add eggs, one at a time, beating after each addition. Mix in flour, lemon and orange zests, lemon juice and vanilla.

3. Pour batter over frozen crust. Bake in preheated oven for 60 to 75 minutes or until the top is light brown and the center has a slight jiggle to it. Let cool on a rack for 2 hours. Cover with plastic wrap and refrigerate for at least 8 hours before decorating or serving.
4. *Decoration:* In a well-chilled mixer bowl, whip cream on medium-high speed until soft peaks form. With the mixer still running, sprinkle sugar into cream and continue whipping until firm peaks form. Pipe a border around edge of cooled cake. Spread raspberry preserves into the center and outward toward the whipped cream. Lay kiwi slices in spirals close to the whipped cream.

Eggnog Nutmeg Rum Cheesecake

SERVES 18 TO 20

I wait patiently every year for the holiday season to start so I can make this cheesecake with fresh eggnog, which gives it a very special flavor.

Tips

Keep canned eggnog in the pantry for making this recipe out of season when you can't wait for fresh cartons of eggnog to be available.

If the cottage cheese has a wet look to it, drain the cheese through a fine-mesh strainer. Too much moisture will change the texture of the cheesecake.

Variation

Substitute cinnamon for nutmeg or use in addition to nutmeg for extra sparkle in the decorating.

- Preheat oven to 350°F (180°C)
- 10-inch (25 cm) cheesecake pan, ungreased, or springform pan with 3-inch (7.5 cm) sides, greased

Crust

2 cups	graham cracker crumbs	500 mL
1 tsp	ground nutmeg	5 mL
⅓ cup	unsalted butter, melted	75 mL

Filling

4	packages (each 8 oz/250 g) cream cheese, softened	4
2 cups	small curd cottage cheese, drained (see Tips, left)	500 mL
2¼ cups	granulated sugar	550 mL
6	eggs	6
1 cup	prepared eggnog	250 mL
½ cup	light rum	125 mL
1 tbsp	vanilla extract	15 mL
1 tsp	ground nutmeg	5 mL

Topping

1 cup	sour cream	250 mL
½ cup	granulated sugar	125 mL
1 tsp	vanilla extract	5 mL
1 tsp	ground nutmeg	5 mL

Decoration

½ cup	whipping (35%) cream	125 mL
2 tbsp	granulated sugar	25 mL
1 tsp	ground nutmeg	5 mL

1. *Crust:* In a bowl, combine graham cracker crumbs, nutmeg and butter. Press into bottom of cheesecake pan and freeze.
2. *Filling:* In a large mixer bowl fitted with paddle attachment, beat cream cheese, cottage cheese and sugar on medium-high speed until very smooth, for 5 minutes. Add eggs, one at a time, beating after each addition. Mix in eggnog, rum, vanilla and nutmeg.

3. Pour over frozen crust. Bake in preheated oven for 60 to 75 minutes or until the top is light brown and the center has a slight jiggle to it. Let cool on the counter for 10 minutes (do not turn the oven off). The cake will sink slightly.
4. *Topping:* In a small bowl, combine sour cream, sugar, vanilla and nutmeg. Pour mixture into center of cooled cake and spread out to edges. Bake for 5 minutes more. Let cool on a rack for 2 hours. Cover and refrigerate for at least 8 hours before decorating or serving.
5. *Decoration:* In a well-chilled mixer bowl, whip cream on medium-high speed until soft peaks form. With the mixer still running, sprinkle sugar into cream and continue whipping until firm peaks form. Ice top of cake with whipped cream or pipe rosettes around top of cake, if desired. Sprinkle with nutmeg.

Maple Pumpkin Cheesecake

SERVES 18 TO 20

Two flavors for the fall that go well together are maple and pumpkin.

Tip

If pure maple syrup is not available you can use about 1⁄4 tsp (1 mL) pure maple flavoring.

Variation

Add 1 cup (250 mL) chopped hazelnuts into the batter for a crunchy texture.

- Preheat oven to 350°F (180°C)
- 10-inch (25 cm) cheesecake pan, ungreased, or springform pan with 3-inch (7.5 cm) sides, greased

Crust

2½ cups	graham cracker crumbs	625 mL
1 tsp	ground ginger	5 mL
⅓ cup	unsalted butter, melted	75 mL

Filling

5	packages (each 8 oz/250 g) cream cheese, softened	5
1 cup	sour cream	250 mL
2¼ cups	granulated sugar	550 mL
6	eggs	6
½ cup	all-purpose flour	125 mL
1 cup	pumpkin purée (not pie filling)	250 mL
1 tbsp	vanilla extract	15 mL
3 tbsp	freshly squeezed lemon juice	45 mL
½ cup	pure maple syrup	125 mL
1 tbsp	ground cinnamon	15 mL
½ tsp	ground nutmeg	2 mL
¼ tsp	ground allspice	1 mL

Decoration

Classic Whipped Cream (see recipe, page 239)

1. *Crust:* In a bowl, combine graham cracker crumbs, ginger and butter. Press into bottom of cheesecake pan and freeze.
2. *Filling:* In a large mixer bowl fitted with paddle attachment, beat cream cheese, sour cream and sugar on medium-high speed until very smooth, for 5 minutes. Add eggs, one at a time, beating after each addition. Mix in flour, pumpkin, vanilla, lemon juice, maple syrup, cinnamon, nutmeg and allspice.
3. Pour batter over frozen crust. Bake in preheated oven for 65 to 75 minutes or until the top is light brown and the center has a slight jiggle to it. Let cool on a rack for 2 hours. Cover with plastic wrap and refrigerate for at least 8 hours before decorating or serving.
4. *Decoration:* Ice top of cake with Classic Whipped Cream or pipe a border around edge of cake, if desired.

Easter Cheesecake

SERVES 18 TO 20

Easter always reminds me of white chocolate and toasted coconut. This cheesecake will be a hit at Easter brunch or any spring party.

Tips

Make sure the chocolate has cooled slightly or the cake will have chocolate chunks in the batter.

Coconut is often burned by a pastry chef. To avoid crying over burnt coconut, follow this technique. Spread coconut in a single layer on a cookie sheet. Bake in a 350°F (180°C) oven for 3 minutes. Check the coconut and stir. Set the timer for another 3 minutes. Repeat until coconut is lightly browned.

- Preheat oven to 350°F (180°C)
- 10-inch (25 cm) cheesecake pan, ungreased, or springform pan with 3-inch (7.5 cm) sides, greased

Crust

2 cups	butter cookie crumbs	500 mL
½ cup	ground macadamia nuts	125 mL
¼ cup	unsalted butter, melted	50 mL

Filling

6	packages (each 8 oz/250 g) cream cheese, softened	6
2 cups	granulated sugar	500 mL
5	eggs	5
1	egg yolk	1
2 tsp	vanilla extract	10 mL
8 oz	white chocolate, melted and cooled (see page 250)	250 g
1½ cups	sweetened flaked coconut, toasted (see Tips, left)	375 mL

Decoration

	Classic Whipped Cream (see recipe, page 239)	
½ cup	sweetened flaked coconut, toasted	125 mL

1. *Crust:* In a medium bowl, combine cookie crumbs, macadamia nuts and butter. Press into bottom of cheesecake pan and freeze.
2. *Filling:* In a large mixer bowl fitted with paddle attachment, beat cream cheese and sugar on medium-high speed until very smooth, for 5 minutes. Add eggs and egg yolk, one at a time, beating after each addition. Mix in vanilla and melted chocolate. Fold in coconut by hand.
3. Pour batter over frozen crust. Bake in preheated oven for 60 to 75 minutes or until the top is light brown and the center has a slight jiggle to it. Let cool on a rack for 2 hours. Cover with plastic wrap and refrigerate for at least 8 hours before decorating or serving.
4. *Decoration:* Ice top of cake with Classic Whipped Cream or pipe a border around edge of cake, if desired. Sprinkle with toasted coconut.

Passover Honey Cheesecake

SERVES 18 TO 20

I love the slight taste of honey in this Passover cheesecake.

Tips

Grind nuts and matzo meal together in a food processor to keep the nuts from turning to butter.

Save the egg whites in the refrigerator for 2 days or the freezer for up to 6 months. Use for meringue or when a recipe calls for egg whites.

Variation

Substitute pecans for almonds for a more complex nut flavor.

- Preheat oven to 350°F (180°C)
- 10-inch (25 cm) cheesecake pan, ungreased, or springform pan with 3-inch (7.5 cm) sides, greased

Crust

2 cups	ground almonds	500 mL
1/4 cup	matzo meal	50 mL
2 tbsp	unsalted butter, melted	25 mL

Filling

4	packages (each 8 oz/250 g) cream cheese, softened	4
2 cups	sour cream	500 mL
2/3 cup	liquid honey	150 mL
6	egg yolks	6
1 tbsp	vanilla extract	15 mL
1/2 cup	chopped almonds	125 mL

1. *Crust:* In a bowl, combine almonds, matzo meal and butter. Press into bottom of cheesecake pan and freeze.
2. *Filling:* In a large mixer bowl fitted with paddle attachment, beat cream cheese, sour cream and honey on medium-high speed for 3 minutes. Add egg yolks, one at a time, beating after each addition. Mix in vanilla.
3. Pour batter over frozen crust. Sprinkle chopped almonds on top of batter. Bake for 60 to 75 minutes or until the top is light brown and the center has a slight jiggle to it. Let cool on a rack for 2 hours. Cover with plastic wrap and refrigerate for at least 6 hours before decorating or serving.

Peppermint Chocolate Cheesecake

SERVES 18 TO 20

During the Christmas holidays I love to serve hot chocolate with a peppermint stick in the warm, creamy drink — a good choice with this cheesecake, too.

Tip

Cool the chocolate before mixing with the cold batter or you will end up with a chocolate chip cake instead.

Variation

Use white chocolate chunks instead of the semisweet chocolate.

- Preheat oven to 350°F (180°C)
- 10-inch (25 cm) cheesecake pan, ungreased, or springform pan with 3-inch (7.5 cm) sides, greased

Crust		
2 cups	chocolate sandwich cookie crumbs	500 mL
⅓ cup	unsalted butter, melted	75 mL
Filling		
6	packages (each 8 oz/250 g) cream cheese, softened	6
2 cups	granulated sugar	500 mL
6	eggs	6
½ cup	all-purpose flour	125 mL
1 cup	sour cream	250 mL
2 tsp	vanilla extract	10 mL
½ tsp	peppermint extract	2 mL
6 oz	semisweet chocolate, melted and cooled (see page 250)	175 g
12 oz	semisweet chocolate chunks	375 g
1 cup	crushed candy canes	250 mL
2 tbsp	all-purpose flour	25 mL
Decoration		
	Classic Whipped Cream (see recipe, page 239)	
¼ cup	crushed candy canes	50 mL

1. *Crust:* In a bowl, combine cookie crumbs and butter. Press into bottom of cheesecake pan and freeze.
2. *Filling:* In a large bowl mixer bowl fitted with paddle attachment, beat cream cheese and sugar on medium-high until very smooth, for 5 minutes. Add eggs, one at a time, beating after each addition. Mix in ½ cup (125 mL) flour, sour cream, vanilla, peppermint extract and melted chocolate. In a small bowl, coat chocolate chunks and candy canes with remaining flour. Fold into batter by hand.
3. Pour over frozen crust. Bake in preheated oven for 60 to 75 minutes or until the top is light brown and the center has a slight jiggle to it. Let cool on a rack for 2 hours. Cover and refrigerate for 8 hours before decorating or serving.
4. *Decoration:* Ice cake with whipped cream or pipe a border around edges. Top with crushed candy canes.

Sweet Potato Cheesecake

SERVES 18 TO 20

Who doesn't like sweet potato pie? Now try my version of this classic as a cheesecake!

Tip

Peel the potato, wrap in foil and bake for 60 minutes in a 400°F (200°C) oven or until soft. Use canned sweet potatoes if fresh are unavailable.

- Preheat oven to 350°F (180°C)
- 10-inch (25 cm) cheesecake pan, ungreased, or springform pan with 3-inch (7.5 cm) sides, greased

Crust

2 cups	pecans, ground	500 mL
1/4 cup	all-purpose flour	50 mL
2 tbsp	unsalted butter, melted	25 mL

Filling

5	packages (each 8 oz/250 g) cream cheese, softened	5
1 cup	sour cream	250 mL
2 cups	packed light brown sugar	500 mL
6	egg yolks	6
1 tbsp	vanilla extract	15 mL
1 1/2 tsp	ground nutmeg	7 mL
6	egg whites	6
4 oz	sweet potato, cooked and mashed, about half a medium-size sweet potato (see Tip, left)	125 g

Decoration

	Classic Whipped Cream (see recipe, page 239)	
1 tsp	ground nutmeg	5 mL

1. *Crust:* In a bowl, combine pecans, flour and butter. Press into bottom of cheesecake pan and freeze.
2. *Filling:* In a large mixer bowl fitted with paddle attachment, beat cream cheese, sour cream and brown sugar on medium-high speed until very smooth, for 5 minutes. Add egg yolks, one at a time, beating after each addition. Mix in vanilla and nutmeg. In a clean bowl, whip egg whites until soft peaks form. Fold in sweet potatoes. Fold into batter.
3. Pour batter over frozen crust. Bake in preheated oven for 60 to 75 minutes or until the top is light brown and the center has a slight jiggle to it. Let cool on a rack for 2 hours. Cover and refrigerate for 8 hours before decorating or serving.
4. *Decoration:* Top entire cake with whipped cream or pipe rosettes around border, if desired. Sprinkle with ground nutmeg.

Sources

Equipment and Services

Calico Cake Shop
7321 Orangethorpe Ave.
Buena Park, California
714-521-2761
(Personal shopping only)
www.calicocakeshop.com
Cake decorating supplies, spatulas, molds and Magic Line Pans.

George Geary, CCP
www.georgegeary.com
Author's website, full of recipes, tips, culinary tour information and teaching locations. Magic Line Baking Pans are sold here.

Golda's Kitchen
866-465-3299
905-712-1475
(Ships worldwide)
www.goldaskitchen.com
Large range of products from bakeware to decorating supplies.

KitchenArt
765-497-3878
(Ships to U.S. only)
www.k-art.com
Privately owned cooking school and cookware shop outside of Purdue University. Full catalog of equipment.

Parrish's Cake Decorating Supplies
310-324-2253
(Ships to Canada)
800-736-8443 (U.S. only)
www.parrishsmagicline.com
Magic Line Baking Pans, cheesecake pans, small hand tools.

The Kitchen Shoppe Inc.
800-391-2665
(Ships to U.S. only)
www.kitchenshoppe.com
Very large family-owned and -operated cookware shop with a large inventory.

Ingredients

VANILLA BEANS

Nielsen-Massey Vanillas
847-578-1550
(Ships to Canada)
800-525-7873 (U.S. only)
www.nielsenmassey.com
Fine producer of high-quality vanilla beans, pastes, extracts and more.

EXTRACTS AND SPICES

Charles H. Baldwin & Sons
413-232-7785
(Ships to Canada)
www.baldwinextracts.com
Pure extracts from anise to peppermint.

Penzeys Spices
262-785-7676
800-741-7787 (U.S. only)
www.penzeys.com
Family-owned and -operated premium spice company. Catalog is full of great facts. Retail stores in 16 states.

The Spice House
312-274-0378
(Ships to Canada)
www.thespicehouse.com
One of the best spice companies. Patty Erd's folks started Penzeys Spices. She carries many different items that can be hard to find, such as maple sugars and flavored flower sugars.

Berries

Driscoll's Berries
"The Finest Berries in the World"
800-871-3333
www.driscolls.com
Website contains berry recipes that the author develops as the corporate chef for the company.

Library and Archives Canada Cataloguing in Publication

Geary, George
The complete baking cookbook : 350 recipes from cookies and cakes
to muffins and pies / George Geary.

Includes index.
ISBN 978-0-7788-0176-4 (bound)
ISBN 978-0-7788-0165-8 (pbk.)

1. Baking. I. Title.

TX765.G42 2007 641.8'15 C2007-902861-6

Index

Note: Recipe names followed by (v) indicate variations.